Hamas and Civil Society in Gaza

PRINCETON STUDIES IN MUSLIM POLITICS

Dale F. Eickelman and Augustus Richard Norton, EDITORS

A list of titles in this series can be found at the back of the book.

Hamas and Civil Society in Gaza

Engaging the Islamist Social Sector

Sara Roy

PRINCETON UNIVERSITY PRESS
PRINCETON AND OXFORD

Copyright © 2011 by Princeton University Press
Published by Princeton University Press, 41 William Street, Princeton, New Jersey 08540

In the United Kingdom: Princeton University Press, 6 Oxford Street, Woodstock, Oxfordshire OX20 1TW

press.princeton.edu

Cover Photos:

Flag image courtesy of Shutterstock

A Palestinian laborer works at a construction site in the northern Gaza Strip. Courtesy of Corbis Images

All Rights Reserved

Second printing, and first paperback printing, 2014
Paperback ISBN: 978-0-691-15967-6

The Library of Congress has cataloged the cloth edition of this book as follows

Roy, Sara.
Hamas and civil society in Gaza : engaging the Islamist social sector / Sara Roy.
  p. cm. — (Princeton studies in Muslim politics)
Includes bibliographical references and index.
ISBN 978-0-691-12448-3 (hardback)
1. Harakat al-Muqawamah al-Islamiyah—Political aspects—Gaza Strip. 2. Harakat al-Muqawamah al-Islamiyah—Social aspects—Gaza Strip. 3. Arab-Israeli conflict. 4. Islamic fundamentalism—Gaza Strip. 5. Jami'ah al-Islamiyah (Gaza) I. Title.
  HV6433.P25R69 2011
  324.25695'308209531—dc22   2010048465

British Library Cataloging-in-Publication Data is available

This book has been composed in Sabon

3 5 7 9 10 8 6 4 2

To Martha

It is not the consciousness of men that determines
their existence but their social existence that
determines their consciousness.
—Karl Marx, *A Contribution to the Critique
of Political Economy*

CONTENTS

Acknowledgments	xi
A Note on Language and Transliteration	xiii
Prologue	xv

CHAPTER 1
Introduction: Structure, Arguments, and Conceptual Framework ... 1

CHAPTER 2
A Brief History of Hamas and the Islamic Movement in Palestine ... 19

CHAPTER 3
Islamist Conceptions of Civil Society ... 51

CHAPTER 4
The Evolution of Islamist Social Institutions in the Gaza Strip: Before and during Oslo (a Sociopolitical History) ... 70

CHAPTER 5
Islamist Social Institutions: Creating a Descriptive Context ... 97

CHAPTER 6
Islamist Social Institutions: Key Analytical Findings ... 161

CHAPTER 7
A Changing Islamist Order? From Civic Empowerment to Civic Regression—the Second Intifada and Beyond ... 191

POSTSCRIPT
The Devastation of Gaza—Some Additional Reflections on Where We Are Now ... 226

APPENDIX
Islamist (and Non-Islamist) Social Institutions ... 237

Afterword to the Paperback Edition	239
Epilogue	261
Notes	271
Selected Bibliography	331
Index	351

ACKNOWLEDGMENTS

THIS BOOK ended very differently than it began. Along the way, many people and organizations have played an important role in its conceptualization, research, and writing, far more than I can or am permitted to name.

Among the people, I will just mention a notable few to whom I am greatly indebted. Foremost is the late Dr. Haidar Abdel Shafi, perhaps the only Palestinian leader who earned the respect and admiration of all factions and Palestinians overall. Years ago, when I needed help with access, I asked Dr. Haidar if he would help me contact some key Hamas officials. I understood that getting to these individuals on my own would not be easy, and that even if I managed to do so, it would take time. With his usual grace and kindness, Dr. Haidar agreed. He made two phone calls—to the late Dr. Ismail Abu Shanab and to Ismail Haniyeh. Within twenty-four hours, I was sitting in their offices, after which additional doors were opened for me. For this, and for so much more, I will always be grateful to the late Dr. Haidar, my dear and cherished friend.

Other people who deserve special acknowledgement are Martha Myers, the late Ismail Abu Shanab, Prime Minister Ismail Haniyeh, Radwan Abu Shmais, Khaled Abu Zaid, Abu Hisham Saqallah, Ramadan (who did not want his last name used), Imad Abu Dayya, Augustus Richard Norton, Elaine Hagopian, Bruce Lawrence, Glenn Robinson, Irene Gendzier, Brigitte Schulz, Leticia Pena, and David Henley.

I am also indebted to the many Palestinians who met with me and allowed me in. They came from inside Hamas and the Islamic movement and outside it—its members and nonmembers, supporters, nonsupporters and detractors, employees and recipients, friends and enemies.

This book would not have been possible without a substantial research grant from the John D. and Catherine T. MacArthur Foundation. I am very grateful to the MacArthur Foundation for their support and for their continued understanding, especially with regard to the changing publication date of this manuscript.

I want to express my heartfelt gratitude to the faculty and staff of the Center for Middle Eastern Studies at Harvard University, which has been my academic home for over fifteen years. Here I want to acknowledge Roger Owen, Steven Caton, Herbert Kelman, Roy Mottehedeh, Susan Miller, Lenore Martin, Cemal Kafadar, William Granara, Susan Kahn, Leonard Wood, William Graham, Alison Howe, Paul Beran, Heidemarie

Woelfel, and Kendra Slaughter. Their constant support and encouragement have been invaluable.

I also want to thank Kate Rouhana for her superb editing and wise counsel.

I am greatly indebted to my editor at Princeton University Press, Fred Appel, whose patience, guidance, and support were deeply appreciated.

As always, none of what I do would be possible without the unqualified understanding and encouragement of my family—my husband, Jay, and daughters, Annie and Jess. Thank you again for tolerating long absences, constant travel, and recurring deadlines. I love you more than I can say.

A NOTE ON LANGUAGE AND TRANSLITERATION

For Arabic terms, names, and expressions that appear relatively rarely in everyday English writing, I have applied a standard method for transliteration: the letter 'ayn is designated by [']; the letter hamza is designated by [']; I omit diacritics.

For Arabic terms that appear in the *Oxford Dictionary* of U.S. English (online edition, 2010), I employ the *Oxford* spelling (e.g., Quran, sharia, Hadith).

For Arabic terms, names, and expressions that appear frequently in English-language academic and journalistic literature, I apply one rendering consistently. For example, an organization known as "The Islamic Center" is rendered as "al-Mujamma al-Islami" (i.e., not al-Mujamma' al-Islami). For persons whose names have more than one English-writing format (e.g., al-Gannuchi, al-Gannushi, al-Gannouchi), I apply one common format consistently.

When quoting an outside source, I spell Arabic words as they appear in the source.

PROLOGUE

> The voices of those from the Middle East . . . [are] telling us that they do not recognize themselves in the image we have formed of them . . . Western scholars look on the world they study as passive or lifeless, incapable of creating a self-image which will compel them to change the image which they have inherited.
> —Albert Hourani[1]

ON A WARM, sunny day in the spring of 1999, I was touring an Islamic kindergarten in the Gaza Strip with my friend Ramadan, who would sometimes translate for me. After viewing a class in session, we were escorted into the school courtyard, a large, clean space that was serenely, yet surprisingly, silent. As we stood in this empty expanse, a bell rang. Within seconds, scores of children poured into the vast silence, filling it with laughter and play, their joy utterly infectious. The teachers, all women, also laughed at the children's apparent insuppressible excitement.

Our guide, the school director, invited us back inside to continue the conversation. He led us into a room where three men and a woman were sitting at a long rectangular table. "This is our board of directors, and they would like to speak with you." I was surprised and delighted, because I did not expect to have such easy access. With Ramadan translating, I began by thanking them for this unexpected opportunity. The exchange that followed proved to be a critically important experience in my research on Hamas and the Islamic movement.

The conversation turned to the school's operations, curriculum and pedagogy, teachers and their backgrounds, and from there branched out to the local community, the demographic composition of the student body, and family life in Gaza. As we talked, a young woman knocked at the door. She was a student's mother searching for someone, and she abashedly apologized for intruding. Instead of sending her away, one board member, Dr. Ahmad,[2] invited her to enter and join the discussion.

Pointing to me, Dr. Ahmad addressed the young mother and said, "This is *Doctora* Sara from America. She is here to learn about our school and what we teach our children. Would you be willing to answer some of her questions?" In an instant, this young, soft-spoken wisp of a girl transformed into a self-possessed powerhouse of a woman, and it stunned me.

Although she was speaking before the board, she did not seem at all intimidated. She described the school's many strengths. I then asked her to address its weaknesses. Unhesitatingly, she took my question as an opportunity to voice her concern: "I would like more help with taking care of my children after school; I mean programs after school that would keep them busy in more creative ways, and [provide] more ways for me as a parent to be involved with the school." Concerned that I might have somehow compromised her by my question, I looked at the board members to gauge their reaction. All but one were smiling. They thanked her, and she then excused herself and left with a certain confidence she had not visibly possessed when she entered.

"In America, people think that Palestinians are terrorists and that we are backward, that we prefer the gun to the computer," said Dr. Ahmad. "We as a people have always valued education, like the Jews, and like your people, *Doctora* Sara. You are a Christian?" The question was asked more as a formality that aimed to restate the obvious than as an inquiry. Suddenly, the conundrum I had assiduously and, for the most part, successfully avoided in my research with the Islamic community confronted me without escape: Do I admit I am Jewish and possibly risk my ability to work with that community—or do I lie?

Understandably, most Palestinians assume that the (non-Israeli) foreigners among them are Christian, for what Jew would want to befriend Palestinians or live in Gaza, let alone learn about the Islamic movement? Before the first Palestinian uprising in 1987, one of the first questions I was inevitably asked in Gaza was, are you a Christian? I always told the truth. When people learned I was Jewish, there was concern, curiosity, and some suspicion, but rarely, if ever, hostility. Once I explained why I was in Gaza—to learn about Palestinians and their lives—and gained their trust, which surprisingly did not take very long, my being Jewish became invaluable.[3] In fact, it opened many doors that usually remained shut to outsiders. However, as the occupation grew increasingly repressive, beginning with the first Intifada (or uprising), the question of my religious and ethnic background was *never* again raised, not once. The answer was simply too inconceivable.

Turning to Dr. Ahmad, who had so gently asked the question, I answered, "I am not Christian, I am Jewish." The room instantly fell silent. The board members were clearly surprised, even shocked. Ramadan (who himself was not an Islamist but a member of the main nationalist secular movement, Fatah) turned to me and asked incredulously, "You are *Jewish*?!" Tension rose, and the air in the room became thick and stagnant.

I had imagined this moment many times—how I might respond, how others might respond to me, and what I would do if the situation became difficult or hostile. What followed, however, was altogether unexpected. I began: "I understand why you are surprised. But you should know that within the Jewish community there are many people who oppose Israel's occupation and who support the right of Palestinians to live in their own state as free people. Many Jews in Israel, in America, and elsewhere speak out against Israeli policies in Gaza and the West Bank. Jews are not all the same, just as Palestinians and Muslims are not all the same. I am here doing this work not only as a scholar and researcher but as a Jew, as an American, and as a human being. I want to learn more than I have been taught and I am hoping you will help me. That is why I am here."

After a moment, Dr. Ahmad quietly asked, "What are you hoping to learn and leave here with?"

"Knowledge. And perhaps a deeper understanding of your community, your lives, and what you are trying to achieve."

"And how will you use what you have learned here?"

"I shall use it to educate others, or at least try."

"Americans think all Palestinians are terrorists, especially those of us who are religious Muslims. We are not human beings to them, just people who kill Jews. Do you really think you can change that?"

"At a larger level, no, I cannot change that, but at an individual or community level, perhaps I can. What I have always tried to do through my work is give others a different way of understanding this conflict, to challenge the ways of thinking that have been created for us."

I could feel the tension abating and myself relaxing. The one woman on the board, Um Mohammad, then asked me, "*Doctora* Sara, do you have children?"

"Yes, I have one child, a little girl. Her name is Annie."

"When you look at your child, what do you feel?" I looked at Um Mohammad and hesitated.

"I feel indescribable love and joy," I answered.

"Can you imagine that it is different for a Palestinian mother?"

"No, Um Mohammad, I cannot."

"This is what you must teach others. That we are no different than you."

Hamas and Civil Society in Gaza

Chapter 1

INTRODUCTION: STRUCTURE, ARGUMENTS, AND CONCEPTUAL FRAMEWORK

THE ISLAMIC RESISTANCE MOVEMENT or Hamas was established at the beginning of the first Palestinian uprising, which began in December 1987. As the representative of political Islam in Palestine, Hamas has had a long and contentious and, in its own way, remarkable trajectory. Typically, Hamas is misportrayed as an insular, one-dimensional entity dedicated solely to violence and to the destruction of the Jewish state. It has largely, if not entirely, been defined in terms of its terrorist attacks against Israel. Despite the existence of differentiated sectors within Hamas—social (including a nascent economic sphere), political, and military—they are all regarded as parts of the same apparatus of terror.

After September 11, 2001, the U.S. government moved to operationalize this perception when it added Hamas to its list of terrorist organizations on November 2, although President Clinton had already designated Hamas a foreign terrorist entity under Executive Order 12947 on January 23, 1995.[1] A key component of this designation was the belief that Islamic social institutions were an integral part of Hamas's terrorist infrastructure in Palestine. Both the U.S. government and U.S. media perceived the role of these institutions to be largely one of indoctrination and recruitment, as typified by this 1995 description in the *New York Times*: "[I]n the Israeli-occupied West Bank and in Palestinian-controlled Gaza, Hamas has another face. Hamas-run schools offer free classes and Hamas-run clinics charge as little as $1 for private visits to a doctor.... Hamas ... uses schools ... to spread the gospel about their jihad, or holy war, and to recruit young suicide bombers with the lure of martyrdom....[C]ritics contend that the distinction between Hamas terror and Hamas good works is dubious. Charity ... helps raise the political stature of a group that promotes terror."[2]

In the United States, the view that Islamic social institutions in Palestine are inherently evil has only intensified over time, particularly in the post-9/11 moral and political milieu. This has led the U.S. government to wage a determined campaign against them, freezing the assets of U.S.-based charities that had contributed to Hamas's social organizations. Perhaps the most celebrated case is that of the Holy Land Foundation for Relief and Development (HLF) based in Richardson, Texas. In 2001, President Bush said, "Money raised by the Holy Land Foundation is used by Hamas to support schools and indoctrinate children to grow up into suicide bombers. Money raised by the Holy Land Foundation is also used by Hamas to recruit suicide bombers and to support their families.... Our action today is another step in the war on terrorism."[3]

In his testimony in the case against the HLF, Matthew Levitt, former deputy assistant secretary for intelligence and analysis at the U.S. Treasury, further argued: "the social wing is the foundation for Hamas. It's what supports its grassroots support. It's what enables it to have political support. It carries on its back the military wing by providing day jobs, logistical and operational support and perhaps most importantly, financing."[4] More specifically, "The *zakat* [almsgiving] committees are Hamas's most effective tool, period. They build grassroot[s] support for the organization. They create a sense of indebtedness among people who benefit from their support. Someone who doesn't have very much and is able to get over the hump by the assistance of an Hamas charity welcomes the chance to do something back. So if they are asked to do a favor, they are happy to do so. It provides a logistical support mechanism to the terrorist wing. It provides jobs for militants and terrorist alike. It facilitates Hamas's stature. They are more likely to get your vote if you are getting their financial support."[5]

On August 7, 2007, the U.S. government blacklisted the al-Salah Islamic Association, one of the largest Islamic charities in the Gaza Strip. Designated a "key support node for Hamas,"[6] al-Salah had its bank accounts frozen, which suggested a new U.S. strategy to target individual Islamic institutions in the occupied territories. In fact, al-Salah was the first "Hamas-related charity" to be added to the U.S. government blacklist since August 2003, when the Palestinian National Authority (PNA) froze the association's accounts (and "confirmed that al-Salah was a front for Hamas"[7]). The Department of Treasury accused al-Salah of employing "a number of Hamas military wing members."[8] Since 80 percent of the association's estimated $5 million budget came from external donors who relied on the banking system to transfer the funds, the freeze was devastating. By 2007, the association was running schools and medical centers and supporting more than ten thousand children, many of whose families had become impoverished because of the Israeli and international economic blockade of the Gaza Strip.

According to a senior Israeli official, the decision to target al-Salah was political and had originated with the Fatah government of Palestinian prime minister Fayyad, which sought ways to reduce financial support for the Islamic social welfare system[9] (and thereby to reduce the influence of the Hamas party, which had democratically won the Palestinian elections in 2006, toppling Fatah from decades of prominence within Palestinian politics). According to Fayyad's information minister, Riyad al-Malki, the aim was not to compete with Hamas but rather to "set up a network of social security where we will be able to respond to the basic needs of families, to connect these families to the official system, and to prevent them from looking for alternatives from the Hamas network," which U.S. officials referred to as "charitable backfill."[10]

In December 2007 President Abbas, who along with the Fayyad government retained power in the West Bank despite the Hamas electoral victory, subsequently dissolved ninety-two Hamas-linked charity committees in the West Bank in retaliation for Hamas's rejection of the Annapolis Middle East peace conference. The Fayyad government claimed that Hamas "transformed the charity committees into financial empires to serve their political ends and activities" and announced that eleven new charity committees would replace those that were closed.[11]

On February 26, 2008, the Israeli government issued closure and confiscation orders against the Islamic Charitable Society (ICS) in Hebron, a charity that had existed for more than forty years and which, at the time of closure, ran a variety of social service programs. According to the Christian Peacemaker Teams, furthermore, "Soldiers have welded shut the gates of the nearly completed $2,000,000 Al-Huda girls' school, raided and looted bakeries that provided bread to the orphanages and on the first of May, raided the sewing workshop in the girls' orphanage, carting away sewing and processing machines, fabric, finished garments and office equipment . . . all of which they brought to the city dump."[12]

Clearly, the attack against Islamic social institutions was preplanned, coordinated, and multipronged. But what concerns about Hamas's social infrastructure prompted the campaign in the first place? Three were paramount:

- *Financing*: Monies raised for the benefit of Hamas's social sector are illicitly transferred to the military wing to finance its infrastructure and activities. As such, the argument goes, charitable and community-based institutions affiliated with Hamas are intimately involved with the military and its terrorist activities, serving as a cover or screen for the military and nothing more.
- *Indoctrination*: Social institutions are used, as President Bush stated, to indoctrinate—that is, incite violence and recruit potential militants from among charity beneficiaries, which is why, the argument contends, Hamas financially supports the families of suicide bombers.
- *Legitimacy*: Even assuming an ideal separation of the social and military wings, "the mere existence of a network of social

welfare organizations affiliated with an organization that deliberately targets civilians is considered unacceptable. It legitimizes an organization that resorts to patently illegal acts . . . ultimately strengthens it and the ideology and practices it promotes."[13]

This last point on legitimacy is the most damaging, because it assumes that the mere provision of needed social services swells the ranks of militant Islamic radicalism.[14] Good works, therefore, are never truly benevolent but merely a means to recruit, whether directly or indirectly, new supporters for Hamas's wholly violent agenda. Seen this way, Islamic social institutions by definition pose both a political and a security dilemma: Like their political counterparts, they seek to dramatically and violently alter the status quo rather than to coexist within it.

These concerns are based on a number of implicit assumptions, three of which I will take on in this book:[15]

1. The recipient community is deeply integrated into the operations and management of Islamic associations (such that its members are able to be indoctrinated and recruited).
2. Islamic social institutions are somehow uniquely Islamic—a viable and attractive Islamic model in action—and this distinguishes them from secular organizations.
3. The mere provision of (often) free social services and financial incentives and interaction with institutional members suffices to mobilize popular support for the Islamist agenda, whether violent or not.

While there can be no doubt that since its inception in 1987, Hamas has engaged in violence, armed struggle, and terrorism as the primary force behind the horrific suicide bombings inside Israel, it is also a broad-based movement that has evolved into an increasingly complex, varied, and sophisticated organization engaged in a variety of societal activities vital to Palestinian life. Hamas's evolution has been most dramatic with regard to its ideology, organizational structure, role in Palestinian society, and perceived goals—its limitations notwithstanding. This study seeks to challenge the conventional frame of reference that defines Hamas only as a terrorist organization. Here, I pursue a more nuanced view of Palestinian Islamism that deliberately seeks to reinterpret its dynamics, challenging the accepted assumption that all Islamic institutions are parts of a larger terrorist infrastructure and that the people who use them are passive victims of religious fanaticism joined in a desire to inflict harm.[16]

Years before the Bush administration targeted Hamas, I had become interested in the role and operations of Islamic social and economic institutions in the Gaza Strip (and to a lesser extent the West Bank), and I had undertaken field research study on the subject. My research, which grew out of the fieldwork I had been doing since the 1980s on the economy of Gaza,[17] asked whether the dominant and essentialist view of Hamas and the Islamist movement in Palestine—a view that precludes the existence of a nonviolent Islamism and is based on the assumption that Islamist politics (i.e., the failure to separate religion and politics) invariably leads to violence and little else—was justified.

My examination of Hamas focused on its social dimensions and, to the extent possible, on the relationship between its social and political sectors, primarily in the Gaza Strip, where the Islamist movement in Palestine is most concentrated. The underlying thrust of all my research in Gaza and the West Bank has always been toward society—women, children, men, families, neighborhoods, communities—and occupation's destructive impact on them, an area that has never received adequate attention. Given Hamas's increasingly important role as a socioeconomic actor, it was inevitable that I would come into direct contact with it in the course of my earlier fieldwork in Gaza, which I finally did in the early days of the Oslo period. In 1995, for example, I observed the Islamist focus on working with Palestinian youth. Unlike the PNA, which sought to absorb young men into the security apparatus as a source of employment and identity, the Islamist approach stressed creating a religious and cultural framework for community development within which young people could participate and find meaningful identity, belonging, and connection.

The resulting sense of personal identification emerged from civic work and community involvement, not from political power plays or bureaucratic positioning. Perhaps this explains why the Islamic movement generally and Hamas in particular have always been able to inspire high levels of volunteerism, despite the widespread societal impoverishment and economic decline within which it grew. As such, Islamic institutions were not generating employment but creating a space where gradualism was possible and accountability and trust were perceived to be high. Islamic institutions provided islands of normality and stability in a sociopolitical context of chaos, dislocation, and pain. Furthermore, because they worked at the grassroots level, where they were able to build personal and communal ties based on religio-cultural identification, Islamic institutions were creating, in effect, a cultural private sector that felt familiar and safe to Palestinians in an otherwise rapidly evolving, confusing, and oppressive environment.[18] This need among Palestinians for purpose, trust, and solidarity has only grown over the years, and the Islamic response and the way people understand and identify with it should not be underestimated.

Institution building in the face of widespread systemic oppression was a critical function of the Islamic movement in Palestine in general, and Hamas in particular, during the Oslo period. This is little known. That the oppression was both external (Israel) and internal (the Palestinian National Authority) was also crucial to the movement's success (and to its failures, which are also examined). Perhaps most interesting at this time were the ways in which Islamic organizations, particularly those associated with Hamas (the majority), increasingly positioned themselves to play a mediatory role in society, a function historically reserved for the secular political faction, which was then disappearing as a distinct political institution under the pressures imposed by the PNA. Hamas's ability to mediate social disputes evolved during the Oslo period but was restricted largely to the social sphere. Unlike Hizballah in Lebanon, Hamas did not mediate political or military disputes. In fact, it took part in them. It was from the social sphere primarily—not the ideological one—that Hamas derived its legitimacy and constructed a broad popular base. Over a decade later, that base gave Hamas its stunning electoral victory.[19]

Given the dramatic decline in Palestinian economic and social conditions during the Oslo period, I began to ask how vital Islamic social institutions were to community development and economic well-being and, possibly, to internal stability and political order. I probed many questions, few of which have previously been examined in the Palestinian case, although they have in other regional contexts (see "Conceptual Framework," below).[20] In order to explore these questions in some depth, I spent as much time as I could inside Islamic social and economic institutions in Gaza, making multiple field trips over a period spanning 1995 to 2000 although the most intensive period of fieldwork occurred during the spring and summer of 1999.[21]

Time Frame of the Study

While this study takes a broad look at the evolution of Islamism in general and Hamas in particular in Palestine, the findings from the field research focus on what I refer to as the Oslo period—that brief era of hope that began in September 1993 with the signing of the first Oslo Accord between Israel and the Palestine Liberation Organization (PLO) and ended abruptly in September 2000 with the outbreak of the al-Aqsa, or second, Palestinian Intifada, or uprising. Many analysts view the first Intifada (1987 to 1993) as a critical period in Hamas's history, because it was during that period that the organization—the political and military embodiment of the Muslim Brotherhood in Palestine—was born and institutionalized. While this is certainly true, I believe that the first Intifada was critical for Hamas for another, ultimately more important reason: It localized and consolidated Hamas's control over the Islamic social sector and provided the foundation for the emergence of new social institutions, which the Islamists were better positioned, and in some cases uniquely poised, to support. This strengthened Hamas's presence and legitimacy at the grassroots level (and with certain international organizations and NGOs working in the occupied territories) and subsequently earned (or gained) it entry into new areas of socioeconomic activity during the Oslo period that followed. This access proved crucial to Hamas's political survival at a time of extreme repression and weakness.

The Oslo period also was a critical time in the evolution of Islamic social institutions because it was then that a formal political institution was established—the Palestinian National Authority—that transformed the political environment and Hamas's position within it and consequently expanded the role and purpose of Islamic associations in Gaza and the West Bank, altering the relationship between the Islamist political and social sectors. It was during this period especially that Hamas demonstrated its capacity for change and moderation. It was also a time when the Islamist social sector played an important role not only within society but within the Islamist movement as well. As such, the Oslo period was arguably far more defining for Hamas as a political and social organization than any other historical period except 2006, when it won the Palestinian legislative elections and assumed control of the government, and 2007, when it violently assumed control of Gaza.

The Oslo period is pivotal for understanding the Palestinian Islamist movement in its social and political dimensions because it was, without question, a discrete and unique period of time in which critical and dramatic changes were occurring within the movement overall and within Hamas specifically. It was also a time, albeit limited, of relative openness that I was extremely fortunate to access and study. The changes I describe remain largely unseen and underresearched. Moreover, they contradict conventional wisdom, which has consistently viewed the Palestinian Islamic movement and Palestinian Islamism as singularly destructive and immutable forces. Fundamentally, these changes illustrate Hamas's capacity for moderation, accommodation, and transformation, as well as the limitations and constraints that have consistently plagued it.

Scope of the Study

Over the course of my fieldwork, I researched a broad range of Islamic social organizations in Palestine—primarily in Gaza but also in the West Bank. I also surveyed some economic and political institutions. Some institutions made themselves more open and accessible to me than others, while others remained completely closed. My research included those institutions with some form of affiliation to Hamas—the presumed majority—and those that claimed none at all—the presumed minority—(a claim that was difficult, in the final analysis, to substantiate). I include both categories and refer to them collectively (perhaps unfairly) as Hamas social institutions because I aim to convey some sense of the breadth and depth of the social institutional universe and the nature of Hamas's role therein.

Social institutions that I surveyed included charitable societies, schools, community outreach programs, libraries, research centers, orphanage programs, day care centers, women's centers, youth centers, homes for the elderly, specialized care centers, health clinics, summer camps, Islamic committees in the refugee camps of the Gaza Strip, and *zakat* committees. I spoke with a diverse range of people involved in these institutions, including officials, staff, and clients, and observed some of their internal operations firsthand.

Economic institutions I visited included investment companies, banks, retail businesses, factories, and private entrepreneurs. (The Islamic economic sector was never as clearly delineated or defined as the social sector, which created many difficulties that are discussed in chapter 5.)

I also spent time in Islamic political organizations. For this, I spoke with officials, members, and supporters of Hamas and Islamic Jihad, many of whom were very willing to meet with me while others were not. Some of the officials and residents with whom I spent time have been killed. Of those still living, not all remain within the Islamic movement. Over the course of my inquiry, I encountered various problems. Many, with time, were surmounted; others never were. They are described throughout this work, for they clearly informed my analysis.

A Note on Terminology

Throughout this study I use a variety of terms: Islamic movement, Islamist movement, Hamas social institutions, and Islamic social (and economic) institutions. These terms can be confusing and therefore require definition.

Technically, there is an analytical difference between the "Islamic movement" and the "Islamist movement" in Palestine. The *Islamic movement* refers not only to its political sector in which Hamas predominates (but which also includes other Islamic political factions such as the Islamic Jihad) but also to the social, economic, cultural, and religious sectors of the movement, which may or may not have direct links to the political. Hence, the use of the adjective "Islamic" does not automatically imply or assume any political affiliation. The *Islamist movement* refers only to the Islamic political and military sectors in Palestine and is meant as a form of political identification and affiliation. However, since Hamas has long defined and shaped the Islamic movement in Palestine, I use the term "Islamist" to refer to all its sectoral parts, not just the political or military.

Hence, in my examination of the Islamic social sector, I refer to "Islamic social institutions" and "Hamas (or Islamist) social institutions" interchangeably. Conceptually, I use the terms interchangeably for two reasons: because from what I could determine, the majority of Islamic social institutions in Gaza fall within Hamas's domain in some form; and because the work of the Islamic social sector as a whole has directly and indirectly benefited Hamas politically. But I acknowledge a problem with this usage: It assumes—as many observers have argued—that all who establish, direct, work, participate, support, and benefit from Islamic institutions, be they aligned or unaligned, are politically motivated Islamic activists. However, my research shows that most arguably are not.

Conceptual Framework

The conceptual framework used in this study goes beyond standard approaches to the study of Islamist movements (including Hamas), which often employ social movement theory or democracy and Islam as their conceptual paradigms. While this study certainly draws from these critical frameworks, it extends them by reframing the approach to include the notion of civism (and civil sentiment) in Islamic and Islamist thought and practice. Civism is here defined as support for, commitment to, and strengthening of an organized society, economy, and polity with attention to the following features: *ahli* institutions, community life, order and stability, law, accepted social usages, individual and collective rights, the public good, productive relations with the "state," and so forth. As such, the conceptual framework examines the concept of social agency in Islamic/ist thought and how Islamists conceive of civil society (including the central role of the Islamic faith in generating civil sentiment) in an attempt to try to understand Palestinian Islamism *from within its own framework*—to understand Islamists as they understand themselves.

In its early years, Hamas had a clear frame of reference: Palestine is Arab, Islamic land that fell to colonial control with the demise of the Ottoman Empire. Hamas viewed the establishment of the state of Israel as a way to perpetuate colonial authority over the Muslim homeland and therefore as illegitimate. As victims of colonialism, according to Hamas,

Palestinians had the right to struggle to regain their homeland and freedom. The Hamas Charter, which is undeniably racist and anti-Jewish, articulates Hamas's reference point. A clear set of objectives was also set forth, but the accompanying discourse was sometimes confused, in part because it derived from the need to fight the occupation and compete with secular political trends within Palestinian society.

More than two decades after its establishment, Hamas has matured and grown in size and popularity. While its frame of reference and objectives remain unchanged, its political discourse has become refined and streamlined particularly with regard to (1) relations with local groups, political factions, and other religious communities and nations; (2) resolving the Palestinian-Israeli conflict and political compromise with the state of Israel; and (3) the nature of the political system it envisages for a Palestine free of occupation.[22] Since Hamas's victory in the January 2006 legislative elections, there has been a further evolution in its political thinking—as evidenced in some of its key political documents—characterized by a strong emphasis on state building and programmatic work, greater refinement with regard to its position on a two-state solution and the role of resistance, and a progressive de-emphasis on religion.[23] In a May 2009 interview with the Hamas chief, Khaled Meshal, the *New York Times* described Hamas's willingness to accept a two-state solution with Israel along the 1967 borders.[24] Commenting on the Hamas Charter and a Palestinian state, Meshal stated: "The most important thing is what Hamas is doing and the policies it is adopting today.... Hamas has accepted the national reconciliation document. It has accepted a Palestinian state on the 1967 borders including East Jerusalem, dismantling settlements, and the right of return based on a long term truce. Hamas has represented a clear political program through a unity government. This is Hamas's program regardless of the historic documents. Hamas has offered a vision. Therefore, it's not logical for the international community to get stuck on sentences written 20 years ago."[25]

A good deal has been written about Hamas and the Islamist movement in the last few years.[26] Although these studies (among others) collectively and individually provide important analyses of Hamas and Islamist politics in Palestine and the moderating dynamics within them, they do not systematically explore the more pragmatic and constructive role of Hamas as seen in its social institutional work.

Furthermore, while the disciplines of Middle East studies and political science, for example, have considered such issues as the positive and negative roles of Islamist movements worldwide, the field of Islamic economics, and the nature of Islamic social and economic work in some Arab countries (e.g., Egypt, Jordan, Turkey, and Yemen), there has been little if any substantive attention paid to the socioeconomic role of Islamists in the Palestinian context. In this regard, Khaled Hroub, one of the finest analysts of Hamas, writes, "Hamas's concern with social issues found expression in the extensive infrastructure of charitable social services the movement established for the poor.... Subsequently, these social services became one of the most important sources of influence that Hamas had with broad strata of the public. Nevertheless, the literature on this subject, either by Hamas or others, remains meager."[27]

My research, which forms the core of this book, attempts to fill this void by examining four broad lines of inquiry, each briefly described below.

The Islamic Social (and Economic) Sector

The Palestinian Islamist movement especially in Gaza is defined not only by political/military organizations such as Hamas but also by a range of social service institutions, many with a long history in the area. In the Gaza Strip, for example, Islamic institutional social activism is over six decades old and is varied and complex, with a tradition of community development work that long predates the emergence of political and radical Islam. As such, the Islamist movement is not homogeneous but rather quite diverse, both in its constituency and in its institutional leadership. Institutions also differ in their missions, objectives, philosophies, approaches, and achievements.

This study addresses the social components of the Islamist movement, the nature of Islamic socioeconomic work, and the impact of this work particularly on community development and stability. It also looks at certain institutions' agendas and work methods, administration, clientele, and operational spheres. Some representative questions explored are

- What types of organizations in Gaza and the West Bank were considered "Islamic" and in what ways were they Islamic? To what extent and in what ways were these institutions "Hamas"? Were these labels synonymous?
- What work did Islamic social organizations actually perform, and what impact did it have on the community or on a collective (Islamic) identity? What were their key objectives, goals, and priorities?
- How "extremist" were these social institutions, and were they directly linked to the instigation of violence?

The study examines the nature of Islamic social (and to a lesser extent, economic) work during the Oslo period, particularly with regard to its strengths and weaknesses, the possibilities created by the institutions themselves, and the external constraints imposed. The actual, presumed, or desired social role of Islamist institutions is discussed against assumptions about the parallel role of the state or similar authority, and in the continued absence of such an authority as well.

As part of its examination of the social and economic sectors, this study takes a particular interest in the notion of change from below and working from the bottom up—the inclusion of women, minorities, and non-Muslims (nonbelievers); the role of (political and religious) ideology versus practice, and religion versus professionalism; the interrelationship between Islamist social institutions; and the nature of Islamic civism particularly as it regards the role of Islamist associations in strengthening or weakening state-society relations and in promoting or delimiting an ethos of civic engagement.

Interrelationships between the Social and Political Sectors

Very little of a systematic nature has been written on the Islamic social sector. Similarly, there have been few serious attempts to clarify the relationship between the social and political spheres of the Islamic movement, especially with regard to the work they do, the clientele they serve, or the beliefs they hold.

Toward this end, the book explores the ways in which Islamic political institutions interact with and/or influence social institutions and vice versa; the nature of Islamic social and political mobilization in Palestine and the links, if any, between them; the changing nature of Islamically legitimized action in the public and political spheres; and the slowly emerging secularization of religious discourse as a way of adapting to existing social and political realities. Attention also is directed to the nature of the ties that do exist between the social and political spheres, and an attempt is made to understand what those ties are and how they are operationalized. The military wing, which is highly decentralized, secretive, and autonomous, and largely West Bank–based, is not included in this analysis.

The political meaning of Islamic social institutions in Palestine has long been a hotly debated topic. To reiterate, the commonly accepted belief is that Hamas has used its extensive social service network—mosques, schools, kindergartens, orphanages, hospitals, clinics, and sports and youth clubs—to further its primary political agenda, which is assumed to be the mobilization of beneficiaries into political action aimed at destroying Israel; it has also been assumed that Hamas has been successful in doing so.[28] As such—and to paraphrase the former U.S. secretary of state Madeleine Albright—Islamic social institutions have long been perceived as a part of the "Islamist terrorist infrastructure." The political intensity with which this belief is held is matched only by the lack of research devoted to it. This study examines questions such as

- Was the Islamic social sector in fact a social wing of an Islamic political movement (i.e., Islamic activists trying to reform society according to Islamic law and create an Islamic model for a state), or were these activists merely Muslims wishing to realize and live by Islamic social values?
- What, if any, formal institutional links existed between Islamic social institutions and their political counterparts?
- What was the basis for bringing institutions and clientele together? Was it enough to encourage sustained action in support of political or radical Islam (i.e., what was the relationship between Islamic social and political activism)? Were institutions and clients joined by their mutual support for Hamas or by shared interests that were expressed symbolically in a common Islamic idiom?
- How important were ideological versus nonideological factors in influencing client communities? To what extent were Islamic social and economic institutions ideologized (i.e., what was the relationship between ideology and praxis)?

Critical Internal Processes of Change within the Hamas Movement over the Past Fifteen Years

Hamas's ability to reinterpret itself is a pronounced and common theme in this book. Different forms of accommodation, adaptation, and transformation are examined within the political and social sectors of the Islamic movement during the Oslo period especially and the second Intifada. During the Oslo period, for example, the long-dominant political (and military) sector receded in favor of its social counterpart, representing a shift, albeit gradual, from an Islamic political movement to collective action in a Muslim society. This shift was in part characterized by a return to the gradual reform tradition and to the ethical-moral aspects of Islam, and by an approach that sought to "prepare the mind" through social activism. In this regard, this book examines the connections between competing (Islamic versus secular) visions of a Palestinian social and political order and competing definitions of legitimacy. The synergy between these competing forces has characterized the history and growth of Palestinian Islamism.

The book addresses the radicalization and de-radicalization (and demilitarization) and reradicalization of the Islamists, the ways in which these processes compare, contrast, and coexist, and the relationship between the Islamic social and political sectors. It also looks at why Hamas failed to persuade Palestinians to adopt political Islam as a national goal, its electoral victory notwithstanding.

The Characteristics of a Future Islamic Society and Body Politic in Palestine

The features of a future Islamic society and polity are vital to explore in light of several key factors both internal and external to the Palestinian-Israeli conflict. To name just a few: the inclusion of Hamas in the Bush administration's global war on terrorism; Israel's 2005 disengagement from Gaza and continued settlement expansion and building of the Separation Wall in the West Bank; the growing embrace of religion and use of Islamic idiom by Palestinian society generally and secular social and political organizations specifically, and the emerging Islamization of Palestinian society and politics, a trend with some precedent;[29] Hamas's electoral victory and control of the PNA followed by the imposition of international sanctions, which has crippled the economy with damaging social effects; the summer 2006 Lebanese-Israeli war in which Hizballah emerged the unofficial victor; and the June 2007 factional war between Fatah and Hamas that resulted in Hamas's seizure of Gaza, the disbanding of the unity government, the establishment of a new emergency and subsequently institutionalized government in the West Bank that formalized and concretized factional divisions into political practice; the June 2007 intensification of the sanction regime imposed on the Hamas-led government one year before; and Israel's three-week assault on Gaza that began on December 27, 2008.

Some Findings

Despite some negative experiences, the more time I spent inside Islamic institutions, the more I came to understand the contradiction between my firsthand experience of them and the impressions I was receiving from secular Palestinian friends and colleagues, let alone those of foreign analysts.

By the end of the 1990s I had observed that Islamic social service institutions and economic enterprises in the Gaza Strip and West Bank avoided radical change. Their behavior was less dogmatically "Islamic" than was often assumed. Rather, they seemed to advocate a more piecemeal, moderate, and systematic approach toward change that valued order and stability, not disorder and instability. This approach was marked within Islamic social organizations whose clientele consisted of people belonging to very different social classes with a range of political outlooks who had no history of acting collectively in support of radical Islam. The mass base of the Islamic movement, as opposed to its political and military leadership, appeared neither ideological nor radical.

During the Oslo period especially, the strength of Hamas increasingly lay in the work of Islamic social institutions whose services, directly and indirectly, reached tens if not hundreds of thousands of Palestinians, helping them to survive. They provided services that the Palestinian Authority was unable to provide adequately, if at all. This base supported Islamic institutions largely because they met basic needs for economic sustenance and community well-being with a focus on health and education, community support, and service delivery. Islamic institutions were increasingly viewed as community actors in a context where few such actors existed. They sometimes went beyond their traditional social roles, engaging in more creative and innovative forms of community action. Hence, Islamic institutions did not emphasize political violence or substate terrorism but rather community well-being and civic restoration, a role that was (and remains) vital in a context of steady deterioration.

Indeed, given the steady socioeconomic deterioration that followed the implementation of the peace process, the balance of power between social and political Islam shifted even further in favor of the former, particularly at the grassroots level, where the majority of people interacted with the movement. This was a defining—and largely unrecognized—feature of the Oslo period. Islamic social institutions had, by the admission of the Hamas leadership itself (and despite clear structural limitations of their own), a greater capacity to mobilize people during the Oslo period than did their political counterparts.

Perhaps most importantly, it was not religious congregations that Islamic social institutions were attempting to create but civic communities, despite the larger religious framework that inspired institutional programs. Indeed, during the Oslo period there was a clear and deeply committed attempt by the Hamas political leadership to stimulate a social, cultural, and moral renewal of the Muslim community in Palestine. This was not an ad hoc measure but a real, if unofficial, strategy of incremental reform. The Islamist goal of social reform through community development was couched not only—or even primarily—in religious terms but in terms that were cultural and, at times, universal.

Organization of the Book

The book is divided into seven chapters. The first three provide the necessary context and conceptual frameworks for understanding the data.

Chapter 1, "Introduction: Structure, Arguments, and Conceptual Framework," explains the origin of the study and introduces key research questions, arguments, and areas of analysis. Chapter 2, "A Brief History of Hamas and the Islamic Movement in Palestine," provides background and a general context for examining Hamas's specific role as social actor. Chapter 3, "Islamist Conceptions of Civil Society," articulates a conceptual framework for ideas about Islamic civil society and explores the meaning of civil society to Islamists themselves.

The next three chapters present the main findings from my fieldwork. Chapter 4, "The Evolution of Islamist Social Institutions in the Gaza Strip: Before and during Oslo (a Sociopolitical History)," explores the evolution and role of Islamist social institutions in Gaza (and the West Bank), beginning with the reformist work and philosophy of the Muslim Brotherhood and continuing through the first Intifada and the Oslo period. Emphasis is given to the primary role of the social sector (e.g., the Islamist institutions' contribution to community development, order, stability, and civic engagement—what I define as civism); the political role and meaning, if any, of Islamist social work; and the impact of institutional work on grassroots development, community cohesion, and civism.

Chapter 5, "Islamist Social Institutions: Creating a Descriptive Context," introduces the reader to some of the major social and economic institutions that existed in the territories during the Oslo period—types, roles, services, target audiences served (clientele), organizational structure, legal status, and funding sources. Most importantly, it explores the social agenda that the Islamists had during the Oslo period and attempts to examine what constituted "Islamic authenticity" during that time and whether that aligns with the various widely held assumptions about Hamas and the Islamists.

Chapter 6, "Islamist Social Institutions: Key Analytical Findings," explores the main outcomes of my research with regard to the work and impact of the Islamist social sector, the nature of the Islamist social project, and the successes and failures of Islamist mobilization at the social level.

The last chapter considers the evolution of Hamas, its social institutions, and the Israel-Palestine conflict generally in the post-Oslo period. Chapter 7, "A Changing Islamist Order? From Civic Empowerment to Civic Regression—the Second Intifada and Beyond," assesses the political impact on the Islamist movement and its social institutions of the following: the second Intifada, Israel's 2005 "disengagement" from Gaza, Hamas's 2006 electoral victory, the subsequent international boycott of the Hamas-led government, and Hamas's June 2007 military takeover of Gaza. Particular consideration is given to how the role of social institutions changed after the second Intifada and after the 2006 elections.

Finally, the postscript offers a brief commentary on the implications and repercussions from Israel's 2008–2009 attack on Gaza, which occurred while this book was being written, and on Gaza's current situation.

A Note on Method

Having spent twenty-five years engaged in some form of research on the Gaza Strip and West Bank, I have always made it a priority to live among Palestinians and "walk in their shoes" to the extent that I was able and for as long as I could. My observations and interpretations over these two and a half decades provide the foundation for this book.

Hence, a central feature of this study is ethnographic. This book attempts to render visible—often through visual description—the social institutions of Hamas, their interrelationships, and their role in creating a collective existence among Palestinians. Having spent time among Islamic institutions and the people who run and use them, I want this book to give them voice. It is important for Palestinians to speak in their own words, not only through mine. As Augustus Richard Norton wrote in his two-volume study of civil society in the Middle East, "[s]cholarship on the Islamists . . . has been overly textual, too inclined to report the words of the ideologue and the spokesman, and insufficiently sociological, in terms of failing to look at the motives of those who lend their support to the Islamist movements."[30]

Despite all that has been written about them, Palestinians remain little known to the world; Hamas and those people identified with it, arguably more so. To the extent possible, I try to provide a sociological profile of both those who run Islamist social institutions and those whom they serve—that is, the people who live and work outside and well below Hamas's well-known circle of political and military leaders. My aim is to present a more dynamic depiction of Palestinian society, challenging the static and distorted one we typically get, allowing Palestinians to speak about Hamas, and from within it, about their everyday lives and what it means to be occupied and deprived. In presenting this more dynamic depiction, I tried to resist resorting to categories or dichotomies (although some are delineated for analytical purposes), since reality is always far more complex, differentiated, and irreducible than the stereotypes that are typically constructed for us. The imperative, as I see it, is to make *more* distinctions, not fewer.

In this book, therefore, I have tried not to speak *for* Palestinians but *from* them by incorporating into my analysis personal stories and accounts in the voices of individual Palestinian men, women, and children who are part of the Islamist social sector. In so doing, I have attempted "to apply," as Loren Lybarger has written, "a disciplined scholarly perspective that resists ideology in the interest of truth—truth always conditioned by the observer's historical and social location, his [or her] relation to power, the accidents of his life course, and the choices for alignment that flow from prior political commitments, experiences, and values. This truth is a reflexive one—seeking understanding of the other and of the self."[31] While I might substitute "accuracy" for "truth," the meaning is undeniably the same: rendering visible the complexities of Palestinian life and, in so doing, providing a more differentiated understanding of the forces that shape it. I do this while acknowledging that all interpretations can—and should—be challenged, recalling what Paul Ricoeur once wrote, "[n]either in literary criticism, nor in the social sciences, is there . . . a last word."[32]

Chapter 2

A BRIEF HISTORY OF HAMAS AND THE ISLAMIC MOVEMENT IN PALESTINE

I DO NOT INTEND TO provide a detailed history of Hamas, nor of the individual personalities within it. Others have already done this,[1] and such a discussion is not this study's focus. What follows, then, is an overview of key developments in the history of Hamas and the Palestinian Islamic movement that I feel are pertinent to the arguments presented in this book.

The Islamic Resistance Movement (Harakat al-Muqawama al-Islamiyya) or Hamas (an Arabic acronym meaning "zeal") was born with the first Palestinian uprising, or Intifada, in December 1987 (although the exact date of Hamas's establishment is still debated). The birth of this organization represented the Palestinian embodiment of political Islam in the Middle East. Although Hamas itself is a relatively recent phenomenon, it is rooted in a decades-old history of Islamic activism that began with the establishment of the Muslim Brotherhood in Gaza City in 1945. Hamas's evolution and influence were primarily due to the nature of Hamas's participation in that Intifada: the operations of its military wing, the work of its political leadership, and its social activities.

Since its inception and even after its 2006 electoral victory, there has been a great deal of debate regarding Hamas's actual strength and political power. Many have maintained that during the early years of its popularity, between 1988 and 1994, Hamas became the main rival of the PLO and had the support of 40 percent to 50 percent of the Palestinian population. In my view these assessments are too high, although it is correct to say that, as a political movement, Hamas's importance during this period was real and derived from the fact that its public, largely grassroots support was often far greater than its membership base and organizational and institutional structure.

Hamas's popularity in the late 1980s and early 1990s rose as Fatah's declined. The same factor accounted for both: Hamas increasingly came to embody the condition of resistance, while Fatah increasingly failed to do so.[2] Hence, Hamas's appeal derived primarily from its nationalist rather than its religious orientation. Khaled Hroub further notes:

> From another perspective, the "Islamism" of Hamas is a manifestation of the phenomenon of the strong rise of Islamic movements in the Arab and Islamic world since the late 1970s ... just like the

leftism of many Palestinian resistance organizations in the 1960s and 1970s [was] a reflection of international ideological trends sweeping the Middle East. Thus, Palestinian nationalist movements in the twentieth century can be seen from two different aspects: first, as resistance to occupation . . . ; and second, as manifestations of ideologies dominant in the Middle East region at the time . . . [which then] are pressed into service of "the resistance project," thus establishing a dialectical link between resistance and social change.[3]

This dialectical link between resistance and social change in the evolution of Hamas and political Islam in Palestine lies at the core of this book.

THE MUSLIM BROTHERHOOD IN PALESTINE AND ITS IDEOLOGICAL TRANSFORMATION: 1945 TO 1987

Hamas has its roots in the Society of Muslim Brothers (al-Ikhwan al-Muslimun), also known as the Muslim Brotherhood (MB) or just "the Ikhwan."[4] The history of Hamas fundamentally starts with the Muslim Brotherhood in Egypt and its concern with the Palestine problem. The Muslim Brotherhood was founded in Egypt in 1928 by Hassan al-Banna (1906 to 1949), a teacher who was deeply committed to the comprehensive reform of the *umma* (the community of Muslims, a social unit beyond the religious with a defined identity). He started the Brotherhood as an educational movement to redress what he saw as the corruption and decline of Egyptians, which resulted from what he viewed as their political, economic, and cultural subordination to the dominant colonial powers. He faulted not only the regime but also the traditional university of al-Azhar, the center of Islamic teaching and scholarship, which he believed had failed, ultimately, to protect Islamic values from Western encroachment.[5] Al-Banna's long-term goals were to rid the Islamic homeland of foreign occupation and to establish an Islamic state within the Islamic homeland.[6]

The importance of Palestine to the movement was demonstrated by a visit of al-Banna's brother to the region in the early 1930s. By 1946 the MB had a central office in Jerusalem, formalizing its presence in Palestine.[7] The question of Palestine was the primary force behind the regional expansion of the Muslim Brotherhood, which participated politically in events surrounding the revolt of 1936 and the war of 1948. Before his death in 1935, Sheikh Izz ad-Din al-Qassam, an Ikhwan member after whom Hamas's military brigades are named, organized violent resistance to Zionism. In fact, the political awareness and nationalistic spirit of the Brotherhood in the years before the 1948 war were so great that political issues predominated over the organization's traditional focus on social work and proselytizing. By 1949, the Brotherhood had established two thousand branches throughout Egypt with 500,000 active members and at least as many sympathizers.[8]

The loss of most of Palestine in 1948 and the placing of Palestinian territory under Jordanian and Egyptian control had a profound impact on the Brotherhood in Palestine, shaping its development in each territory and severing its links with the Arab world. In the West Bank, which Jordan annexed in 1950, the Brethren merged into the Jordanian branch of the Muslim Brotherhood. Through 1967 and after, the Muslim Brotherhood was a legal political party and acted as a loyal opposition to the Hashemite monarchy, given their shared commitment to social traditionalism and rejection of revolutionary Arab nationalism as personified in Egypt's President Nasser.[9] In fact, between 1948 and 1967, the Muslim Brotherhood was the only continuously legal political organization in the West Bank, tolerated by the regime as a possible counterweight to nationalist and leftist forces. Perhaps this was due to the fact that the Brotherhood folded its political activities into its social agenda of gradual Islamic reform, notably through education.

The Muslim Brotherhood in Gaza encountered a different reality and took a different trajectory than its counterpart in the West Bank. In Gaza, which was not annexed by Egypt, the Brethren formed a separate organization. Contact with their Egyptian counterparts effectively ended in December 1948 because the Egyptian government banned the organization after it was involved in what appeared to be an attempted coup and following several attacks on Cairo's Jewish community (although other sources maintain that some contact between the branches continued). From the beginning, the Gaza branch had a tradition of militancy and engaged in clandestine political and military activities including participation in the 1948 war that aimed to end Israeli occupation. In fact, many studies argue that the MB became the primary political movement in Gaza until 1955.[10]

By contrast, its West Bank counterpart was forbidden by Jordan to engage in violent cross-border attacks against Israel and had no such tradition of militancy.[11] One of the most important features of the Brotherhood's history in Palestine occurred in the early 1950s when certain members of the Gazan branch organized two secret military organizations—Youth for Vengeance (Shabab al-Tha'ir) and the Battalion of Justice [Katibat al-Haq]—most of whose members later became key figures in Fatah and the PLO. Over the next few years, the Brotherhood became the most prominent political movement in the Gaza Strip. By 1954 the Brotherhood in Gaza had eleven branches and over one thousand members, most them students from refugee camps.[12]

In 1954 Gamal Abdel Nasser, the hugely popular president of Egypt, outlawed the Muslim Brotherhood in Egypt (and Gaza), on the grounds that it had participated in a plot to assassinate him. The movement was forced underground, allowing it to gain experience in building decentralized, militant, and secretive organizations.[13] This greatly eroded the Brotherhood's influence in Gaza, where Nasserism had wide appeal. Furthermore, Nasser had encouraged the development of the Palestine Liberation Army, the military wing of the PLO, and had established military training units throughout the Gaza Strip.[14] Nationalism was the defining framework for armed struggle, not Islamism.

Under these circumstances the Brotherhood's program of political confrontation and armed resistance was unworkable, and a new strategy was needed. In 1957 the leadership of the Gaza Brotherhood was invited by Khalil al-Wazir, more popularly known by his nom de guerre, Abu Jihad, to establish an organization close to what would soon become Fatah, which would be dedicated to liberating Palestine through armed struggle. The Brotherhood did not take his request seriously, but when Fatah was formally established in 1958, many Brethren joined. Two years later the mainstream Brotherhood in Gaza, fearing the continued loss of its membership to a number of new political organizations that had emerged in the Strip, adopted an official decision against Fatah and refused to participate in the establishment of the PLO in 1964. According to Khaled Hroub, this decision was historically significant since it resulted in an unprecedented rift between the national Palestinian armed resistance movement and the Palestinian Islamists, a split that would only deepen over subsequent decades. Hence, between 1957 and "the early 1980s, when the foundation for the 1987 emergence of Hamas was laid, the Brotherhood withdrew from the political-national effort to liberate the homeland."[15]

The Brotherhood, instead, chose to focus on preparing the "liberation generation" through proselytizing and religious education. The objective, to quote an analyst of the movement, was to "launch a comprehensive effort at cultural renaissance designed to instill true Islam in the soul of the individual and, following that renaissance, to embark on the path of liberation."[16]

The 1967 war did not alter the thinking of the Muslim Brothers but rather reinforced it. To them, the war represented an ideological competition between the Islamic and Arab nationalist positions. With Nasser's defeat and the loss of more territory, the Brethren in Gaza especially remained convinced that the loss of Palestine was God's punishment for neglecting Islam, highlighting the importance of a preparatory religious education in the confrontation with Zionism.[17] While not unhappy with Nasser's defeat, they now faced the dilemmas posed by Israeli occupation.

The contact that remained (if any) between the Egyptian and Gaza branches of the Brotherhood terminated after the war. The Gazan branch remained in the mosques as it were and did not participate in the growing trend toward armed struggle fostered by nationalist factions.[18] Despite some interaction between the MB branches in Gaza and the West Bank during the late 1960s and 1970s, which was made possible by the fact that both territories were now under the same Israeli administration, the two branches remained quite distinct, reflecting "the inability within the movement to think or behave like a Palestinian-Islamic movement within an explicit arena of Palestinian politics."[19] The development of the mainstream Brotherhood, and subsequently Hamas, was essentially a Gaza phenomenon.

Although Israel's defeat of the Arab states in 1967 generated an Islamic resurgence in other contexts, it failed to do so in Palestine, where the secular nationalist forces led by the PLO were clearly predominant. It was nationalism rather than Islam that defined popular identity, at least during the first decade of occupation. This had a devastating impact on the Brotherhood, which was unable to articulate an effective response to the occupation, the loss of identity, and the loss and settlement of Palestinian land.[20] The movement curtailed many of its activities, recognizing a loss of community interest and support. It was put into a position where it had to rethink its public image and the nature of its message.[21] The nationalist spirit of the time was reinforced by the fedayeen movement in the Gaza Strip and its strategy of armed struggle against Israeli occupation, which was eventually put down by Ariel Sharon in the summer and fall of 1971 after three years of fighting (which ultimately spurred the reemergence of the MB).

Unable to respond effectively to the new reality created by Israel's occupation, the Islamic movement made a conscious decision not to engage with the nationalist movement and turned inward. Between 1967 and 1975, for example, and fueled by rising oil wealth from Saudi Arabia and other Gulf states, the movement launched what came to be known as the period of mosque building, in which the number of mosques in Gaza tripled from 200 to 600 and nearly doubled in the West Bank from 400 to 750.[22] This was followed in the 1970s through the late 1980s by the phase of social institution building, which led to the formation of Islamic student societies in high schools and universities (long the preserve of secular nationalist groups), youth organizations, charitable societies, kindergartens, medical clinics, and other institutions. In 1978 alone, three Islamic Sharia colleges were established in Gaza, Jerusalem, and Hebron, although some of the founders had no formal affiliation with the Muslim Brothers.[23] This network of social institutions was largely based in the Islamic Center (al-Mujamma al-Islami) founded by Sheikh Ahmad Yassin in 1973 in the Gaza Strip and legalized by the Israeli military administration in 1978 (see chapter 4).

The rise to power of Israel's right-wing Likud party in 1977 further encouraged the Islamist movement for two reasons. First, despite its hostility to Palestinians, the Likud's messianic message, which framed the conflict in religious as well as nationalist terms, supported Islamist approaches. Second, beginning in the early 1980s, Israel (like many Arab states) initially pursued policies that aimed to bolster the Islamists over the secular nationalists by allowing the Muslim Brotherhood to organize and mobilize politically and socially.[24] In fact, as late as 1986 the military governor of Gaza, General Segev, stated, "We extend some financial aid to Islamic groups via mosques and religious schools in order to help create a force that would stand against the leftist forces which support the PLO."[25]

Political momentum for the Muslim Brotherhood increased with the 1979 Islamic revolution in Iran and the subsequent spread of political Islam throughout the region, including Hizballah's rise in Lebanon. In the early 1980s, however, the Brotherhood came under increasing criticism from the nationalist camp for its passivity in confronting Israeli occupation, particularly in Palestinian universities, which deeply affected student activists within the Islamist bloc. In the early 1980s, the Islamic Jihad was formed in Gaza by leaders of the Brotherhood who left the mother organization because of its unwillingness to engage in armed resistance with the Israeli occupation. Foremost among them were Sheikh Abd al-Aziz Awda and Fathi al-Shaqaqi, who argued that fighting the occupation and reforming society according to Islamic principles could occur simultaneously.[26] The formation of the Islamic Jihad, coupled with its popularity and military successes, challenged the Brotherhood's dominant position within the Islamic community as well as its strategy toward Israel that emphasized internal social reform before external political action. Increasingly at stake for the Brotherhood was the loss of political influence over the younger generation of activists.

The expulsion of the PLO from Lebanon in 1982 and the nationalist crisis that attended it persuaded the Brotherhood that the PLO was politically and militarily defeated and gave rise to a change in strategy in which the Brotherhood saw itself as a potential political alternative. In 1983 Sheikh Yassin established two paramilitary wings—al-Majd and al-Mujahideen. The former was created as an intelligence unit responsible for surveillance and punishment of collaborators, and the latter was a commando unit charged with attacking Israeli military targets.[27] In 1984 Sheikh Yassin and other leaders of the Muslim Brotherhood were arrested on charges of weapons possession and planning armed operations against Israel. Sheikh Yassin was given a thirteen-year sentence but was released in a prisoner exchange ten months later. It was clear that the arrest of Brotherhood officials signaled a decision by the organizational leadership to engage in armed struggle with Israel. According to Ismail Abu Shanab, a cofounder of Hamas, "The period 1983 to 1987 marked the phase of direct preparation for resistance to the occupation, including armed struggle. Sheikh Ahmad Yassin took the lead in this, and did so independently of the Muslim Brotherhood."[28] It is also important to note that, by the mid-1980s, the PLO had begun to recover from its 1982 defeat and its influence among Palestinians was growing, at the expense of the Brethren's. This was evident from the results of various elections in local professional associations in the West Bank and Gaza Strip, which PLO-affiliated groups won. This, too, weighed on the movement.

Based on the writings of the Brethren at the time, they had three objectives: cadre formation and mobilization, passive resistance, and military action.[29] The inclusion of armed resistance in their strategy indicated a radical shift in their ideology and practice, from reformism to militarism.[30] By the time the first Intifada erupted just a short while later, the constant tension between armed struggle and social reform had finally been resolved: both objectives could be achieved simultaneously. But with the formation of Hamas in December 1987, which eventually took over the institutions of the Muslim Brotherhood, political action and armed confrontation clearly became dominant, representing not a break with, but a reorganization of, the Brotherhood, which effectively was subsumed to Hamas. According to Mishal, "The transition to politics and armed struggle represented by Hamas was intended to complement, not replace, the social activities identified with the *Mujamma*."[31]

Other analysts such as Jeroen Gunning argue that the conflict between social reform and political action was resolved through a compromise of sorts or what Glenn Robinson has termed "an internal coup."[32] Those Brothers who did not agree with the formation of Hamas could remain within the Brotherhood. Those who chose resistance first could join Hamas without having to renounce their Ikhwan membership. By creating a separate but affiliated political movement, the more absolutist and ideologically conservative older guard of Brothers (who tended to be urban, upper-middle-class merchants) who remained outside Hamas retreated in favor of a younger generation of new leaders (university educated, from the lower middle class, and based primarily in the refugee camps[33]), many of whom had been educated in the West or in Western-type schools. As such, a door was opened to the entry of large numbers of activists who were not necessarily ideologically motivated in the same way or to the same degree as the founding leadership.[34]

In effect "Hamas ... represented a shift of emphasis in the Islamic movement's strategy, from reformist and communal to political, and from the spiritual life of the individual to national action."[35]

The First Intifada (1987 to 1993)

The context for the first Palestinian Intifada had been established over the preceding twenty years of occupation and the growing oppression, deprivation, and dispossession associated with it.[36] The spark came on December 6, 1987, when an Israeli settler was killed in Gaza, followed two days later by another incident in which an Israeli truck killed four Palestinian bystanders. Demonstrations erupted in Gaza's largest refugee camp, Jabalya, which was considered the start of the Intifada. On December 9, Yassin met with other members of the Brotherhood leadership in Gaza and founded Hamas. On December 11–12 and December 14–15, Hamas issued its first leaflet in Gaza and the West Bank respectively, calling for the defeat of the occupier—a nationalist, not religious, agenda— and many consider this the beginning of the organization, although it was not made official until late February 1988.

The first Palestinian Intifada dramatically altered the nature of Islamic politics in Palestine. The gradual, reformist, and non-Palestinian approach of the Muslim Brotherhood ceded to an activist form of Islam that was Palestinian- and nationalist-centric but anchored in an Islamic perspective (however, some more traditional Muslim Brothers refused, arguing that Islamic reform was still more vital than resistance). The change resulted from a recognition that good works alone would no longer suffice to build popular support, although the leadership continued to emphasize social service as an important part of their political program. Good works now had to be tied to political and (eventually) violent resistance to Israel's occupation.

The social, political, and military structures created by the Brotherhood were transferred to, and then to varying degrees reorganized under, Hamas. According to the late Ismail Abu Shanab, even greater numbers joined Hamas who had not been fully active or engaged MB members and therefore did not possess the requisite ideological understanding or commitment to the movement; others introduced new ideas (both Islamist and non-Islamist) through their experiences abroad. Abu Shanab, who himself had received his PhD in the United States, argued that this mixture of individuals and perspectives contributed greatly to Hamas's pragmatism and flexibility, allowing the movement to appeal to a wider popular constituency.[37]

It was during the first Palestinian Intifada that Hamas emerged as a political challenge to the PLO and most notably to its dominant party, Fatah. From the beginning, Hamas refused to join the nationalist movement and publicly positioned itself as a political competitor: an activist Islamic organization that was the Palestinian embodiment of political

Islam, claiming to serve the goals of the Muslim Brotherhood, not those of the PLO. Sheikh Yassin argued that Hamas was primarily a political movement whose main goal was to secure the right of self-determination for Palestinians but within an Islamic framework. Yet this political competition with the secularists in large part compelled Hamas to adopt a nationalist discourse. Hamas defined itself as a wing of the Muslim Brotherhood in Palestine—a needed parallel to the PLO's United National Leadership of the Uprising (UNLU)—and established a structure independent of it. Hamas distributed its own leaflets, called its own strikes, and organized its own activities. I was living in Gaza during the second year of the Intifada (1988–1989), and although the thrust of political and social activity was clearly within the PLO's domain, Hamas was a defined presence. How much popular support Hamas actually enjoyed at this time is impossible to verify, since hard indicators were few and of limited methodological value. However, Hamas did draw support from a variety of circles—refugees, the nonrefugee poor, the middle classes, and professionals—and its popular resonance was undeniable. Hamas was constantly competing with the UNLU over leadership, authority, and popular support, but it was some months before it enjoyed visible success.[38]

For well over a year after the Intifada started, Hamas—despite having made clear inroads into the political arena—remained tainted by its early working relationship with the Israeli authorities and by policies that failed to engage the occupation meaningfully beyond issuing leaflets and communiqués that remained Islamic and vaguely antinationalist in orientation.[39] During these early days, Hamas "directed its followers to take only those actions that had religious overtones and thus would be easily understood as integral to Islamic ritual—such as fasting, praying, and exploiting dates of religious significance in order to escalate the Intifada under its leadership."[40] At the time it seemed that, for Hamas, defeating the secular nationalists was at least as important as ending the occupation. However, during the Intifada, this contradiction soon became unsustainable.

The Islamist profile increased, albeit negatively, with the November 1988 decision by the Palestine National Council (PNC)—the legislative wing of the PLO—to formally accept a two-state solution based on the 1947 UN Partition Plan and UN Security Council Resolutions 242 and 338, declaring in effect its acceptance of a state in the West Bank and Gaza. Immediately following the PNC declaration, Arafat renounced terrorism, formally accepted 242 and 338, and recognized the state of Israel, thereby meeting the U.S. government's precondition for meeting with the PLO (heretofore banned), which had wide popular support. People celebrated by dancing in the streets, defying curfew (and thereby risking their lives) as Israeli soldiers stood at a distance, watching in stunned disbelief. People believed that these concessions would finally lead to a state, albeit small, for which they were willing to settle. "I will never forget my home in Palestine; it will always be in my heart," one Gazan told me. "But now, all I want is a factory and a flag."

After the PNC acceptance of a two-state solution, Hamas rejected any initiative based on compromise with Israel, arguing, among other things, that no political settlement with Israel—seen by Hamas as a usurper—was possible, since any concession would constitute a violation of Palestine's status as an Islamic endowment (*waqf*).[41] Further, Hamas argued, the occupation must end as a precondition for any talks. Differences with the UNLU increased tensions. According to Mishal and Sela," On the one hand, Hamas was not eager to aggravate its disagreements with the [UNLU] to the point of a head-on clash, as that would be counterproductive in the struggle against Israel. On the other hand, Hamas did not back away from a confrontation in the future should the [UNLU], together with the PLO, assent to a political settlement that jettisoned the principle of liberating all of Palestine."[42]

Hamas, which three months before (August 1988) had issued its organizational charter—a maximalist and decidedly racist document—began a series of attacks against Israeli soldiers inside Israel, a campaign that did not appear to have the support of the Palestinian majority. Yet several months earlier, in March 1988, Mahmoud al-Zahar (with the apparent support of Sheikh Yassin), then a key Hamas member but not acting officially for the organization, had presented to Israel's then foreign minister, Shimon Peres, a proposal that outlined both a short- and a long-term solution for the West Bank and Gaza. Representing a modification of Hamas's official position, the proposal was rejected by Israel. (This was followed by an initiative in April 1994 by Hamas's Political Bureau that dealt with the establishment of a Palestinian entity in the West Bank and Gaza Strip in addition to other proposals for a conditional cease-fire with Israel in 1995). Although in principle Hamas rejected a permanent settlement of the conflict with Israel, they accepted a temporary settlement as a phase toward the realization of their larger goal.

Khaled Hroub states, "This is the first time in Hamas's history that the movement provided a (non-historic) concept [of a solution] in the form of a proposal or an almost comprehensive solution."[43] In the two decades since, Hamas has continued to make clear its willingness to engage Israel in dialogue over an armistice and interim solution to the conflict (e.g., a full Israeli withdrawal from the occupied territories), demonstrating its pragmatism and flexibility, as well as its ability to adapt strategically and tactically to changing political circumstances.[44]

In an interview with Zvi Sela, the chief intelligence officer of the Israel Prisons Service, Yassin's political position is revealed. According to Sela,

> We held him [Yassin] in Hadarim Prison [near Netanya] on the third floor in harsh conditions. We gave him a very hard time. He was not allowed visits and we kept him tightly locked up for almost five years. He was held in a narrow room where the temperature was 45 degrees [Celsius] in the summer and freezing cold in the winter. His blankets were dirty and smelled. That's how he lived. I found him to be a very smart man, and also very decent. We engaged in a war of minds. We knew that after every battle between us someone would die, either on my side or on his side.
>
> ... I always told him, "Stop blowing up buses, stop murdering women and children." He replied: "Tzvika, listen, we had good teachers. You established a state thanks to your military power. The dead I take from you are for the sake of establishing a state, but you are killing women and children for the sake of the occupation. You already have a state. You are dirty and hypocritical. I have no interest in destroying you—all I want is a state."
>
> (*Ha'aretz*): So the father of the Hamas movement told you he recognized the State of Israel?
>
> Yes. He was smart and brave. Cruel but credible. He gave his life in the war for the freedom of his people. I tend to think that if we had tried for an agreement with him, we would have succeeded. He thought the reason the Israelis were dealing with [then PLO leader] Yasser Arafat is that they were very smart, because we knew we would get nowhere with him.[45]

Although Israel maintained direct communications with Islamist officials for over a year after Hamas's establishment, because Israeli officials continued to view it as a movement dedicated to social reform rather than political violence, this changed dramatically in mid-1989 following the kidnapping and killing of two Israeli soldiers in February and May. Immediately after the killings, Israel arrested hundreds of Hamas activists in Gaza and the West Bank as well as Sheikh Yassin (who was not released until 1997), al-Zahar, and other high-ranking officials, which seriously weakened the movement.[46] By the end of the summer of 1989, Israel halted all meetings with Hamas and, by December, outlawed it. Israel then began a campaign to eliminate Hamas through arrests, deportations, and assassinations.[47] By May 1990 a nucleus of fighters was formed by Sheikh Yassin and Salah Shehada, the first military leader of Hamas.

With Yassin's imprisonment and Israel's elimination campaign, the organization was crippled at the senior leadership level, necessitating an organizational structure that was more decentralized. The political, military, and social sectors of the movement were, in effect, delineated at this time. The relationship between the political and military wings appeared most defined. Social institutions were more loosely affiliated with their political counterparts if at all; indeed, these kinds of connections were deliberately kept to a minimum in order to protect Islamic social organizations from attack.[48]

A similar restructuring occurred in which political decision making and power over the movement's financial resources shifted to the more radical, young, and technocratic leadership based outside Palestine (primarily in Amman, where the Muslim Brotherhood played a visible public role).[49] The existence of dual leaderships not only created structural problems but also ideological ones, as the Oslo period revealed. The external leaders, who did not have to deal with the reality of life under occupation, could afford to be more extreme in their vision of political Islam than the local leaders, who tended more toward moderation.

Another feature of the restructuring was the division of the West Bank into seven subdistricts and the Gaza Strip into five. Each territory had its own headquarters that included four divisions: security, religious preaching (social), political activity, and military activities. Gaza and the West Bank were linked by a coordinating committee under the control of the senior leadership, which consisted of three major committees: political, military, and indoctrination.[50] Military and civilian wings of the organization were now separated, a key change.

The August 1990 Gulf War began what is arguably another phase in Hamas's political evolution, further solidifying Hamas as a political and resistance force. Although Yasir Arafat opposed the Iraqi occupation of Kuwait and advocated, as most Arab states did, that the Arab League resolve the dispute, he opposed the U.S. attack to dislodge Iraq from Kuwait. This alienated the Gulf states particularly, since the United States was not going to allow a diplomatic resolution of the conflict. Arafat's decision to side, in effect, with Iraq against the Gulf states, who were key funders of the PLO, proved to be a political and economic disaster for the PLO, eroding its popular base of support over time. Hamas, by contrast, sought to protect its relationship with the Gulf and with its own constituents. After condemning the presence of Western forces in the region, Hamas subsequently called on Iraq's Saddam Hussein to withdraw from Kuwait, a position for which Hamas was rewarded.

There was considerable speculation that much or all of the monies earmarked for the PLO were being redirected to Hamas and its social sector. According to local sources at the time, from 1990 to 1993 Kuwait and Saudi Arabia contributed $30 million and Iran—a new donor—$13 million.[51] Through the *zakat* committees, Hamas was consistently able to reach the poor who had formerly been subsidized by the PLO. In addition, Hamas allegedly received support from other Islamic movements abroad and informal donations from foreign supporters. Thus the Islamists' financial strength grew in both absolute and relative terms from the start of the Gulf War, and the organization was greatly appreciated and valued by widening sectors of society for providing welfare and social services in an increasingly depleted environment. Hamas, its leadership, and its institutions were also renowned for their honesty, decency, and incorruptibility not only by the Palestinian street but also by international officials, who sometimes relied on Hamas—and, I was told, only Hamas—for the grassroots distribution of donor funds.[52] As political and economic competition intensified, periodic disputes broke out between Hamas and the nationalist factions in Gaza and the West Bank.

Following the October 1990 massacre of seventeen Palestinians at the al-Aqsa Mosque in Jerusalem, Hamas's official military organ, the Izz-ad-Din al-Qassam Brigades,[53] was formed. The Qassam Brigades staged a series of attacks against Israeli soldiers and settlers that was known as the "war of the knives." Within months, the United States was calling for an international peace conference between Israelis and Palestinians—the first public negotiations between Israel and the Palestinians from the occupied territories. Some analysts argued that the American diplomatic initiative was, in part, a response to Hamas's growing political and military power and was an attempt to eclipse it.

The peace conference convened on October 31, 1991, in Madrid. Hamas rejected the conference (as did certain nationalist factions), leading to greater hostility with Israel and greater factional conflict—at times, violent—between Hamas and Fatah.[54] These clashes (then still the exception) surprised and shocked the Palestinian public, who opposed them as they have since.

During the Madrid period (October 1991–August 1993), the peace process faltered for many reasons, including internal Palestinian divisions and internecine conflict. The more pivotal reason was that Israel continued with its policies of settlement expansion, land expropriation, and economic pressure, the latter of which was markedly escalated by the introduction in March 1993 of closure policy (economic blockade) in the occupied territories, which diminished Palestinian life in new and fundamental ways. Hamas successfully capitalized on the obvious contradictions between a diplomatic process allegedly designed to secure peace and on-the-ground policies that clearly undermined it. Hamas benefited not only by presenting itself as a counterhegemonic force and political and moral alternative to Fatah and its political failures, which included participation in the Madrid process—stating at times that its opposition to the PLO was democratic—but also by increasing attacks against the

Israeli military and Israeli civilians. Indeed, as its involvement in the Intifada deepened, Hamas became more militant. (Yet it is important to note that throughout the first Intifada and the Oslo period that followed, Fatah had significantly more institutional resources than Hamas did.)

During this time Hamas attempted to force the release of Sheikh Yassin from prison by increasing its attacks against Israeli personnel. Israel responded by deporting 415 Islamist officials, activists, and supporters to southern Lebanon in December 1992, where they remained for one year. Palestinians in Gaza feared that this action heralded a larger Israeli policy of transfer that would affect them all. The expulsions, which generated intense attention and debate in the territories, represented another critical turning point in the political trajectory of the Islamic movement in general and of Hamas in particular.

First, the expulsion of hundreds of Hamas and Jihad activists was regarded as an act of severe repression against the Islamist movement specifically and against Palestinians generally, creating popular linkages that cemented the nationalist credentials of Hamas and repositioned it domestically as a viable political alternative to the PLO. Second, the attack against the Islamists demanded a real response from the nationalist factions, notably Fatah, which now had to contend with Hamas—perhaps for the first time—as a serious and permanent political actor whose military activity against Israel surpassed Fatah's own. Third, while Hamas's popularity widened as a result of the expulsions, Fatah's was diminishing. The combined effect of the PLO's financial crisis and the faltering peace talks so eroded Arafat's popular support that there were calls for his resignation.

Furthermore, during the deported activists' time in Lebanon, Hamas not only developed relations with Hizballah, "which contributed to a qualitative improvement in their military capabilities,"[55] that were subsequently and devastatingly used against Israel; it also expanded its representation regionally. Eventually, under international pressure, and coerced by (faltering) peace talks that were official (Madrid) and secret (Oslo), Israel allowed the deported Islamists to return, and they received a heroes' welcome.

The PLO now acknowledged a political shift in its relationship with Hamas, a shift that compelled it to engage the organization formally as a serious rival by trying (and failing) to incorporate Hamas into the PLO. The period from roughly 1992 through 1993 was a terrible one especially inside the Gaza Strip, marked by greater factional conflict and the violence that increasingly accompanied it. During this time Hamas began targeting Palestinians deemed collaborators with Israel's security services—a charge that, once made, was virtually impossible to appeal. This introduced an additional layer of fear and insecurity among Gazans.

Conflict continued between Hamas and its Palestinian adversaries but also increased among the secular nationalists. These factions, historically important social actors, were beginning to break down as their disputes increasingly centered on power, not ideology, and as their economic resources declined; the only faction for whom ideology remained central was Hamas. The crisis was exacerbated by declining economic conditions and the PLO's inability—despite its concessions—to achieve a political settlement with Israel, which was systematically expanding its control over the West Bank and Gaza. Arafat's relatively weakened position with his popular base in the West Bank and Gaza compelled his participation in the then secret Oslo negotiations. Doubtless, too, Israel saw in Oslo an opportunity to take advantage of Arafat's compromised position in order to contain (if not eliminate) Palestinian nationalism in both its secular and its religious forms.

The Oslo Period (1993 to 2000)

In late August 1993, it became known that Israel and the PLO had been engaged in secret negotiations to end their conflict, a revelation that stunned Palestinians, Israelis, and the world. On September 13, 1993, the Declaration of Principles was signed, the first of the Oslo peace accords, ending the first Intifada and transforming the political and economic reality of the West Bank and Gaza forever.[56] This had a dramatic impact on the Islamic political movement, triggering an existential crisis. Israel ceded limited autonomy to Palestinians in the Gaza Strip and West Bank (only). In exchange, the PLO, mainly Fatah, recognized Israel's right to exist, ending all claims to pre-1948 Palestine. By June 1994 the PNA, the first internationally recognized Palestinian self-administrative body, had been established, with PLO chairman Yasir Arafat as its president. The international community declared its support for the Oslo process, and the regional community refrained from condemning it. With pledges from twenty-five foreign governments for $2.1 billion in economic assistance to Palestinians in the West Bank and Gaza Strip, the PNA assumed responsibility for a range of administrative, economic, and social services, establishing formal institutions to run the affairs of "state." At the time, it seemed a clear victory for the secular nationalist agenda, posing a profound dilemma for the Islamist sector and its relationship with the grass roots.

Hamas (in alliance with ten other Palestinian factions based in Damascus) vehemently rejected and condemned the Oslo Accords because Hamas considered them a betrayal of Palestinian national and historic rights. Yet popular sentiment in Palestine (and Israel—among Jews and

Arabs) was largely behind Oslo and the hope of peace and normalization with Israel, placing Hamas in a defensive position—in dramatic contrast to the one it had occupied just weeks before. Indeed, within ten days of Arafat's famous handshake with Israeli prime minister Yitzhak Rabin on the White House lawn on September 13, 1993 Palestinian opinion polls indicated that 60 percent of Palestinians favored the PLO leadership and only 17 percent favored Hamas.[57]

How then would Hamas respond to the Oslo Accords, and to the nationalist acquiescence to a secular democratic state in a fraction of historic Palestine, and still maintain its position as the leading opposition force? In the early post-Oslo months, the focus was on maintaining national unity and avoiding any confrontation with the secular nationalists that could bring internal disorder and erode public support. The Hamas leaders understood that Israel's partial withdrawal from Palestinian lands was deeply embraced by the Palestinian public, and they certainly did not want to be seen as having impeded it. They therefore instructed the organization's members to downplay the necessity of jihad under occupation and to emphasize instead the illegitimate and imbalanced nature of the Oslo agreements, which violated UN Resolution 242 calling for an Israeli withdrawal to its 1967 borders. In this regard, Hamas subsequently focused on the PNA's failings—corruption, mismanagement, and political ineptitude.[58] This decision was taken despite fears—which ultimately proved correct—that Fatah and Israel together might at some future point attack and try to destroy Hamas, each for its own purpose, and with international support. That Hamas was the militarily weaker party was clear to all, especially to its own leadership.

One key question confronting the Islamist movement was whether Hamas should participate in the new Palestinian government, a question that derived in part from the movement's preference for coexistence (albeit uneasy) over conflict. According to an internal report Hamas prepared after the Oslo signing, there was no consensus on the issue of government participation, and the leaders openly acknowledged their inability to prevent implementation of the accord or confront the PLO, thereby derailing the process. They further conceded their inability to provide an alternative political platform consistent with national and Islamic principles.[59] In a somewhat prescient description of Hamas's current reality, the document stated: "We opt for confrontation, but shall we confront our people? And can we tilt the balance in our favor? And if we succeed, will we be able to offer the people an alternative, or will success only intensify the offensive of occupation?"[60]

As a result, Hamas opted for participation through unofficial presence in the PNA's administration, and it did so by encouraging its supporters to work for the Authority on a personal (as opposed to an official) basis. According to Mishal, "[Hamas] ... justified this by distinguishing between two perceptions of the PA: as a sovereign political power, but also as an administrative apparatus geared to provide services to the public. While the former image represented political principles and national symbols, the latter was perceived to be instrumental, linked to reality. As a political center ... the PA was denied Hamas's legitimacy. However, as an administrative apparatus designated to enforce law and order and provide employment and services to the community, the PA could be acknowledged."[61]

Hamas adopted a three-pronged strategy: armed (but controlled) violence[62] against Israel and its continuing occupation; political (as opposed to military) confrontation with the PNA while maintaining open communication with Fatah; and building support for the Islamic movement politically and socially. The movement felt that this cautious approach was justified as long as the final outcome of the peace process was indeterminate.

Another of Hamas's priorities was to protect its social institutions, a key factor in its strategy of nonconfrontation with the Authority's police and security forces. Concomitantly, though, Hamas continued its attacks against Israeli civilians and soldiers, especially in the period leading up to the implementation of the May 1994 Cairo Agreement and the implementation of limited autonomy in Gaza and Jericho. Because Hamas viewed the Oslo Accord and Cairo Agreement as existential threats, it was unwilling to abandon armed struggle against Israel (and would defend it as a form of self-defense against Israel; as a way to avenge the murder of Palestinians; and as a form of pressure on Israel to withdraw from the West Bank), although the attendant risks were clear: economic and military retaliation by Israel and the PNA, internecine conflict, and eroding public support.

For its part, the PNA—and Yasir Arafat specifically—responded with a policy of open confrontation when it perceived Hamas as a threat; a policy of controlling and containing Hamas, since co-optation and elimination were not possible; and continued security cooperation with Israel. It was also clear that the two sectors were periodically talking to each other and, despite their clear animosity, attempting to maintain open channels of communication. In fact, Hamas agreed to what amounted to a ceasefire, particularly during the 1995 Oslo II negotiations that transferred to the PNA limited autonomy over certain restricted areas of the West Bank.

Hamas's strategy of continued armed struggle against Israel was strengthened by the massacre of twenty-nine Palestinians by a Jewish settler in the Ibrahimi Mosque in Hebron on February 25, 1994 (during negotiations over the Cairo Agreement). In response, the Qassam Brigades launched a series of revenge suicide bombings and targeted attacks inside Israel—in Afula and Hadera in April, in Tel Aviv in October, and in Ramat Gan and Jerusalem in the summer of 1995—that took the lives of many Israeli civilians.[63] While these attacks were justified to the Palestinian public as avenging the deaths in Hebron, they were also designed to strengthen Hamas's bargaining position with the PNA as a viable opposition force.[64]

A severe crackdown ensued, first by Israel and later by the PNA. This included mass arrests of Hamas and Jihad activists, assassinations of key officials, and intensified closures of Gaza and the West Bank, which imposed enormous economic hardship on an increasingly impoverished population—a fact that continually plagued Hamas. Both Hamas and the Islamic Jihad accused the PNA of working with Israel against their organizations and in assassinating key members of their military wings. On November 18, 1994 (one month after Israel and Jordan signed a peace treaty), a terrible incident occurred in Gaza that some Hamas officials argued changed the internal Hamas-PNA dynamic forever. Known as Black Friday, Palestinian police opened fire on Islamic activists who were planning a protest following prayers at Gaza's Filastin Mosque. The protest turned into a riot, and fifteen people were killed, two hundred were injured, and hundreds more arrested.

The combination of popular fear over rising internecine violence and Israel's damaging economic restrictions as well as popular expectations surrounding the second Oslo agreement, known as the Taba Accord, compelled both Arafat and Hamas to try to settle their differences (notably over the use of violence against Israel) in talks that took place in Cairo during the fall of 1995. After the signing of the Taba Accord on September 28, 1995 (which fragmented and cantonized the West Bank), Hamas's internal leadership temporarily suspended attacks against Israel because they did not want Hamas to be viewed as having disrupted Israel's planned withdrawal from major Arab localities. In fact, under great pressure from Israel and the PNA, neither Hamas nor the Islamic Jihad carried out any suicide attacks between August 1995 and February 1996.[65] While no formal agreement was signed at the end of the Arafat-Hamas talks in December 1995, a tacit agreement was reached, informed in part by Hamas's calculations after Taba. The agreement stipulated that Hamas could continue its armed struggle against Israel (no doubt a form of pressure on Israel that Arafat did not oppose) as long at it did not do so from PNA-controlled territories.

Hamas's position in these talks largely reflected the thinking of the political leaders outside Palestine who opposed accommodation with the PNA and a cease-fire with Israel. The internal political leadership, however, opted for a less militant approach in favor of one that would allow Hamas to compete for political power within a changed, PLO-dominated order that was increasingly and dangerously positioned against it. The internal Hamas leaders were responding primarily and with great alarm to growing Israeli pressure on Arafat to eliminate Hamas and its social institutional infrastructure. The threat to the Islamic social sector was critical in moderating their position. Since 1995, Hamas's senior political leaders in the country had not only proposed conditional cease-fires with Israel and an accommodation with the PNA to preempt intra-Palestinian disputes; they had also increasingly redirected their strategic emphasis away from political and military action to social and civic development (see chapter 4), recognizing the PLO's relative strength. This accommodationist position was rejected by Hamas's military wing, leading to threats against some political leaders and growing tensions between the "inside" and "outside."

That Hamas pursued a dual and seemingly contradictory policy of limited, cautious engagement with the PNA and outright opposition is further seen in its approach to the January 1996 Palestinian elections and to what was perceived by most as a push for peace under a secular-nationalist agenda (Israeli prime minister Rabin's assassination two months earlier by a radical right-wing Orthodox Jew opposed to the peace process had arguably strengthened the need for a secular approach to negotiations). Hamas's possible participation in these elections as a separate political party under the auspices of Oslo was intensely debated in the first two years of the peace process between those favoring such participation (led by Sheikh Yassin) under certain specified conditions, and those who rejected it outright.[66] Just before the January elections, Hamas announced that it would not participate and would passively boycott the elections, although it encouraged some of its members to run as independents. In this way, Hamas could participate unofficially without granting legitimacy to the PLO and to the PLO's negotiations with Israel,[67] thereby avoiding complete political marginalization in what its leadership understood would be a popularly supported event.[68]

Indeed, one month before the elections, polls showed Hamas with 15 percent compared with Fatah's 40–45 percent of the vote.[69] So Hamas's decision to boycott yet encourage individuals to participate was not only political but tactical, since certain key Hamas officials understood that an electoral victory was unlikely and could compromise them politically and ideologically but so too might a blanket rejection of the elections. Rather, the internal political leadership chose to reposition themselves away from being "rejectionists" toward being an "opposition from within." Over time, this evolved into a policy of working with the PNA as an administrative entity providing needed services to the population but opposing the PNA (and Arafat) as a sovereign political power with the right to represent and speak for Palestinians.

Whatever agreement there was to maintain quiet ended with Israel's assassination of Yahia Ayyash on January 5, 1996, a key figure in Hamas's military wing and known as "the engineer" for his expertise in explosives.[70] Ayyash's assassination two weeks before the Palestinian election followed that of Islamic Jihad leader Fathi al-Shaqaqi in Malta on October 26, 1995. Not only did these attacks elicit acts of revenge from both organizations; they effectively extinguished any possibility of an agreement between Arafat and the Islamists over ending attacks against Israel, which may have been Israel's intent.

The revenge attacks, which had been planned by Hamas military cells in the West Bank, began in February and March 1996 after the Palestinian elections. A series of suicide bombings occurred in several major Israeli cities including Jerusalem, Ashkelon, and Tel Aviv, with devastating results. In less than three years since the start of the Oslo peace process, more than one hundred Israeli civilians and soldiers had been killed and hundreds more injured. Not only did these operations underscore the autonomy of Hamas's military wing (whose leaders were distinct from the domestic political leadership operationally, strategically, and in social and political background); they increased the tensions between the inside and the outside leadership, and highlighted the weakness of the (internal) political sector.[71]

This time the PNA responded not only by imprisoning some of Hamas's political leaders but went further, closing down some of its charitable institutions—a policy it had long resisted. Under mounting pressure from Israel and the United States, the Authority began an all-out offensive against Hamas in both Gaza and the West Bank. The PNA effectively weakened the military wing by arresting and imprisoning over one thousand Islamist officials and activists, many of whom were tortured and killed.[72]

The PNA's crackdown had its desired effect, and Hamas did not recover until the start of the second Intifada in 2000. One immediate outcome of this terrible wave of violence was the election in Israel of the rightwing Likud leader Benjamin Netanyahu in May 1996 over his Labor rival Shimon Peres. Some analysts posited that Hamas aimed in part to defeat Peres since he had ordered "the engineer" Ayyash's assassination in an attempt to boost his electoral chances. With Likud in power in Israel, the Oslo process, flawed as it was, lost even the illusory appearance of success.

Given Netanyahu's opposition to Oslo and his more openly hostile posture toward the Palestinians and the PNA, Arafat wanted to avoid further internecine conflict with Hamas and so focused more on repairing their strained relationship. Although suicide operations abated for almost a year, they resumed in March 1997 with an attack in Tel Aviv followed by attacks in Jerusalem in August and September, leading to further and harsher PNA crackdowns.

By early 1998, tensions between the PNA and Hamas had increased dramatically, particularly after the murder of three senior military commanders of the Qassam Brigades. Although Hamas held Israel responsible for the killings, it also accused the PNA of collaborating with Israel in their execution. This collaboration was no doubt spurred by what the Palestinian leadership hoped would be a successful conclusion to the upcoming Wye River Accord, which called for the redeployment of Israeli forces in the West Bank. Signed by Israel and the PNA on October 23, 1998, the Wye agreement angered Hamas since it predicated Israel's transfer of land on the PNA's commitment to fight terrorism and disarm combatants, and secured PNA agreement to having the United States monitor the accord's implementation.[73] More attacks by Hamas (and Islamic Jihad) ensued, and the PNA responded with arrests of Hamas activists (Sheikh Yassin was placed under house arrest) among other repressive measures, further weakening Hamas politically and militarily.

In May 1999, the Israeli elections for prime minister brought the Labor party leader Ehud Barak to power. Together with President Clinton, Barak (prematurely) insisted on holding a peace summit with Arafat in July 2000 that aimed to end the conflict but, predictably, ended in failure.

The Second Palestinian Intifada, Hamas's Electoral Victory, and Its Seizure of Gaza (2000 to Present)

Following the demise of the July 2000 Camp David summit, which attempted, in effect, to formalize and institutionalize the losses imposed on Palestinians by the Oslo agreements, the second Palestinian uprising erupted in September. It was only with the start of the second Intifada that Hamas, together with other political factions, was able to reassert itself politically and militarily. Several political factors contributed to the Islamists' reascendance: the militarization of the Intifada (i.e., ending the occupation through violent confrontation); the emergence of a younger generation of more militant Fatah activists who assumed leadership of the Intifada (and increasingly eclipsed the role of the older generation of PNA/PLO elites); internal and seemingly irrevocable political splits within the Palestinian national movement; and widespread corruption of Fatah and the ruling political structure. These factors among others, including the subsequent U.S. and Israeli campaigns (military, political, and economic) against Yasir Arafat and the PNA—themselves derived from a policy designed to preclude the emergence of a Palestinian state—allowed Hamas to rebuild its political/military infrastructure and pursue a form of militancy (as seen in the spate of suicide bombing attacks in Israel between 2002 and 2004; see chapter 7) that initially went beyond Fatah's own.[74]

During this period, which was characterized by Israel's invasion and reoccupation of the West Bank, the building of the separation wall, and increased repression of Gaza, Israel assassinated several of Hamas's key leaders. The first, Sheikh Salah Shehada, a member of the Political Bureau and head of the first military wing of Hamas, was killed on July 23, 2002, when an IDF (Israel Defense Forces) F-16 dropped a thousand-ton bomb on his apartment building in al-Daraj, a densely populated neighborhood of Gaza City. His wife and several other people were also killed. Ismail Abu Shanab, a leading member of the Hamas Political Bureau and perhaps the most moderate among the Hamas leadership, was killed on August 21, 2003, by five missiles fired into his car, incinerating him. Abu Shanab's assassination was followed by Sheikh Yassin's on March 22, 2004, when an IDF rocket struck him as he was leaving a mosque after prayers. His successor, Dr. Abd al-Aziz al-Rantisi, was then killed by a helicopter missile strike the following month on April 17, 2004, after returning from a visit to his family. At this point, the locus of power within Hamas began to shift outside the occupied territories to Khaled Meshal in Damascus. There is no doubt that Israel's assassinations did weaken Hamas locally inside Gaza and enhanced Meshal's power within the organization and his assumption of control over the military wing.

These assassinations, among other factors discussed above, not only catalyzed the Islamist factions and their radicalization, but slowly shifted the balance of power in their favor—particularly after Israel's 2005 disengagement from Gaza—culminating in their electoral victory in January 2006, a vote that was less *for* Hamas and far more *against* Fatah.

Indeed, it was the United States and the international community that pressed the Palestinians for legislative elections after Israel's redeployment knowing full well that Hamas-backed candidates would run for office and, according to some U.S. officials, welcoming Hamas's participation under the Change and Reform Party. President Abbas voiced little if any objection to Hamas's electoral participation. The acceptance of Hamas's entry into the political process was based on two key factors. First, in exchange for its participation, Hamas offered to cease all suicide bombings against Israel. Second, few believed that Hamas would win a parliamentary majority; rather, the expectation was that Hamas would gain a minority presence—even if sizable—and, through its formal incorporation into the government, be de-radicalized and more easily controlled. Yet according to the Hamas leader Usama Hamdan, the Hamas leadership expected an electoral victory.[75]

Hamas's democratic victory, however, was short-lived not only for Hamas but for the Palestinian people, followed as it was in June 2006 by an Israeli and U.S.-led international political and economic boycott of the new Palestinian government. The boycott amounted to a form of collective punishment against the entire Palestinian population and, to my knowledge, was the first time in the history of this conflict that the international community imposed sanctions on the occupied rather than the occupier. By imposing international financial and economic sanctions and attaching conditions to desperately needed aid, the boycott aimed to compel Palestinians to overthrow the government they had democratically elected and embrace one they had clearly rejected. The Bush White House was unwilling to accept, or incapable of understanding, that Fatah had been defeated politically for its years of corruption and ineptitude and that no amount of coercion could reverse that.

The tragic irony is that Hamas made it very clear that it wanted to govern normally without sanctions and the constant threat of Israeli attacks, which continued long after Israel's 2005 redeployment. These attacks culminated in Israel's aerial bombardment of Gaza, officially in response to the abduction of an Israeli soldier, Gilad Shalit, by Palestinian militants on June 24, 2006. During this time Israeli soldiers captured sixty-four Hamas members, many of whom were democratically elected legislators in the West Bank, incarcerating them indefinitely (seventeen were still held at the time of this writing in 2010). Even before its election victory, Hamas had effectively suspended suicide bombings and was unilaterally observing the proposed cease-fire with Israel (approximately eighteen months), thus proving its ability to implement a ceasefire when Israel fully reciprocated (the cease-fire lasted from March 2005 to June 2006; see chapter 7).[76] In fact, during 2006 Israel killed 657 Palestinians—half civilians—and Palestinians killed 23 Israelis.[77] Hamas also made it clear that it could (and did) deal directly with Israel on more mundane matters (e.g., the delivery of municipal services) and even, albeit indirectly, on more substantive ones. It also made it clear that it would "abide by any agreement ratified by popular referendum."[78]

Instead, in what has become known as the "Gaza Experiment" and the "Gaza Laboratory," Palestinians found themselves largely sealed off from the rest of the world, unable to work or move, a growing majority dependent on international relief, facing shortages of food and medicine, with little if any recourse or redress. The Hamas-led government was weakened—cut off from the international funds it needed to pay the salaries of its 162,000 employees and facing a Fatah-dominated bureaucracy hostile to its presence. With 100,000 laborers effectively unable to work, unemployment levels nearing 50 percent in certain regions of Gaza, and 35,000 new entrants to the labor force each year, Palestinian youngsters had few options for employment other than in militias and gangs. Palestinian institutions suffered enormously and were threatened with collapse.

As pressures mounted and already limited resources evaporated even further, people fought over those resources that still remained, namely power and money. This accounts in large part for the terrible factional warfare between Hamas and Fatah, which began in April 2006 and escalated in May[79] and June 2007[80] despite the establishment of a coalition government two months before—a government that functioned under an ongoing and repressive Israeli occupation.

By June 2007, Hamas-Fatah violence had been ongoing for fifteen months, taking the lives of around seven hundred Palestinians and injuring over a thousand more.[81] This interfactional violence also was rooted in a U.S. government plan to undermine and eventually overthrow the Hamas-led government, initiated soon after Hamas's electoral victory. While the Palestinian leadership—both Fatah and Hamas—must assume responsibility for the chaos they have created and continue to create, external powers have also contributed directly and perniciously to the conflagration, which Hamas consistently and correctly viewed as an attempted coup against its democratically elected government. Indeed, in a confidential "end of mission" report leaked to the public, the former UN Middle East envoy, Alvaro de Soto, revealed that after its electoral victory Hamas wanted to form a broad coalition government with Fatah and other political groups. The United States, he argued, discouraged Palestinians from joining.[82] "We [the UN] were told that the U.S. was against any 'blurring' of the line dividing Hamas from those Palestinian political forces committed to the two-state solution."[83]

He further stated:

> I want to stress that, in effect, a National Unity Government with a compromise platform along the lines of the Mecca [the agreement that resulted in a unity government between Hamas and Fatah] might have been achieved soon after the election, in February or March 2006, had the US not led the quartet [i.e., the United States, European Union, Russia, and the United Nations] to set impossible demands.... At the time, and indeed until the Mecca Agreement a year later [February 2007], the US clearly pushed for a confrontation between Fateh and Hamas—so much so that, a week before Mecca, the US envoy declared twice in an envoy's meeting in Washington how much "I like this violence," referring to the near–civil war that

was erupting in Gaza in which civilians were being regularly killed and injured, because "it means that other Palestinians are resisting Hamas."[84]

The American plan to roll back a national unity government and unseat Hamas by arming Fatah so it could fight Hamas for control of the government (and thereby ignite internal fighting), which Israel itself viewed as unworkable folly, was initially promoted by Elliot Abrams, the American deputy national security adviser, laid down by General Keith Dayton, the American coordinator of security between Israel and the Palestinians, and approved by Condoleezza Rice.[85] (However, it was strongly criticized by the Pentagon, the CIA, and the U.S. Embassy in Israel, but was implemented nonetheless.) Reports indicate that President Abbas, who initially resisted pressure from the United States and from within Fatah itself to violently confront Hamas and was even willing to work with a Hamas-led government, eventually conceded when the pressure became too strong.[86] Indeed, less than a month after the Mecca Agreement was signed, "Abbas was told to scrap Mecca at every subsequent meeting he ... had with Israeli prime minister Ehud Olmert or with U.S. Secretary of State Condoleezza Rice and Abrams."[87]

Confirming what many observers already knew, in April 2008 *Vanity Fair* magazine published "The Gaza Bombshell," in which the American plan was exposed. The article cites David Wurmser, Vice President Cheney's former chief adviser on Middle East affairs: "It looks to me that what happened [in June 2007] wasn't so much a coup by Hamas but an attempted coup by Fatah that was preempted before it could happen."[88]

The United States (and Abbas) had allegedly asked Israel to approve the shipment of weapons, ammunition, and armored vehicles into Gaza and the West Bank to support Fatah's Presidential Guard, a policy that threatened and inflamed Hamas leaders and supporters.[89] (Other accounts maintain that Israel notified the Americans that it would prohibit weapons from entering Gaza for fear that Fatah would lose them, which is what happened as Israel did allow some arms deliveries including two thousand automatic rifles and two million bullets.) In fact, the United States designated $86.4 million in security support for the Presidential Guard.[90] Another source citing a U.S. government document describes a $1.27 billion program (over five years) that would have added 4,700 men to the 15,000-member Guard.[91] According to the document, "The desired outcome will be the transformation of Palestinian security forces and provide for the president of the Palestinian Authority to be able to safeguard decisions such as dismissing the cabinet and forming an emergency cabinet."[92]

This arming of Fatah (in which Egypt and Jordan also participated) was explicitly aimed at destroying Hamas and its military infrastructure.[93]

In June 2007, believing time was not on its side, Hamas responded brutally and, according to many in Gaza, horrifically (or, as some analysts have put it, grossly overreacted).

According to *Ha'aretz*, "The primary reason for the break-up [of the unity government] is the fact that Fatah, headed by the Palestinian Authority Chairman Mahmoud Abbas, has refused to fully share the PA's mechanism of power with its rival Hamas—in spite of Hamas' decisive victory in the January 2006 elections. Fatah was forced to overrule the Palestinian voters because the entire world demanded it do so. The United States, the European nations, most of the Arab leaders and, of course, the State of Israel, warned Fatah not to share power with Hamas."[94]

In fact, after Hamas fighters took over the PNA security buildings in Gaza, they discovered documents linking Fatah to the CIA. According to a Hamas spokesman, "The CIA files we seized, which include documents, CDs, taped conversations, and videos, are more important than all the American weapons we obtained the last two days as we took over the traitor Fatah's positions."[95] The identification of Fatah with the CIA further weakened the cause of Palestinian secularism. Following Hamas's takeover, the United States announced that the training of the Presidential Guard would be transferred to the West Bank despite its "disappointing performance in the Gaza Strip."[96]

By mid-June 2007 the Palestinian National Authority was effectively shattered,[97] and both factions, Fatah and Hamas, were seemingly committed to eliminating each other, a reality that was altogether new and frightening. Fatah was clearly in turmoil, splitting between those officials in Gaza who wanted to negotiate and cooperate with Hamas and those who did not. It was also clear that Abbas did not have full control over Fatah or its political organs, especially the Central Committee. Although Hamas was now the unchallenged power in the Gaza Strip, it, too, was not without internal divisions. The terrible violence perpetrated during mid-June (7 to 14) that led to its military takeover of Gaza was allegedly ordered by Khaled Meshal at the urging of certain Arab states and groups who remained unidentified. Ismail Haniyeh, the prime minister and recognized head of Hamas inside the territories, had apparently opposed Meshal's decision, as did his Syrian benefactors. Haniyeh's opposition was based on his fear of creating deeper divisions between Hamas and Fatah and within Hamas itself, a fear that was painfully realized. (This likely accounts in part for Haniyeh's subsequent overtures to Abbas for talks.)

It may also be that Hamas had been, for some time and likely under Meshal's direction, preparing to attack Fatah's security institutions formerly headed by, and still under the influence of, Mohammed Dahlan, now Abbas's national security adviser. Dahlan, who was supported by

U.S. officials, has been a bitter enemy of Hamas since his 1996 crackdown on the movement. He consistently refused to accept the Palestinian unity government brokered by the Saudi government in the Mecca Agreement "and made his opposition intolerable to Hamas when he refused to subject the security forces under his command, armed and trained by the U.S., to the legitimate Palestinian unity government as agreed between Hamas and Fatah."[98] Alistair Crooke, a former Middle East adviser to the EU foreign policy chief Javier Solana, similarly observed, "Dahlan refused to deal with [the independent interior minister appointed to the unity government], and put his troops on the streets in defiance of the interior minister. Hamas felt they had little option but to take control of security away from forces which were in fact creating insecurity."[99] Hence, Hamas was not attempting a coup against the government or the Fatah organization as a whole but only against Dahlan's U.S.-funded militia (and individual Fatah loyalists it blamed for the murder of Hamas members).[100]

With Hamas's seizure of Gaza on June 13, 2007, President Abbas dissolved the unity (but Hamas-dominated) government the same day, dismissed Prime Minister Haniyeh, declared a state of emergency, and formed an emergency government in the West Bank, a decree that Hamas bitterly rejected as unconstitutional. Abbas also canceled all decisions made by the Hamas government. Apparently, Abbas asked Hamas officials not to touch his home in Gaza and was willing to work with them to resolve the tension. Haniyeh pleaded with the head of Hamas's military wing to leave the president's home untouched but was rebuffed, and the house was taken over. According to insiders, Abbas was greatly offended and hurt by this and took the action personally.

On June 17 Abbas swore in a new cabinet of technocrats, a move that one day later resulted in the lifting of the international economic and political boycott that had been imposed by the United States and the European Union (a boycott that was subsequently intensified against the Hamas-controlled Gaza Strip). Other economic and diplomatic restrictions were also removed, including those on the $562 million in back Palestinian tax monies Israel owed the PNA, which Israel committed to release in installments. Abbas also banned Hamas's militia, the Executive Force, and its military wing, the Qassam Brigades, which he deemed illegal given their "military coup" in Gaza.[101]

Although Hamas still retained a sizable majority in the Palestinian legislature (74 out of 132 seats) in June 2007, it had only 36 voting legislators (because 38 were imprisoned), far short of the requisite quorum of 66 required for it to convene the parliament. Because Hamas could not obtain a quorum, power in parliament devolved on the Fayyad government. Abbas further suspended clauses in the Palestinian Basic Law that required legislative approval of the new emergency government, and he stripped Hamas of its representation in the National Security Council. Abbas subsequently announced plans to amend the existing electoral law, which was, in fact, later changed. The new law stated that in order to run for office, a party must recognize the PLO as the sole legitimate representative of the Palestinian people and also must recognize all previous treaties and agreements, including Oslo and its recognition of Israel. These changes, of course, made it difficult if not impossible for Hamas to win legislative elections.[102] Although it is unclear whether Abbas had the constitutional authority to issue such decrees,[103] the fact remains that in backing him and his new government, the United States and the international community openly supported the dismantling of a democratically elected government in the Middle East, one that they had helped to install. Israel took a similar stance, with Olmert stating that he intended to start final status negotiations with the Palestinians on the condition that Abbas fight Hamas.[104] Furthermore, the international community committed to terminate aid and revenue transfers from Israel to the Fayyad government if it engaged in talks with Hamas. The president's office also put together a plan that called for a continued struggle against Hamas, which entailed refusing to negotiate with the Hamas leadership, arresting Hamas officials in the West Bank, and closing Islamist social institutions in the West Bank. The United States, the European Union, and most Arab states promptly expressed support for the Abbas plan.

The clear separation between Gaza and the West Bank and the creation of two authorities was something Palestinians greatly feared. On the other hand it was a reality that the Israeli government, particularly under former Prime Minister Ariel Sharon, had long pursued. On June 15, 2007, the *New York Times* wrote: "Mr. Olmert is expected to tell Mr. Bush that Israel favored sealing off the Israeli-occupied West Bank *from the infection of Gaza*, continuing to prevent contact between them"[105] (emphasis added). This perception, strongly propagated by Israel and the United States especially, but also by Fatah, that the two territories must be viewed as separate entities—politically, economically, financially, diplomatically, and administratively—one evil and the other good, one deserving of food and the other not, has had dire consequences, particularly for an already acutely impoverished Gaza Strip. Gaza was positioned as the "counteroutcome," the tangible result of noncooperation. Subsequently, the Palestinian ambassador to the United Nations, Riyad Mansour, blocked a UN resolution calling on Israel to lift its devastating economic blockade of Gaza (and in November 2007 circulated a draft UN resolution calling Hamas a "terrorist organization").

Similarly, it was clear that U.S. State Department believed it could undermine Hamas in the eyes of Palestinians in Gaza by improving the economic situation among Palestinians in the West Bank. This was essentially the same failed strategy that had informed the international boycott of the Hamas-led government in 2006. Toward this end, *al Quds al-Arabi* reported:

> [We] learned from sources working for NGOs in Palestine yesterday that they have received from the USAID organization a request for them to present large-scale project proposals for financing [by USAID] in the West Bank on an accelerated basis. According to these sources, USAID ... requested, less than 12 hours after the appointment of Dr Salam Fayadh to form an emergency government, ideas for huge projects to be carried out in the West Bank, on condition that these projects be capable of showing quick results in the life of people in the West Bank and that they involve large numbers of Palestinian workers. The sources told [us] that these are [supposed to be] projects in which it will be apparent that there is large-scale American funding for improvements in the life of the people of the West Bank, and that this [American connection to the quick improvements] should be readily apparent to the eye and tangible on the ground....
>
> The sources said what is being asked of them is to convince the people of the West Bank that they are fortunate having the government of Fayadh and the decision of Abbas to form this government, in contrast to Hamas which controls Gaza. Concerning the possibility of carrying out any projects in the Gaza Strip, sources who asked not to be identified by name said they are being told it is not allowed to let even one dollar reach the Gaza Strip.[106]

Having taken control in Gaza, Hamas suddenly found itself responsible for far more than a government. Immediately following Hamas's takeover, a Palestinian colleague wrote from Gaza: "Hamas realizes it is stuck with a surprise outcome on a greater magnitude than it faced after its landslide victory in the elections of January 2006. They need help and they are asking for it. I think, though, this time people like us, moderates in Gaza particularly, have to talk to both (and they [Hamas] are calling for ideas) to help end this incredibly dark turn of events."[107]

In the immediate aftermath of the takeover and despite the great uncertainty that accompanied it, Hamas was praised for its behavior: "rank and file Fatah members are not being lined up against walls.... Newspapers are not being closed or businesses shuttered. Schools are not being told what to teach and there is no purge. This is not an Islamic revolution but simply a political party attempting to defend itself against the militia of an unelected warlord backed by foreign powers."[108]

Many people described an initial sense of greater personal security. Soon after the takeover, my colleague wrote, "Gaza now is in a complete standstill; literally, complete. About the only positive that came out of this whole thing is that the blackmailers, extortionists, criminals, drugs and arms dealers, and outwardly corrupt figures are out or neutralized. We hardly see armed persons on the street. All intersections are manned by Hamas guys, helping run traffic. The Executive Force seems to have minimal presence, at least, in our area. They are completely non-intrusive and not visible either. Car thefts, kidnappings among families and civil crime all seem to have disappeared or have been minimal. Other than that, Hamas has thrown everyone in Gaza into a dark and mysterious abyss."[109]

Several months later, reports out of Gaza were far less sanguine. Some described terrible human rights violations including the looting of private businesses and homes and the confiscation of entire office buildings and homes belonging to Fatah officials, the imprisonment and torture of Fatah members and supporters, and growing censorship.[110] The Palestinian Human Rights Monitoring Group and the Palestinian Centre for Human Rights in Gaza have documented many abuses committed by the "dismissed government" (and by the Fatah government based in Ramallah) including interfering with the functioning of the Gaza Municipality and other municipalities in the Strip and the takeover by Hamas of the civilian judicial system in Gaza by establishing illegal judicial bodies that are not independent.[111]

Hence, despite its "victory" Hamas lost a good deal of its popularity and credibility with civil society because it increasingly came to be seen as having abused its power in much the way that Fatah did, particularly after the June violence. Gazans already began to speak of the "Fatahization" of Hamas. Four months after the seizure, a former spokesman for the Hamas government, Ghazi Hamad, wrote that the takeover was a "serious strategic mistake that burdened the movement more than it can bear."[112] Yet, since June 2007, Hamas has firmly taken control of Gaza despite the enormous pressures imposed by Israel, the international community, and the Fatah-based PNA to undermine and destroy it (see chapter 7 and my postscript).

Given that Islamism is now the dominant political dynamic in the region, perhaps the greatest mistake of Western and Israeli policy is the ongoing demonization and isolation of the Islamists in an attempt to bar them from the political process. Hamas's continued resilience—even after Israel's massive assault on Gaza from 2008 to 2009—attests to this. In fact, there can be no credible peace process with a Palestinian government that excludes the party elected by Palestinians to govern them. As this book argues, Hamas not only remains open to sharing power;[113] it also has a history of nonviolent accommodation and political adaptation, ideological reflexivity and transformation, and political pragmatism that the West should welcome.¹¹⁴ The alternative portends disaster, as it threatens to strengthen the more regressive elements within Hamas and radicalize Palestinians overall, further destabilizing a situation that is already fraught with unbearable tension.

A Concluding Note

In a 2007 confidential report issued by a European think tank assessing emerging issues for policy research in the Middle East, the authors refer to the "predominance of a moralising political discourse" that has "preempted discussion of Middle East policies on the basis of evidence." This discourse, in effect, constitutes a diversion, a political and intellectual justification for policies and practices that are informed by the need for conformity, not by the reality they are purportedly there to address. With regard to the importance of talking to Islamists, the authors write:

> [I]s it knowledge we seek or pressure we seek to exert? Do we want to pressure them to change their ideas (e.g. on the right of Israel to exist) or have a dialogue based on listening, not just dictating? Perhaps we should be trying to find out what is their agenda, their priorities? It is important to remember not to juxtapose Islamists as radical in contrast to "moderate" regimes in the region. This is simply misleading: in most cases these are authoritarian regimes and in most cases Islamists will moderate on many issues (peace with Israel is not the only criteria of moderation).
>
> And on what issues should we engage? All issues can be on the agenda, and it is key to talk about problematic issues—Israel, minorities, women—but it is just as important to find out what is their policy on democracy, political reform, development, i.e. issues that are very high on their own agenda. There is lots of evidence that these are effective entrepreneurs, both political organizers and in business. Yes, dialogue can deal with the problematic areas (e.g. jihad, war and terror) as these are political issues and any dialogue should be a dialogue about solutions, e.g. Palestine problem.¹¹⁵

The question then arises, "what are the entry points to help (re)-establish a more evidence-based policy discussion?"—a question whose answer is made all the more urgent by the growing political vacuum in the region and by the failure of domestic transitions in places such as Palestine, Lebanon, and possibly Egypt and Algeria.¹¹⁶ By examining the socioeconomic work of Islamist institutions in Palestine—a side of the movement seldom seen let alone understood—and the seemingly fluid relationship between Islamist social and political sectors, I hope to provide, at least in part, the kind of evidence that reveals the possibilities for moderation and transformation within the Islamist movement (as well as those factors constraining it), those areas of common understanding, and shared objectives that must also inform policy if it is to be effective and purposeful, evidence that is more of an imperative now than ever before. As the next chapter will show, Islamic social institutions are rooted philosophically in Islamic conceptions of civil society and civic life, which have a long, albeit misrepresented, history.

Chapter 3

ISLAMIST CONCEPTIONS OF CIVIL SOCIETY

THE CHOICE OF a civil society model as an informing framework for this study originated with my respondents, particularly those who worked in Islamic associations. They would often characterize their work as either being part of civil society—fundamentally that intermediary space between the ruler (the state) and the ruled (the private sphere), in which institutions operate independently in their own fields for community benefit—or as contributing to its development. When asked what they meant by civil society, how they defined it, and the role of religion within it, their answers, while varied, had common themes:

One was that an Islamic civil society does not differ in certain ways from a non-Islamic or secular civil society but embraces some of the same values (e.g., civility, tolerance) and roles (e.g., independent entities compensating for the deficiencies of the "state").

Another quite prominent theme was that Islam, both as a religion and as an expression of cultural identity, should not be relegated solely to the private sphere but should also be situated squarely in the public sphere, given its emphasis on justice, equality, and modernity; in this regard, respondents emphasized that religion is not an obstacle to the development of a vibrant civil society but rather a core feature of it. In their view, therefore, Islam is an integral and inseparable part of daily life and livelihood.

A third theme stressed compatibility between Islam and civil society, arguing that Islam contains all the requisite elements to form a civil society and that traditional Islamic society (and the notion of the *umma*) was indeed a version of civil society. And lastly, given their strong and consistent ties to the local grass roots, Islamic social institutions provide a stronger foundation for building a civil society than their secular counterparts, which have, in many cases, loosened those local ties in favor of a more global constituency.

The literature on civil society, and more specifically on civil society in the Arab and Muslim world, is now vast and well beyond the scope of this study.[1] It was during the 1980s and 1990s that the (Western) concept of civil society, itself an "intruder to Islamic political thought,"[2] became more relevant to the Arab world owing to the global changes precipitated by the end of the Cold War and the rise of Islamic radicalism. Amr Hamzawy describes four issues that characterized the Arab literature on civil society: the applicability (and hence universality)—or not—of Western political concepts, particularly the concept of civil society; the (re)interpretation of Arab-Islamic political history and its impact on the relationship between state and society, especially with regard to secularism and the role of religion in politics; the definition of civil society in the Arab context; and the impediments to establishing a democratic civil society.[3]

For the historical evolution of civil society as a concept in the history of ideas, I refer the reader to others.[4] My aim here is to briefly but critically explore the role of Islam in civil society and the role of civil society in Islam in order to underscore that Islamist thought on this issue is neither monolithic nor uniform, and thereby to challenge common essentialist representations, as well as to situate Hamas within the diverse schools of thought that exist.

Majority Islamic Perspectives

The debate over civil society and Islam is typically subject to essentialist interpretations by the "right" as well as the "left."[5] These interpretations (many of them imposed by outsiders) lack nuance and fail to address certain questions, including one continuously debated among Muslims and others that asks not only whether Islamic and Islamist groups are part of civil society[6] but whether they even *can* be—that is, can civil society be constructed in Islam?

Theoretically, at least, there has long been a debate among Islamic thinkers, indeed since the time of the Prophet, centered on the relationship between what could be termed civil society (religious, professional, and tribal units) and political authority or the state. This debate has been carried over into contemporary Islamic fundamentalist discourses, with a majority of writers, jurists, theologians, and even some philosophers calling for strengthening civil society (as an organizing principle for establishing an Islamic state) and a minority opposing it.[7]

For example, Muhammad Salim al-'Awwa, a lawyer and prominent figure in the Egyptian Muslim Brotherhood committed to the Islamic awakening (*al-sahwa al-islamiyya*),[8] argues that since the establishment of the first Islamic state, despotism has been rejected in Islamic thinking and never really succeeded in denying the legitimacy of free thought despite concerted attempts by the Arab state system to do so.[9] He (among others) calls for "reviving Islam, depicting its contemporary condition as an archeological relic that requires renewal without destroying its essence," a process in which civil society institutions are free to develop without interference. "This essence is eternal and embodies faith, worship and moral values" and represents "a quest for cultural authenticity along with a need to adapt to changing realities."[10]

Ahmad Moussalli, who is a professor of political studies at the American University of Beirut and a leading scholar on political Islam, argues that "[a]lthough it might seem that the concept of civil society is Western and imposed on the non-Westerners in order to keep local systems in subjection to the West, this is not entirely true, at least in terms of the functions of civil society."[11] This majority, in fact, assigns civil society a role far greater than that of government itself. Muhammad Abduh (1849–1905), an Egyptian religious scholar and liberal reformer who is regarded as the founder of Islamic modernism, wrote: "Every individual has an opinion about politics and the social organization of the nation.... Thus, many Muslims now believe that the call to caliphate, which is in accordance with religious laws, is against their interests, considering such an advocate not only their enemy but an enemy to Islam as well."[12] John Voll states it thus: "The evolution of the Islamic social order emphasized the ideal of a community that is integrated as a whole through personalized associations. Although there were rich and poor, leaders and followers, elites and masses, the social groupings did not create entities (like class, church, or state) that stood 'between the individual and the community of the faithful' as a whole. The sense of belonging to the *ummah* became a central feeling, and for the Sunni majority, that sense had a higher claim than loyalty to a particular state. That tradition of social order has helped to shape modern socio-political development in the Islamic world."[13] In this regard, Moussalli correctly argues that the concept of civil society, which marks the transition from the natural to the civil or political condition, must be examined within a general theory of politics.

While the practical application of these theoretical precepts favoring civil society has fallen short, the theory underlying the potential role of civil society in Islamic thinking is nonetheless critical to examine, given the intense debate, controversy, and profound misunderstanding surrounding Islamist politics and Islamic political culture. Although traditional Islamic societies did not experience the kind of civil society that later emerged in Europe, they did possess those conditions necessary (albeit insufficient) for the development of a viable civil society and associational life.[14] The Tunisian Islamist Rachid al-Ghannouchi (who is the exiled leader of the [opposition] Tunisian Islamic al-Nahda [Renaissance] party) characterizes it thus: "Civil society was proposed as a counter to the natural state that preceded it. Humans in the natural state were said to have been dominated by anarchy, power, oppression, and hegemony, whereas the newly conceived civil society is founded on a contract among free individuals."[15] These ideas formed the theoretical and political foundation for modern Islamist debates on the role of civil society and could, under better political conditions in Palestine and the region as a whole, act as forces of moderation, stability, and development.

According to Moussalli, the first Islamic community was referred to as a civil society—*al-mujtama' al-madani*. "Civil" in this context described a city where Muslims were allied on tribal and geographic lines as were Jews and others. The resulting social structure was therefore characterized by a variety of religions and outlooks, a pluralism that was accepted not only by the Prophet but by the first Islamic constitution (622 CE), which legalized the right of people comprising each minority to live according to their own laws and scriptures and run their own affairs, as long as they did not threaten the state. In fact, the constitution, which effectively established the first Islamic state, was written in order to end terrible intertribal fighting; it provided for a set of rights for the Muslim, Jewish, and pagan communities of Medina, bringing them together within the context of one community, the *umma*.[16] Hence, the Jewish tribes were part of the same community with Muslims but had their own religion. Perhaps more importantly for purposes of this discussion, each religious and tribal group was allowed its own representative leadership who, like their Muslim counterparts, would mediate between the state and the people as necessary. This was seen clearly during the Ottoman period in laws that codified the rights of Christian and Jewish minorities to run their own affairs and gave their leaders latitude as government intermediaries.[17]

In the history of Islam, the role of social intermediary was embraced by more than one segment of civil society and is linked to the Quranic concept of *hisba*, the duty to do good and shun evil (*al-amr bi'l-ma' ruf wa'l-nahy 'an al-munkar*), which morally and politically demanded the active involvement of civil society in social and political affairs.[18] In fact, several Islamic social institutions in Gaza including al-Mujamma al-Islami, contain statutes with the following Quranic verse: "Let there arise out of you a band of people inviting to all that is good, enjoining what is right and forbidding what is wrong. They are the ones to attain felicity."[19]

The importance of the intermediary role (especially for purposes of this study) lies in the fact that historically different civil society actors were able to exercise legitimate social authority outside state control in roles that were vital to community well-being and to safeguard that authority against state interference or trespass. For example, the notables (*al-ashraf*), who were connected historically to the Prophet and therefore had enormous social prestige and influence, often intervened with political authorities on behalf of the people. Their social role was, to varying degrees, tied to that of other social organizations such as guilds (*asnaf*) and Islamic charitable trusts (*awqaf*), which enjoyed marked autonomy from the central government.[20]

Because the notables' authority in the community was often tied to the marketplace, the notables and the craftspeople were aligned and united economically and politically in a complex web of interrelationships. So linked, these groups "had created a multi-layered framework through which individuals belonged to each local community, and they connected this framework to the more general ideal of the Islamic community (the *ummah*)."[21] The resulting structures and rules served to protect individuals and certain civil society actors from state abuses, ensuring for society a high degree of independence.[22] It was a society based on "freedom and voluntary cooperation politically, where authority is not repressive, as well as socially and culturally, that is with regard to relations among its individual members."[23]

The writers Wajih Kawtharani and Khalid Ziyada, both Lebanese historians, and Burhan Ghalyun, a Syrian political scientist,[24] embrace a prominent role for civil society in Arab society under more open political conditions. They analyze it thus: Despite the expansion of state-dominated structures, which tried to appropriate and instrumentalize Islam for their own political purposes, the "true emancipatory essence of religion remained intact and was protected through the institutions of the traditional intermediary sphere,"[25] which preserved the organizational and cultural variety of the *umma* in a medieval social contract. Thus, under the auspices of religion, a civil society could develop that provided not only services but also protection from a repressive state. Kawtharani further calls for the revitalization of civilian associations, such as religious endowments, as a way to build a social contract within Arab societies.[26]

The legitimacy and centrality of civil society in Islamic history is further evidenced by the role of legal-religious scholars who played the powerful intermediary role of representing popular grievances before the state.[27] Since the Prophet Mohammad did not provide for a priesthood or similar religious institution, nor was any official after Mohammad considered to possess prophetic or infallible religious powers, a body of men gradually developed with specialized religious functions focused largely on the Quran and the Hadith (the sayings of the Prophet). As Muslim law came to occupy a central place in Islam, these religious figures increasingly merged with legal scholars and jurists, eventually producing an identifiable body of ulama—scholars, jurists, and teachers educated in the Islamic sciences, particularly during the early part of the Abbasid period (749–1258).[28] Given the focal and historical role of law in Islam, "the leaders of the *'ulama* concentrated on the development, exegesis, enforcement, and teaching of Islamic law, a law that embraced not only matters that Westerners would consider 'religious' but most aspects of the life of a believer."[29]

Thus, legislation was not considered a function of government but rather the domain of civil society as interpreted by the ulama. In theory, the ulama, who eventually organized into different legal schools, played an important role in the affairs of the state, and their primary goal was not to govern so much as to establish law and order (by issuing legal opinions), which in turn would facilitate the implementation of the sharia (the eternal principles of religion and revealed law). Because the ulama derived their legitimacy from civil society and not from government, their role was not only legal but moral and beyond the reach of a coercive state.[30] Traditionally, religious scholars played two roles: They "legitimized despotic rule (as long as its representatives respected the shari'ah in all aspects of society and continued to allow scholars access to the masses)" and simultaneously "protected the people from repression and despotic excesses by systematically limiting the scope of politics."[31]

Munir Shafiq, a Palestinian writer (and Christian convert to Islam), describes it this way:

> Ever since the founding of the Umayyad Caliphate [661–749], the gap between the *'ulama* (scholars) and religion on the one hand and the state on the other gradually began to widen.... Since then, and until the end of the Ottoman period, the regime was described as the "rule of avarice and conquest." ... The *'ulama* had become the authority to whom the people turned in times of crisis and difficulties, when oppression and degradation became totally unbearable.... Some sort of deal, a settlement, was struck between the *'ulama* and rulers. The *'ulama* did not incite rebellion against the rulers even though they despised the "disagreeable" separation between ruler and religion. At the same time, they did not condone deviant practices, and thus concentrated their efforts on consolidating the role and position of religion in society. In a sense the *'ulama* were the last line of defence for the people in times of crisis and tribulation.[32]

Hence, the ulama sought acceptance from society, not from government, and their power (particularly as the "guardians of public morality"[33]) depended on their followers, not on a ruler, who had no authority over the opinions of the ulama. Law was civil in nature, resulting from the interaction between scholars, who were known to be quite assertive,[34] and different segments of civil society, although it often dealt with political concerns. Not surprisingly, governments would often impose their will on an unreceptive population, but the right to legislate, theoretically and practically, still resided with society, although the relationship between ruler and ulama was characterized by periods of conflict over the past 1,400 years.[35] In fact, "most political doctrines and religious issues were settled ... away from the intervention of governments. When a legal opinion of a scholar became widely accepted in society, it became a part of the legislative compendium of the community that the government had to honor and fulfill."[36]

Furthermore, according to al-Ghannouchi, Shafiq, and others, this period of ideal Islamic rule (when scripture and the will of the community were superior to the ruler's will; the state was accountable to society; legislation remained the responsibility of the scholars; and the ruler's power was limited by the sharia, the ulama, and popular consensus) was also a time when a variety of other institutions (e.g., public, judicial, educational, and cultural), funded by the *awqaf*, were able to maintain a high degree of independence from the state.[37]

It was a period in the Islamic experience when the relationship between the state and society "afforded society a wide scope for initiative, organization, and self-sufficiency."[38] The Lebanese sociologist Khalid Ziyada states that this separation of politics and religion led to a consistent pattern of functional differentiation, whereby the state assumed responsibility for certain tasks such as tax collection and the preservation of social order, and civil society (through the religious institutions) focused on the provision of services and the cultural reproduction (i.e., the transmission of values) of the *umma*. Yet the two authorities were not entirely isolated from each other but linked by their interdependence, however delicate.[39]

With colonialist intervention in most of the Arab and Islamic countries (notably through modernization/secularization campaigns) and the emergence of the modern territorial state in the nineteenth and twentieth centuries, the traditional Islamic citizens' society and its characteristic institutions—the traditional intermediary sphere, which al-Ghannouchi argues was the precursor for democracy in the Arab world—were destroyed. With the rise of the externally imposed nation-state, the classical separation of power between the ruler and the scholars ended, as did the functional distinction between the political and religious/social spheres.[40]

For example, under colonial rule, the *awqaf* and many religious educational institutions in many Arab and Islamic countries were seized by the state and placed under its control. Shafiq argues that the worst assault came after independence and the establishment of secular Muslim regimes, which placed all religious institutions and associations under government control, stripping them of independence. (However, Meir Hatina argues that these institutions maintained an "ethos of religio-political unity [that] became the ideological *raison d'etre* of the twentieth-century Islamic movements, which transformed faith into an assertive force aimed at bringing about sociopolitical change by evolution, or if necessary, by revolution."[41])

> Whereas in the West the relationship between secularism, the church, religion and the state stabilized through an historic accord that left the church and its charitable, educational and media institutions completely independent, the secularist authorities in the Muslim

world have not agreed to any settlement with Islam and its institutions; instead, they have sought to eliminate Islamic rivals or at least subdue them through a process known as "drying of the springs."[42]

So degraded, religious institutions became instruments for rulers to use to further their own (secular) goals. The ulama, says al-Ghannouchi, could either defer to the new authoritarian structure and hopefully secure certain freedoms, particularly in education, or oppose the ruling regime, as the Muslim Brotherhood did in Egypt (through both peaceful and violent means).[43]

Incapable of preserving its institutional authenticity, Islamic civil society was replaced by a political and economic order that was unable (and unwilling?) to reproduce the civil roles once played by the ulama and others, precluding the transition to democracy.[44] Nawaf Salam, the current Lebanese ambassador to the United Nations, argues that what was being asked of society was nothing less than its own demobilization: trading political rights to participation for social justice and national dignity enforced through coercive government methods.[45]

The obstacles to democracy in the Arab world are not limited to foreign influence alone but emanate as well from extremist thinking within the Islamic movement, according to al-Ghannouchi. The strategies of violence used by Islamist groups in the 1980s and 1990s failed, and they contrast profoundly with the concept of gradual change in Islamic thinking. Like many secular thinkers, al-Ghannouchi argues that a complete rejection of modern social structures in favor of an essentialized religious formation is a political and social dead end. He opposes the militant paradigm espoused by Sayyid Qutb (see below), which he regards as ahistorical and ill-suited for adaptation to current social realities. (However, al-Ghannouchi argues that such extremism is not organic to Islam but results from an environment of political repression. Hence, in a more open, inclusive political system Islamic radicalism will mitigate.[46])

In this way, al-Ghannouchi and other Islamist intellectuals such as the controversial scholar and dean of the Sharia faculty at the University of Qatar, Sheikh Yusuf al-Qaradawi,[47] and the Egyptian activist Kamal Habib call for a reevaluation of the nature of political involvement within an Islamist frame of reference,[48] that is, shifting away from the decades-long obsession with politics in favor of social and cultural rediscovery in order to lay the groundwork for Islamic reform, notably the "moral re-education of the individual and the articulation of a moral-ethical civilizatory project."[49] They view this sort of gradual political reevaluation as being possible only in "intermediary social and cultural spaces between the state-controlled official politics and the individual sphere ... allow[ing] [Islamist] movements to become acquainted with the pluralist features of modern civil societies."[50]

Clearly, Islam, like all belief systems, is not (politically or theoretically) monolithic and rigid but contains within it (opposing) trends—both authoritarian and participatory[51]—for addressing the ongoing tension between tradition and modernity that are expressed differently in different contexts. The political philosophy embraced by Hamas illustrates these different trends, drawing as it does from both authoritarian and participatory traditions.[52] Such trends are visible in modern Islamist discourses on civil society, ranging from those that reject any societal role that challenges Islamic doctrine and allow for only one (divine) interpretation (the minority), to those (including Hamas) that allow for pluralistic interpretations of doctrine and view society as the ultimate source of legitimacy, assigning it the right to oversee and challenge political authority (the majority). Meir Hatina terms the latter centrists.[53]

Islamist discourses on civil society—be they radical or moderate—do advocate certain common beliefs such as the Quranic injunction to enjoin good and forbid evil—although they differ profoundly in their understanding of how best to actualize it. Perhaps the most powerful commonality regards sharia and the need to restore it (largely, but not always entirely, rejecting Western legal thought) as the basis of law and the foundation of an Islamic order or society (and ultimately an Islamic state).

Similarly there is consensus around the belief that government must ensure an Islamic life and enforce Islamic law; that Allah, who is the maker of law and who defines good and evil, is the source of authority and sovereignty in society; that this authority is then delegated by Allah to the nation or community and by the community to the ruler, hence the community has the authority to apply God's law and is the source of all power; and that the ruler, whether a caliph, imam, or president, is the "mere representative, agent or employee of the community that elects, supervises and if necessary deposes him [should he violate the community's trust and fail to execute God's law], either directly or via its representatives."[54] Indeed, it is tyranny—secular or religious—that is a core concern for both the radical and the reformist. That said, there are clear theoretical differences over the relationship between the ruler and the ruled, the role of civil society, and the obligations of the state to the society and to the individual (and over the parameters of legitimate state behavior).

The Radical and Moderate (or More Progressive) Schools of Thought

I should say at the outset that the use of the terms " radical" and "moderate" is problematic: Each term implies attributes that may not necessarily apply, and both terms are loaded politically. For example, in the Middle Eastern context "moderate" often refers to regimes politically allied to the United States. Furthermore, some individuals considered moderate might be better termed traditionalist. And, as Samuel Helfont argues, there is a difference between thought that is modern and moderate—the former does not necessarily lead to the latter.[55] "Radical" and "moderate" are used here to delineate certain important differences in philosophical approaches (e.g., flexibility in interpretation).

One school of thought, which Moussalli terms radical Islamic fundamentalism, is based on a few exclusivist concepts: "authenticity, onesidedness of truth, purity, superiority and above all salvational knowledge."[56] By contrast, the progressive school represents a more modern and moderate trend and is characterized by pragmatism and adaptability. This school allows more than one interpretation of Islamic legislation and argues that the legislative process must reflect a society's beliefs and interests. The progressive discourse addresses the need for change in terms of "religious and social criticism, the Islamic understanding of politics, the attitude to political rule and the necessity of dialogue with secular forces."[57] Voll similarly argues that these different schools or "styles of Islamic action and response" represent the "interplay between the challenge of adapting to changing conditions and the steady adherence to the fundamentals of the faith,"[58] reflecting a struggle to balance the demands for continuity with the need to accommodate change.

Collectively these two schools offer a range of positions and understandings of civil society and its role in Islamic life and illustrate the variety of thinking on this issue.[59] However, it is also clear that an absolute or binary delineation in theory and position are problematic, since one often finds seemingly contradictory positions in a given school or in intellectual representations of that school.[60] Furthermore, and most important for this study, the scholar Gudrun Kramer makes the point that "it is not possible to talk about Islam and democracy in general, but only about Muslims living and theorizing under specific historical circumstances.... There are certainly essentials of the faith... accepted by all who consider themselves to be Muslims and who are recognized as coreligionists. But these thinkers differ considerably as to how an Islamic society should be organized. What is required, therefore, is specificity."[61] And by "specificity" Kramer argues for the critical importance of understanding Muslims from within the specific political, economic, and social contexts that define their daily reality.

The Radical Discourse

The radical school is perhaps best illustrated by the political philosophy of Sayyid Qutb and his adherents. It is characterized by a set of conditions and assumptions that collectively negate the possibility of a pluralistic civil society or an independent associational life. Qutb argues that divine will can be expressed only through the free choice of the people. Thus the power to rule derives from men, not from God, since it is delegated by God to the people, not to the state. Thus, the state's authority is given and legitimized by popular consent and social agreement and not by divine ordination.[62] Submission to popular will is therefore a religious obligation. People grant the ruler authority because they believe he will follow the law and act in their interest. According to Qutb, *shura* or the idealized Islamic concept of "participation qua consultation" will ensure "human control of human affairs within the bounds of the law."[63]

Within this paradigm little if any value is assigned to individual freedom; individual rights are subsumed to community rights and deferred to the state, which in turn is responsible for ensuring social unity, social harmony, and moral order. Nothing that could disrupt or otherwise threaten social unity or the general will is allowed; political parties, associations, and civil institutions must therefore represent the majority view and work harmoniously together.[64]

Hence, only the community can represent the individual, and communal interests—represented and implemented by the state—are paramount. Consequently, only the state represents and embodies the public will—itself contracted freely between the ruler and the people—and has the right to control the life of the individual and of society. The community, therefore, has no right to challenge, let alone supervise, the government as long as it remains faithful to Islam.

Since the sharia was seen by Qutb as a complete system[65] that needed only to be applied, a legislature was considered unnecessary, a position Hamas does not hold.[66] (Qutb also believed that through sharia man becomes complete and finds true freedom, a belief Hamas does share.)[67] Should the state violate the legislative substance of the Quran and act godlessly, people do have the right to disobey and use violence against the state as the only means of change. (Anwar al-Sadat's assassination was justified in this way.) Qutb states, "According to Islam, the most serious injustice is luring people from the worship of God and forcing them to deify those rulers who empower themselves to legalize what God has prohibited and to prohibit what God has allowed."[68] Framed in this way, the only legitimate society is one that is religiously Islamic. Any violation of this society becomes a violation of religion itself.

For Qutb, groups that do not believe in Islam are denied participation; religious minorities are tolerated but disempowered; and individual freedom of expression is directly tied to the individual's ideological understanding of Islam (which led Qutb to believe that most existing societies were *jahili* or pagan[69]). Hence, while voluntary civil institutions are important and the state is secondary, those institutions must serve communal interests and not the particular needs of individual segments of civil society, which Qutb considers illegitimate.[70]

The commitment to Islam as a comprehensive, indivisible system negating individuality and differences of all kinds is a characteristic thread of the radical Islamist discourse on civil society.[71] Similarly, the radical discourse views human rationalization, analytical deduction, group consultation, or any attempt to interpret, adjudicate, or intellectualize problems outside an Islamic framework or away from their divine source as not only invalid but illegitimate and heretical. Such deviation is not only a violation of the law; it is a violation of the faith. Furthermore, since sovereignty belongs only to God, all differences within the community—political, economic, or social—must be adjudicated solely by referring to Islamic texts and opinions. For the radical Islamists, therefore, only those civil institutions that follow Islamic religious injunction are acceptable.

The Moderate Discourse

Another, more progressive school of Islamist thought, the moderates (for want of a better term), is more open to non-Islamic systems, beliefs, and institutions and to multiple modes of interpretation.[72] The moderates attribute social ills and violence to the absence of pluralism and democracy within civil society, which, they believe, are critical to individual and community well-being. Rather than insist on the exclusivity and superiority of Islamic thought, the moderates insist on the need to "harmonize religion and the world"[73] since Islam is more than just religion; it is society. They argue therefore that the conflict between the East and the West is not due to religious or cultural factors but to political ones (i.e., colonialism and imperialism); as such, it can be resolved.

Certain themes characterize the moderate Islamist discourse. One is the importance of, and need for, pluralistic (rather than purely dogmatic) interpretation of doctrinal texts and methodological flexibility, given that no one human being can produce a definitive interpretation of God's laws. Abdelwahab El-Affendi, a scholar of Islam at the University of Westminster, writes:

> If we were to identify the most problematic feature of traditional Islamic thought in general, and political thought in particular, we could call it "textualism," that is, the tendency to seek solutions (only) within the confines of earlier precedents or expertly sanctioned conduct.... Modern Islamic writers, chief among whom ... [is] Sayyid Qutb, have contributed to this confusion, especially by emphasizing the notion of "God's authority" within the Islamic state. They seem to create, by this formula, the illusion that the conflicts

taking place in Muslim polities are between God and some people, and not, as has always been the case, between different groups of people, none of whom disputes God's authority, but all dispute that of each other. To say . . . that "authority belongs to God alone," is to bypass the basic question at issue: who should exercise this authority and how?[74]

Jamal al-Din al-Afghani (1838–1897), Muhammad Abduh (a disciple of al-Afghani), and Rashid Rida (1865–1935, a disciple of Abduh), all key figures in the modern Islamic reform tradition, attempted, in their own ways, to reinterpret traditional Islamic ideas in order to address the challenging and painful problems brought about by the growing interaction and confrontation between the Christian West and the Islamic East. They rejected pure traditionalism and pure Westernism (i.e., uncritical imitation of the West) and sought to reinterpret Islam and the Islamic past in new modes that were modern and nationalist,[75] focusing on what became a characteristic feature of Islamic modernists: the need for articulating pragmatic values in a rapidly changing world. These values included the "virtues of reform and self-strengthening,"[76] "political activism, the freer use of human reason, and efforts to build up the political and military power of Islamic states."[77] As Amr Hamzawy states, they sought "to develop the fundamentals of a contemporary and civilizatory societal project in harmony with Islam, with intellectual horizons that call into question both the unthinking copying of the West and the uncritical following of the *salaf as-salih* (the forefathers)."[78]

Hamas similarly recognizes that while the sharia must be the basis of legislation, providing a set of general principles that address the needs of the individual as well as the community, it needs to be augmented by other legal systems and sources of knowledge, which include Western as well as Islamic legal traditions. In an interview I had with Ismail Abu Shanab in 1999, he also stated that Islamists must study Western systems, critique them, and incorporate what is meaningful in them into their own system.[79]

Hassan al-Banna (1906–1949), the founder of the Muslim Brotherhood in Egypt, had, as a priority, the creation of an Islamic order (*al-nizam al-islami*), a model of society that is based on the authentic Islamic principles but grounded in modernity. Concerned far more with the nature, reform, and future of Muslim society (in the twentieth century) than with any specific political order (including the historical caliphate, which was abolished in 1924) or the establishment of religious government, al-Banna stressed the importance of the individual (and his spiritual awakening) to the community and to the nation. Once the individual has become Islamized, so will his family and eventually the nation. Nations will always suffer as long as individuals suffer; nations cannot reform until individuals do.[80] The goal was not only to modernize life but to Islamize life along modern lines.[81]

For al-Banna, Islam was far more than the sum of its legislation; it was a system that allowed for individual and collective reformulations and adaptations of its laws to modern life. Thus, legislation must reflect the interests and convictions of society as it exists today. (The state, however, was necessary to protect Islam). The Quran needed to become more relevant to the modern life of Muslims and therefore required new interpretations. Furthermore, al-Banna and the Brothers "claimed to offer the contemporary Muslim freedom from tradition,"[82] freedom from the past, even a rejection of it, if "the attribution of sacredness to the old stands always in the path of every renaissance."[83]

In this way, Islamic law becomes more flexible and universal in outlook, articulating principles "necessary for progress and happiness in all times and places."[84] One of these principles was that of *ijtihad* or interpretation in order to help Muslims address the needs of the community. There was also "analogy" (*qiyas*) and "consensus" (*ijma'*) in order to make Islam more relevant to modern times. The Muslim ruler's authority to legislate in the interests of society[85] derives from the people and must reflect their interests, a relationship al-Banna described as a social contract. If the ruler fails to honor this contract, the nation is freed from obedience and loyalty to him, a belief shared with the radical school.[86]

In an oft-cited statement, al-Banna summarized it thus: "We believe the provisions of Islam and its teachings are all inclusive, encompassing the affairs of the people in this world and the hereafter. And those who think that these teachings are concerned only with the spiritual or ritualistic aspects are mistaken in this belief because Islam is a faith and a ritual, a nation (*watan*) and a nationality, a religion and a state, spirit and deed, holy text and sword.... The glorious *Qur'an*... considers [these things] to be the core of Islam and its essence."[87]

Central to the implementation of social will are individual freedom and the greater importance of the community—a key source of legitimacy—compared with the state, which plays a limited role and is accountable to the people. Although the state must adhere to religious teachings, Shafiq and al-Ghannouchi argue it must articulate policies that best serve and reflect the interests of the community as opposed to the ruler's (or ruling class's) own.[88] In a similar manner, Abu Shanab stated: "In the Islamic system, the Head of State [*al-khalifah*] represents the nation, not God. The community does not choose *al-khalifah* except to be their representative ... so he does not derive his authority except from representing the community which has ... the right to watch him and forbid him from getting beyond the borders of his brief."[89] Hence, the ruler possesses representative, not religious authority.[90] Furthermore, according to Jeroen Gunning, Hamas places "representative authority above religious authority—on the ground that the Prophet's successors derived their authority from having a popular mandate ... while allowing representatives to draw on religo-legal expertise where needed."[91] Hence, for Hamas it is more important for political authority to obtain popular trust than religious sanction.

In fact, for Hamas two critical conditions of legitimate authority in an Islamic state are *shura*, whereby the ruler consults with his people, allowing them to shape policy, and *ijma'*, the need for consensus. Elections are essential to maintaining the consultative process for they guarantee the freedom to chose and express opinion. But *shura* must also be practiced daily so that leaders can remain in constant touch with their constituents. "It is this *shura* model that informs much of Hamas' internal practice as well as its behavior during the municipal and legislative elections."[92]

Hamas further argues that a divine contract without a social contract is illegitimate, as is the social without the divine, further underlining the importance of consent and consultation. In the former the people's sovereignty is denied, and in the latter God's sovereignty. Hence, "[t]he dual contract is the foundation of Hamas' political theory":[93] "one between the people and their representatives (safeguarding free will), and one between the people and God (safeguarding divine design)."[94] (Embedded in this duality, however, is the tension between individual freedom and submission to God's design.)[95]

Whereas the radical discourse insisted that strict adherence to textual stipulations is enough for the creation of a proper Islamic society, the moderates argue that adherence to doctrine in the absence of social awareness will fail to bring about a revival along Islamic lines. What is called for is a reinvigoration of Islamic thought and institutions based on greater openness, dialogue, and even cooperation. Says Shafiq, "One should also note here that the adherence of the Muslim mind to the textual frame of reference necessitates an interaction with life and reality from a strictly objective standpoint characterized by what typifies the scientific approach to learning and to the discovery of phenomena.... [In this way], [t]he mind, which ... appears to be restrained by the text ... is nevertheless given wide scope for innovation."[96] Underlying social awareness is the need to recognize the existence of many belief systems, not just one. There is a recognition that God created difference and that this difference is good for humanity and the Muslim community (as long as it remains within an Islamic framework).[97]

In this regard many Islamists including al-Ghannouchi, al-Qaradawi,[98] al-Banna, al-'Awwa, Sheikh Muhammad al-Ghazali (an Egyptian cleric and scholar, 1917–1996), Muhammad 'Imara (Egyptian intellectual), and

Hassan al-Turabi (Sudanese Islamic political leader) reject a one-party system as unviable and call for multiparty politics and representative parties as critical forces in the revival of the Islamic community (although for many, such as al-ʿAwwa, these parties would have to adhere to Islamic values).[99]

Al-Ghannouchi (like some leaders of Hamas[100]) argues not only that pluralism is sanctioned by religion—even to the point of allowing parties that advocated communism[101] and atheism—but that religion and democracy are not contradictory. He argues that Islam, which is the distinguishing feature of an Islamic civil society, has a civilizing influence on its members and consolidates civil society through a belief that all people are equal and judged according to their deeds; a belief in the value of hard work, which is considered a religious duty; the principle that preserving life and bettering the community as a whole is more important than preserving individual wealth; a passion for freedom; and the belief that the authority of religion is based on the freedom of *ijtihad*, which values innovation and creativity.[102] This means acceptance of Islamic societies engaging in a process of mass political participation (including in the establishment of a secular democracy[103]) in order to gain access to power without violence, if possible, and rejecting Qutb's approach. Says al-Ghannouchi, "Power sharing in a Muslim or non-Muslim environment becomes a necessity in order to lay the foundations of the social order."[104]

Saʿid Hawwa (1935–1989), a Syrian Muslim Brother and a leading figure in the Islamic movement in Syria under the Baath party, also was concerned about the state of Islam—the nature of Islamic decline and the need for its revival—under (heretical) secularized state regimes.[105] Although he rejected some of Qutb's formulations, he advocated a return of Islam to the example of the *salaf as-salih* as a way of freeing it from Western dominance, but he did not do so uncritically. He argued, for example, against a one-party system. People should be free to form political parties (without insulting Islamic beliefs and values), which must be allowed to articulate positions and publish without censorship. Should conflicts arise, they must be resolved through rational discourse and reasoning—not by government but by the courts—a position the radical school rejects. Popular participation and freedom of association, then, is not only sanctioned but ensured. In this way among others, the citizen in an Islamic civil society becomes a force for positive change, understanding the value of voluntary belonging.[106]

Hence, for the more progressive Islamist thinkers a proper Islamic society is one that seeks popular political participation and freedom of association, particularly with regard to the formation of civil institutions. The former is guaranteed through the institution of *shura*, which obligates the head of state to engage with the elected community leaders, and which is often presented as the functional equivalent of a Western parliamentary system and indicative of acceptance of the principle of majority decision as the basis of an Islamic democracy.[107] According to al-Ghannouchi, Shafiq, and Hawwa, Islamic society tolerates diversity, pursues social justice, and protects human dignity. Because authority (after God) belongs to and is retained by the community, the state must yield to civil society and its institutions—which are free to organize as necessary—and to the sovereignty of law.

Relevance to the Present Study of Islamist Social Institutions in Palestine

Important concepts run through the moderate discourse that are particularly important for, and characteristic of, the work of Hamas social institutions. First, Islam in general is dynamic, inherently flexible, and open to a range of interpretations—an essential foundation for building and sustaining a viable civil society, including innovation and experimentation. This dynamism is expressed in a desire to combine cultural and religious renewal with the changing realities of modern day life (albeit within limits that do not violate religious belief or moral conduct). This refers to the dynamic interaction of the Islamists with their sociopolitical environment and its attendant constraints.[108]

Second, and related to the first, is the value assigned to rational thought and rational debate, human reasoning and insight, human (and enlightened) *ijtihad*, and to the widening of the parameters of intellectual discourse (and pluralism) that this implies. Third, knowledge and expertise are valued in the pursuit of one's goals. Fourth is the concern for the human being, for human dignity and well-being, itself derived from Islam's recognition of man's special status and his responsibility for improving human society but within parameters strictly defined by devotion to God and morality—creating a "sound (moral) Muslim."[109] Fifth is the importance of engaging in and with the community, both for individuals and for the realization of political goals.

Sixth is the importance of institutions as (autonomous) social actors pursuing the revival of Islamic society, a society characterized by gradualism, social justice, human rights, respect for law, and the preservation of human dignity. In this sense, the moderate mainstream Islamic discourse is more moral than political and, like its secular counterpart, also speaks to the idea of a shared "faith" that is not only religious in nature but ethical as well. I define it here as a set of values that animates civil institutions and contributes to the development of political, social, and professional life. Indeed, active, pluralist participation in social and cultural institutions in particular "represents the most promising strategy for gradual reform in accordance with Islam."[110]

The key question, then, is how to secure democracy and freedom for Muslim societies as they exist and not as they are supposed to be according to one vision or another.[111] Furthermore, some Islamists "held that society must rely on varied personal and informal ties, which are the distinctive characteristics of an authentic traditional community. [Hence], political parties, professional associations, investment companies and charitable organizations fill a central role in the transition to democracy ... and should be encouraged rather than restricted."[112]

Seventh is the concept of enlisting society in the practical resolution of its own problems. That is, while the commitment to religious doctrine and the ideological boundaries of Islam on the part of society are essential, without a clear commitment to social and political values and activism—to the value of mundane (and not only divine) action, as al-Ghannouchi states it—religiosity and traditional jurisprudence alone become meaningless.

Eighth, it follows that society is the primary institution in Islam tasked to enjoin good and forbid evil—revitalize the community—and must be allowed to do so without interference. Ninth, the role of the individual and of individuals in the renewal of Islamic society is recognized and cannot be violated, underlining the importance of voluntary belonging and voluntary action. Tenth, the revitalization of society cannot occur without social consensus and is in fact predicated on it. Eleventh, nonviolence is an unquestioned value, providing the overall framework for good works.

Implicit in all this is the belief that civil society is a precondition for achieving other desirable goals: political and social democratization, economic growth and development, justice, cultural identity, and, if necessary, popular resistance. In Iran, the liberal religious author Majid Mohmmadi describes those advantages of civil society as including greater popular participation in decision-making processes, the institutionalization of public affairs, strengthening mutual trust in society, and the desecularization of individuals and groups in power.[113]

Why, then, are the structures of civil society in most Muslim polities so weak?

Some would argue that this weakness is endemic to these societies and their religious and cultural orientation. El-Affendi argues something different and characterizes the weakness of civil society as "a dynamic reality which is being created and recreated daily in front of our very eyes. At this very moment 'civilised' acts of oppression are taking place in tens of Muslim capitals and countless other cities, where a frontal assault is being launched on the organs of civil society: schools, private associations, civic organisations etc., under this pretext or that. The destruction of civil society in Muslim lands is, to reiterate, not a relic of history nor is it the consequence of culture or ideology. It is an outright act of vandalism, which is reproducing itself daily, with increasing violence."[114]

Stated differently, Moussalli asks: "Are the moderate fundamentalists—the majority of whom are denied the right to form political parties, even when they represent substantial segments of society [as they arguably do in Palestine today]—in any way responsible for the tyranny and lack of democratic civil institutions in the Arab world?"[115] An examination of Islamist civil institutions in Gaza (and the West Bank) will argue for the possibilities created by moderate reformist Islam in Palestine, possibilities embodied in associations that, despite limitations of their own, have long represented moderation and stability and even creativity in a consistently declining and increasingly fractured society.

Chapter 4

THE EVOLUTION OF ISLAMIST SOCIAL INSTITUTIONS IN THE GAZA STRIP: BEFORE AND DURING OSLO (A SOCIOPOLITICAL HISTORY)

IT IS BY NOW AXIOMATIC when speaking of Hamas social institutions to think of them as part of a larger political and military network engaged in terrorism. It is equally axiomatic when reviewing the historical development of these institutions to draw a dichotomy between social institutions interested in *da'wa* (religious preaching, education, and community-oriented work aimed at the Islamization of society) before Hamas was established and those committed to jihad (political activism and military struggle) afterward.[1] While it is certainly true that Hamas as an organization has consistently emphasized political objectives over social ones—although this changed visibly during the Oslo period—the same cannot be said of the Islamist social sector. The primary transformation within this sector was not in objectives that suddenly changed from social to political, from nonviolent to violent, from reformist to revolutionary, but rather in orientation—from one that had long focused on religious and educational initiatives dedicated largely if not entirely to proselytism to one that increasingly became more broad-based and development-oriented (an approach that was supported by key members of the political leadership and may, in some cases, have derived directly from their initiatives).

Hence, the primary change that occurred between the periods before and after the signing of the Oslo Accords lay in the nature of the work carried out by Hamas social institutions, not in their politicization. This will be explored in chapter 5, by examining how Islamist social institutions operate and gain popular support. Furthermore, under Hamas control, many Islamic social institutions—over time—became less proselytizing and less rigid ideologically than they were prior to 1987, and more open and innovative.

Of course no one can deny the political framework in which these social organizations operate and their role—direct or indirect—in the political strategy of the Islamists. This became especially true after the June 1967 war with the beginning of Israeli occupation and the defeat of secular, nationalist Arab regimes. Although their defeat established a framework for the gradual revival of Islamist movements in the Gaza Strip and West Bank, it took at least a decade before this resurgence actually became marked. As discussed in chapter 2, Islamism did not emerge powerfully in Palestinian society in the immediate aftermath of the 1967 war,[2] because it could not compete with the strength of Palestinian nationalism (and it was not until 1973–1974 that the Islamic movement dominated by the Muslim Brotherhood [MB] began to reassert itself publicly after the defeat of the fedayeen movement in 1971). Rather, its slow and quiescent appearance initially complemented that of the secular nationalist PLO. Thus, during the first decade of occupation, the Brotherhood focused on reorganizing and reasserting itself as a religious organization dedicated to social reform.[3] In this regard, Beverly Milton-Edwards writes: "The group was influenced by the dynamic of Islamic resurgence regionally but was unable to generate the necessary internal political climate for change. [During the first decade of occupation], [i]t did not find a politically receptive audience nor would it do so without the catalyst of external actors such as the occupation authorities."[4] This catalyst emerged after 1977 when the political impact of Islam began to be felt at the mass level, especially in the Gaza Strip, which became the focus of MB activity.

There is no doubt that the Muslim Brotherhood has long used social institutions to spread its ideas and increase its influence. The MB's success was tied in large part to the fact that, until the first *Intifada* in 1987, the Brethren largely refrained from violent resistance against the occupation. Consequently, the Israeli authorities did not interfere in their activities, a lesson learned from the Brotherhood's experience in Egypt. In fact, because of their political invisibility at the time in both Gaza and the West Bank, Israel did not consider the Brotherhood a threat and actively supported its work as a counterweight to secular nationalism, a policy that Israel would later regret. The MB's success also derived from working in sectors, notably education and welfare, often neglected by the institutions of the national movement.[5]

Some Key Institutions before 1987

The Muslim Brotherhood has always believed that societal (and ultimately political) change is an evolutionary and gradual process that must begin with the reform of the individual—from infants to the elderly—and a return to Islam. Only a reformed, properly Islamic society would be prepared to undertake meaningful resistance and a prolonged armed struggle. The MB's ideology was not indigenous and did not focus on

Palestine. Rather, it was Egyptian, and it focused on the writings of al-Banna and Qutb and on the creation of a community of believers ruled by sharia law that would lead to the establishment of an Islamic state and a resurrected caliphate (i.e., political leadership for the *umma*—a successor to the Prophet Mohammad). As a movement, the MB's orientation was Muslim, not Palestinian, something that changed irreversibly with the first Palestinian Intifada and the establishment of Hamas.

Consequently, the Brotherhood promoted a conservative approach that emphasized Muslim piety and the creation and fortification of a proper Islamic society through Islamic reform, an approach that resonated at the popular level as the failures of Arab nationalism became increasingly stark. As such, the work of the Brotherhood prioritized religious practice, the family, women, education, and charity (over resisting Israel, for which it was no match)—*da'wa* over jihad. The Brotherhood established a variety of institutions both large and small during its first four decades in Palestine: nursery schools and kindergartens (often attached to mosques), religious schools (typically run by charitable associations), youth clubs, sports clubs, orphanages, neighborhood libraries, day care centers, health (medical and dental) clinics, and nursing homes.[6]

However, it was not until the 1970s that the Muslim Brotherhood in Gaza—with the acquiescence and support of the Israeli authorities—had developed a marked institutional and social infrastructure. This began, in effect, with the establishment in 1973 of al-Mujamma al-Islami by Sheikh Yassin among others (see chapter 2). Its most prominent leaders other than Yassin were Ibrahim al-Yazuri, Abd al-Aziz al-Rantisi, and Mahmoud al-Zahar.[7] The Mujamma leadership were all men who came from refugee families; as such, they were barred from internal political structures that were the domain of Gaza's old and landed elite. They received a secular education in Egypt and the United States and returned to Gaza as professionals—doctors, dentists, pharmacists, engineers, and educators—with skills desperately needed by the community. As a group they lacked formal religious training but later came to religion through politics. As Milton-Edwards put it, "Their religiosity and spirituality is realized through a path that is political rather than metaphysical."[8]

Established as a voluntary institution that linked education and religion within a service construct, the Mujamma stated that its aim was to provide Islamic education and sports for Gaza's youth, and welfare assistance and health care for Gaza's poor. Encouraged by Israel's policy of noninterference, the Mujamma expanded its institutional base through which it continued to provide needed social services, creating a public sphere that would rival that of the "state." (It was also through the Mujamma that the message of reformist Islam was transmitted). Branches were established throughout the Gaza Strip, particularly in the refugee camps. These branches ran nursery schools, kindergartens, play groups, health clinics, sports and youth clubs, a nursing school, a center for women's activities, a drug rehabilitation program, and other social centers and religious activities.

The Mujamma operated in the poorest areas of Gaza, renting buildings and establishing programs for the local population, an approach that typified its community work. In Khan Younis, for example, the Mujamma established a medical clinic that was staffed by its own membership, set up a dental service in the nearby refugee camp, and ran a kindergarten.[9] Most activities were centered around the mosque, "combining worship, education, and social welfare with subsidized services such as medical treatment, children's day care, free meals, and sports clubs."[10] Typically, a mosque would have a kindergarten and Quranic school attached to it; some mosques also had their own medical clinics and mobile medical units. "In each area, on a particular day, *Ikhwan* medical specialists in the different branches of medicine would provide free medical consultations on a voluntary basis. Meanwhile *Ikhwan* pharmacists would dispense medicine at cost or lower. There was also a day when boys could be circumcised without charge and the *Ikhwan* would organize and pay for the customary celebrations."[11]

With the financial assistance of the Israeli authorities, Gulf donors, institutional members and supporters, and the mushrooming of *zakat* committees that emerged from the need for systematic fund-raising, the Mujamma built new (non-*waqf*) mosques or rehabilitated old ones, which spurred the rapid increase in Gaza's mosques during this time. The Mujamma's focus on sports, especially football and the martial arts, was strong; Center-owned stadiums or grounds were located throughout the Gaza Strip.[12] As *zakat* committees flourished and often worked in association with a given mosque, the Muslim Brothers were able to provide assistance to thousands of needy families who thereby benefited from traditional Islamic institutions. Over time, thousands of children attended Ikhwan-run schools and kindergartens, while others enrolled in Palestinian and Arab universities were receiving Ikhwan loans.[13] Through the Mujamma, therefore, the Muslim Brotherhood in Gaza was able, in fairly short order, to establish an infrastructure of social institutions based on personal friendships, trust, and group solidarity, cementing its presence and influence at the grassroots level in a manner other political groups found difficult to match, let alone surpass.

Yassin began modestly by creating three-member cells throughout the entire Gaza Strip, many reaching the neighborhood level. As the movement grew and its societal penetration increased, the territory was divided into five subdistricts under an established and rigid chain of command that was hierarchical and authoritarian.[14] Eventually, the Mujamma succeeded in establishing a large-scale social program consisting mostly of schools and religious classes teaching the Quran. Social activities focused on individuals, groups, and communities and were all conducted according to Islamic norms. Adhering to an Islamic way of life was a central aim of the Mujamma's social program, particularly as it regarded the family and women. A key emphasis was placed on the poor and the duty of *zakat* "as a central avenue for social infiltration and expansion of its public support among the needy."[15] Critical links were established with small traders and merchants inside the refugee camps.[16]

The Islamists also attacked what they considered to be immoral behavior at the societal level, which included alcohol and drug use, prostitution, pornography, and activities that young men and women participated in together. Weddings and appropriate behavior seemed to be a focus of attention as well.[17] Violence was sometimes used to impose Islamic norms. I remember that during my first visit to Gaza City in 1985, I was shown its only cinema, long closed, which the Islamists had attacked years before.

In 1976 another key institution, al-Jam'iyya al-Islamiyya (the Islamic Association) was founded by Ahmad Bahar, an *alim* (scholar) and former imam at the Palestine Mosque in central Gaza, and Abu Shanab, who also was a civil engineer. The association was effectively an instrument of the Mujamma. Article 3 of the Jam'iyya's statute clearly describes its mission: "The aim is to lead the people to the True Islam [*Al-islam al-hanif*] and to work spiritually through worship, and intellectually through science, and physically through sports, as well as socially through charity."[18] The Jam'iyya provided a framework for religious and communal activities and established branches throughout the Gaza Strip with kindergartens, health clinics, summer camps, computer centers, and a variety of religious and social activities. It should be noted that not everyone involved with Islamic charities had MB connections.

During this time, other key Islamic social institutions began operations including, in 1978, the Jam'iyyat al-Salah al-Islamiyya (the Association of Islamic Prayer), which ran programs similar to those of its predecessors. In 1981 the Mujamma established the Jam'iyyat al-Shabbat al-Muslimat (Young Women's Muslim Association or Society) as an institution providing training in traditional areas such as sewing and embroidery but also computer skills, religious instruction, and literacy. In addition, several other, smaller institutions emerged that provided a variety of social services in health, education, and basic assistance. Because the Mujamma did not control all the groups claiming membership in the Muslim Brotherhood, power struggles did emerge over the control of resources and social influence, but the Mujamma clearly remained "the spearhead of the MB's mainstream in the Gaza Strip."[19] These charities, no matter their activity, emphasized Islamic education and social justice and generally adhered to the principles espoused by al-Banna and the early Egyptian Brotherhood.[20]

During the 1970s and 1980s, the Muslim Brotherhood via the Mujamma and other institutions positioned themselves as critical social actors, at times indispensably so. In addition to their providing a range of social services, I personally remember stories of the role they played in mediating clan disputes (often without charge), which became a key area of focus and means of consolidating ties with the grass roots, particularly with the more marginalized elements of society who had no other source of appeal. Not only did their mediatory role accord the Islamic institutions great social prestige, especially in a society where customary law prevails (in the absence of civil law); it enabled them to empower the poor and provide them with a greater sense of equity and fairness in a system that had extremely limited options. This was critically important.

The Brotherhood consistently sought to legalize the movement's social and religious activities by gaining formal legal recognition for its associations with the objective of developing a civil society along Islamic lines. Initially, the Israeli military authorities rejected requests by the Mujamma. A key factor working against the organization in this period was the opposition of more traditional Islamic bodies such as the Jam'iyyat Tahfiz al-Qur'an (Association for Teaching Memorization of the Quran).[21] However, in 1978 and 1979 the Israeli authorities granted the Mujamma a license, which was crucial to its institutionalization and strengthened its ability to influence the public discourse and agenda. Concomitantly, the Brotherhood encouraged its followers to join a variety of voluntary and public institutions, professional associations, and unions, where they were relatively successful in winning support and increasing their political influence.

The Brotherhood used the Mujamma as an institutional framework within which to pursue most of its activities. Effectively, this meant that all religious institutions belonging to the Brotherhood (including a growing number of mosques) were under the Center's authority and leadership.[22] Composed of seven committees working in preaching and guidance, welfare, education, charity, health, sports, and conciliation, the Mujamma became "the base for the development, administration, and control of religious and educational Islamic institutions in the Gaza Strip, under Yassin's supervision."[23]

During the 1970s and 1980s, the Muslim Brotherhood also established itself firmly in the area of higher education with the founding, in 1978, of the Islamic University in Gaza (IUG). Considered a key node of support for the Brotherhood in the Strip, the IUG provided preachers for local mosques in Gaza and the West Bank and educated a generation of Muslim leaders that assumed positions in different sectors of Palestinian society. In this way, the Islamic movement was able to reach further and deeper into the Palestinian community by providing needed services in employment and training as well as education. Arguably the most visible expression of social penetration through institutional means, the IUG was established in response to Egypt's decision to deny Palestinians access to Egyptian universities. This decision was taken in retaliation for the PLO's condemnation of President Sadat's peace treaty with Israel.

Initially the university, which was meant by its founders to be run according to Islamic principles, was under the effective control of the PLO. However, a budgetary shortfall eventually compensated by external Islamic sources and channeled through the Mujamma ultimately resulted in an Islamic takeover of the university (although not all staff or faculty were members or supporters of the Islamic movement).[24] By the early 1990s, more than five thousand students attended the IUG, with the Mujamma playing a central role in its administration.[25]

Islamic student groups were also able to compete successfully, although not easily and increasingly violently, with nationalist student groups in other (nationalist) universities, particularly in student council elections, capitalizing on growing student disillusionment and anger. Calling themselves al-Qutla al-Islamiyya (Islamic Bloc), these students had close links with the Muslim Brotherhood and its social institutions. They were particularly active in the West Bank, especially after the 1979 Iranian revolution, when Muslim leaders and activists urged university (and high school) students to pay greater attention to political issues.[26]

In fact, during the decade preceding the first Palestinian uprising, relations between the Islamic and nationalist movements became increasingly hostile rather than accommodative, which in part reflected the rise of religious revivalism in Gaza and the West Bank. The growing violence between them—seen, for example, in the burning by MB members of the Palestinian Red Crescent office in Gaza in 1980—was spurred by several factors including Israel's open, albeit benign, support for the Muslim Brotherhood over the nationalists and the formation and growth of the Islamic Jihad (some of whose members broke off from the Ikhwan), which not only advocated political violence against the occupation but in doing so placed Palestine together with Islam at the center of its discourse on the Islamic struggle for liberation.[27] As such, the Islamic Jihad positioned itself as a revolutionary, antiestablishment force within the Islamic movement, creating tensions with the MB that did not abate. The Muslim Brotherhood for its part continued to emphasize defeating the PLO—considered heretic and traitorous to Islam—over confronting the occupation; members remained adamant in their insistence that liberation could be achieved only through the Islamization of Palestinian society and the establishment of an Islamic state. A Mujamma slogan at the time read, "How can uncovered women and men with Beatle haircuts liberate our holy places?"[28]

Indeed, perhaps the greatest challenge facing the MB at this time was how to persuade Palestinians to reject secularization at the personal level and nationalism at the political level. Considerable efforts would be made to change the secular nature of Palestinian society, often by challenging the nationalist movement through elections within their own institutions such as professional associations, unions, and universities. (The Islamic challenge was strengthened by the weakened and dislocated state of the nationalist movement, particularly Fatah, after Israel's 1982 invasion of Lebanon, which forced the PLO into exile in Tunis.)

Although it would be incorrect to say that the Ikhwan had a transformative social impact on Palestinian society in Gaza, it would be equally incorrect to assert that the Brotherhood's presence was unnoticed, particularly in a society where it was certainly not anomalous to practice a form of politics that was inspired by Islam. Teasing out the two—the direct impact of the Brotherhood on social life and the general tendency within society toward Islamic practice—is difficult, if not impossible. Yet this raises an important point about the relationship between cultural Islam and politics in the Palestinian context. Gaza's socially conservative culture is often assumed or treated as a given. However, to a certain—perhaps large—extent, Gaza's social norms have been imposed by various forms of coercion exercised by different forces, including the MB and Hamas.

By the outbreak of the first uprising, there was palpable evidence—both positive and negative—of the MB's social program, especially in Gaza: an institutionalized social infrastructure that reached into most areas of the territory; a welfare system that addressed the poorest (refugee and nonrefugee) segments of Gazan society; the tripling and near doubling of the number of mosques in Gaza and the West Bank respectively between 1967 and 1987; control of the Islamic University in Gaza and the Brotherhood's presence in student councils in other universities; the closing of cinemas and restaurants selling alcohol; increased donning of Islamic over Western dress; and violent attacks on nationalist institutions (a strategy that the Islamic Jihad rejected).

Hence, as it became a more formal and prominent institutionalized presence in the Gaza Strip, particularly during the decade prior to the first Intifada, the Mujamma and its adherents began to play a more politically activist and violent role in society, which contradicted the MB's emphasis on education, religious teaching, welfare, and gradual reform.[29] Tensions were building within the Brotherhood between those who advocated traditional approaches and those who—under growing pressures from the Ikhwan's younger ranks and Palestinian society as a whole—were pressing for military action.³⁰ Despite this, the debate over the value of armed struggle and military action against the occupation continued until the start of the first Palestinian Intifada, when any such refusal became indefensible.

By the end of the decade, Islam had emerged and transformed into a political force increasingly capable of mounting a challenge to secular nationalism. Yet it also was clear that Palestinians could not be easily persuaded of the Islamic vision or its gradual, reformist approach. As the occupation turned twenty years old, the ability to win hearts and minds depended less on the establishment of an Islamic state and far more on ending Israel's occupation through armed struggle. It was this understanding and quest for authenticity and the need to secure a popular base of support (especially among the young) that contributed to a dramatic strategic shift within the Islamic movement, powerfully expressed during the first Palestinian Intifada, away from the problems of social development toward political and military resistance and a focus on Palestine. The eventual result was the creation of the Islamic Resistance Movement (Harakat al-Muqawama al-Islamiyya) or HaMaS.³¹

Islamic Social Institutions under Hamas: The First Intifada (1987 to 1993)—Social Reform in the Service of Political and Military Struggle—Territory before Community

With the formation of Hamas during the first Intifada, the thrust of activity within the Islamic movement had finally shifted from the social/civil to the political (and, later, military) realm, reflecting a dynamic that had been strengthening particularly during the five-year period preceding the first uprising. Although prioritizing social development (i.e., longer-term religious and community reform) as a means to effect long-term political change remained important for the Islamic movement—reflecting the fundamental connection between the social and the political in Islamist thought and practice—social change was no longer prioritized over political change, as it had been before 1987. Rather, during the first Intifada, the activities of the Islamic social sector (identified largely with the Mujamma) were meant to complement, strengthen, localize, and institutionalize Hamas as a political actor and solidify its position within Palestinian society as the natural heir of the more traditional Ikhwan. Political action—resistance and martyrdom—was primary, not social reform or building an Islamic society (although the latter remained critical for the former). The nation assumed primacy over the individual. Khaled Hroub observes: "Hamas combined Islamic social-instructional discourse with the discourse of nationalist resistance, placing each at the service of the other. The commitment to an Islamic code of conduct served the objectives of resistance and liberation. At the same time, enlistment in the *Intifada* and the resistance effort became a religious commitment."[32]

The goal was not so much to change the nature of social activity but rather to maintain and strengthen it, in order to address new economic exigencies created by the Intifada and respond to the population's immediate needs. In this way, Hamas was able to secure and expand its popular base of support and political stature. By linking community activism with religious-nationalist doctrine, Hamas was able to territorialize the conflict—that is, carve out its own "turf" for action—and compete with other political actors.

As such, Hamas reinforced the Muslim Brotherhood's (conservative and largely successful) social program, which had evolved considerably over the preceding decade. Additionally, competition with the PLO and pressure from Israel compelled Hamas to expand the program's political and social infrastructure and develop a bureaucracy to support it in a manner that was foreign to the Ikhwan. Hamas's strategic emphasis on conservatism—maintaining a strong connection to Islamic values—and continuity also had another purpose: to consolidate and standardize Hamas's control over the Islamic social sector, something that did not occur immediately but over time. As Mishal and Sela observe: "Initially intended to be an autonomous organization within the MB movement, Hamas practically turned into the hard core of the Islamic movement, with its own ideological and political stature, which soon overshadowed and in fact coopted the MB mother movement."[33]

That Hamas's social program remained fundamentally unchanged from that of the Ikhwan can be see in Hamas's 1988 Charter, which called for the creation, through religious education, of a properly prepared society that would be capable of fighting (and ultimately ending) the occupation. Articles 15 and 16 state:

> When an enemy usurps a Muslim land, then *jihad* is an individual religious duty on every Muslim.... That requires that Islamic education be given to the masses locally and in the Arab and Islamic spheres.... The education process must involve scholars, teachers, educators, communicators, journalists, and the educated, especially the youth of the Islamic movement.... Fundamental changes must be made in the educational system to liberate it from the effects of the ideological invasion that was brought by the Orientalists and missionaries.... We must train the Muslim generation in our area, an Islamic training based on performing religious duties, studying

God's book very well, and studying Prophetic tradition (*sunnah*), Islamic history and heritage from its authenticated sources with the guidance of experts and scholars, and using a curriculum that will provide the Muslim with the correct world view in ideology and thought.[34]

Practically, Hamas translated its social vision in several ways. Emphasis continued to be given to the work of the Islamic social service network established by the Ikhwan, which Hamas expanded in an effort to penetrate civic life and civil society. Writing in 1995, I observed that Islamic social and economic institutions had continued to grow. Long experience, religious commitment, and continued funding allowed them to become some of the most effective service-delivery institutions in the Gaza Strip.[35]

A common focus was children—especially orphans—and families, including collaborators' families. For example, by 1995, between seven thousand and ten thousand orphaned children in the Gaza Strip received some form of support from various Islamic associations. Through its many committees and organizational branches in the refugee camps, villages, and towns in the Strip, the Islamist movement was able to identify children who needed assistance. Orphans included both parentless children and fatherless ones as well. Typically, individual cases took twenty-four hours to two months to review; once approved, an orphaned child received a monthly stipend of about $33 through age sixteen.

Each year, according to local sources, Islamist associations were spending between $2,772,000 and $3,960,000 on orphan support. Clothes, basic school supplies, and, when needed, food rations were also provided. Social workers would make periodic follow-up visits to children and become part of their lives. Some Islamic charities established programs connecting overseas sponsors with needy children. Such community outreach was a long-standing feature of Islamic social programs that contributed mightily to earning the trust of the poor. Similar services were provided for approximately five thousand of Gaza's neediest families, who were ranked and helped according to need. Typically, these included families of martyrs and prisoners in Israeli jails, and families with no breadwinner and widows.

An important focus of Islamist social programs particularly toward the end of the Intifada period was the wives and children of men killed for collaborating with the Israeli military authorities. Collaborators were reviled by Palestinian society, and many were killed by Palestinian factions including Hamas. In keeping with cultural traditions, which confer an individual's shame on his or her entire extended family, the families of collaborators were ostracized. Islamic charities made a concerted and, I believe, almost singular effort to reintegrate these "collaborator" women and children into society, not only through the provision of basic relief but by incorporating them into other Islamic-sponsored activities in which the larger community participated. In this way, they were slowly "relegitimized."

Education, however, remained the key area of focus, given its central role in building an Islamic society. Under Hamas, the Islamic movement maintained its prominent role in Gaza's educational system and incorporated not only religious studies but a standardized government curriculum. Hamas's educational role assumed different forms (which I was able to view): formal education (i.e., Islamic schools), extracurricular classes devoted to Quranic study and to remedial tutoring in various subjects for children of all ages, and informal classes devoted to religious teaching in Islamic social institutions; there were also professional organizations and unions (I did not witness the latter two).

One example of how the Islamic movement penetrated the educational system in Gaza can be found in the refugee camps, where 35 percent of the population lived. By the end of the Intifada, Islamic committees had been established in each of the Gaza Strip's eight refugee camps. Each committee had several branches within individual camps, and there was some, albeit limited, intercamp coordination between committees. In Nuseirat camp, for example, where an estimated forty thousand people lived at the time, the Islamic committee had five branches, each with a staff typically consisting of a director who was a teacher, an administrator, a social worker, a secretary, an accountant, and teachers. The Islamic committee ran kindergartens for 1,200 boys and girls who attended school from eight to eleven in the morning in classes of 35 to 40 children. Several of the kindergartens—by some accounts, the majority—were housed in mosques.

The curriculum consisted of reading and writing in Arabic and English, religion, and recitations from the Quran. Every child, regardless of his or her family's political orientation, was welcome to attend. (When I asked about this, the director just laughed.) The annual tuition was IS 120 (Israeli shekels, or US $40) per child; with transportation, it increased to IS 170 (US $57). These fees, which paid for staff and teacher salaries as well as toys, were high for impoverished camp residents, but they were willingly paid because the kindergartens were highly valued for their educational quality and discipline—attributes that also characterized the many nurseries, kindergartens, and day care centers run by Islamic organizations outside the camp system. Parents of all social classes, including the wealthy, sent their children to these schools. Parents I interviewed (none of them devout Muslims) clearly indicated their preference for an Islamic curriculum and the moral teachings of Islam. The parents in Nuseirat camp requested that more Islamic-run kindergartens be established, while the kindergartens run by the secular political factions in Nuseirat were forced to close because of low enrollments. At the time of the research, the only other kindergarten available was government run.

Another reason that the committee kindergartens were popular was their involvement of parents in the educational process: Mothers would meet monthly to voice concerns, and parents were asked to evaluate teacher performance. When I asked one completely veiled mother how the Islamic committee could improve its educational services to the community, she responded: "We desperately need day care facilities. There is one in [the village of] Zuweida but that is not nearly enough. We need toys that will cognitively challenge young children, and we need more computers. We only have one. If our children are going to compete in the twenty-first century, they must be computer literate." Job openings for kindergarten teachers were advertised in mosques. Applicants, usually women, were required to have a high school education and some teacher training. They were interviewed and selected by a committee of professionals.

Another feature of committee services was free remedial tutoring after school. In Nuseirat camp, one hundred children in the fifth through twelfth grades received tutoring in math and English. Tutors, all volunteers, were usually (but not exclusively) camp residents who taught in government and UNRWA schools. Not all were members of Hamas or Islamic Jihad or even devout Muslims. The only precondition for volunteering was qualification and interest. A limited number of Islamic associations both inside and outside the refugee camps also provided computer courses to boys and girls for a nominal fee. Additionally, teenage boys and young men were offered extracurricular sports (e.g., soccer, table tennis), usually in or through the mosques, which included prayer and religious instruction. At the time I visited Nuseirat camp in 1995, a sports center was being built above one mosque by camp volunteers.

Committee staff and volunteers also would regularly visit prisoners, martyrs' families, and the sick, which contributed mightily to creating personal bonds with the community. Programs existed for blood donation and free medications for the needy. Islamic charities and associations ran public health clinics that offered free medical and dental care to widows and orphans, and comparatively low-cost services to others. The al-Salah Islamic Association, one of Gaza's best known (see chapter 5), also arranged, with foreign donations, for children with Intifada-related injuries to be treated in France, Germany, and the United Kingdom.

Like its counterparts in other camps, the Islamic committee in Nuseirat had several affiliated women's groups and engaged in activities centering on the family and women's roles. Programs focused on counseling and training. Typically, female "coaches" visited female camp residents to counsel them on proper health care and nutrition, as well as adolescent development and challenges. Very poor wives and mothers were coached in basic household management. These programs were staffed almost entirely by female volunteers who first learned about them in the mosque, from other participants. The mothers of children enrolled in Islamic kindergartens were also invited to volunteer, and all who accepted received appropriate training. As of March 1995, there were three hundred women volunteers in Nuseirat camp working through the Islamic women's committees. With this number of volunteers, it was not unreasonable to assume that the Islamic committee may have been providing services to a majority of households in Nuseirat camp,[36] a pattern that could be found in other camps as well.

Other women's associations combined training with religious instruction. The Women's Islamic Association in Gaza City, for example, offered courses in skills such as knitting, sewing, and secretarial work that women could use to earn some income and help their families. A six-month sewing course cost IS 120 (US $40), and a four-month knitting course cost IS 100 (US $33). The poor were exempted from tuition. Fees only partly covered teacher salaries and other running costs. About eight to twenty-five women participated in each sewing class and twelve to fifteen in knitting class; all came from the poor and lower classes. Women would bring their own materials and keep whatever they produced. Sometimes exhibits were held where trainees could sell their goods. By 1995, nearly four hundred women had taken various courses.

Activities for men were kept totally separate to secure the women's reputations and safety. In Gaza's very traditional and conservative society, the mere presence or absence of men could single-handedly determine whether a woman would receive vocational training. Participants, who had to be literate, came from nearby areas and surrounding refugee camps. The director of one branch insisted that market studies were carried out before courses were offered so that women would be trained only in skills for which there was sufficient demand to make them marketable after their training. An essential and mandatory part of the program was instruction in Islamic culture, philosophy, law, and religion. Quranic verses had to be memorized, and students were required to pass an examination in the Quran in order to graduate. Two classes per week were therefore devoted to these subjects, the purpose of which was to educate women in proper Islamic behavior and housekeeping.

Another important way that Hamas sought to implement its conservative social agenda and thereby institutionalize and buoy its local political role was by continuing to adjudicate social (including legal and financial) disputes, a role the Islamic movement had historically played. Sheikh Yassin, in particular, became known for his acumen and skill as a mediator.

His quasi-legal judgments, based on religious law, were respected and honored, and the popular legitimacy he commanded may have been one reason the occupation authorities arrested him in 1989. I personally remember hearing many stories from friends in Gaza at the time—none of them supporters of Hamas and some, in fact, extremely hostile to the Islamists—attesting to Yassin's wisdom and fairness.

Islamic leaders settled a range of disputes, from those inside the home to compensation for families of automobile accidents (thereby inhibiting a cycle of retaliation and counterretaliation). They would address conflicts over transactions involving land, breach of contract, employee treatment, and lesser acts of wrongdoing. They met with varying degrees of success, but their role was quite visible and accorded them considerable moral authority (itself enhanced by the fact that they often received no compensation). This authority no doubt made it easier for Hamas to advocate a conservative social agenda that emphasized proper Islamic conduct and religious norms inside and outside the home: praying regularly, fasting during Ramadan, Quranic study, proper dress for women, and appropriate behavior for women and girls, especially in public.

Hamas pursued its social agenda without apparent coercion. Although I witnessed (in 1988 to 1989) some public incidents (generally involving women who were reprimanded for improper appearance) and was myself the object of one such reprimand, the overall approach of the Islamists was arguably noncoercive and was often recognized as such by the community. The incidents were described to me as the work of rogue elements. In discussions, various Hamas officials offered reasons for the lack of coercion that were both philosophical and strategic. Not only did such an approach violate Islamic values and beliefs, they said; it would also erode the moral authority and influence that Hamas had worked so hard to build within the community. This influence was further consolidated in often successful attempts by Hamas to gain official representation in a range of local institutions including professional and student organizations, labor unions, and chambers of commerce.

During the Intifada, the Islamist imperative was to deepen the connection to Islamic values through social service and welfare provision and to use that connection to bolster Hamas's political stature as the authentic representative of nationalist aspirations and communal needs. In this the Islamists were reasonably successful, especially when one considers the consistently greater strength of the nationalist secular forces. However, the political successes Hamas enjoyed during the Intifada were threatened and began to erode with the advent of the Oslo period and the establishment of the PNA. This reality, while described in the literature, is not, in my view, fully appreciated or understood, particularly with regard to its impact on Hamas's own rethinking and restrategizing of its future course, evidenced in a palpable shift in focus *away* from the political and military spheres *toward* the social sphere, where further, more innovative changes were slowly but visibly being introduced.

Hamas Social Institutions during Oslo (1993–2000): From Political Activism and Armed Struggle to Civic Activism and Cultural Accommodation—Reprioritizing the Community and Its Development

By the admission of its own leadership in Gaza, Hamas was measurably weakened by 1998 (and probably earlier). In response, the leadership was slowly undergoing a process of de-radicalization and demilitarization and searching for political and social accommodation within the status quo of Palestinian society. There was a pronounced shift in emphasis within the movement in Gaza and the West Bank away from political-military action to social-cultural reform, and political violence was slowly but steadily being abandoned as a form of resistance and as a strategy for defeating the occupier. The shift to the social realm—and retreat from the political—was dramatic and, by the admission of the domestic Islamist leadership itself, reflected, more than anything, the successes of Israel and the PNA in weakening the Islamic political sector and defeating its military wing. With Oslo, the environment was more hostile to Hamas; and with its influence clearly waning, it became more difficult and costly to compete politically and violently.

The thrust toward the social, furthermore, was not simply a return to old forms of social service provision commonly associated with the Islamic movement and the Muslim Brotherhood but included entry into new areas of community and development work that pointed to an emerging new logic between state and society.[37] This new logic was characterized by a need for more innovative ways of thinking and a focus on civil society, since it was there that the Islamists were most competitive—if not more so—with the secular nationalists. Their greatest strength still lay in their mass base and in their embrace of the community as the strategic core of their political program. Hence, Hamas did not only aim to address certain problems but sought more creative ways of doing so.

As stated earlier, during the Oslo period the political and military sectors of Hamas were substantively weakened by a combination of factors. Most significant was the sustained intense pressure through arrests, imprisonment, torture, and execution imposed by Israel and the PNA under Arafat. In addition, these same pressures were imposed on Islamic social institutions, the so-called "terrorist infrastructure," which resulted in the closing down of many charitable societies including the Jam'iyya and the

Mujamma (some of which later reopened), a pattern that continues to this day under the Abbas-led government in the West Bank (with similar attacks against Fatah-based institutions by the Hamas-led government in Gaza [chapter 7]).

Another critical factor was the Palestinian population itself, the mass base of support for Hamas, who could no longer tolerate extremism in any form. The economic costs of Hamas's military operations and terrorist attacks, particularly the spate of suicide bombings inside Israel, became too high in an eroding socioeconomic environment, and widespread popular opposition to such attacks played an important role in ending them. Another consistently overlooked factor contributing to Hamas's declining influence at this time was the defection of its younger activists who were disillusioned by the failure of their leadership to achieve any meaningful political change.[38] Some of these younger members who had run and promoted Hamas's political infrastructure and bureaucracy during the first Intifada told me at the time that their wish was to leave Palestine and live in a free country like the United States where they could practice their religion and never have to deal with politics again.

Hence, not only did the leadership have increasing trouble controlling the militancy of younger activists (as seen in the attacks of the military cells); the organization also suffered from an eroding membership. Indeed, the diminished ability of Hamas's senior leadership in Gaza to maintain control over their rank and file was a serious problem. This further demonstrates that the ideological commitment to Islamism was challenged from within and that Hamas's fundamental base of support derived from communal, not political, activism.

Hamas's internal malaise also was due to growing popular alienation from politics—all politics—perhaps especially, political Islam. Political ideology—which had apparently exhausted its options to effect genuine change—had little place in Palestine at that time. Instead, people increasingly turned to cultural and religious practice, expressing the need to return to the ethical and moral traditions of Islam because these were the only belief systems left with any legitimacy. This was made very clear to me by a wide range of people inside and outside Hamas. Interestingly, a key figure in the Islamic movement in the West Bank emphatically told me that people were not turning to religion in greater numbers or even becoming more observant. They were, he said, simply seeking greater comfort in practicing Islam,[39] a pattern that only became more pronounced as time went on and living conditions progressively worsened.

Popular alienation was no doubt deepened by the absence of any alternative political channels of expression and by the PNA's increasing militarization of society. Moreover, with the end of the Intifada and the initiation of the Oslo period, the resistance component of the Palestinian struggle—so critical to Hamas's political thinking and action—was effectively co-opted and undermined. This had direct repercussions for Hamas's social theory and practice, which were largely if not wholly developed and shaped by the praxis of resistance during the Intifada. For Hamas, social and political activism were inextricably linked, a belief traceable to its Muslim Brotherhood roots. With the removal of the resistance/opposition component from Palestinian political imperatives, what role remained for Hamas? The resulting problem confronting Hamas (and the Islamist movement generally) was fundamentally one of survival, not one of resolving doctrinal contradictions between Islamic precepts and nationalist goals.

My interviews with several senior leaders at the time strongly suggest that they were desperately seeking ways of ensuring their survival as a movement, which they felt was threatened by the PNA's military superiority and by overwhelming popular support for the peace process. How, in light of its own internal weakness, general popular disaffection, and environmental constraints, could Hamas remain the primary opposition force capable of mobilizing and maintaining popular support? Justifying a strategically altered political and ideological position did not appear to be a principal concern.

In response (and despite the fact that many in the Islamic political sector remained active and fully committed to political and military action), there was a slow but steady shift in emphasis, both ideologically and strategically, away from political and military action to social work and community development.[40] This shift was characterized by more nontraditional and creative approaches, in addition to the propagation of Islamic values and religious practice.

Strategically, Hamas in particular and the Islamist movement generally attempted to carve out public space in which they could operate without too much harassment from the Israeli or Palestinian authorities, and provide highly sought after services to an increasingly needy (and appreciative) population through a well-developed institutional infrastructure. It was through practical and increasingly novel programs rather than ideological principle that the Islamists would maintain their presence and influence within Palestinian society. This approach was, in effect, dual: It represented a search for accommodation and consensus within the status quo and an experiment of sorts in redefining the Islamic social agenda.[41] This is not to say that tensions and contradictions between the "old" and the "new" did not exist; they did. But, arguably, the idea of articulating and putting into action a domestic social reform program that (in some cases) went beyond conventional or stereotypical Islamic/ist ideas began in earnest during this period. It was this social program—and Hamas's ability to interpret Islam in multiple ways—that no doubt provided the foundation for Hamas's social agenda during the 2004–2005 municipal and 2006 legislative elections.

It became increasingly clear, therefore, that in the two- to three-year period before the second Intifada the Hamas leadership in Gaza was no longer seriously calling for political or military action against the occupation but was instead shifting its attention to societal rehabilitation and change. So pronounced was the shift that some of Hamas's political leaders stated their outright opposition to violence as a form of resistance, in effect rejecting the strategy of violence as a way to defeat the occupier. Also apparent was a shift in language and ideas, notably, a growing acceptance of civil society as a concept—of a society in which Islamist institutions functioned as part of an integrated whole with their secular counterparts.

While this was consistent with Hamas's long-standing program of socializing people into what Gunning has called "willing the Islamic state" (i.e., internalizing the principles of Islam, which it did through its programmatic emphasis on community, education, and consultation),[42] it also represented the beginning of a change in Hamas's conception of what constitutes an Islamically prepared society and what role the community should play in it. Hamas slowly but increasingly accepted that dissent was appropriate within the community and that it should play a role in determining practical/policy outcomes at the societal level (chapter 6).[43] As a result, a more broad-based understanding of society and the role of "citizens" was slowly evolving, creating in turn a new, more constructive discourse of empowerment (opposed to a destructive one of violence) that paralleled the retreat of Hamas's long-dominant political sector. In this way the Islamists gained entry to, and legitimation by, the existing order, which it appeared they were seeking or at least accepted.

Although social action has a political and revolutionary purpose in Hamas's political ideology, Islamic social activism, as it was evolving in the Oslo context, was becoming increasingly incorporated within the mainstream (which, of course, was one way the ruling authority controlled the Islamic sector, but it worked to the advantage of both). Some of the clearest examples of this dynamic were found in education, health, and banking.[44]

In education, for example, Islamic kindergartens, reputed centers of intense political proselytizing if not brainwashing, taught, as stated earlier, a standard curriculum that was approved by the Palestinian Ministry of Education. This was also true for new Islamic schools at the elementary and secondary school level. Islamic schools also taught a religious curriculum that was their domain alone. However, the Education Ministry had standardized, regulated, and approved its own religious curriculum, which, as far as I could determine, was not imposed on Islamic schools. Interestingly, one principal in a Mujamma school in Gaza commented to me how impressed he was by the ministry's religious curriculum. According to Ministry of Education officials at that time, 65 percent of all Gazan educational institutions below the secondary level were Islamic.

In the health care sector, Islamic medical facilities began offering tertiary and highly specialized care. For example, one of the most sophisticated hospitals in the West Bank and Gaza, located in Hebron, was founded, administered, and financed by the Islamic and Islamist leadership during the Oslo period (see chapter 6). Although small hospitals had been founded by the Muslim Brotherhood years earlier, they did not compare with the scope of the Hebron facility.

In the economic sector, an Islamic banking network was established, with four Islamic banks and more than twenty branches in the occupied territories, Islamic investment houses, and a range of business enterprises. As far as the banks were concerned, it was highly unlikely that Hamas had any control, direct or even indirect, over them, given its own limited organizational structure and the tight regulation of such activities by governmental agencies. Officials interviewed at the Palestinian Monetary Authority (PMA) at the time were adamant that Hamas had no role whatsoever in the Islamic banking system. (On April 21, 2009, the Islamic National Bank opened in Gaza, the *first* bank to operate outside PMA control, and it is widely understood to be affiliated with Hamas. The bank is not considered to be a legal entity, since it did not apply for a banking license from the PMA and is not subject to any financial or administrative regulation or supervision. Capitalized for $20 million, the bank opened with six thousand personal accounts for civil servants; however, clients dealing with this bank were told they would be doing so at their own risk. The American government has imposed sanctions on the Hamas-owned bank.)[45]

In all these cases, Islamic institutions were working with and were regulated by the appropriate Palestinian ministries and agencies and, in many cases, had what appeared to be good working relationships with the governmental sector (see chapters 5 and 6). Also important is the fact that people seeking the services of Islamic NGOs did so not because they supported Hamas (or any other Islamist faction) but for the simple reason that they needed the services. Furthermore, as I maintain in subsequent chapters, accepting the service did not automatically or necessarily translate into political support for the Islamist movement.

Arguably, these expanded or new areas of Islamist social activity represented the normalization, institutionalization, and professionalization of the Islamic sector in the education system, the system of health care delivery, and banking and finance. Indeed, Islamic social service organizations typically

- had no (political) ideological criteria as conditions for access to Islamic social services, or for membership in Islamic social organizations;
- evinced no desire or intent to create a strictly Islamic society or to implement any Islamic model;
- desired greater practical cooperation with the Palestinian government, itself reflecting an openness on the part of the Islamists for better state-society relations and not an attempt to challenge, alienate, or sabotage state authority;[46] and
- prioritized professionalism over ideology.

This approach steadily legitimized Islam, however slowly, as part of the dominant paradigm. In fact, I consistently found that Hamas preferred to operate openly and legally, which is not unusual for Islamic movements in other national contexts where they are tolerated.

In fact, the Islamic sector was not advancing a policy of isolation but was calling for greater accommodation and cooperation with national/local and international actors, including certain counterpart professional institutions in Israel, the United States Agency for International Development (USAID), European governmental agencies, and United Nations organizations among others. In one Islamic community center I was visiting, I was invited to sit with the board of directors to discuss their expansion plans for the center. One of the first questions I was asked by the chairman of the board, himself a well-known Hamas official, was whether I had any contacts with USAID. They also wanted my assessment as to whether an application from their center would be evaluated fairly. It was apparent that the board was interested in applying for a USAID grant if there was a real possibility of winning one, a trend I found in other (but not all) Islamist organizations as well. In another health care institution in Gaza, the al-Wafa Rehabilitation Hospital, which was considered "Hamas" since some members of its management team were political members or supporters of the organization, the medical director proudly described a training program inside Israel to which he sent some of his staff (chapter 5).

This position advocating greater social integration with non-Islamic actors, both internal and external, appeared widespread among officials in the Islamist social sector and was the stated position of some members of the political leadership. Hence, the work of the social sector was not regarded by either its members or its beneficiaries as a political battle against the state. This begs the question of whether there were direct ties between Islamic political and social institutions. The debate over the answer has been intense since the birth of Hamas. Accepted belief argues that Hamas has controlled all Islamic social institutions and used them for political indoctrination and military recruitment. Yet, despite this control, Hamas's relationship was not always as direct (hands-on) and routine as is commonly believed, nor as nefarious. However, it cannot be denied that the work of Islamic social institutions, be they aligned or nonaligned, did bolster the position of Hamas.

Thus, the organic interconnection between political and social action in Hamas's ideology meant that expanding the social sector served the movement's objectives even if the social institutions involved claimed no linkages to Hamas. Islamist organizations were judged by their social and economic performance, not by their political ideology. As such, Hamas's internal shift arguably represented the beginning of a new ethos of civic engagement, a limited pluralism, as it were. It further points to what the scholar Amr Hamzawy calls the "inner secularization of the religious discourse"[47] as a means of adapting to existing social, political, and economic realities.

The shift to social action, to a social (and, hence, modified political) domestic agenda, to new forms of social engagement, and to the normalization, incorporation, and institutionalization of the Islamist agenda during the Oslo period represented an important change within the Islamist movement, not simply a policy of political adjustment. What was occurring was no less than the creation of a new space in Islamist thinking away from national action toward communal development and reformist initiatives. Hence, the changing focus to the social sphere was practical and pragmatic and accompanied by a need to rediscover Islam and its ethical and moral relevance for society. It appeared that Hamas or its successors were slowly moving away from the political extreme toward a more centrist position, trying to position themselves between the corruption of the PNA and its donor-linked development projects, on the one hand, and violent Islamic militants and the impossibilities they came to represent, on the other. This position was not unlike that of the moderate reformist stream of Islamic thought discussed in chapter 3.

Hamas, perhaps, was trying to limit the arbitrary political power of the PNA, not through political or military confrontation, which had failed and was costly, but through mobilizing people at the social/cultural level and allowing the social part of the movement to define, pragmatically and nonviolently, the Islamist agenda for some time into the future. And, while the transformation from militancy to accommodation was incremental and uneven, it was, without question, occurring.

Concluding Reflections

Hamas's emerging shift to the social sector, though not widely examined, has been observed by other analysts. In their important study, Mishal and Sela write: "The Hamas leaders ... realized that the PNA's security and police forces were waiting for a pretext to abolish Hamas as a military movement, especially following the incorporation of Fatah into the PNA's bureaucratic and security apparatus. To these considerations were added strategic ones—namely, the collapse of the Soviet Union, the weakness of the movement's allies in the Arab and Muslim world, and the need to adapt to the new reality, which meant *narrowing the movement's activities to social and political domains*"[48] (emphasis added).

Khaled Hroub further and correctly argues that because it evolved within the occupied territories, Hamas has had difficulty with the intellectual production of new ideas that could parallel the expansion of its popular base.

> [A]fter the uprising ended, *there was no corresponding evolution in Hamas's thought to reflect the passing of one era and the beginning of another*, in which the basic variable was the presence of the PNA in parts of the Occupied Territories.... This was reflected in a new social atmosphere akin to the dominant one in the region, under which the sense of an external threat (Israel in this case) is replaced by an internal governmental authority–society conflict.... By imposing heavy legal regulations on Islamic and other charitable institutions, monitoring their funds, interfering in their internal affairs, and eventually putting them under the supervision of the security services, the overall social atmosphere became charged with fear and occupied by the PA apparatuses. *Hamas was thus deprived of functioning freely within one of its most cherished domains of work* [emphases added].[49]

My findings depart in some qualified measure from both these positions. That considerable constraints existed on, and within, Hamas, limiting its development at the social level, is not in dispute, nor is the absence of an evolutionary model of social or political change. However, Hamas was beginning to articulate new ways of addressing those constraints. The Islamist reorientation toward the social sector was arguably easier to effect than often believed because Hamas's true ideological support base was always small, especially when compared with its popular support base. Its primary constituency was nonideological and secured by its long history of community work, where Hamas was most competitive with the PNA. This is in good part why Hamas focused its critique on the social and economic deficiencies of the Oslo process and PNA programs and why it was able to maintain its base within the Palestinian community. That is also why Hamas, as a movement, chose to expand the parameters of programmatic activity beyond those historically defined, to adopt new ways—alongside the old—of engaging in traditional areas of work, and to reach out to mainstream, non-Islamic actors for professional, technical, and financial support.

This reorientation was not only an attempt to "take cover," as it were, and avoid retaliation by the PNA or Israel, nor was it a random, self-serving demonstration of "openness, flexibility and willingness to adopt new options in accordance with changing political circumstances."[50] Rather, it was the beginning of a serious reorientation in social and political strategy that went beyond a purely pragmatic, reactive adjustment to a new reality. Although this strategy lacked specific goals and objectives and was not made official or public in any formal or institutionalized manner, evolving instead beneath the level of political rhetoric, it was undeniably taking shape. It represented a rethinking, albeit slowly, of Hamas's role in the changed post-Oslo context. And, as such, it challenges, in my view, the contention that no such evolution in thought occurred in any manner after the end of the Intifada.[51]

Hamas's strategic rethinking not only sought accommodation with the status quo but also attempted to deepen and widen its social program within the community through greater professional and programmatic engagement, which I examine in the following chapter. Hamas always believed in a "private sphere outside the state's reach in which the law has no power and alternative visions of the good life are tolerated, on the ground that this is between God and the individual."[52] Hence, the shift did not represent a narrowing to the social domain (or increased restrictions on functioning in that domain) as much as it did a widening and restructuring of activity within that domain, expanding the concept of community activism and engaging in new ways of problematizing issues. Although the constraints were many and some insurmountable, the approach toward addressing them *prioritized communal development over the creation of an Islamic society, which became secondary.* Because of this Hamas (and the Islamist movement generally) increasingly encouraged expansion, change, and even experimentation within the social sector, allowing greater room for creativity and retreating from ideology and proselytism, limitations notwithstanding.

Hamas's social strategy was not only a tactic that helped it maintain a presence in a range of civil activities but also, in my view, an increasingly serious attempt to widen the parameters of civic life and mobilize collective action in a constructive and developmental manner that would challenge the parallel structure and, potentially, the legitimacy of the PNA, which sought the exact opposite. In this way, too, Hamas was perhaps beginning to rethink and possibly redefine what it meant to be a mass movement.

Toward this end, some Islamist officials and many institutional staff expressed less concern with official dogma and maintaining ideological and political consistency than with simply doing good work, which was defined in different ways. Even the imposition of religious doctrine was mitigated. Furthermore, the PNA, by the admission of its own senior leadership, often refused to coerce Islamic institutions—indirectly (or perhaps directly) assisting them—because of the important community work they did, which PNA officials openly acknowledged to me. (The closing of twenty Islamic institutions in 1997, for example, occurred under considerable pressure from the United States; many, if not most, were subsequently reopened.)

During the first Intifada, therefore, Hamas aimed to secure and intensify its political role, extolling sacrifice and martyrdom; its social sector was secondary. Throughout this period Hamas sought to localize its political presence not by changing the parameters of activity in the social sector but by securing them, which was accomplished by strengthening existing institutions and building new ones (in order to compete with the PLO's greater institutional base). The goal was not change or reform but the solidification of Hamas's political role. During the Oslo period that followed, however, the social sector came to define the political with an emphasis on moderation, community development, and innovation.

In a 1992 internal document circulated among Hamas's senior officials analyzing a range of alternatives for dealing with the end of the Intifada and the possible establishment of a Palestinian Authority and interim self-rule, Hamas stated its primary goals for the coming phase:

- Preserving the movement's popular base so that it can strongly support the continuation of jihad in the next campaigns. . . .
- Adhering to jihad as the way to liberate Palestine from the occupation, which will remain during the implementation of interim self-rule.
- Resisting normalization and further negligence and surrender of the Palestinians' rights. This might be the most important factor in determining our choice . . . [sic]. It must be bound to our goals and interests in every historical phase . . . [sic].[53]

I argue that what actually evolved at the social level over the next few years was somewhat different. Rather than *resist* normalization with the status quo, Hamas came to *seek* it, as is made evident in the widened scope of its programmatic work at the social level. That is, while the movement strenuously sought to preserve its popular base, it did so not in order to mobilize future violent activity against the "state" but to secure a form of political and social accommodation in an environment increasingly and dramatically positioned against it. Because of this, the Islamist social agenda aimed to strengthen community development in ways that were both traditional and new, potentially redefining the notion of participation at the individual and collective levels. The next two chapters examine and analyze how.

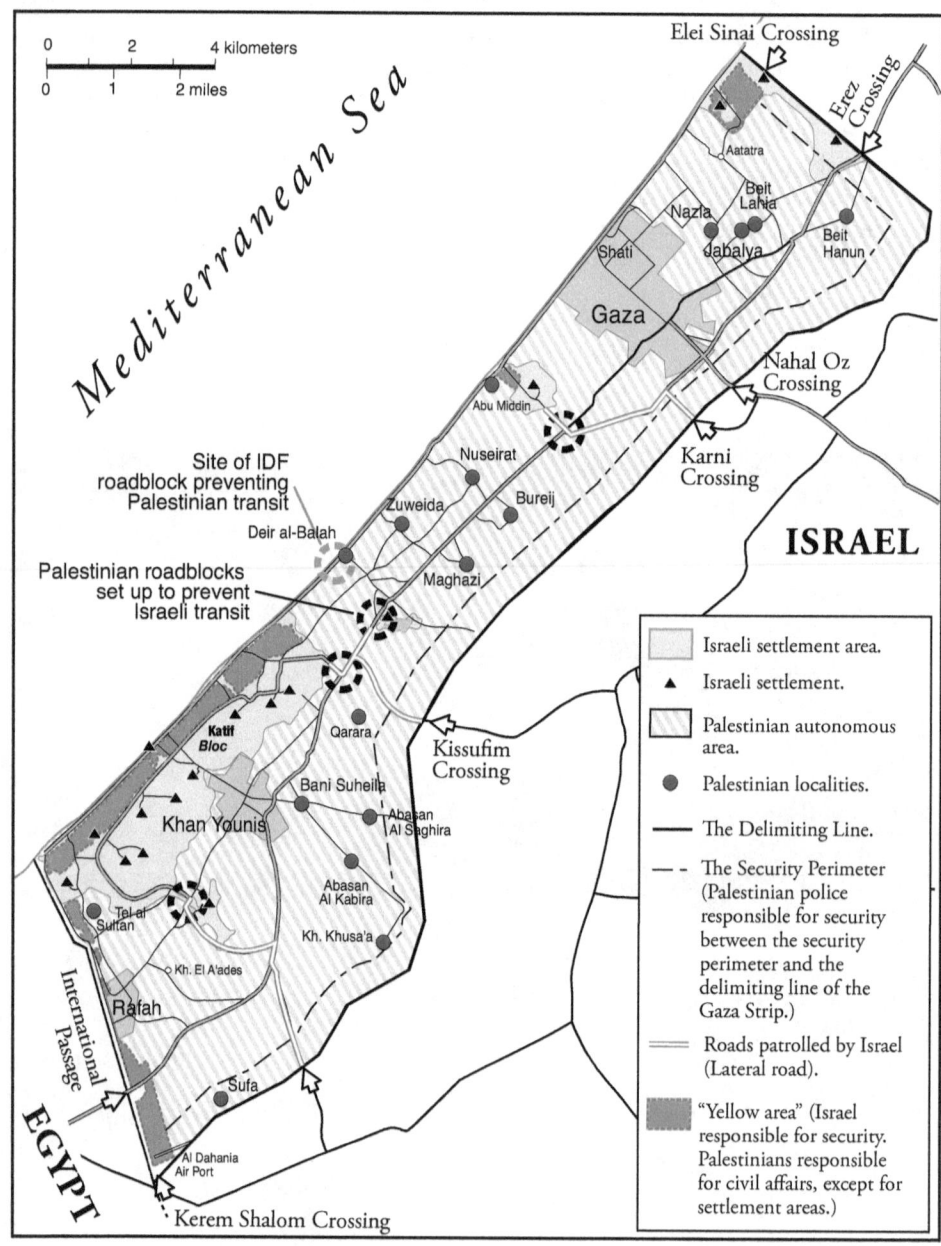

Map 1. Gaza Strip, July 1998. Source: Foundation for Middle East Peace (www.fmep.org).

Chapter 5

ISLAMIST SOCIAL INSTITUTIONS: CREATING A DESCRIPTIVE CONTEXT

> A rising mass movement attracts and holds a following not by its doctrine and promises but by the refuge it offers from the anxieties, barrenness and meaninglessness of an individual existence. It cures the poignantly frustrated not by conferring on them an absolute truth or by remedying the difficulties and abuses which made their lives miserable, but by freeing them from their ineffectual selves—and it does this by enfolding and absorbing them into a closely knit and exultant corporate whole.
> —*Eric Hoffer*[1]

ON MONDAY, NOVEMBER 24, 2008, U.S. federal prosecutors won sweeping convictions against the Texas-based Holy Land Foundation (HLF) in a retrial of the Muslim charity after having lost their original case in a mistrial in October 2007. This was the largest terrorism-financing case in the United States since the September 11, 2001, attacks. According to the *New York Times*, "the five defendants, all leaders of the Holy Land Foundation for Relief and Development . . . were convicted on all 108 criminal counts against them, including support of terrorism, money laundering and tax fraud. The group was accused of funneling millions of dollars to the Palestinian militant group Hamas, an Islamist organization the government declared to be a terrorist group in 1995."[2]

Prior to its shutdown by the U.S. government in December 2001 and the seizure of its assets, the HLF was the largest Muslim charity in the United States. At the trial, lawyers for the defense argued that the HLF's work was humanitarian, providing aid for a range of community welfare programs and particularly for Palestinian orphans living under Israeli occupation.

Yet it was the provision of this humanitarian aid—amounting to approximately $12.4 million—to Islamic charities and schools controlled by Hamas that was deemed criminal. The prosecution argued that HLF monies were "provided in support to Hamas and its goal of creating an

Islamic Palestinian state by eliminating the State of Israel through violent *jihad*."³ Hence, the government argued, by supporting schools, charities, hospitals, and other Islamic social welfare organizations, the Holy Land Foundation was spreading Hamas's ideology, strengthening its political agenda, and allowing Hamas to divert monies to support terrorist violence. Indeed, the prosecutor, Barry Jonas, described the Islamic charities supported by the HLF as centers for the recruitment of terrorists that were part of a "womb to the tomb" cycle."⁴

It is important to note that the HLF leaders, some of whom have family ties with Hamas political officials,⁵ were not accused of directly financing terrorism. Rather, they were accused of illegally contributing to Hamas through its social welfare structure after its 1995 designation as a terrorist organization.⁶ Patrick Rowan, the assistant U.S. attorney general for national security, stated: "For many years, the Holy Land Foundation used the guise of charity to raise and funnel millions of dollars to the infrastructure of the Hamas terror organization. This prosecution demonstrates our resolve to ensure that humanitarian relief efforts are not used as a mechanism to disguise and enable support for terrorist groups."⁷ A witness for the U.S. government, Professor Bruce Hoffman of Georgetown University, further maintained "that 'almost without exception,' successful terrorist groups throughout history have relied on charitable front groups to raise money and build goodwill among those they seek to control—in Hamas's case, the Palestinians. These front groups rarely openly advertise their affiliation, but the people they help 'know there is this connection.'"⁸

On May 27, 2009, the Holy Land chief executive officer, Shukri Abu Baker, and chairman and HLF cofounder, Ghassan Elashi, were each sentenced to sixty-five years in jail while two other HLF officials—Mohammad el-Mezain and Abdulrahman Odeh—received fifteen years and another, Mufid Abdulqader, was sentenced to twenty years.⁹

Underlining the illegality of allowing any distinction between Hamas's political violence and its social sector work was the November 12, 2008, designation by the U.S. Treasury Department of the Union of Good, a Saudi-based umbrella organization that works with over fifty Islamic foundations worldwide, as a "specially designated global terrorist entity."¹⁰

The Union of Good is regarded as a significant source of support for Hamas (a view shared by the PNA); as such the government of Israel outlawed the organization in February 2002. Furthermore, on July 7, 2008, Israel issued an order declaring as illegal thirty-six global Islamic funds and foundations belonging to the Union of Good that raise money that "supports Hamas in building a political alternative to the PA and maintain a terrorism-supporting system."¹¹ More specifically, the 2008 order states that the money sent to Hamas's "civilian infrastructure ... [which provides] legal camouflage for its activities ... is used to support terrorism, including suicide terrorism."[12] According to Israel's Intelligence and Terrorism Information Center, a research institute closely linked to Israel's Defense Ministry,[13] Hamas's civilian infrastructure supports terrorism in the following ways: "The da'wah uses 'education,' preaching, inciting the populace to terrorism and violence and spreads radical Islamic propaganda within the battle for hearts and minds [which] Hamas achieves ... through its independent education system." Furthermore, the "da'wah supports Hamas's terrorist operatives (wanted terrorists, prisoners, and the wounded) and the families of 'shaheeds,' including suicide bombing terrorists. That is done directly, with cash payments, or indirectly, through health, welfare, religious and educational services."[14]

In its own designation, which came just before the HLF verdict, the U.S. Treasury maintained that the Union of Good was created by Hamas leaders in 2002 in order to "[facilitate] the transfer of tens of millions of dollars a year to Hamas-managed associations." Furthermore, the Union of Good "acts as a broker for Hamas by facilitating financial transfers between a web of charitable organizations ... and Hamas-controlled organizations in the West Bank and Gaza."[15]

On December 3, 2008, in another landmark ruling, the Seventh Circuit Court of Appeals in Chicago upheld a judgment against three U.S.-based Muslim charities—the American Muslim Society, the Islamic Association for Palestine-National, and the Qur'anic Literacy Institute—accused of financially supporting Hamas through their support of Hamas's social welfare institutions. The court ruled that charities are liable if they support organizations that engage in terrorist acts even if the donated funds were earmarked for humanitarian purposes. The case centered on the murder of David Boim, a teenager killed by Hamas in 1996. Boim's family sued the charities, and a lower federal judge ordered them to pay $156 million in damages.

This ruling was subsequently overturned by a federal appeals court, which said that an "adequate causal link" between the charities' activities and Boim's killing had to be shown. But the December 3 ruling overturned this and agreed with the lower court that no proof of a linkage was necessary. Judge Richard Posner, writing for the eight-to-two majority, argued: "Anyone who knowingly contributes to the nonviolent wing of an organization that he knows to engage in terrorism is knowingly contributing to the organization's terrorist activities. And that is the only knowledge that can reasonably be required as a premise for liability.... Giving money to Hamas, like giving a loaded gun to a child (which also is not a violent act), is an 'act dangerous to human life.'"[16]

Hence, the mere successful provision of services is regarded as propaganda—providing "over arching legitimization and cover for what is ultimately a terrorist organization"[17]—capable of directly mobilizing the poor into political acts of violence. The conceptualization of the Islamic social sector as a terrorist infrastructure that recruits, proselytizes, and radicalizes beneficiaries and mobilizes them into political and military action in support of Hamas, diverting humanitarian aid to military use and strengthening the political role of Hamas, is not new; it certainly did not arise with any of these trials but rather with the emergence of Hamas over two decades ago. As these cases show, the equation of Islamist social institutions with violence and the belief that the work of these institutions is merely a guise for promoting terrorism and its attendant agenda as well as other forms of abuse remains deeply embedded and uncritically embraced at many levels of American society including the U.S. Supreme Court.[18]

The reality, however, is far more complex and, I would argue, challenges some key common assumptions. This chapter and the next will analyze why. This chapter begins with a descriptive account of the Islamist social institutions (ISI) in Palestine that I surveyed and their characteristic features, including some ethnographic data on individual organizations, the people who work in them, and those who seek their services. (Again, I use the terms "Islamist" and "Islamic" interchangeably. The former refers to the fact that the Islamic social sector falls under Hamas's domain, while the latter is a term that is used by respondents to describe their institutions.) It is my intention here to provide a representative sampling of institutions, some of which I spent days and weeks with and others, just hours (or less). As stated in chapter 1, while my focus is on ISIs in Gaza, I also include some from the West Bank in an effort to compare Islamic institutions in the two areas. Furthermore, in addition to those social institutions with some form of affiliation or tie with Hamas, I include those that claimed none at all, admittedly a minority. I do so not only to convey a sense of the breath and depth of the Islamic social sector but in an effort to better understand Hamas's role therein. This is followed in chapter 6 by an analysis of my key findings with regard to the Islamist social sector and the nature of Islamist mobilization.

Defining a Typology of Islamist Social Institutions

"We work under the sun," said the director of one ISI in Gaza, referring to the broad range of activities undertaken by the Islamist social sector. Indeed, my research found that Islamic institutions play roles in a wide range of areas: relief and charity work; care of orphans,[19] which includes all aspects of their life from infancy to age sixteen; care of the elderly; care and placement of "illegitimate" children, who come to them as abandoned infants; youth-based programs, including sports and the arts; preschool, primary, elementary, high school, and university education; literacy training; vocational and computer literacy training; library development; education and rehabilitation of physically and mentally disabled children and adults; primary and tertiary health care; specialized health care; women's income-generating activities; and women's empowerment and civic participation programs. In 1999 Islamic institutions accounted for 10 percent to 40 percent of all social institutions in the Gaza Strip and West Bank, according to various sources including Palestinian ministries, Islamic and secular NGOs, and Palestinian research institutions. And for individual sectors in Gaza such as education, these percentages appeared to be much higher.[20]

The exact number of ISIs was impossible to determine with any accuracy. To my knowledge, no official numbers existed. (I am told this remains the case.) For example, an official with the General Union of NGOs in Gaza said in 1999 that there were about 200 NGOs in Gaza and 800 in the West Bank. Although some Islamic NGOs belonged to the Union, this official did not know how many were actual Union members but claimed that 16 NGOs "belonged" to Hamas. Another Union official maintained that there were fewer than 14 Islamic NGOs in Gaza, excluding branch organizations. The deputy minister of NGOs in the PNA's Ministry of Interior in Gaza indicated that there were 700 NGOs in the West Bank and Gaza, only 40 of which were Islamic. (His hostility to Islamic institutions was very clear in our exchange, and he asked rather incredulously whether my research was sanctioned by Harvard.) The deputy minister in the PNA's Ministry of Non-Governmental Organizations in Ramallah (which was abolished in 2002) stated at the time that there were over 1,800 NGOs in the West Bank and Gaza but only 600 to 700 were "real" or operational. He, too, did not know what percentage were Islamic.[21]

In its excellent study of Islamic social welfare activism in the occupied territories, the International Crisis Group (ICG) indicated that in 2002 the number of "Hamas-affiliated social welfare organizations" in the West Bank and Gaza fell between 70 and 100 (excluding branch organizations).[22] I should make clear that, for PNA officials especially, "Islamic" was synonymous with "Hamas," and ISIs were unequivocally viewed with hostility; affiliation with Hamas was assumed but never delineated. Little if any allowance was made for, or significance attributed to, any distinction between the social and political sectors of the Islamic movement or to nonaligned ISIs.

Islamic social organizations have been categorized in somewhat different but equally accurate ways. The ICG divided ISIs into two broad categories: charitable and service institutions.[23] The former engage primarily in the provision of food and cash assistance, while the latter provide a wide range of services primarily in welfare, education, and health. The two sometimes overlap programmatically. Glenn E. Robinson, a scholar of Hamas, provides a somewhat different typology of Hamas's institutional network, dividing it into mosque-based or religious-based institutions (which are predominated by the Mujamma), other medical and educational institutions, and explicitly political institutions such as student political parties at universities that are designed to mobilize support for Hamas.[24]

Ismail Haniyeh, the former head of the Islamic NGO sector in Gaza and the current prime minister of the Hamas-led government in Gaza, divided the work of the Islamic social sector into education, health, sports, women's affairs, and youth-based activities. Ismail Abu Shanab similarly categorized the work of the social sector into religious-based activities, health and educational services, and charity.[25] (I was unable to obtain exact numbers from either of them.)

While all these typologies are valid, I would offer another typology that clearly emerged from my fieldwork, one that views ISIs not only from the perspective of their programmatic work but also from the strategic or methodological approach they take to their work. Here I am referring to the way a given ISI approached and interacted with the people who used their services: either as "mere" recipients or as participants in a process of community-based development. The former generally characterized the approach of charitable institutions, while the latter was more often found among institutions that provided community services.

Hence, I would offer a typology that categorizes ISIs as traditional/nonactivist and developmental/activist. These categories are certainly not absolute, and the lines between them were sometimes crossed. However, the former tended to focus on addressing the basic needs of individuals and families—where institutional initiatives were defined by need, not vision—while the latter emphasized civic empowerment through community participation and were inspired by a longer, more articulated view. Traditional institutions typically included charities, religious-based institutions, and some service (educational and health) institutions, while developmental institutions embraced various service organizations including those engaged in formal and informal education, the delivery of health care, certain women's organizations, and sports and cultural programs. The examples below were chosen because they typify the work of ISIs in each category and because it is not possible to include a descriptive account of every institution visited (see appendix).

Traditional Institutions

Islamist social institutions are defined more broadly to comprise "a wide range of institutions providing a large variety of services to Palestinian society."[26] They can be very small, shoestring operations consisting, say, of a group of volunteers distributing food or larger, more sophisticated organizations such as a specialized medical facility or vocational training center with a board of directors, employees, and fund-raising operations. Some are individual organizations and locally based, while others are branches of a larger organization often headquartered in Gaza City. Examples of such institutions, collected during my fieldwork in the late 1990s, are described below.[27]

The House of the Book and the Sunna (HBS), centrally located in the Khan Younis/Bani Suheila area of the Gaza Strip, was strictly engaged in humanitarian work. The HBS had several programs typical of traditional ISIs: relief (food, clothing, cash assistance) for the needy, orphan support, a school, and a health clinic. With a staff of forty, most of them volunteers (although paid workers received only IS 600 or US $150 per month), the HBS claimed to reach approximately ten thousand people directly and indirectly through its various programs. Their school had 180 male and 180 female students enrolled full time in grades six through twelve. Classrooms were segregated, with boys taught by male teachers and girls by females, given the institution's very strict religious orientation. In fact, before I was allowed inside, my companion, Ramadan, entered alone and was asked if I was appropriately covered or was wearing any makeup, especially lipstick.

Boys and girls learned different subjects. Boys learned Arabic language, religion, computer science, handicrafts, and ceramics. Girls learned sewing, cooking, and some computer skills. There was a rather impressive library—in fact, we entered through the library—that contained only religious texts, "nothing analytical," the head of the HBS proudly proclaimed, an elderly man whom I will call the *Haj*, since he would not give me his name. He told me that girls and boys could use the library free of charge but girls could come only on designated days and never mixed with boys, which was not necessarily the case in other ISIs. This segregation appealed to many parents for both cultural and religious reasons. Because the HBS served a poor population, student fees were minimal and sometimes waived.

The HBS relief program had long supported around 5,000 people in the Khan Younis area with food, clothing, and cash assistance, but this number was later reduced to 2,500 owing to economic constraints. Its orphan program served 700 children whose families received a monthly stipend of $50, but I was unable to determine the criteria for selection or the length of the support. The program had Muslim, Christian, and international donors, primarily the United Nations Development Program (UNDP).

Lastly, the HBS ran a health clinic that received twenty to thirty patients a day. The *Haj* told me, in no uncertain terms, "We prefer Muslim doctors, but we will take anyone who is qualified." The staff consisted of five MDs (one of whom was female), including a pediatrician, orthopedic specialist, and general practitioner with an ENT specialty. The clinic had a lab and a pharmacy and received some of its drugs from the NGO Pharmacists Without Borders. It charged very little for its health services—five new Israeli shekels (NIS) or US $1.25 to use the clinic, and two NIS (US $0.50) for medicines, a fraction of what a government clinic would have charged at the time.

The HBS had a huge facade with a big sign proudly announcing its presence. The facility was extremely clean and spacious, even cavernous, but quite austere. Every room had a computer, a characteristic feature of most ISIs. I encountered only male staff, which was somewhat atypical, and they wore both traditional and Western attire. However, I was allowed to speak only with two men: the *Haj*, clearly the organization's patriarch, who was stern and suspicious (although he began to relax as the interview progressed); and a younger, more outgoing male assistant who clearly deferred to his superior.

Throughout the interview, the *Haj* would not look at me or address me directly; he interacted only with my (male) companion, Ramadan. I would ask a question and the *Haj* would direct his answer to Ramadan. While it was typical for male staff in ISIs not to shake my hand, this interview was the only instance in which I experienced such punctilious treatment, which derived from the *Haj*'s religiously orthodox character and no doubt set the tone for the whole institution. I should add that this sort of orthodoxy was the exception among the Islamic institutions I visited. Indeed, throughout our discussion, the *Haj* insisted that the HBS was more authentically (i.e., religiously and strictly) Islamic than other ISIs, something that my research confirmed.

The Qatar Charitable Society (QCS), which was headquartered in Gaza City, was an Islamic charity funded largely by the Qatari government and affiliated donors. The QCS claimed no affiliation to Hamas whatsoever. It administered some of its programs through the al-Salah Islamic Association (see below). The then head of the Society, a lovely, gentle man known as Abu Hisham, had earlier headed Gaza's *zakat* committees and still worked closely with them.

The QCS engaged in strictly humanitarian work. It assisted the very needy, sick, disabled, and marginalized with money, clothing, and food. It also had a program for orphans and needy university students that subsidized fees and other costs. Decisions were based entirely on need according to various criteria (which did not appear to be consistently applied) including household income, number of family members working, and number of sick, disabled, and elderly family members.

During this time in Gaza, not only were economic conditions declining, but the direct funding of many NGOs was ending, with monies being redirected through the PNA in an attempt to strengthen the ruling authority during the Oslo period. In effect, what this did was cut off funds or reduce the funding of many viable NGOs, undermining their ability to work. Thus, given the QCS's limited resources, more people were turned away than could be helped.

Typically, needy Gazans would come to the QCS office seeking assistance. Potential clients who were physically unable to travel or could not afford to do so were visited at home by Abu Hisham. He would often approach wealthy businessmen and shopkeepers, asking them to offer longer-term support for an individual child or help defray a specific cost, such as a medical procedure or educational expense.

QCS's office staff was no more than three people, but it had a larger constellation of field-workers. I was fortunate to sit with Abu Hisham in his office (in the Rimal section of Gaza City) while he received clients and to accompany him on many of his field visits throughout the Strip. Clients coming to the QCS office were invariably women asking for assistance. All were fully covered but not veiled (although a minority had their faces covered). Women who came for help of this kind were almost always desperate and sad and ashamed of their position, especially the younger ones. Abu Hisham spent a great deal of time gently turning people down, explaining that there were not enough funds to help everyone, even the most grief stricken and destitute.

During one of these exchanges, I was sitting across from Abu Hisham. These encounters made me painfully aware of the terrible poverty confronting so many in Gaza. That afternoon, three different women, two of them sisters, were in the office. When the sisters realized that Abu Hisham could not help them, they approached me, pleading that they each had disabled children and no money to care for them. The third woman was weeping because she could not pay her rent and her landlord was going to evict her family. Even after she left the office, I could hear her sobs fading into the street below. When I visited a local *zakat* office (*zakat*, one of the five pillars of Islam, is an obligatory tax levied on Muslims and given to the poor) with Abu Hisham, a similar scene unfolded with a woman and her ten-year-old daughter. After being told there was no money to help her, she shoved her daughter toward me saying, "Take her to America, please. At least you can feed her." The little girl, fearing perhaps that I would, clung desperately to her mother.

In yet another encounter in the Nuseirat refugee camp, a young mother came in to speak with Abu Hisham. She was holding her toddler boy and explained that he had cerebral palsy, something that was entirely plausible given his unusually small size at the age of two or three. She was asking for money to buy him Pampers. Abu Hisham spoke softly to the woman, and then she left looking a bit relieved. "What are you going to do," I asked? "We are going to buy her Pampers."

Abu Hisham would see how upset I would get after some of these visits and would say in a gentle but resigned manner, "You just get used to it." Visiting his clients in their homes was a similarly disquieting experience. These individuals were among the poorest and most marginal in Gazan society. One such family of nine lived in three small rooms in the Deir al-Balah refugee camp. They were classified as needy because the father, a young man, was epileptic and had been severely beaten by Israeli soldiers during the first Intifada. They had two sons, both of whom were deaf. At the time of our visit, the mother was in the hospital undergoing surgery. The person who affected me the most, however, was the father's mother, who sat on the floor wordlessly, listless to the point of being nonresponsive. Despite her detachment, her profound sadness was searing. She clearly hated being viewed in this way by me and the two other foreigners with us, two Asian nuns. I felt ashamed for violating her dignity in this way, for taking away what little she had left, and quickly walked out of the shelter. Abu Hisham told me that they receive only NIS 200 (US $50) per month, "very little, I know, but better than nothing at all." Social workers would visit the family once every three months.

Two other families assisted by the QCS were totally destitute. One family of nine lived in Deir al-Balah village in a shelter consisting of four crudely made walls and a dirt floor. The entrance was the only source of natural light. The interior was dark, damp, and clammy. There was no electricity or working appliances. They cooked over an open fire. Running water was the only apparent amenity. A doorless, broken refrigerator in the common area was used as a makeshift wardrobe. The disabled father sat alone in one "room"; his two sons sat in another area, and his daughters remained separate, huddled together in what passed as a kitchen—a hole in the dirt floor probably used to light a fire. A pail was used to wash dishes. Beyond a few salutations, no one spoke; they just stared. This family received NIS 200 (US $50) per month.

Another family I have never forgotten were squatters, homeless people who lived under the constant threat of eviction. Their "home" consisted of three tents: one for eating (which contained some floor mats and a small, decrepit cupboard), one for sleeping, and another where they kept odd pieces of clothing strewn in piles. The mother was clearly ill, suffering from some sort of respiratory disorder. Her children, including a set of twins, were all filthy and poorly clothed, and some also appeared to be sick. A makeshift oven existed outside and was used to bake bread. This family was entirely without means of support, marginalized within, and by, their own society. In addition to a monthly stipend of NIS 200 (US $50), Abu Hisham would provide them, when possible, with donations of clothing and food.

The QCS supported several other programs, none of which appeared to be part of a larger strategic or institutional plan; rather, support would be given to discrete projects if a compelling need or purpose was identified particularly by Abu Hisham. (When I asked Abu Hisham what he would do if he had more money, he said simply that he would help more needy and sick families.) The QCS supported 240 needy families (those who were poor, disabled, or had an ill or disabled father), some through the al-Salah Association and others with the help of external donors.

It also provided financial support for the construction of a mosque in Rafah, which I was taken to see. The mosque had three floors: the first for praying, the second for women's activities, and the third for youth activities. Plans also included building a bed-and-breakfast facility for mosque visitors.

QCS grants were also given to support six (out of twenty) rehabilitation centers for disabled children—in Gaza City and elsewhere in the Strip. Previously, the grants had been given directly to disabled children's families, but when QCS staff found that the money was not being used for the child, they decided to give it only to certified rehabilitation centers. One such recipient was the Nuseirat Rehabilitation Center (NRC) in the Nuseirat refugee camp. The NRC ran a program for disabled children aged six to fourteen—sixty-eight physically disabled children, forty-five deaf boys and girls, and an undetermined number of children with brain damage. The Center ran several programs, including one that taught sign language to children and their parents; another specifically directed at teaching brain-damaged children; a computer training course for both boys and girls; and vocational training courses that aimed to give children vocational skills. Children were allowed to remain in the school until they attained a specific skill, in some cases, as long as ten years. Teachers, primarily women, were all UNRWA trained and had had one year of specialized study, and those I met had taught for at least six years. For some subjects but not all, boys and girls would be taught separately. All told, the QCS provided support for several hundred disabled children.

Although he never admitted this to me directly, it became clear that Abu Hisham largely decided which centers the QCS would support based on his visits to the centers, discussions with teachers, degree and quality of teacher training, and the way in which children were treated. Adherence to Islamic religious law was not the most important criterion affecting his decision; professionalism was, although I was not able to obtain any specific criteria used by Abu Hisham other than his experience, intellect, and common sense. In fact, Abu Hisham told me on more than one occasion that beyond the issues of appropriate dress and "respectful behavior," he did not pay much attention to religious purity. "If we do good work and help others, then we are doing God's work." He also would reiterate, "If we discriminate we become fanatics." Once, referring to the al-Ihsan Association for Disabled Children (chapter 6), a center run by Ahmad Hijazi, a well-known Muslim religious figure and preacher in Gaza City who was known to be affiliated with the Islamic Jihad, Abu Hisham argued that if Hijazi did not improve his substandard rehabilitation facilities for disabled children, the QCS would cease to support him. In my subsequent discussions with Hijazi, I confirmed this and found that there was no love lost between the two men. In July 2008, the QCS was one of the thirty-six Islamic organizations outlawed by the Israeli government.

The Young Women's Muslim Society (YWMS) was established in 1981 by the Mujamma and had branches throughout the Gaza Strip. It served females aged eight to sixty. Each branch offered the same vocational training, computer training, religious instruction, and literacy programs. In addition, the society offered kindergarten classes, summer camp programs, and a relief assistance program.

Vocational training courses were geared to providing women with income-generating skills and were largely focused on traditional, culturally acceptable areas: sewing and knitting. These activities were defined by popular, cultural norms, not by Hamas. A typical class had eight to ten women per class and would last six months. During their training, women would receive lectures on religion, particularly on how to run an Islamic home and the importance of religious values, and also on gendered issues such as appropriate child-rearing methods, child health care, and maintaining proper health during pregnancy. The number of classes offered depended on demand and institutional resources at any given time.

The Society also offered computer training courses (in DOS, Excel, Access) that were certified by the Palestinian Ministry of Education. Also emphasized to me was the fact that the YWMS had a license from the Palestinian Interior Ministry and was legally registered. (At the time of my fieldwork, the Rimal branch, which had been closed by the PNA two years earlier, was still operating unofficially with the full knowledge of the authorities.) The main center in Gaza City offered three-month computer courses. In order to make the most use of their six computers, instructors—all of whom were female and had their *tawjihi* (matriculation exam)—would teach one girl per computer for 1.5 hours three times per day.

Another program for women aged fifty to sixty provided vocational training for females who were functionally illiterate, together with literacy classes jointly administered with the Red Crescent Society. Interested trainees could receive additional training for several more years. When I visited, I observed a class of women in their third year of study who seemed very cohesive and visibly proud of their achievements. The sense of connectedness among them was palpable. The public was informed of the classes through advertisements in local newspapers and by word of mouth via Society members who had strong community connections. The Society made an effort to offer enough classes so that all interested women could enroll.

The YWMS also coordinated training programs with other Gazan organizations, partnerships that might originate with YWMS or vice versa. For example, the Society proposed a training course in food preservation to the Palestinian Ministry of Agriculture, which agreed to collaborate and sent staff to help plan the course. These courses were subsequently offered in Rimal, Tuffah, and Jabalya and proved quite popular; demand exceeded capacity. Similarly, the Women's Affairs Center, a secular organization in Gaza, approached the YWMS seeking help organizing courses in business administration and planning, while the Palestinian Center for Micro Projects codesigned with the Society a training program about microfinance for women.

The YWMS also ran popular kindergarten programs in three areas: Gaza City (one program), Deir el-Balah (one), and Khan Younis (two). Each school enrolled 120 children with five to six teachers in ten-month sessions from August to June. There were also three nursery schools, one each in Rafah, Deir al-Balah, and Gaza with nine students per class. These schools had excellent reputations. Children from both rich and poor families attended, although the former were charged more. Typically, poor families were charged NIS 30 (US $7.50) annually.

A particularly important YWMS program was Quranic recitation. Both staff and parents highly valued this program. For the staff, the program helped lay the foundation for a proper Islamic way of life; for many parents, it gave their children something constructive to do and a valuable way of filling their spare time. This is not to say that parents did not value such religious training—some clearly sought it—but it was not necessarily a priority. Part-time courses in Quranic instruction, which were licensed by the *waqf*, were offered at the introductory, intermediate, and advanced levels. Each student received a certificate upon completion. The House of the Book and Sunna provided materials and sent teachers and supervisors to administer tests on how to recite the Quran. After my experience with the *Haj*, I felt certain that these tests were quite rigorous!

Females aged eight to sixty were eligible, and classes of fifteen to twenty students were arranged by age. Courses were held in thirteen sites, including mosques, kindergarten classrooms, and other facilities where space could be found, often close to where students lived. For younger students (aged eight to fifteen), classes were held after school throughout the school year. For older women, they were held in the morning and afternoon. Classes involved one and a half to two hours of memorization. Each student received a free Quran. There was no charge for these classes except for those teaching intensive Quranic memorization.

On a visit to the YWMS branch in the Tuffah section of Gaza City, which was a small and rather sparse rented space, I found the place throbbing with activity. All the women, both staff (who numbered four) and students (around twenty), were conservatively dressed in long cloaks or loose-fit coats (*jilbab*) and head scarves (*hijab*). The branch was open to local people, and the staff made a point of saying that anyone including the nonreligious was welcome. When I visited, sewing courses were in session, and a minority of the female attendees did not wear head scarves, although the staff encouraged them to do so. The facilities were rudimentary but clean, with wooden tables, chairs, and sewing machines on cold tile floors. The only decor was color photographs of the summer camp program, which were displayed everywhere. Overhead costs were funded by class fees, and money was always an issue, given rising expenses.

Another core program was dedicated to providing financial assistance, food, and clothing to very poor "hardship" cases. Families were chosen on the basis of need, and the identification and selection process was officially based on standard criteria. However, the needy were often identified through the Society's connections with the local community and via word of mouth. As with the QCS, families would also approach the Society seeking help. While not rigorously scientific, the identification process worked. I was told that records on each family were carefully kept and shared with other ISIs in order to prevent beneficiaries from obtaining aid from multiple sources, a common problem mentioned by many ISIs engaged in relief work. The Tuffah branch alone served two hundred needy families, although the average was sixty to one hundred per branch. Also, the Palestinian Ministry of Social Affairs occasionally sent female hardship cases to the YWMS for training courses. In fact, PNA-ISI relations would sometimes exceed the "merely" bureaucratic (licensing, registration) and extend into rather cooperative professional relationships, as confirmed to me by some ministry officials.[28]

During the summer, the YWMS offered an extremely popular fifteen-day camp program for girls in UNRWA schools throughout the Gaza Strip—including Rafah, Khan Younis, Deir el-Balah, the Bureij and Jabalya refugee camps, and Gaza City. There were forty summer camps, each hosting from one hundred to five hundred girls aged eight to fifteen. Orphans were actively recruited for the camp and often accepted without charge. The staff was largely female. The camps offered sports, handicrafts, health awareness, English language, and computer skills. Computer training was especially popular. Field trips included a tour of Gaza—which, for some children, was their first excursion beyond their neighborhoods—and organized trips to parks and other municipal sites, which were facilitated by the Gaza municipality free of charge. A nominal fee of NIS 10 (US $2.50) was charged to attend, with an additional NIS 60 (US $15) fee for the computer course.

I attended one of these camps in Gaza City. Hundreds of children filled a huge outdoor space. Many wore YWMS T-shirts (I still have mine), and they were divided into groups based on age, each engaged in a specific activity. There was great joy, laughter, and excitement, and I remember thinking how profound their happiness was.

These summer camps also featured exhibitions of products made by women enrolled in YWMS vocational courses, a source of great pride, as the women told me. After being exhibited, these products would be sold locally, and the proceeds would go to the women.

The Islamic Charitable Society (ICS) was a traditional ISI in the West Bank town of Hebron (Al-Khalil in Arabic), which one of my secular Khalili friends referred to as a "Hamas factory." My first trip to the ICS began with a lecture from the director, Abdel Khaleq Natsheh, a spokesman of Hamas in the West Bank, about the true definition of terrorism (a discussion spurred by a prior foreign visitor who had asked him whether Hamas would threaten U.S. interests). Terrorism, he told me, can take many forms: demolition of homes, denial of medicines, uprooting of people, construction of settlements, and expulsion of residents. "We have a right to defend ourselves under international law. After liberation, there will be no excuse for fighting or violence." Once the occupation ended, he argued, Palestinians could focus on strengthening their civil society with the Islamic movement playing a major role. "Islamic institutions in Palestine have long assisted people, especially in Hebron. For thirty-eight years, no one considered these institutions terrorist, but the U.S. can freely bomb Iraq and Sudan." He clearly considered it a grave insult that anyone would define his charity as anything evil or violent and resented the need to defend it against such accusations.

Founded as a service organization in 1962 by fifteen locals who were orphans, the ICS was dedicated to orphan care, offering education, health, housing, and relief. With five branches throughout the West Bank, the ICS had 140 employees and nine volunteers at the time I carried out my research. This included 42 teachers for boys, 50 for girls, and 9 supervisors (and 6 chefs). They were all involved with policy formulation, planning, and the administration of several schools for approximately one thousand orphans and five hundred nonorphans (either needy or the children of prisoners). Students were male and female, with male teachers for boys and female teachers for girls. All women and girls were appropriately dressed. The schools were religiously observant but not extreme or rigidly traditional like the House of the Book and the Sunna. The ICS claimed to be the biggest school of its kind for orphans in the entire West Bank and Gaza Strip; while this may have been true, I was never able to verify it.

The first six grades were for orphans only. After grade six, the schools opened to anyone based on merit. Children attended through age eighteen and the completion of the *tawjihi*. Both the school and the dormitory (for six- to fourteen-year-olds) were free of charge for orphans; others were charged nominal fees. When dormitory students reached age fourteen, they had to go live with relatives. Although orphans and nonorphans received the same services, those who lived in the dormitory were provided with pocket money, clothes, stationery, books, and transportation. Day students received much the same; however, instead of transportation they received food, which they ate in school.

ICS schools in villages, which went through grade five, did not have boarding facilities, although they did provide food, uniforms, and extracurricular activities. All ICS schools were approved by the Palestinian Ministry of Education and the Islamic *waqf*, especially the curriculum. The ICS, like all Islamic schools, used the government-approved curriculum through grade twelve. However, the ICS curriculum also taught various aspects of Islam and used guidelines established by the *waqf*. For example, at the elementary and preparatory levels, children were taught about Islamic values and the life of the Prophet. Beginning in grade ten, they were taught sharia.

The two schools (one for boys and one for girls) on the main campus in Hebron were quite impressive (the former larger than the latter): Rooms were large, clean, and nicely decorated, often with photos of the institutional founders and sayings from the Quran. There was a large, rather stately library, which I was told contained seven thousand books on Arabic language and literature, English, science, and religion. The school campus also had separate dormitories (rather spartan but clean and comfortable), dining halls, kitchens, rooms for prayer that were attached to each school, and a huge lecture hall with beautifully painted murals of Hebron, Jerusalem, Mecca, and Medina on the walls. Both the boys' and girls' schools contained computer, chemistry, physics, and biology labs and classrooms, which were clean but simple with old desks and chairs, had walls decorated with photos of the *nakba* (the catastrophe of 1948), sayings from the Quran, and posters of English grammar rules. Hallways were almost festive, decorated with student artwork depicting a variety of themes—largely, but not exclusively, Islamic.

As with most Islamic schools I visited, the director claimed that popular interest in, and support for, the school was very high. This was sometimes confirmed in interviews with parents and other locals. At the time of my research, the ICS had graduated twenty-seven classes, and "many of those [graduates] were MDs, engineers, professors, teachers, and workers in industry and trade," according to director Natsheh.

Like other charities, the ICS solicited local and foreign sponsors for individual orphans. The latter could be either Muslim organizations (such as the now-shuttered Holy Land Foundation) or Christian organizations. At the time of my research, a wealthy local resident had donated a parcel of land on which a new school was being built, and another promised donation was to be used to build a new girls' school, which was closed by the Israeli government in 2008. The ICS was largely dependent on local grants and donations to cover running costs. When I asked about financing, the director looked at me and responded, "Here comes the question about terrorism."

Other sources of funding or in-kind support included local *zakat* committees (which would donate cash or blankets) and charitable associations and NGOs (both Islamic and non-Islamic, local and foreign), which sometimes gave food and donations from abroad, particularly the United States and Canada. The ICS had a public relations officer who told me he spent much of his time writing project proposals and trying to get them funded by applying to donor agencies directly or through NGOs. "We will take money from anyone," he told me, another common theme among ISIs.

It became apparent that, like many other Islamic charities, the ICS was in good part dependent on the financial resources and goodwill of the local community. For this and other reasons, the staff clearly worked hard to maintain the comparatively high quality of their services and a reputation for honesty and service. The ICS was also very open about the fact that, as a registered NGO, the staff regularly dealt with different Palestinian governmental ministries and international organizations. They described a proposal they had submitted to the UNDP via the Palestinian Economic Council for Development and Reconstruction (PECDAR), which was established by the World Bank, for the construction of a new school (which I subsequently confirmed with PECDAR). Although the proposal was turned down by the UNDP, PECDAR had agreed to fund the construction of one floor. Natsheh also described how Yasser Arafat had visited their Society and had lunch and dinner with its board. The ICS had never been shut down by the PNA but had been closed several times by Israel. Some of its former students and teachers were among those deported to Lebanon in 1992. On those occasions when it was shut down, classes would be held in local mosques.

Interestingly, when I asked about its relationship with other Islamic institutions, I was told that the ICS generally had more interaction with non-Islamic organizations than with Islamic ones. Natsheh answered, as did officials in other ISIs, that their work with other Islamic institutions was largely a matter of coordination—comparing lists of recipients to ensure that beneficiaries were not receiving support from multiple sources—again, a common finding. In some cases, ISIs coordinated care of a specific child, but this was often done at the personal, not institutional, level.

The ICS was extremely well known in the Hebron area and rarely had to recruit; instead people came seeking its services, especially schooling. If the number of children exceeded availability, then priority was given to children with no father and secondarily to children with no mother. Two to three times a year the ICS would deliver food supplies—rice, sugar, oil, tea, canned and fresh meat—and clothes to the families of its students who were orphans, thereby maintaining a link with the student beyond the school. Services were also extended to about 1,000 additional needy families who would receive clothes, food, blankets, shoes, and cash about two to three times a year. Given that the average family had no fewer than four people, at least 4,000 people, including at least 2,000 to 2,500 children, were assisted. In addition, the ICS sponsored a small income-generation project for poor women and a workshop for sewing clothes that employed several women from nearby villages. In 1999 the ICS established a library in Hebron, which is described in the next chapter. On the more entrepreneurial end, it owned a commercial building in which it leased space to other businesses and ran a popular local market in which people would rent stall space to sell inexpensive clothes and shoes. Over the last ten years, the ICS also began operating two bakeries, a dairy, a physical therapy clinic, and a Boy Scout troop.

Almost all—if not all—ISIs, even those I would consider "developmental," had a strong charitable component, which is consistent with Islamic values. In Palestine, as in other parts of the Arab and Islamic world, charitable institutions are often associated with *zakat* committees, which are a defined presence in the world of charitable support in Gaza and among the most established Islamic institutions in Palestine. However, it is difficult to determine how large a role they play financially or organizationally. As the ICG explains: "*Zakat* is not a formal tax in Palestinian law nor is it collected by the P[N]A. Because Muslim Palestinians are thus free to determine whether, to what extent and how to disburse *zakat* payments, it is for all intents and purposes impossible to determine what percentage of the population participates in this practice, or how much money is raised on an annual basis."[29] It is also impossible to determine to what extent, if any, *zakat* money provided a financial resource for Hamas (as the committees did for the Mujamma prior to the first uprising), although there has been considerable speculation on this issue.

Zakat committees have long existed in both Gaza and the West Bank. According to the PNA, there were sixty-two *zakat* committees in the occupied territories in 1998, while an unpublished UN study found thirty such committees in 2001, sixteen of which were in the Gaza Strip.[30] These committees, which have been under the direction of the PNA's Ministry of Religious Affairs since 1996, serve primarily low-income families in which the husband/father is permanently disabled, chronically ill, unemployed, or imprisoned, and families headed by widows and divorced women. Beyond individual payments from local residents, *zakat* committees receive money from diverse sources, including voluntary donations from individuals, governments, corporations, organizations, and from *zakat* funds abroad.

By 2003, the Gaza *zakat* committee claimed over fifty employees and distributed "cash assistance, food, medicine, free health care, and interest-free loans for housing and university education"[31] to more than five thousand people. Specifically, the *zakat* committee had a program for needy families and sick people. Recipients were identified through various means, but most common were the personal connections between *zakat* officials and the community. These connections were absolutely critical in identifying the needy, especially those who were incapable of accessing the system or otherwise disempowered or vulnerable. Word-of-mouth referrals were important, as were more systematic methods of identification that included information sharing with other ISIs and NGOs. Typically, needy families would periodically receive locally purchased food parcels consisting of three kilos of rice, sugar, lentils, cooking oil, and two cans of meat. The *zakat* committees would also distribute meat to the poor on special occasions such as holidays, and needy students would get money for school fees.[32]

Residents also sought assistance from the *zakat* for specific medical problems. During one of my visits to the Gaza *zakat* committee, a young woman came in with her medical records, pleading that she needed to purchase equipment for a kidney ailment, while another requested funds for orthopedic surgery. Typically, a steady stream of people would visit with medical complaints. Abu Majid, director of the Gaza *zakat* (and a friend of Abu Hisham), admitted that some complaints were false but attributed the lies to simple desperation, not some nefarious motive. Medical requests were referred to physicians for validation. For those in genuine need, assistance was provided as available and as allowed by the committee's financial capacity, or alternative arrangements were made, if possible, to identify a local sponsor to finance the medical care.

Community outreach and networking for funds were important functions of *zakat* committee work. In fact, at the time, one legendary woman in Gaza contributed US $100 per month for each of seven families. However, demand far exceeded available resources, and in many cases there was little the *zakat* committee could do.

The Gaza *zakat* committee also had a program for orphans that serviced the entire Gaza Strip "from Beit Hanoun to Rafah."[33] The program had 3,000 registered orphans—1,400 had sponsors both local and foreign, which meant they were receiving aid (approximately US $25 to $50 per month distributed every three months), while 1,600 were placed on a waiting list. Abu Majid allowed me to look through a pile of applications from the families of orphans; each contained photos of the child, the family, and financial data. He also showed me receipts for donations with a list of signatures from recipients—usually the mother. If the mother was illiterate, a fingerprint was taken, and proof of receipt was sent to the donor. Records appeared to be carefully kept and filed, although not computerized.

The Rafah *zakat*, headed by a fellow named Abu Ahmad, had a similar though far smaller program supporting 154 orphans largely with donors from Jordan and Saudi Arabia. There appeared to be little coordination with the Gaza *zakat* program. Children were selected on the basis of need, health status, and family circumstance. Again, since these committees worked in communities of which they were a part, clients were often identified through personal connections. Families would also seek out the *zakat* committee for assistance. Unlike the office in Gaza, the Rafah "office" was literally a one-car garage space, poor and sparse. The sole decoration was a photo collage of the *zakat* committee's activities: meat distribution, sheep slaughtering, and distribution of gifts and school supplies to children.

Sponsors of orphaned children, whether local or foreign, were provided with data on "their" child, which I was shown: birth certificates, a biography, father's death certificate, monthly income, information on the mother (alive or dead, employed), present guardian, level of education, school address, mother's ID card, photos of the child and the family, health reports, and sometimes more extensive reports on the health and economic status of the child's family. Donors apparently preferred to sponsor children younger than age ten. Some supported the same child for several years. A minority supported older children. Funding stopped at age sixteen. However, it was more common for donors to give for six months or one year. At that point, the *zakat* committee had to find another donor. Officials in the Palestinian Ministry of Social Affairs at the time told me that since they did not have a specific program for orphans, they would sometimes refer individual cases to the *zakat* committee or other ISIs. Conversely, depending on the service they were engaged in, ISIs would solicit the Palestinian Social Affairs Ministry for assistance, as did the al-Ihsan Charitable Society in Hebron, which provided services for the mentally and physically disabled and ran a school exclusively for the deaf. Al-Ihsan sought help for thirty-five disabled children and received a one-time payment of US $50 per child.[34]

Most donors sponsoring children under age ten were local (including Arabs from Israel), although foreign sponsors (both institutional and individual) typically came from Kuwait, the United Arab Emirates, Saudi Arabia, Jordan, the United States (HLF), and the United Kingdom (Interpal, Islamic Relief). A common complaint was that before the establishment of the PNA, the *zakat* committee received money from such organizations as World Vision, the UNDP, and Catholic Relief Services; since, monies were redirected to and through the PNA, a financial loss for ISIs and other NGOs.

Sometimes foreign donations were earmarked for specific items: that summer, Kuwaiti money was being used to purchase 1,800 school bags. During one of my visits with Abu Majid, the transaction was being finalized. I asked if I could examine one school bag. On it was written (in English):

> What I try to say through my work is simple. My message is as follows: Love all creatures, love everything that has life. I have been trying to express in different ways through my work the message such as "preserve nature" "Bless life" "Be careful of a civilization that puts too much stock in science" "Do not wage war" and so on.

When I asked Abu Majid about the quotation, he did not even know it was there. He had purchased the school bags because he had gotten a good deal on them and did not really care or notice what was written on them. He asked me to explain what the saying meant and was even more pleased with his purchase after I did. A similar purchase of school bags by the *zakat* committee in Rafah included copybooks, pencils, a writing tablet, a calendar, and some simple toys that were distributed free of charge.

Foreign donors, in particular, would receive a follow-up report on "their" child every six months. The average monthly payment was NIS 100 (US $25), although some children received more depending on need and sponsor wishes. At one of the distribution days that I attended when women would collect their checks, they were all conservatively dressed in the *hijab* and *jilbab* and some were entirely veiled, which was not common in Gaza at the time. Checks were issued through different banks depending on where donors were located. On this particular day, I saw checks that were drawn on the Cairo-Amman Bank and Israel's Bank Leumi.

Again, the primary form of interaction and coordination between the *zakat* committee and other ISIs (and some non-Islamic institutions) was around the issue of duplication. It was well known that recipients would go to more than one charitable organization seeking aid. Hence, duplication of benefits was carefully screened by ISIs and other NGOs. In fact, this was the primary and, for many, the only form of coordination ISIs engaged in with each other.

During a visit with Abu Hisham to the Rafah *zakat* committee, Abu Ahmad took us to meet a young girl with clubfeet for whom the Rafah *zakat* committee had raised US $1,000 for surgery. Unfortunately, she was not at home when we arrived. However, an interesting thing occurred during this attempted visit. The same building housed the Muslim Women's Youth Center (MWYC). Given my keen interest in Islamic institutions, both Abu Ahmad and Abu Hisham asked if I would like to visit the Center. I immediately agreed, and we entered. I had assumed that the two men were familiar with the MWYC and that was why they had suggested we visit. I was surprised to discover that neither of them knew about the Center and had never previously visited it, something I had not expected given the local character of life in Gaza and Rafah's comparatively small size. (Throughout my research, I repeatedly found that this sort of "expected" relationship often did not exist, and that the world of ISIs was far less integrated or coordinated than I had initially assumed.)

When we entered, a young and assertive woman, whose head and body were covered, quickly approached us. It was clear from their subsequent exchange that this woman did not know either Abu Ahmad or Abu Hisham. After they explained who we were and the nature of my research, she invited us in.

The MWYC facility was small, but every square inch of space was used. We saw at least five activities: artificial flower making; a shop selling products, some of which were produced by the Center (including plates, cups, teakettles, oil canisters, clothing, framed religious sayings, and serving platters); another shop selling children's books and school supplies at reduced prices; a classroom filled with school uniforms; and a day care facility for twenty to thirty children "of working mothers." Abu Hisham appeared quite impressed and complimented the director (whose name we were not given), who was clearly pleased. On this particular day, only a few female staff were present, all of whom were covered but not veiled. We made our visit brief given that we had unexpectedly interrupted their work. Outside the entrance to the MWYC, an Arabic sign indicated that Save the Children and USAID had contributed funds.

Developmental Institutions

By definition, developmental ISIs are more complex and sophisticated than their traditional counterparts, although they sometimes work in the same sector. They have a more integrated and longer-term strategy that views the development or betterment of the community as an ongoing and multidimensional process. While many of these institutions are large and relatively highly capitalized, some are not. An excellent example of a developmental ISI is the al-Wafa Medical Rehabilitation Hospital, which is discussed in some detail in the last section of this chapter. Here I briefly profile two others, the al-Salah Islamic Association and the al-Rahma (Mercy for Children) Association.

The al-Salah Islamic Association was established in 1978. The main center was located in Deir al-Balah with branches in Gaza and various refugee camps. Each branch ran the full range of association programs. By 2000, al-Salah employed 35 paid staff and 50 volunteers, including the board of directors. By 2006, one year before it was blacklisted by the U.S. government, al-Salah employed 270 people.[35]

The longtime director (through at least 2007), Ahmad al-Kurd, is a well-known figure in the Gaza Strip. An Arabic teacher in the UNRWA schools for thirty years who also taught English at the Mennonite Central Committee, al-Kurd was elected mayor of Deir al-Balah as a Hamas candidate in 2005 and is currently the Hamas-appointed minister of social affairs. It became clear to me that he was the catalytic force behind the organization and its many programs.

Al-Kurd was very clear about his institution's objectives: to reduce poverty, improve living conditions, and empower recipients. He saw its most important program as orphan support, which he considered a crucial expression of the Islamic imperative to help the needy and which remains, to this day, a central institutional focus.[36] Of the 12,000 orphans throughout the Gaza Strip at the time, 10,000 were registered, according to al-Kurd. Al-Salah provided for 5,000 orphans, making it the single largest provider in the territory; as such it was regularly consulted by, and interacted with, the Palestinian Ministry of Social Affairs. According to al-Kurd, these 5,000 orphans were equivalent to 2,000 families, and by helping them the association affected approximately 20,000 people over varying periods of time (from several months to several years), depending on individual need. Each supported child in a family (often more than one) received around US $25 to $30 per month. Determination was made through an evaluation process (not detailed to me) that aimed to strike a balance among needy families. As part of its evaluation process, al-Salah did share information with other ISIs about families already receiving assistance.

Al-Salah's monies derived from international donors, mostly Muslim (but also some Christian) NGOs in the United States, Canada, France, Jordan, Saudi Arabia, and Kuwait but also private individuals. In the case of the latter, al-Salah would match children with donors, actively fostering a relationship between them. This relationship was considered vital for the child not only financially and economically but also psychologically and socially. According to al-Kurd, knowing that other people cared for and were interested in the child lessened his or her sense of abandonment and vulnerability. Typically, donors provided support until the child reached the age of fifteen,[37] but some kept up support through university education, an indication of the depth of the bond that was established between the child and the donor.

Not only would individual donors receive, in typical fashion, a report on their child every six months including a letter from the orphan, a photograph, school certificate, and a report detailing the child's status, but sometimes donors would finance specific items such as computers for "their" child. If the family's circumstances improved, the monthly stipend might be reduced. In such cases, donors were asked to help other, more needy families. Often they would demur unless "their" family agreed, again showing a valued relationship. Sometimes donors would refuse outright to support other children because they insisted on supporting their child.

The office of the orphan program was run-down and not very clean, although the secretaries (all covered but none veiled) were among the most efficient I encountered in my research. Most of their data were computerized, but there were also handwritten charts documenting the receipt of funds. They showed me rosters containing, for each supported orphan, the child's name, donor's name, donor's country of origin, the amount of support, the recipient's signature, and the date of receipt.[38] These receipts were sent to donors every month, as accounting was done on a monthly basis. On one visit I observed clients coming in to pick up their checks. All were women, very poor, young and old, and conservatively dressed despite the terrible summer heat. Pictures of the Temple Mount adorned one wall, and Quranic inscriptions were hung on two others.

According to al-Kurd, al-Salah was audited annually by an accredited firm, Saba Financial, and the results were given to the PNA. Although I am not an accountant, I was given a stack of papers (which I could not assess) regarding the audit including the final report, which summarized the findings most favorably. The walls of the main office had big boards laced with color photos of other activities (again, common among these institutions): soccer, volleyball, and basketball games; kindergartens; formal dinner functions; and food served during the feasts. Al-Salah also arranged for a variety of cultural activities for orphans and their families, including events that were open to the public, in which children and their mothers participated and celebrated religious and national holidays. They also had cooking classes for orphan girls and were planning a children's library (presents for orphans often included books) and a summer camp ("youthful play is a priority for children"[39]).

I was able to accompany one of al-Salah's social workers named Leila from the Gaza branch[40] on her visits to some of her client families. Leila focused on the health and educational needs of the child, cultural issues, and religious instruction. Although social workers were required to visit families twice a year, they often wound up spending more time with individual families while addressing specific needs. In one day, Leila would visit six to seven families for one hour apiece.

For example, on a visit to one (distressed but not destitute) family (that was not one of her formal follow-up visits), Leila spent considerable time inquiring about family members' health; when she discovered that the family did not have health insurance coverage, she arranged for the mother to visit the Gaza office so that al-Salah could arrange coverage through the Ministry of Health. The mother clearly appreciated Leila's attention and concern and, despite our polite protestations, kept insisting that we remain and eat something. This sort of response from a family was not uncommon in our visits. It was clear to me how powerful these simple acts of assistance were; they created linkages between human beings and between individuals and institutions that mitigated vulnerability, providing recipients with some sense of recourse, some option, in an environment where little if any existed.

Because it was summer and school was not in session, Leila and one of her coworkers described to me the educational follow-up they do for orphans (something Abu Hisham later confirmed[41]). Social workers, for example, would often visit children at school to see how they were doing. If problems were found, the social worker would try to get the child remedial help, which was relatively easy to do, or arrange for special courses, which apparently was more difficult. Sometimes teachers, both religious and not, who wanted to help would volunteer their time for remedial classes. Typically, these classes were for children aged eight to fourteen and were often held in al-Salah kindergarten classrooms. The association also had a literacy training center.

Alya, who was another social worker in the Deir al-Balah headquarters, engaged in similar follow-up programs and would sometimes visit families with Leila. Alya would also arrange courses for weak students that would meet three times per week after school at the Deir al-Balah offices. She told me that she identified weak students among her orphans by reviewing their school report cards. "We have great ambitions for our orphans, but limited funds." Al-Salah held a ceremony at the end of the school year to acknowledge students who had done well and worked hard. Social workers would also visit orphans' families during feasts, and observations were all recorded in formal family evaluations.

Clearly follow-up was an important part of al-Salah's program and something that Abu Hisham, as a contributor to al-Salah, had emphasized.[42] Alya held monthly meetings for the mothers of orphans, many of them widows, both young and old (note: an orphan was also defined by al-Salah as a child whose father was disabled or incapacitated). She focused on a variety of issues regarding health, education, social problems, and religious practice. One session I viewed focused on teenage behavior and how to deal with it. The discussion elicited expressions of concern similar to those one might hear anywhere and, at times, laughter, which could not help but make one smile. Discussions dealt with a range of related issues including the relationship between a woman's children and her husband, her own relationship with him, and home maintenance.

Women would share stories and advise each other. The practical information conveyed at these sessions no doubt possessed a certain utility, but they appeared to be far more important for the emotional and psychological (and perhaps social) connections they created among some of the women, even if these connections ultimately proved transient. The sessions also created a certain link with the social workers, who clearly had established respectful, caring relationships with some of these poor Gazan women, no doubt a rarity in their daily lives. It would be hard to imagine that their relationships with Leila or Alya were unimportant to both the women and their children.

Alya and some other social workers I met consistently emphasized women's emotional health as a priority concern, whether the woman was the mother of an orphan or impoverished or otherwise compromised (e.g., her children had been killed in political violence or her husband had been disabled). She told me: "The psychological problems of women are serious. They are under constant pressure with no psychological relief. [Their problems] result from three things: poverty, disease, and a living situation that is very limited and difficult, sometimes ten people living in a small space, which creates many problems. For women especially there is much nervous[ness], tension, and stress. There are also physical problems [such as] nutritional problems, thalassemia, and vision problems. They have suffered a lot, and we want to compensate them."[43]

Al-Salah would assist women in two ways: by empowering them to help themselves and by providing some resources directly. Empowering them meant providing clients with the names and addresses of women's associations and organizations (both Islamic and non-Islamic) that could help them find work or obtain needed assistance. A common referral was to the (decidedly secular) Gaza Community Mental Health Program, whose services were free for the poor. Women were also referred to a local psychology clinic run by a respected professional. Information sharing between al-Salah's social workers and their female clients—and showing women how to advocate for themselves—was a critical component of their relationship. It built high levels of trust between women and al-Salah's social workers. This accessibility to the staff both reduced the women's isolation and empowered them at the same time. On Thursdays women had an open invitation to visit the office, speak with a social worker, discuss their problems, use the phone, photocopy documents, and find whatever organizational help they needed.

Another way that al-Salah assisted its clients was by arranging counseling sessions for women with its own social workers. Although the social workers were not trained psychologists and had limited therapeutic skills, they still provided an emotional resource that seemed to be valued and appreciated by many clients, who perhaps felt less marginalized and vulnerable after being seen. For some women the relationship seemed to have a sense of intimacy, a familial quality that superseded ties to al-Salah as an organization but that clearly forged a link with it. Other women, however, were less sanguine, some expressing frustration with inadequate services.

The institution also had a program for 500 needy families[44] (defined as families in which the father was unemployed or parents were disabled). These individuals received a modest monthly stipend (NIS 200 or US $50), also funded by private donors, and their children's school fees (including university) were covered. During the first month of school, for example, al-Salah would distribute supplies to 2,000 needy children in Gaza, in addition to their standard 5,000 orphans. Furthermore, they would distribute winter clothes and foodstuffs, including lamb from Australia and canned meat from New Zealand, to around 6,000 families; approximately 2,000 families received flour rations.[45]

Education was another focal point of al-Salah's program. One of my interviews with al-Kurd took place at a brand new school, the al-Salah Benevolent School (for boys), which was still under construction at the time but which opened in the fall of 1999. This project had been initiated by the board of directors and licensed by the Palestinian Ministry of Education.[46] The school began at third grade and was planned to run through high school. There were eighteen classrooms with 30 boys per class for a total student body of 540 boys. Orphans would pay no fees. Although al-Kurd had hired twenty teachers for the start of the school year, his hope was to ultimately employ fifty. He indicated that a separate school was planned for girls, but he did not sound very enthusiastic or convinced of its actualization.[47] The planned curriculum would be heavily weighted toward the hard sciences, but it would also include computer literacy,

English, and religion. The facility consisted of three new buildings, all designed, Mr. al-Kurd said humorously, by a "Fatah architect/engineer." We held our interview in one of the administrative buildings. Another contained a cafeteria (all meals would be free), library, and cultural center in which events would be held. The third building contained rooms for science and computer labs in addition to some administrative offices. The building and grounds were lovely.

Up until the establishment of the Benevolent School, the core of al-Salah's education program was its eight kindergartens, all fully licensed during direct Israeli rule, in Deir al-Balah, Maghazi, Bureij, and Rafah. Families were charged NIS 200 (US $50) per year, and registration was open to the public. Given its reputation for higher quality standards, al-Salah's schools had approximately 1,500 children whose families were poor and rich, secular and religious, educated and illiterate, professionals, and PNA officials. Although I was unable to see the schools in session, I did speak with a range of people from refugee families to PNA officials, many (but not all) of whom favored Islamic schools over their secular counterparts and enrolled their children in them.

Like other ISIs engaged in education (all of which were private), al-Salah taught a standardized Ministry of Education curriculum and a religious curriculum that was not standardized (or regulated) but institution-specific. (This no doubt contributed to the varied reputations of different Islamic schools as well as official concerns that Islamic schools were being used for purposes of indoctrination and recruitment.) Religious instruction in the Quran and in Quranic memorization was an important part of the religious curriculum taught in all kindergartens and in other cultural activities. At the higher educational levels, religious classes were held separately for both boys and girls every day during the summer and four times a week during the school year. The hall in which these classes were held had walls with hand-painted drawings of the Dome of the Rock in Jerusalem and other religious and nationalistic scenes. The hall, which was located next to the new school, was quite colorful and cheerful, with multicolored chairs creating a visually pleasing environment.

However, what distinguished al-Salah from other secular schools, according to al-Kurd and some of his staff, was the way subjects were taught. Islamic schools "emphasized human and Islamic values, good behavior, proper conduct, and an appreciation for the arts and literature."[48] This distinction, they felt, also applied to other ISIs, including the Mujamma and the Jam'iyya, although they did not want to comment on other ISIs in any detail. Al-Kurd continued, "Islamic organizations work in parallel with each other. We cannot judge the philosophy of others."

Anecdotally, my friend Ramadan (who was avowedly secular) had two nephews; one went to an al-Salah kindergarten and the other to a secular kindergarten. He told me his family really saw the difference between the two boys: "The one who attends al-Salah has learned to memorize the Quran, has learned skills for dealing better with other children, has stopped using bad language, is better behaved, uses no political slogans, [says] nothing about Israeli soldiers, and talks about his ancestral homes in Palestine. In the secular school, my other nephew learned songs and his behavior was not as good."

At the time of this research, al-Salah operated one medical clinic in the Maghazi refugee camp, which was established in 1994. By 2003, it had established three more, for a total of four clinics, which employed ninety-seven people, one-third women.[49] Women served as doctors, nurses, and pharmacists and treated both male and female patients, although the latter constituted two-thirds of the patient load. Throughout my research, the Islamic health officials I interviewed insisted that the primary criterion for hiring staff was qualification for the job (not favoritism, nepotism, religious orientation, or any other subjective criterion), "and this is precisely why people prefer Islamic clinics."[50]

Al-Salah's clinics offered general medicine, dentistry, optometry, gynecology, physiotherapy, pediatrics, and small surgery (circumcision) in addition to laboratory and pharmaceutical services. The organization did not discriminate along any lines, political or otherwise. In 1999 the Maghazi clinic was seeing two thousand patients per month who were charged NIS 5, compared with NIS 30 in government clinics, for what was commonly regarded as comparatively high-quality health care. Those who could not afford to pay were given free care, although al-Salah staff conducted their own fieldwork to determine who was truly needy and who was not, again a feature I found in other ISIs as well (hardship cases would be evaluated on an individual basis). By 2006, the four medical clinics were reported to be seeing one thousand patients daily.[51] Mohammad Abu Asaker, who conducted fieldwork with the al-Salah clinics (in 2005 and 2006), reported that the "[m]edical clinics receive about U.S.$500,000 annually; this money goes to buy new equipment, salaries, and [for] building new facilities. This money is received from different sources, the biggest part is from regional and international Arab and Islamic foundations and bilateral donors like [the] European Union and the United States Agency for International Development (USAID)."[52]

The clinics were established to supplement the health services offered by UNRWA and government clinics, which operated from 8:00 a.m. to 2:00 p.m. The al-Salah clinics opened after 2:00 p.m. and remained open into the evening, a pattern found among other Islamic health clinics as well, although some would be open from 8:00 a.m. through 10:00 p.m. They aimed to provide medical services close to where people lived, making these services easily accessible and improving community well-being.

Such supplementary hours also allowed the clinic staff to form relationships with their patients outside the clinic through home visits to check on sick patients, make condolence calls, and perform general follow-up procedures.

Unfortunately, I was unable to visit any of the al-Salah clinics, but I did visit another Islamic clinic on more than one occasion, visits that have remained with me. Located in one of Gaza City's poorer quarters, it was known as the al-Huda Clinic and was one of three Islamic clinics in the area. The street where the clinic was located was literally dirt and sand; there were no paved roads, which is one indication of how poor, disadvantaged, and underserved an area it was. The director was Dr. Taher al-Lu'lu' ("pearl" in Arabic), a pediatrician who had worked in the clinic for thirteen years and did most everything medically. Al-Huda was a poor facility, quite run-down and not particularly clean but extremely well run. There was one large room where patients were seen and small surgeries performed, another area that housed a pharmacy, and Dr. al-Lu'lu''s office, which had some posters of Kosovo on the wall and an expired calendar. There were no other hangings or decorations, Islamic or otherwise, on any of the walls. There was also a rather shabby courtyard where people would wait.

The clinic was open from 5:00 p.m. to 9:00 p.m. (after the government clinics closed). During that period, a steady stream of people (from surrounding neighborhoods and some refugee camps) came in with a variety of complaints and questions. All patients were walk-ins; no appointments were taken. The clinic was open to the public, and people were seen in turn. Some came in for reassurance about their condition, which they often received, at times with a gentle scolding about taking better care of themselves. Others sought free medicines, which were not always given, and some walked away quite angry. In addition to Dr. al-Lu'lu', one other doctor worked there, as well as a nurse and a pharmacist, but they were not always there at the same time. Dr. al-Lu'lu' almost cringed when I asked whether his staff was "Islamic," by which I meant religiously observant. He insisted that he chose his staff on the basis of their skills and that was why they were trustworthy. He also emphasized the close supervision that he gave his staff, again a theme I repeatedly encountered in other ISIs, although I did not see much evidence of it during my visits.

Although I believed Dr. al-Lu'lu' when he said that being religious was not a criterion for selection, I believed that it would act as a deciding factor between two equally qualified candidates, one religious and one secular. Although the clinic was almost rudimentary in appearance, it was remarkably efficient. But it also possessed a certain familiarity, almost intimacy, that was expressed between the doctors and some of their patients, sometimes with humor and wit. This made the compromised condition of the place seem less important. While there was no doubt that patients felt comfortable using an Islamic institution or one that was religiously based, I saw over and over that it was not religion that drew people (or the staff) to ISIs as much as quality service, the personal commitment of the clinicians, and the assignation of worth to their patients, which people deeply appreciated and, I suspect, seldom received elsewhere. That is not to say that people did not have complaints—they did—and they usually centered on inadequate services.

I remember sitting just outside Dr. al-Lu'lu''s office watching men, women, and children go in and out when a man came in with his young son who was no more than three years old. There was a pleasant exchange between this man and al-Lu'lu'. What struck me about their brief exchange was the virtual absence of hierarchy between them. Then, almost unexpectedly and with lightening speed, the little boy was placed on a table, his pants removed, and a circumcision performed. The child screamed, was quickly dressed, praised by the adults for his bravery, given a candy, and ushered out of the clinic, whimpering but calm—all in less than fifteen minutes! Next came a man with a piece of metal lodged in his finger, which Dr. al-Lu'lu' removed almost as quickly as he had performed the circumcision. The patient was charged NIS 10, and he thanked the doctor profusely. Al-Lu'lu' claimed that at Shifa Hospital the patient would have been charged at least NIS 150. (The circumcision was free.) The clinic's revenue was largely based on fees and donations.

Dr. al-Lu'lu' said that a part of his work involved follow-up visits to particularly sick patients in their homes as well as condolence calls, although I did not have the opportunity to accompany him on any of these visits. A key advantage for some of the patients who visited the clinic was the ability to see the same doctor over time. Clearly, that the al-Huda clinic could function as it did required a rather extensive informal social network of people—patients, volunteers, funders—to keep it going.

The al-Huda clinic, like those of al-Salah and other ISI clinics, periodically held a "Medical Day" for the neighborhood when al-Huda would provide free medical care and free medicines for any problem that could be addressed in the clinic (these free clinics have a relatively long history in Gaza). During the most recent event, according to al-Lu'lu', 270 people were seen. Doctors, both men and women (and occasionally a Christian doctor), would volunteer their time. These events were not coordinated or planned with other ISIs. It appeared that Islamic clinics operated in much the same manner as other ISIs: as independent, localized entities with a neighborhood client base and with no apparent or automatic organizational or bureaucratic connection to each other (or to governmental clinics). Another illustration of this decentralized approach lay in the fact that some Islamic health clinics were very eager to accept free medicines from the organization Pharmacists Without Borders, whereas al-Lu'lu' totally rejected them, although he did not tell me why. Relations between Islamic clinics and the Palestinian Ministry of Health (MOH) were typically standardized. However, in al-Huda's case personal conflicts between Dr. al-Lu'lu' and the director general of the Health Ministry compromised the clinic with regard to certain benefits afforded other ISI clinics such as free MOH drugs.

Dr. al-Lu'lu' was a member of the Islamic Jihad, which no doubt contributed to al-Huda's reputation as an Islamic clinic.[53] But what primarily defined al-Huda as Islamic was its commitment and its proximity to the people it was serving despite its obvious limitations.

The al-Rahma Association was one of the most interesting ISIs I encountered, because it was the only organization in Gaza (and one of two or possibly three in all the occupied territories at the time) that cared for "illegitimate" children also known as "infant[s] of unknown parentage."[54] Located in one of Gaza City's poorer neighborhoods, al-Rahma was well known as a "Hamas" institution, because the then director and board members were known Hamas members. The director in 1999, Ahmad al-Zahar, was Mahmoud al-Zahar's brother.

The problem of children born out of wedlock was rarely if ever discussed openly and had no public face in Gazan society, given the extreme social costs associated with it. In a traditional society where the behavior of women is considered a critical marker of male honor and family honor and status, illegitimate births can have devastating consequences for both mother and child, including death. Despite the horrific price paid for illegitimacy, when such births do occur, they pose a terrible dilemma for a society so ill-equipped to deal with them.

Between its establishment in 1993 and the time of my visits in the spring and summer of 1999, al-Rahma received, on average, one illegitimate child a month, a rate that largely still obtained through early 2010. In that five-and-one-half-year period, al-Rahma had taken in approximately 66 babies (and by early 2010 had received 171 infants).[55] Of these, 40 were placed with families in Gaza, and some additional placements were pending at the time of my visit.[56] Some of the children placed were not infants but youngsters between ages one and five who had been living at al-Rahma. Children who did not get placed for whatever reason—usually because they were disabled—would remain at al-Rahma until they were of marriageable age or were able to work or attend vocational school or university. Although the institution was relatively young at the time, the board's stated intention was to care for these children, fulfill their health needs, educate them, and help them marry.

Babies would arrive in various ways: abandoned on the doorstep, deposited by a "third" party, or delivered directly from the hospital immediately after birth. Sometimes, alerted to the presence of an illegitimate infant in a neighborhood, ISI officials would go out to the neighborhood to locate the child and bring him or her to al-Rahma for protection and care. Typically, al-Rahma received newborns aged one to three days old.[57] Immediately after receiving an infant, al-Rahma would apply to the Ministry of Social Affairs for a birth certificate. The child would be given a name and, according to al-Zahar, a normal birth certificate without any indication of illegitimacy. The names of the parents would be "filled in" once the child was adopted.[58]

The institution's overriding objective was to reintegrate these children into society. "It's not their fault they are illegitimate," said al-Zahar. For children who were healthy, the placement process would begin immediately. Al-Rahma had a waiting list of childless families, and when a child became available, an individual family would be contacted and vetted. One official, Mr. Abu Nasser Kujuk, investigated families who applied for "adoption" and, based on a description of his tasks, clearly performed the functions of a social worker. He claimed to perform a thorough investigation, although he did not specify what that meant. Priority was given to childless couples who could "provide a good life, have good morals, and a good reputation [and are] financially secure."[59] It was rare for al-Rahma to turn down a family, but it did so on at least two occasions; in one case, the couple was deemed too old; in another, the mother worked outside the home!

A formal adoption entailed multiple steps, each one requiring documentation. First, the family had to be approved by al-Rahma, which took about one month. Then the family had to go to the Ministry of Justice to obtain a license of legal custody. The custody would subsequently be registered with the Ministry of Social Affairs, with which al-Rahma appeared to have a good working relationship. Lastly, a contract was drawn up between the family and al-Rahma. I was given time to look through the institution's adoption files. They appeared to be organized, neat, meticulous, and quite hefty, with detailed application forms, bureaucratic/governmental forms, in-house evaluations, personal recommendations, photos, and so on.

According to al-Zahar, a child that was placed in a home was considered a child of the family once it suckled its adopted mother's breast or the breast of the father's sister. Once this happened, the child became bound to the family and could not marry siblings. Furthermore, if the adoptive parents changed their will, the child could also inherit (although this had to be done with children two years of age and younger).[60] When I asked al-Zahar and some of the board members whether they encouraged parents to change their wills (and, in effect, circumvent Islamic inheritance law), they responded by saying this was up to the individual family itself but that they, as an institution, did not oppose it.

Although I was unable to substantiate this with any of the adoptive families themselves,[61] al-Zahar and other board members indicated that al-Rahma followed up with the family twice a year until the child turned sixteen. If problems arose, they would work with the family to resolve them, either through their direct intervention or by arranging specialized assistance from other sources. Serious problems, they told me, were very rare.

Al-Rahma financed the care of its illegitimate children through direct donations from a variety of organizations: the American Near East Refugee Aid (ANERA), church groups including the World Council of Churches, international NGOs and other international organizations, and foreign governments (e.g., Germany, Canada, the United Kingdom, Finland, France, Kuwait, and Qatar). Financing was also generated through individual sponsors. Once a child was adopted, sponsor monies would be shifted to other purposes; in this way, al-Rahma covered running costs and projects.

The institution also ran a typical sponsorship program for 450 fatherless orphans (through age sixteen), providing a family with US $40 to $45 monthly per child. Families would be visited twice a year, and donors would receive regular reports. Al-Rahma also provided some temporary residence—three months to two years—for hardship cases, who were children deemed to be in danger for whatever reason. This largely referred to children whose families were too poor to care for them.[62]

The facility was sparklingly clean but not sterile. It was well lit and received lots of natural sunlight. There was color everywhere, and the rooms were child-friendly and inviting. There were two floors of rooms that included sleeping areas for the children, a play area, a laundry room, and staff sleeping quarters. In addition to children's rooms, there was a big function room for special occasions with a large red table, small multicolored chairs, and shelves of neatly stacked toys and stuffed animals donated by ANERA.[63] There was one caretaker for every four or five children and a volunteer nun from Finland. The children were all clean and nicely clothed and appeared well cared for. There was a great deal of interaction between the staff and the children—lots of physical contact with the babies—and a great deal of affection as well. I did not see much didactic interaction with the older children, most of whom were disabled in some manner. The two male staff members did not shake my hand. All the female staff wore head scarves and long robes but none were veiled, while one of the males had Western-style clothing. The walls had little religious symbolism save a framed print with some Quranic sayings.

At the time of my research, al-Rahma had applied for and received permission from the Palestinian Ministries of Interior and Education (a fact I confirmed with both) to build a nursery school and kindergarten for the children who came to al-Rahma. The institution was also planning a children's library to be located in Gaza City's more affluent section, Rimal. Its primary aim, which was consistently reiterated to me, was to "integrate and streamline"[64] disadvantaged children. This was a key institutional objective and a prominent theme among other developmental ISIs as well. The school was planned to accommodate seventy-five children and four teachers.

The school and the library were to be part of a larger, seemingly self-contained village that also included a new and larger building for al-Rahma, since the one it was in was rented and increasingly inadequate to institutional needs. I sat with four members of the board of directors who showed me architectural drawings for this new building, which consisted of two wings—one for girls and the other for boys. They appeared quite excited about the plans and gave me a copy of the drawings, asking me if I could possibly assist with suggesting some funding sources and explicitly asking me to approach USAID. "You would take money from the U.S. government?" I asked. "Of course. Why not? We are a professional organization and we have projects that are important for the community." The project represented an attempt to improve the lives of the children at al-Rahma, create a sense of family among them, and integrate disadvantaged children with the community. The idea for this project was the board's alone and another example, in my view, of the absence of a larger social program among the Islamists.

Like the al-Wafa Rehabilitation Hospital discussed below, al-Rahma is an excellent example of an ISI that defined a problem and a niche within the community that few if any other institutions were addressing. (Currently, al-Rahma remains the only institution in Gaza receiving abandoned children, whose numbers are increasing given Gaza's severe socioeconomic decline.) I became persuaded that al-Rahma's principal aim was to care for the children in its charge and to mitigate their disadvantages, be they physical or cultural. Its goal for children born out of wedlock, for example, was the same as the goal for the families of collaborators (which other ISIs focused on)—to relegitimize and reintegrate them socially, which al-Rahma worked closely with a variety of ministries to accomplish. I asked al-Zahar whether extended families had ever tried to threaten or remove out-of-wedlock babies who wound up at al-Rahma in order to kill them for the sake of restoring family honor, as I had heard a vivid story about such a situation elsewhere. "Never," he responded, leaving me to ponder why.

Organizational Features

General Structure

I found that Islamic social institutions, whether traditional or developmental, shared certain common characteristics, exceptions notwithstanding. For example, management and staff were typically well educated, highly trained, and professional (some individuals held advanced degrees from Western universities). Similarly, the services provided by Islamic NGOs were generally of high quality and were perceived as such by the population and by the National Authority.[65]

Furthermore, Islamic NGOs almost uniformly defined niches and worked in sectors and localities where considerable needs were largely unmet. Their constituencies were mostly the poor and marginalized (e.g., widows, orphans, children born out of wedlock, families of collaborators, the elderly), and in some localities of the Gaza Strip and West Bank, Islamic NGOs appeared to be the only ones working with these groups. Another common feature (albeit with minor exceptions) was the insistence of the Islamist and ISI leadership that anyone, regardless of socioeconomic, religious, or political background, could participate in their social programs. (Typically, this question elicited laughter from the respondent.)

Islamic NGOs were also officially and legally registered with the appropriate Palestinian ministries, as they had been with the Israeli authorities before 1994 (see below). Furthermore, they took monies from a variety of sources willing to support them, religious or secular, including the U.S. and European governments, and international organizations.

ISI staff usually lived in the communities they served. They invariably were religious, by which I mean they observed basic Islamic rules regarding appropriate behavior, dress, prayer, and so forth. Men and women often worked together (e.g., doctors and nurses, teachers), although their tasks were sometimes separated; it depended very much on the nature of the ISI (some interpreted Islamic codes more rigidly than others, while some were barely distinguishable from secular institutions) and the kind of service provided. Beneficiaries were often the poor and working classes from nearby villages, camps, and towns. Some were religious in the orthodox sense, but most appeared not to be.

However, the ISI client base could encompass a broad range of socioeconomic (religious and political) backgrounds from the very poor to the very wealthy; I found this was especially true for the Islamic educational sector. The clear majority of parents whom I interviewed over time made it clear that they did not send their children to Islamic schools because their families were devout (although they were traditional and conservative); they did so because the schools offered the best education available and taught Islamic values. Parents were often impressed by the fact that teachers in Islamic schools were not only better trained but willing to work for lower salaries than their counterparts in secular schools. This was evidence of real commitment and dedication, which parents understandably valued.

Perhaps the most common feature of ISIs was their decentralized and local character. ISIs existed in a decidedly local construct and assigned considerable value to a localized milieu. They deliberately resided in and near their client base—a feature with a long history—which facilitated access and fostered structural connections with the community that were absent in the larger society, especially in Gaza (see chapter 6). This was a critical reason for the success of Islamist social organizations. Because they were local and localized, ISI programs were often institution-specific, reflecting the absence of a comprehensive social (and economic) vision or plan within the Islamic/st movement as a whole. This lack of vision was commonly attributed to the occupation, the absence of a state, and shortage of funds, not to any theoretical weakness in Islam. In the absence of vision, however, Islamists were "working hard to build confidence with people, to promote a grassroots base, to build trust, a clean and modest life ... filling in the gaps not filled by the Israeli government or the PNA."[66]

Indeed, in the absence of a unifying vision or agenda, the more common forms of inter-ISI cooperation—themselves limited—seemed to be information sharing about beneficiaries receiving assistance, the identification of recipients, and referrals and sharing of medical supplies and medicines in the health sector. ISI-secular interactions usually were around referrals of disabled children from secular to Islamic programs or schools and sharing statistical data on disabled kids, donation of equipment (e.g., wheelchairs) for rehabilitation centers, sharing of specialist staff (e.g., speech therapists) who might work part-time at an ISI, and the participation of ISI staff in professional training programs at secular institutions. This sometimes occurred in the educational sector where, for example, the Jam'iyya teachers and administrators would visit other secular and Islamic kindergartens to learn and took UNRWA training courses.[67] There were also cases, although few, where ISI staff were non-Islamic or non-Islamist.[68]

The apparent lack of horizontal connections between ISIs meant that it was not unusual to find that one institution did not appear to know what another was doing (or did not know about other Islamic institutions at all). This also appeared to be true for the Jam'iyya and al-Salah, which, as two of the largest and best-known ISIs in Gaza at the time, seemed to have little if any institutional interaction with, or detailed programmatic knowledge of, one another. It became clear to me that, as a rule, ISIs did not want to discuss other ISIs with no particular reason given. (I suspect this reticence derived in part from not wanting to appear ignorant of other ISIs, especially in front of a foreigner.) When the issue of institutional cooperation was raised, the lack thereof was often acknowledged and attributed, simply, to a "difference in philosophy, although services may be the same."[69]

Indeed, according to Dr. Aziz Duweiq, professor of urban geography at An-Najah University (who received his PhD from the University of Pennsylvania) and who subsequently became speaker of the Palestinian Legislative Council on January 18, 2006, "[there is] no network, no coordination, no one mind making decisions."[70] The fact that Abu Ahmad and Abu Hisham—both important figures on the *zakat* committees in Gaza—did not know anything about the Muslim Women's Youth Center (whose office was in the same building as the home of one of their beneficiaries), for example, was a "disconnect" I would encounter repeatedly in my research with Islamist NGOs. In some communities such as Hebron, I was told that competition between well-known families (e.g., Natsheh, Duweiq, Jabari) over social service provision would also work against the emergence of coordinated networks. Over time, it became a source of considerable discomfort for me when, in interviews with ISI officials, I seemed to know more about other ISIs and what they were doing than the people I was interviewing.

Another example of a disconnect—an institution that few in the ISI universe appeared to know of (or, perhaps, acknowledge)—was the Hebron Women's Union (HWU). Headed at the time by Iffat Jabari, who was known to be affiliated with the Islamic Jihad and who (correctly) defined herself as an Islamic feminist and activist and claimed to be "the first woman to drive a car in Hebron," the HWU focused on women's empowerment through a reinterpretation of Islam that was modern and liberating, no small task in a town as conservative as Hebron.[71] Although Jabari's work was part of a pattern of growing Islamic female activism within the Islamist movement (which included integrating women into Hamas's political structure), it was not accepted by everyone in the political leadership or by the more traditional forces within Hamas and outside it, especially in Hebron. Her principal goal was to use religion to educate women about social problems and promote a more progressive interpretation of sharia. If women knew their rights in Islam, she felt, they could empower themselves. For Jabari, tradition, not religion, was the primary problem, and this belief led to some innovative programs on her part.

Through the HWU, Jabari, who attended the Beijing Conference on Women in 1995, promoted activities that elevated the role of women (many of them poor and uneducated, young and old, from Hebron and the surrounding villages) in their community and increased their participation in the public domain. These activities covered a broad range of programs from the traditional to the nontraditional, including sewing, knitting, hairdressing, first aid, literacy, maternal health, pregnancy health, computer literacy, workshops on women's rights in elections, sports (table tennis), fitness classes (the HWU fitness center was quite state-of-the-art, and dwarfed its very small library), and karate and self-defense classes. Some of these programs were carried out in conjunction with local universities and medical and political organizations.

Using Islam to justify why women should work outside the home, receive an education equal to that of men (and appropriate to level of need), and run their own businesses (but not without certain restrictions mandated by religious law, e.g., the family must always come first), the HWU developed a strategy for women's empowerment that Jabari proudly admitted angered the more orthodox members of her community—both male and female—who nonetheless tolerated it. Gunning similarly writes, "many of the female supporters I spoke with in the 1990s credited Hamas with having given them the courage, opportunity and sometimes the financial aid to break with tradition and persuade their families to allow them to attend university."[72]

A key part of Jabari's strategy was to educate, to the extent possible, the men—husbands, fathers, brothers—related to her female clients. She claimed that she often met with secular women's groups and found common ground with regard to such issues as women's education and right to inherit. They would, however, disagree over other issues such as the right to work without restriction and on polygamy. Regarding the latter, Jabari told me, "I don't like it but it is in the Quran and one cannot ignore it or fight to have it deleted. But even with polygamy, it can only occur in special cases and under tough conditions,"[73] again a qualification not universally accepted within the Islamic movement.

Thus, rather than the typical representation of Islamic social institutions as a cohesive, homogeneous, monolithic, well-oiled, highly integrated, and superbly functioning (and therefore subversive) machine, I found a group of organizations that—despite many excellent examples among them and a reputation for effective service delivery—were largely decentralized and disconnected, characterized by a range of programmatic initiatives (in terms of both sector and quality) and approaches, intense competition for resources and clients, and territoriality. In fact, I found that many ISIs had stronger organizational and bureaucratic links to the PNA than they did to each other.

If ISIs in Palestine were linked to each other in some way, it was through a broadly shared notion of Islam and Islamic values. This begs the question, What makes Islamic institutions in Palestine Islamic? And here, too, when I put this question to my respondents, I received a range of answers. For example, an ISI official with a charity in Hebron replied, "conscience, trust, honesty, behavior, nonradicalism and to a lesser degree dress—but what's in an outfit? I don't have to dress in religious garb or have a long beard. Islam should be modern." For many others such as the *Haj* at the House of the Book and the Sunna, being an Islamic institution had a great deal to do with appropriate dress and behavior; for another, "raising well-behaved children." For some, being an Islamic entity meant a stronger emphasis on teamwork and volunteerism. Still others referred to the name of the organization and whether the ISI constitution contained Islamic regulations or the word "Islamic." One staff member argued that if the institutional founders were members of the Islamic movement, then the institution was Islamic.

When I asked Dr. Duweiq what makes an institution Islamic, he first answered, "Not much actually." But after thinking a moment, he went on to state, "how the directors behave, attitude, motivation, humility, trust, application of Islamic values (e.g., are nurses covered), saying '*b'ismillah al-rahman al-rahim* [in the name of God the all-merciful]' before touching a patient, prioritizing religious and collective goals over personal ones, and having a desire to please God." For a doctor working in an Islamic health clinic, being Islamic meant a "greater commitment to people that is measured more in terms of [our] approach than substance," which included a decision-making process based on consensus (*ijma'*), something I heard repeatedly from ISI staff and recipients, especially those working in the health and educational sectors. Hence, for some, the difference between an Islamic and non-Islamic institution came down to philosophy.

Mr. al-Kurd of al-Salah echoed these ideas when he said that one thing that made his institution Islamic was "our way of teaching"—i.e., with greater care and concern for the individual. Another official expressed it a little differently when he said that, in an Islamic institution, "there is a strong commitment to the poor, and the dignity of the poor is protected. At other institutions people are forced to stand in line and are humiliated." For Husam, the owner of a "Hamas" factory (see below), being an Islamic entity had strictly to do with adhering to Islamic practices such as "praying" at the appropriate times and segregation of the sexes as well as high-quality production. For Iffat Jabari, being Islamic meant "opposition to Oslo" as well as "appropriate dress and a vision toward women and Islam." For others, it meant honesty, "that money is used appropriately," a common theme, and that "beneficiaries get all their rights." In one ISI, the director said, "What makes this institution Islamic is the fact that I am running it!" For Ismail Abu Shanab, "the difference between Islamic and secular organizations is that we do what we do out of religious conviction [and a] sense of obligation to the community."[74] Officials in non-Islamic NGOs and in the PNA almost invariably defined an Islamic

NGO as one that had Hamas officials on its board of directors; almost all such respondents believed that ISIs were politically affiliated with and directly controlled by Hamas. They also argued that the ISIs' adherence to higher quality standards was an attempt to lay a professional foundation for usurping political control.

Legal Status

In contrast to the popular image of a nefarious network of institutions operating in some illegal, unofficial underground, Islamic social institutions in Gaza and the West Bank have long been visible and registered, operating as independent, legal organizations or as branch organizations of a legally registered "parent," as ISIs do in other Arab or Muslim countries. Prior to the establishment of the PNA in 1994, ISIs were registered with the Israeli authorities, and the majority were considered charities. After 1994, the new Palestinian government mandated that individual ISIs had to obtain an additional license from the appropriate government ministry (e.g., education, health, social affairs). Ironically, this caused some to encounter their first governmental interference. For example, the al-Salah Association was licensed by Israel for sixteen years, from its founding in 1978 until the PNA was established, during which time it reportedly encountered no problems. It subsequently received an operating license from the PNA, which closed the association for a short period in 1997.

In 2000, under Law No. 1 on Charitable Societies and Civic Associations, all social organizations (NGOs, PVOs, charities) were required to obtain new certificates of registration from the Palestinian Ministry of Interior (which proved easier for previously PNA-licensed organizations than for those that were new or unrecognized), a move that was regarded with considerable alarm by the NGO community, since it was viewed as a form of PNA intrusion into NGO affairs and a violation of NGOs' independence.[75] The then Ministry of NGOs in Ramallah argued that the Interior Ministry was designated for this role because of its greater institutional capacity, given its bureaucratic presence in towns, villages, and rural areas.[76] In fact, officials in Gaza's Ministry of Education told me in the summer of 1999 that they would no longer issue licenses to any educational institution before it obtained one from the Interior Ministry. When I asked a high-ranking official at Gaza's Ministry of Interior why kindergartens must first obtain a license from the ministry, he answered, "the NGOs belonging to Hamas do political activity under the cover of social work. All social institutions are political. Most of their activities [are found] in kindergarten work; this worries Arafat—that they do political activities through kindergartens. [He] does not want the kids to be taught fundamentalism."[77] When I asked him if he had ever entered and observed an Islamic kindergarten, he admitted he had not.

Indeed, Law No. 1 stipulated organizational transparency, designed to prevent the illicit movement of funds. It further required "registered organizations to appoint a certified accountant to supervise their budgets, keep detailed and verifiable records of all income and expenditures, and submit 'detailed' and independently audited accounts (along with full accounts of all activities) to the PA on an annual basis."[78] If an organization failed to adhere to these requirements (or violated its approved charter), the PNA had the legal right to close it down, seize its assets, and disburse those assets. However, with the second Intifada and the virtual destruction of the PNA by 2002 or 2003 (see chapter 7), the law was never fully enforced.[79]

Having said this, the ironic fact is that the Islamic social sector was comparatively more compliant with the law than its secular counterpart and was often the first to register organizations. As I have argued earlier, during the Oslo period ISIs went out of their way to avoid confrontation with the Authority as part of their desire at the time for accommodation and integration.[80] Because of this they cooperated fully with all legal requirements. Furthermore, ISIs were not viewed by the PNA as a threat in the way some secular organizations were, especially those secular groups engaged in human rights work and in activities that directly challenged the PNA's authority.[81] The services provided by Islamic institutions complemented rather than competed with the PNA, especially in the health care sector. In this way, the ISIs assisted the Authority by addressing needs that the PNA could not.[82] After the PNA temporarily closed sixteen "Hamas social organizations" in 1999 (likely due to external pressure), a Ministry of Interior official told me: "Even though Islamic institutions have been 'closed' for some time, we look the other way. They work anyway and we let them work because they offer support to the people. [They] indirectly support the PNA through their work [and] take a burden off the PNA. We close our eyes to them."[83]

Gunning further points out that the Hamas-affiliated charities he investigated all held elections to select and legitimize their leadership; registered members would elect an executive board or administrative council of around seven to nine members. Given that this sort of selection process was not stipulated under the law, "the fact that charities have chosen to adopt [it] is highly significant."[84]

Sources of Finance

How does Hamas reproduce itself? The Gulf states and Iran are clearly sources of funding for Hamas, and this became noticeable during the first Gulf War when aid to Fatah was virtually terminated. The Muslim Brotherhood International is another funding source, as is the Union of Good.[85] In May 2009, Sheikh Naim Qassam of Hizballah revealed Hizballah's broad financial support for Hamas, although no details were given.[86] It is believed that Hamas also raises funds from *zakat* inside Palestine, although this is empirically difficult to prove and little is known about the total amount of funds raised. Another source, of course, derives from donations outside Palestine despite restrictions increasingly placed on foreign NGOs by Israel, the United States, and Europe.[87] Again, although it is difficult to prove, it appears that Hamas has been relatively successful in avoiding dependence on political rents and that, historically at least, its funds have not remained in the hands of an elite encouraging clientelism and corruption.[88]

Common arguments maintain that Hamas directly funds the Islamic social sector, which comprises by far the largest component of the movement, absorbing 90 percent of its activities, according to Reuven Paz.[89] A typical response from U.S. government officials during the Oslo period was that Hamas spent most of its $70–90 million budget on its social institutions.[90] While it was never possible for me to determine with any accuracy the size of Hamas's budget, or how much proportionally was assigned by Hamas to ISIs and in what ways, it is clear, as the ICG maintains, that the "indirect involvement of Hamas in the process through 'mediation' can be assumed to be vital for any number of such institutions."[91]

Perhaps this is why questions about institutional sources of financial support often elicited stern and sometimes hostile responses. In the Jam'iyya, this question abruptly terminated the interview, with my respondent, Sheikh Ahmad Bahar, yelling at me: "Why are you asking me this? You are all the same; you just want to say we are all terrorists!"[92] In some institutions I was given more of a chance to explain why I was asking the question; and this sometimes would contribute to a more fruitful exchange, but not always. Some ISI officials were visibly insulted by the presumed implication that they were being used politically or to promote a violent agenda.

However, despite the fact that I was unable to obtain an exact answer to the funding question, certain patterns did emerge. First, funding of individual ISIs appeared very much to be an independent exercise, with each institution responsible for securing its own financing (or large percentage thereof), "technically only accountable to their own membership (which includes non-Hamas members)."[93] This was consistent with the decentralized nature of the social sector overall.

Second, ISIs almost uniformly insisted that their financial support derived from a combination of local, regional, and international donations from individual and organizational contributors. Some donations derived from explicitly Islamic sources while others came from a variety of nonreligious sources, although a large percentage were from charities in the Gulf region. For example, Hebron's al-Ihsan Charitable Society received funding from a variety of sources (as did al-Rahma): the PNA Ministry of Social Affairs, an Italian PVO, charities in the United Arab Emirates and Qatar, the United Palestinian Appeal in the United States, and Medical Aid for Palestinians in the United Kingdom. The organization's treasurer reiterated an almost universal theme: "We are a humanitarian organization and we will take money from whoever will donate, foreign and domestic. We accept money with no political or religious conditions."[94] In the lobby of the al-Ahli (Islamic) Hospital in Hebron (chapter 6), plaques were hung with the names of individual and organizational donors that included OPEC, the Arab Fund for Social and Economic Development, MBC/London, the European Union, local donations from wealthy Palestinian families and from the Arab community in Israel, the Holy Land Foundation, ANERA, UNRWA, the United Nations Development Program (UNDP), Muslim Aid–London, the Welfare Association, and the UK-based Palestinian Relief and Development Fund (INTERPAL).[95]

Third, according to the ICG report, ISIs "also benefit from informal support networks. In some cases, Palestinian expatriates are approached [by donors] with cash donations and asked to distribute them to Palestinians in the occupied territories."[96] A local ISI is identified and is asked to provide a list of eligible recipients and an institutional representative to "witness and confirm the disbursements. Such funds are as a rule not transferred to the budgets of the organizations involved, but are nevertheless perceived as part of their activities."[97] This, too, points to the localized, decentralized nature of ISI activity. These organizations also had the added the advantage of being able to use cultural and religious factors to raise money, which were not necessarily or as easily available to secular organizations.[98]

Fourth, and impossible for me to verify, was the argument that Islamic economic enterprises helped subsidize service and relief activities in addition to other domestic and foreign sources (see below).

Fifth, both Hamas and ISI officials (at least those who were willing to speak on the subject) were adamant that there was no direct funding between them, and everyone strenuously rejected the thesis that social funding was diverted to Hamas for political and military purposes—a commonly made claim for which there is debatable evidence, states the ICG.[99] Hamas argued that ISIs were independent and insisted on maintaining that independence, wanting no formal connection, in order to protect the social sector. One senior Hamas official who asked not to be identified argued that while Hamas may have provided some financial support to individual institutions, it did not possess the bureaucratic capacity to centralize, manage, and finance the entire social sector, a fact I found plausible given the apparent lack of comprehensive information about the ISI sector among the senior Hamas leadership.

Furthermore, it was argued, ISIs were professional organizations fully capable of raising their own funds independent of Hamas. ISI officials made similar arguments, consistently emphasizing their professionalism and insisting that they, like all social institutions in Gaza, were governed by PNA laws demanding transparency and accountability and, absent that, would not be allowed to operate. Similarly, some of the international funding organizations interviewed, particularly the UN agencies, stressed the professionalism of various ISIs and their preference for working with these institutions over others when necessary.

Political Affiliation

Political affiliation is a problematic concept, especially in a society where the majority of people are affiliated with a political movement in one form or another. Some ISIs and secular NGOs claimed total independence while others claimed some sort of political affiliation, whether with Hamas, Islamic Jihad, Fatah, the Popular Front for the Liberation of Palestine (PFLP), or even the PNA itself. Affiliation can take different forms and is often a matter of degree. Some institutions, such as the Mujamma kindergartens, were clearly known to be within the Hamas orbit.[100] In others, such as the al-Wafa Medical Rehabilitation Hospital and the al-Rahma Association, the institution was considered to be Hamas because one or more individuals—the founder or director or board member(s)—were known Hamas officials, members, or supporters. And in other cases, such as the Qatar Charitable Society, no affiliation was assumed. In fact, none of the institutional charters I viewed made any reference to or mention of the Hamas charter. Addressing the issue of political affiliation, a USAID official asked: "Can you assign 'political affiliation' to an organization if it does not have a political agenda and its leader is not affiliated to the extent that he acts on behalf of a political movement as opposed to his institution?"[101]

Friends and colleagues would often tell me that I should visit a particular institution, school, or factory because "it was Hamas." When I asked what made an institution "Hamas," people would typically reply, "It's known to be" or "The director is a supporter," and not much more. The quality of affiliation would grow increasingly gray when individuals who were identified with Hamas in some way—and even that was sometimes subject to dispute—sat on the institutional boards of either independent or decidedly nationalist secular institutions such as the Society for the Care of the Handicapped (SCH) in Gaza City, which aimed to have a governing board more politically inclusive and representative of the community it was serving.

Hence, Khaled Abu Zaid, the SCH director and a Fatah loyalist, included on his board of directors an Islamist who happened to be disabled. Did this man, as a Hamas member, exert any political influence on the SCH? Abu Zaid laughed outright when I asked him the question. Furthermore, because Ismail Haniyeh was then a friend of the SCH, any physically disabled member of the SCH (which claimed four thousand members!) was allowed to attend the Islamic University in Gaza without charge. And for those SCH members who were considered hardship cases, the university agreed to pay for books and supplies as well. This certainly did not make the SCH a "Hamas" institution. Similarly, the Jala' Society for Culture and Art in Gaza City, which treated traumatized children through participation in the arts and theater, had one board member who belonged to Hamas. Because of this, the U.S. government refused to fund Jala' despite the fact that it received funding from the European Union, Japan, and Save the Children and had been vetted by USAID as nonpolitical.[102]

When I was able or deemed it appropriate,[103] I would ask ISI officials and staff members, "What does it mean to be regarded as a Hamas institution?" Uniformly, they would reject any direct relationship with Hamas or any notion that the political sector influenced or otherwise used their institutional resources in any manner. On the other hand, some acknowledged their own personal support for Hamas or that others within that particular ISI supported or sympathized with the movement. As one ISI staff member told me (a sentiment often expressed), "We have a right as private individuals to support whatever party we want, just as you do in America. But inside this institution we are professionals with a job to do."[104] According to Gunning, "although there is considerable overlap in personnel and interests, each charity is operated by its separate Administrative Council. While charity representatives sit on Hamas' *Shura* Council, the charities do not appear to be directly controlled by Hamas."[105] Haim Malka further points out that although ISI officials and staff may be members or supporters of Hamas, "[i]deological affinity plays a more crucial role in mobilizing Hamas's network than does formal affiliation."[106]

Furthermore, when questioned about ISIs, many Islamist leaders—including Haniyeh, who was then in charge of Islamic NGOs—did not appear to have a clear sense of the ISI universe at all (although Haniyeh, at least, was well informed about specific ISIs) and often did not really know (or appear to know) the range and variety of programmatic work in which ISIs were engaged. Abu Shanab, for example, told me on more than one occasion, "I don't know what they [ISIs] are doing, but they practice and teach Islam, so they further Hamas's goals; it will all come together in the end."[107] Abu Shanab also insisted that there was no formal connection and that the real connection between the social and political sectors was one of philosophy, a theme other respondents also expressed. "Since the roots of social work [in Islam] are not political, there is no necessary [organic] connection between them," one ISI official argued. He acknowledged that the service work of the social sector would generate support for Hamas, but the primary interest of the Islamic movement was "building the human being"[108] and, hence, the community.

In fact, the emphasis on the human being and the perceived attack against him in all spheres of life and against Islamic culture during the Oslo period was a pronounced theme among ISIs and among the Islamist leadership. As discussed earlier, disaffection with the political leadership from within Islamist ranks was palpable at this time. Violence had achieved little and had imposed considerable costs on both society in general and Hamas in particular. One ISI official characterized the program of the political wing as one in which "they stand still or limp." Society was in bad shape and attention, catalyzed by the weakening of the political and military sectors, was shifting from the political to the social. The former head of the political wing of Hamas, Sayyid Abu Mussameh, said: "We are a pragmatic movement, not just an ideological [one]. Our priority today is not to clash with the PNA. Who rules is of less importance right now. This doesn't mean we don't care, but we do not want conflict." The sense of political weakening and military defeat was real among the inside Islamist leadership. "We must also change mentality, thinking, the mind. This is not because of Israel or the U.S.—the problem is within us."[109]

Mahmoud al-Zahar, now the foreign minister of the Hamas-led government, similarly spoke of the need to focus on "the palm leaf [not] the cigarette."[110] By this he meant working at the local level with communities, shunning the elite and what they had come to represent. In his view, the Islamists needed to work on rehabilitating society at the grass roots: "We are reconstructing the poorer classes—raising their living standards and improving their quality of life to the extent possible; the *sulta* [here he was referring to the PNA] created a new rich class, that's all. A room in a mosque, that's all we need." For many respondents, their greatest fear was a society slowly spinning out of control.

Many of the people I spoke to within the Islamist movement believed that the Oslo process was absolutely destined to fail, so time was on their side. The new battle was not military but ideational, over ideas and values—"we fight by changing ideas through Islam," was a typical response. The new emphasis was on "laying the groundwork for the next generation. Again, to quote al-Zahar, "the Palestinian position is weak, people are weak, [and] we must accept the current situation [regarding] Oslo and the PNA. We must fight resignation; we must work for change or no prophets will succeed, no artist will create any art, no one will build a house. In this era, we will sacrifice ourselves, but we must leave a legacy through our children and use the present situation as a field, planting our ideological seeds for the future."[111] And by "sacrificing ourselves," al-Zahar clearly meant ceding the Islamist political vision for the time being to this new social priority—changing the mind of people through grassroots initiatives aimed at improving the quality of life and creating a more Islamic way of life. Social progress, though difficult and slow, was the main vehicle for changing people's minds. "The main force of the Islamic movement is Islamic projects and the people's belief in the social project."[112] This was a consistent theme at the time.

Hence, "the Islamic struggle was not a matter of fighting," I was told by Dr. Mohammed el-Hindi, a pediatrician and former leader of the Islamic Jihad, "but of thinking, a matter of mind. It was no longer a question of invading the other but of invading the mind. Force was not military but cultural."[113] Facing a formidable foe in the PNA, the Islamists clearly adopted a strategy that focused on areas over which they had control, could operate relatively unencumbered, and had popular appeal. Furthermore, with the creation of a Palestinian National Authority as specified by the Oslo peace accords, Islamists also argued that they could experience themselves culturally in ways that had been denied them during direct Israeli rule. And as argued earlier, it also enabled the Islamists to carve out a space in society that was less threatening to, and more protected from, the *sulta* and Israel—in effect, finding a meaningful accommodation with the status quo. In this strategy, the Islamist social sector played a key role. Hence, if a linkage existed between the social and political sectors of the Islamic movement, it was for many of its members "spiritual not organizational,"[114] one of philosophy not politics, "principle not practice."[115] That is one reason why ISIs were willing to take grants from any source willing to assist them and why they appeared to have better working relations with the PNA than they did with each other.[116]

"Hamas" Economic Organizations[117]

As far as I could determine at the time, no Islamic economy or distinguishable Islamic economic sector existed separately from the larger Palestinian economy. What I did find was a collection of economic entities—small (and a few large) businesses, factories (including subcontractors for Israel), retailers, and wholesalers—that identified themselves as Islamic according to much the same definition (in contrast to ISIs) and functioned as a formal part of the larger economy, including trade with Israel. Although my research on Islamic economic entities (IEEs) was greatly limited by restrictions on access (which I did not encounter nearly to the same degree with ISIs), it became increasingly clear with time (although more research was required to substantiate this) that what distinguished IEEs from ISIs was the relatively greater cohesion of inter-IEE relations and networks and the desire among IEEs, almost without exception, to remain invisible—either unseen or unidentified as Islamic or "Hamas." In fact, many of the Islamic or "Hamas" factories I visited were physically located in areas not visible from main streets—almost hidden from view. On both accounts, the contrast with social institutions was striking.

The desire among IEEs to remain invisible—physically and politically—derived, I believe, from two factors: (1) to be identified as Islamic or Hamas-affiliated would jeopardize business, especially inside Israel but also in the West Bank; and (2) such an identification would bring unwanted exposure to the internal networks that appeared not only to help sustain IEEs but arguably gave them a competitive economic edge (see below). Indeed, the key question regarding IEEs was not whether an Islamic economic sector existed but how Islamists were organized economically and to what purpose or end their business enterprises were used. As stated above, a common belief among people in Gaza that I could not substantiate was that Islamic economic production activities helped subsidize the work of ISIs.

Because of access restrictions (and ultimately time limitations), I was unable to determine the exact nature of IEE networks and how specifically they functioned, which would have provided greater insight into the relationship between IEEs and ISIs and between IEEs and the Islamic political sector. Clearly, however, these networks existed in some form.

Islamic economic enterprises in Gaza consisted primarily of small businesses and factories, which produced for the local market and for export to the West Bank and Israel. (Raw materials and finished products were imported from Asia and Europe through middlemen via Israel and Jordan.) The small businesses typically included grocers (which did not sell cigarettes or alcohol), novelty shops, bookstores, and wholesalers and retailers involved in the import and export of food items, clothing, accessories, textiles, and stationery. A few larger businesses were engaged in construction and contracting and in financial investment (largely around land, which during the Oslo period became highly speculative and, for a time, lucrative). Islamic factories traditionally produced clothing (for women and children), women's handbags, foam, pharmaceuticals, heating equipment, and dental products.

Unlike their social counterparts, IEEs defined themselves as Islamic in consistent terms—according to religious practice and appropriate behavior: segregation of the sexes, praying, fasting, and dress. Some of the smaller merchants would not sell items prohibited by religious law. However, many respondents also tacitly associated "Islamic" with "high quality," whether goods, services, or human resources. And "Islamic" institutions were also identified by close working relationships, including those between supervisors and workers, and by their locations in areas considered traditional Hamas strongholds (particularly factories). All the factories I visited were located in poor areas of Gaza known as centers of support for Hamas.

Not surprisingly, although it was relatively easy to identify a given business or factory as Islamic, I was not able to determine whether an IEE was Hamas-affiliated. Again, it was the Gaza street that would often identify a specific factory, wholesaler, or retailer as "Hamas" because the owner or manager was known or believed to be a member or supporter. In some cases but certainly not all, I was able to determine that the owner or director of a given IEE was somehow affiliated to Hamas; what this meant beyond that affiliation was not possible to ascertain. In some cases where owners of IEEs were willing to identify themselves politically, I heard more references to the Muslim Brotherhood than to Hamas specifically.

One such example was Husam, the owner of a sewing factory in Gaza whose brother, Tarik, was an old friend of mine in Gaza. Tarik[118] was a Fatah supporter; Husam was a member of Hamas.

Husam owned his own sewing factory, which had six employees. In addition, he subcontracted work to four other factories in Gaza (with sixty employees) and had a strong working relationship with them. Husam's factory would largely design and cut pieces for children's clothing—jeans, shirts, pants, jackets, and underwear (he would also import underwear and diapers and sell them locally). He would then subcontract other factories to do the sewing. Most of the sewing work was carried out in the subcontracted factories. For six to eight months of the year, these subcontractors worked only for Husam. All products were produced locally, and all transactions were handled by local banks. The finished products would then be returned to Husam, who would arrange for distribution.

Husam would then market the clothes to retailers in Gaza (primarily his friends) and to somewhere between twenty-five and thirty wholesalers in the West Bank and Israel (largely the Arab community inside Israel), subject to Israeli approval. According to Husam, he had been trading with the same people for twelve years. The West Bank occupied the largest share of Husam's business (50 percent), followed by Gaza (40 percent) and Israel (10 percent). Husam indicated that many of his contacts in Gaza, the West Bank, and Israel were Muslim Brothers. Tarik claimed they were all Hamas supporters.

In Gaza, Husam also marketed basic foodstuffs, which he imported from Israel, Jordan, Turkey, Brazil, and Egypt through middlemen. Stationery (e.g., pens, pencils, rulers, calculators, writing tablets, printer paper, schoolbags especially for the *zakat* committees, children's books, religious books[119]) was another major item, which Husam imported from Japan, France, Sweden, Taiwan, Malaysia, and China, also through Israeli middlemen. He would market his stationery to wholesalers in the West Bank and Gaza who in turn would sell it to around one hundred retailers in each territory. Textiles accounted for 50 percent of his revenue stream, while stationery brought in 30 percent and food the remaining 20 percent.

When I asked Husam what distinguished his factory and business ventures as Islamic, he responded in two very different ways: "praying, separating men and women," and "higher-quality products" for which he asked comparatively higher prices. In this regard, Husam argued that there were no differences between Islamic and non-Islamic businesses in terms of their goals—i.e., profit—only in how these goals were reached. IEEs were unequivocally profit-driven. "I will make miniskirts if people want them," Husam told me. "Our first priority is to get the work done." This sentiment was common among other IEEs I visited. Husam lamented how difficult it was to maintain his critical trade connections outside Gaza, which were absolutely crucial to his revenue base—given growing Israeli-imposed closure restrictions. He told me that he would be happy if he could just break even.

"How these goals were reached" by an Islamic business, Husam explained, had several dimensions. The most obvious were integrating prayer into the workday (secular hires were encouraged to pray), segregating the sexes, and veiling women. For cultural reasons, women workers were far fewer and more transient and short-term (e.g., there was a high turnover of women due to marriage). In two factories, some women employees, all conservatively dressed, worked in separate areas—a cultural as well as religious practice. In one factory, women and men worked in separate rooms divided by a sliding door. Both sexes were allowed to enter through the same door, but women arrived after the men. When I visited Husam's factory, there were no women working there, which I questioned. He claimed to want to hire women, but he said none, except the poorest, were willing to work there, because such labor was considered *haram* (shameful), a reality I often encountered.

Husam's six employees worked eight to twelve hours per day and were very skilled at sewing. I watched them carefully working at their machines. Husam found his workers, all locally trained, through "referrals or friends of the family." Tarik—and no doubt others in the community—believed that all employees "were Hamas," either through membership or support. The factory, which was more a huge workroom, was modern, very clean, organized, and comfortable, but certainly not elaborate or sophisticated. I saw nothing religious on the walls or anything overt to suggest that this was an Islamic entity; however, other factories did have the ninety-nine names of Allah and Quranic sayings on the wall. One thing that struck me was how hardworking and efficient the workers were and how content, almost happy, they seemed. I remember thinking that perhaps one function, whether intentional or not, of an IEE was to provide workers with a set of values and rules to which they were held accountable, to provide a structure and sense of order, standards, and expectations in a localized milieu that was otherwise chaotic and volatile.

In all the Islamic factories I visited (some of them established in the late 1960s and early 1970s), supervision of workers was an important issue. Many had worked for the same employer for several years, including Husam's employees. Turnover was low. Workers received a marked degree of personal attention, which struck me, and were quite closely supervised. On-the-job training appeared to be an important component of employment. When I asked various managers including Husam what qualifications (beyond skill) they sought in their employees, the near-uniform response was some combination of trustworthiness, honesty, appropriate behavior in the workplace, cleanliness, and punctuality. A typical reply: "Do they come to work on time? What do they do with scraps of material? How do they behave in the workplace?" This contrasted with what I had seen in the many other factories I had visited in Gaza over the years.

Husam and Tarik took me to several other factories (including one operated by one of Husam's subcontractors), wholesalers, and retailers that were self-defined IEEs. They included an underwear factory, a jeans factory and attached retail store, four sewing factories, a handbag wholesaler, and a fabric wholesaler. Husam knew all the owners/managers personally. The sewing factories, which specialized in children's, women's, and men's clothing and were historically quite lucrative, varied in size from large, spacious workrooms comfortably housing thirty to forty employees to small operations with only five people. The larger factories performed all parts of the production process: design, cutting, sewing, finishing, pressing, packaging, and shipping (all fabric was imported from or via Israel). In one factory 40 percent of output was entirely produced in Gaza while 60 percent was designed and cut in Israel, sewn and packaged in Gaza, and shipped back to Israel. Smaller factories would sometimes do everything except the actual sewing. There was a clear division of labor and specialized functions. On average, workers were paid US $300 to $500 a month, a relatively good wage in Gaza at the time.

CREATING A DESCRIPTIVE CONTEXT 149

Uniformly, working conditions were very good, and space was efficiently used. There appeared to be little waste. Work areas were clean, organized, and well lit. Despite intense summer heat, they were also cool and comfortable. The smaller factories with five and ten employees, for example, produced 2,000 and 2,700 finished pieces of clothing per month respectively. The former (with five employees) exported 60 percent of its product to the West Bank and Israel and marketed 40 percent locally. The latter sent all its products to Israel. Larger factories with twenty workers produced on average 8,000 pieces per month; those with thirty to forty employees could nearly double that output. The Israeli market was a key source of revenue for IEEs. They all acknowledged that the main historic reason for their commercial viability was the Israeli market (and Israeli middlemen).

For some time, Gazan producers had been able to compete with their Israeli counterparts on the basis of cheaper labor (and other production-related) costs, lower prices,[120] lower profit margins, and quick turnover. However, even back when I did my fieldwork, concern was expressed over numerous trends that had begun to converge and impinge on the Gazan economy: Israel's tightening of closure restrictions, which increased production costs for Palestinians and made them less reliable trading partners; Israel's establishment of competitive sewing factories inside Israeli settlements in the occupied territories, which would employ Palestinian labor and then outcompete Palestinian producers in the market; and the pressure of cheaper labor costs in Jordan, which drained production orders away from Palestinian factories to Jordanian ones. (Jordanian-produced goods were then marketed in Israel, the West Bank, and Gaza, and Gazan businesses had a hard time competing in local markets.) All were ominous indicators of the dramatic economic decline that would follow.

Although my sample was painfully small, my interviews revealed something quite interesting that clearly merited further research: IEEs appeared to coordinate their activities, albeit informally, in order to share risk and perhaps mitigate (but certainly not end or even avoid) competition. It became increasingly clear, for example, that some Islamic sewing factories[121] produced only children's clothing while others concentrated on women's clothing and still others on clothing generally. In some cases but not all, they also seemed to target different markets—the West Bank alone, Gaza alone, Israel only, or some combination (typically, Israel and the West Bank) thereof. In more than one interview with factory owners and wholesalers, I was told that many IEEs would try to carve out individual market niches in order to avoid competing directly with other IEEs. There appeared to be an informal "gentlemen's" agreement to avoid unnecessary competition where possible, but implementation was often imperfect.

For example, one of the largest fabric wholesalers in Gaza (out of six in the Strip at the time) whom I shall call Mohammad (son of a well-known Hamas official) told me that he sold only to retailers in Gaza (60 percent) and Israel (40 percent) but not the West Bank. In fact, Husam bought much of his fabric from Mohammad. When I asked Mohammad why he did not trade with the West Bank, he simply refused to answer. Another sewing factory owner in Jabalya stated that while competition among IEEs (and others) could be fierce, there were attempts to "interact" with other factories informally, often on a personal level. This interaction, he said, could assume different forms, from attempts to lessen or prevent competition in a given market to using social (and, quite possibly, political) networks to exert pressure in order to achieve a desired outcome. The language was deliberately vague, and no direct reference to Hamas was made.

However, it may have been that IEEs and the network of which they were a part somehow informally (and imperfectly) divided the market among themselves in order to help one another maintain position and profit margins, soften the impact of losses, and provide a limited competitive edge vis-à-vis other Palestinian and Israeli businessmen. I deeply regret that I was unable to research this appropriately, but the indications I observed of such arrangements did suggest that it was not an Islamic economy that was being created but rather increased leverage within an increasingly adverse economic environment. As such, IEEs were not trying to separate ideologically or doctrinally from the larger Palestinian economy—which would have been impossible in the highly constrained and distorted environment of Gaza—but rather to carve out a better collective negotiating position within it (not unlike ISIs), possibly using their social and economic (and political) networks in the Islamic movement to do so.

Although it would be methodologically incorrect to generalize from my small sample of IEEs, I was nonetheless struck by the apparent interconnectedness of the businesses I visited, the close personal ties between the owners and operators I did meet, and the personal relationships these men claimed to have with other IEEs—the ways in which they consulted one another and shared information, including about the recruitment of workers.[122] This pointed to the existence of Islamic networks for recruitment and training, and possibly distribution and marketing. In this regard IEEs stood in stark contrast to the way ISIs typically worked, a difference that I would attribute, in part, to their smaller size collectively and their greater vulnerability economically.

Hence, IEEs were subject to the same forces, vagaries, and restrictions of the market and of Israeli policy as were other Palestinian enterprises. As economic units, IEEs were defined by their owners and managers—just like most other Palestinian institutions—and not by the doctrinal imperatives of an Islamic economy. They may have enjoyed a certain competitive edge vis-à-vis their secular counterparts with regard to the recruitment of highly trained labor, higher worker retention levels, access to certain wholesale and retail outlets, perhaps a certain degree of inter-IEE regulation over competition, and low overhead costs. But economic and financial imperatives clearly trumped ideological or political ones.[123] Indeed, Israel was a critical market for many IEEs, and some of the businessmen I met claimed strong and long-standing trading relationships with Jewish Israelis, which they clearly wanted to retain.

A Glimpse inside a Hamas Social Institution

One institution that was widely and popularly known to be "Hamas" was the al-Wafa Medical Rehabilitation Hospital (al-Wafa or WMRH) in Gaza City. An excellent example of a developmental ISI, al-Wafa was one of the most professional institutions I encountered in my work with Palestinian NGOs, Islamic or secular, and one of the most humane. Al-Wafa worked collaboratively with certain institutions in Gaza—the Islamic University and the Society of the Care of the Handicapped—but also had a professional relationship with Tel Hashomer Hospital in Israel and various Norwegian NGOs specializing in rehabilitation and in the care of those with traumatic brain injuries.

The institution began as a nonprofit NGO, the al-Wafa Elderly Nursing Home, founded around 1979 to address the needs of the largely underserved poor, elderly (age sixty or older) population of the Gaza Strip. Based on economic and social need, patients were given a place to live supplemented with comprehensive social and medical services and, if needed, rehabilitation services.

During 1995–1996, al-Wafa Medical Rehabilitation Hospital was established on the same premises as the nursing home but specifically targeted patients with head and spinal cord injuries as well as other neurological disorders. The rehabilitation hospital was initially established in part to help defray the costs of the nursing home, but by 1999 "there ha[d] clearly been a shift in emphasis so that it ha[d] . . . taken on an independent and important role as the first and only in-patient rehabilitation center in the Gaza Strip."[124]

The hospital was housed in a somewhat run-down and overcrowded building, and more space was needed, which was subsequently built between 2007 and 2008. However, all areas of the facility were very clean and neat. Every room had two beds and bathroom facilities. Sayings from the Quran and Hadith were posted on the walls in the hallways, and a prayer area was provided. My primary contact was the medical director, Dr. Medhat (who, under the Hamas-led government, went to work in the Palestinian Ministry of Health), although I spoke at some length with the board members, nursing staff, patients, and their families.

Although housed together, the nursing home and the rehabilitation hospital served different functions and existed as discrete entities. Between 1980 and 1999, about 222 elderly persons had had the nursing home as their permanent residence for varying time periods. By 1999 the nursing home had a capacity of thirty beds with an occupancy rate of 100 percent. I saw fifteen old men and fifteen old women there. Apparently these people had no family to care for them. Technically, if an elderly person had no sons willing or able to care for him or her, al-Wafa would accept that person if space allowed. I was told that before coming to al-Wafa, some patients had been abandoned and homeless. Almost all the elderly could have been living in a normal home setting except for their social situations, and many if not most were not in need of al-Wafa's specialized medical services.[125]

The government or occasionally a private donor covered the cost of nursing home care (approximately US $40 per day in 1999), which included medical and dental care for the residents. While I was there, a resident approached Dr. Medhat, smiling with delight and thanking him for the new dentures he had received. The respectful way that Dr. Medhat responded touched me deeply. The nursing home was spare but clean. One thing that struck me was the absence of an institutional smell. There was absolutely nothing fancy or decorative about the rooms, however; they were more functional and utilitarian than warm and personal. Although the staff had a decidedly medical character and the nursing home was not the focus of their attention, there was a reasonable amount of interaction between the staff and the elderly, largely around mundane rather than more creative activities.

The rehabilitation hospital was a very different entity. It served severely disabled persons, many of whom had complex medical problems. The majority had acute and chronic physical and cognitive disabilities. Patients were admitted with new injuries or referred from another hospital that was unable to meet that patient's rehabilitation needs. Overall, al-Wafa's patients' medical issues were far more complex than those treated by counterpart institutions in the West Bank, most notably the Abu Rayya Rehabilitation Center in Ramallah (which I visited several times) and the Bethlehem Arab Society for Rehabilitation, both key specialized centers.[126]

The medical problems of inpatients generally fell into the following categories: cerebrovascular accidents (CVA) (30 percent), spinal cord injuries (SCI) (21 to 30 percent), traumatic brain injuries (17 percent), orthopedic cases (10 percent), and other conditions, including cerebral palsy, amputations, and neurological and neuromuscular problems.[127] During the three-year period from 1996 to 1998, the hospital served some 419 inpatients divided by case category as follows: CVA (126), SCI (89), pressure sores (64), traumatic brain injuries (61), orthopedic problems (37), cerebral palsy (15), neuromuscular diseases (10), amputations (9), and other medical problems (8). The average length of stay was 47 days for the three years, which was higher than for comparable centers in the West Bank, and the range in length of stay was 1 to 681 days.[128] Up until 2004, there were no other rehabilitation facilities in the Gaza Strip that could receive any of these patients. Combined with three specialized centers in the West Bank, the al-Wafa Hospital reached over two hundred communities comprising 30 to 40 percent of the Palestinian population in 1999.[129]

By 2006, al-Wafa had one Inpatient Department with around fifty beds (forty of these beds were apparently donated by a "U.S. organization") and one Outpatient Department. The former had separate wards for men, women, and children. The staff consisted of doctors, nurses, nurses' aides, physiotherapists, occupational therapists, speech therapists, a social worker, and psychologists. There was a lab for basic blood and urine chemistry and simple x-ray equipment for chest and skeletal pictures.[130]

Because many of the patients had complex medical problems on top of their primary diagnoses, their rehabilitation process was extremely challenging. This was not an easy or simple patient population but one that would have been difficult and challenging in any setting, even one with far better resources than Gaza's. According to a Swedish specialist,

> To begin with 21 in-patients with problems of this nature constitutes an extremely heavy work burden. These patients require staff-intensive resources, especially the nursing staff, as well as technical aids, such as lifts, to lessen the burden of the work, which in fact were not available at WRMH.... [T]hey are working very much with medical problems, much less with medical rehabilitation and to an even lesser degree rehabilitation.... When the medical problems become extensive and you are not a part of a larger hospital where such resources are available, then there is a strong possibility that rehabilitation will ultimately get lost or have low priority among the medical expertise.... That a small rehabilitation center, physically removed from a larger hospital, should take on such work is debatable unless you have extensive resources.[131]

Furthermore, given Gaza's high population density and the fact that al-Wafa was for many years the only center of its kind serving the entire Gaza Strip, annual admissions were typically higher than they were in

West Bank institutions of comparable size. In 1997 these comparable-size admissions were 20 percent higher at al-Wafa.[132] And yet the number of yearly admissions increased, from an average of 140 in 1999 to 180 in 2004 (after four years of Intifada). Around two-thirds of the patients were adults, and the rest were children.[133] The children brought to al-Wafa often suffered either traumatic brain injuries because of traffic accidents or Intifada-related injuries.

I saw children aged five to six with brain stem injuries from being hit by cars, a common problem both in the refugee camps and in the crowded streets of Gaza. These children had no hope of recovery. One child I spent time with during the summer of 1999 could not speak and was unable to move his limbs. His mother was in the room, and the anguish on her face was heartbreaking. Dr. Medhat escorted me through the wards but would sometimes leave me alone to observe. I watched therapists massaging and exercising children's leg and arm muscles so they would not atrophy. One little boy whom I visited several times had a brain injury and was on a breathing machine. He had not made any progress but was clearly well cared for. In fact, according to one external evaluation, given al-Wafa's specialized experience working with spinal cord injuries—especially the urological aspects—it was recommended that children with spina bifida be added to al-Wafa's patient pool.[134]

Occasional miracles did occur: One girl who had been in a coma for seven months suddenly woke up and was able to communicate to some extent. The staff, who were very kind, paid an exceptional amount of individualized attention to these children, which was particularly important because some had not received adequate family care. Some children had been abandoned, leaving al-Wafa to provide chronic and sometimes terminal care, which they provided for adult patients as well. All the children I saw were extremely clean, well groomed, and nicely dressed. I asked Dr. Medhat whether I could look under their covers; each time I did, the bed was clean. Although I am not a medical doctor, I saw no evidence of bedsores or other skin infections, a fact confirmed by foreign specialists (see below). Occasionally there was toy or playful decoration in a room, but these rooms, like those in the nursing home, were quite clinical and modest.

During the summer, the rooms housing the elderly and the children were air-conditioned, but the rest of the institution was not. Although al-Wafa was the only place able and willing to provide long-term care for patients with spinal cord and other neurological injuries, the goal was to get them home, especially the children, and train the family to care for them. In reality, this did not happen often enough, and the center wound up caring for some of them indefinitely. The hospital was financially supported mainly through patient fees covered by the Ministry of Health or by insurance agencies, and partly through donations.

Al-Wafa also had an Outpatient Department that worked primarily on rheumatology. From 1996 to 1998, 2,158 people were treated on an outpatient basis for largely orthopedic problems.[135] In 2004 the outpatient clinic saw about seventy patients a day (a rate that remained constant through at least 2007), four days per week, for physiotherapy treatment.[136] Spinal cord injuries represented only about 2 percent of outpatients, indicating poor follow-up on discharged SCI patients, a problem al-Wafa was seeking to correct with help from Norwegian NGOs.[137]

In 1999 two Norwegian NGOs specializing in rehabilitation evaluated al-Wafa as a candidate organization for a comprehensive rehabilitation program they wanted to implement in the Gaza Strip. According to their evaluation report, "Initially, the three national centres chosen for this scheme were all located in the West Bank. With time, however, it became increasingly clear that access to these [specialized] services for the population of Gaza was nearly impossible. One centre located in Gaza, namely the El Wafa Medical Rehabilitation Hospital ... was therefore considered as a potential national resource and incorporated into the program."[138] In 1999 an external review found:

> Finally, concretely, concerning patients at WMRH, many positive observations must be mentioned. As far as I can judge from this limited visit, the patients, despite their complicated problems, are receiving extremely competent care. From the medical rounds and medical records you could see that patients with previously serious problems were doing surprisingly well. The staff on all levels appeared to have a good basic knowledge of their field of work. They are dedicated and work very hard. The patients appeared also to be very well taken care of by the nursing staff, even when you looked under the sheets! I saw no signs of bed sores or poor skin care, for instance, general signs of negligence. The patients were all well groomed and their bedding and clothes were well cared for and clean.[139]

To develop the rehabilitation process at al-Wafa, the Norwegians set up staff training in conjunction with the Sunnaas Rehabilitation Hospital in Norway, a collaboration that continues as of this writing.[140]

From available data including external reviews, the al-Wafa staff was overall quite strong. Although institutional policy aimed to create a multidisciplinary rehabilitation staff, constraints on finances and human resources resulted in a staff dominated by the traditional medical specialties, doctors and nurses. In 1999 there was one medical director, three full-time doctors, and two volunteer interns. "But in general the medical doctors [were] a central and strong group in the Center, who also [carried] a heavy load because of the number and complexity of the patient group."[141] By 2003 there were seven doctors on staff, but none were specialists in rehabilitation medicine.

In 1999, according to Dr. Medhat, there was a program for ongoing training in the field of rehabilitation, both in-service and externally, whereby several doctors spent six months training at the Tel Hashomer Hospital Center in Israel and another in specialist training in Austria.[142] In fact, some members of the senior medical staff told me that it was easier to link up with relevant institutions inside Israel than it was with counterpart institutions in the West Bank.

The nursing staff represented the single largest professional group. Between 1999 and 2003 the number of nurses—both male and female—increased from approximately twenty-four regular nurses (and seven nurse's aides) to fifty nurses. In 1999, turnover among nurses was high—with a more than 50 percent loss annually—because they carried an extremely heavy load with a very difficult patient population, although external reviews indicate they were "doing a very good job."[143] In addition to workload considerations, other employers, particularly the government, seemed to offer better salaries and benefits. The nurses themselves emphasized the need for better transportation to and from the center, given its location on the periphery of the city, especially for the evening and night shifts. They also asked for some staff rooms in the center, including a cafeteria.[144] Nurses were clear about the difficulty of their workload, which they felt could be eased through more and better contact with the families of their patients. Some of the female nurses were completely veiled, while others had only their heads covered.

At the time of my research, the physiotherapy group consisted of only one full-time and one part-time specialist. They worked largely with outpatients, leaving the far more challenging inpatient population to ten assistants who were receiving training at the Islamic University in Gaza (IUG). By 2003 there were twenty physiotherapists in both the In- and Outpatient Departments.[145] (In fact, by 2005 al-Wafa had plans for establishing a master's program in rehabilitation with the Islamic University and had requested assistance for this from international donors.)[146] The Norwegians reported a lack of technical aids and equipment, all of which came from Israel. Equipment was expensive, and when it broke there were no repair facilities available locally.

The occupational therapy group was also weak in 1999, with only one "very competent specialist and one assistant with a two-year rehabilitation course."[147] Yet when I viewed them working with patients, they were wonderful—lively and upbeat, often playing certain games to help patients improve their manual dexterity.[148] By 2003 there were fourteen occupational therapists working at al-Wafa in addition to a part-time speech pathologist, who worked four hours per day, and a psychiatrist who visited the center twice weekly. Later psychologist(s), social worker(s), educators, and recreational therapists, all essential to a multidisciplinary approach to rehabilitation, joined the institution.[149] However, continued limited availability of professionals in these areas has weakened the institution's ability to provide comprehensive care.[150]

Although follow-up on inpatients continued to be a problem for al-Wafa that was no doubt exacerbated by restrictions on travel and mobility that Israel imposed on Gazans after 2000, the hospital's follow-up efforts did make progress.[151] By 2003 there were two outreach programs; by 2004 discharged patients enjoyed greater follow-up owing to greater cooperation between al-Wafa and the Community Based Rehabilitation (CBR) team in Gaza. Al-Wafa also ran a four-month course for the CBR rehabilitation workers on the rehabilitation of patients with SCI and CVA among other program initiatives.[152]

As the political situation deteriorated, al-Wafa had limited if any interaction with comparable facilities in the West Bank but had many more professional contacts with foreign NGOs and other international institutions. A growing challenge involved dealing with an ever-increasing population of severely sick and injured patients who were transferred shortly after being injured or undergoing surgery, or who had severe complications including tracheostomies, chest infections, and bedsores.[153] Given its focus on rehabilitation, al-Wafa certainly did not have enough adequately trained personnel to deal with these medical problems. A significant minority of the patients, around 25 percent,[154] were severely injured, some in a vegetative state. These patients remained in the hospital's care owing to lack of nursing home facilities or other follow-up programs. In a report issued by the Sunnaas Rehabilitation Hospital in Norway, with which al-Wafa was working to improve its treatment program, the staff expressed "the need for teaching nurses and patients about prevention and treatment of bed sores, bladder training, nutrition and chest infections. They also had several patients with tracheostomy that needed close follow-up. Urologic and urodynamic examinations and advice for neurologic patients were limited.... Cognitive rehabilitation was also very limited and only recently they had employed a psychologist educated in the USA, but without experience in neuropsychology. They wanted very much to see the treatment protocols for the different patient groups. In terms of establishing a Masters program in rehabilitation in Gaza, they were interested in getting in contact with potential visiting lecturers."[155]

In conjunction with their Norwegian colleagues, al-Wafa's board of directors further proposed establishing a small mobile rehabilitation team to visit referral hospitals and teach them how to initiate early rehabilitation for patients requiring continued hospitalization because of their medical condition. The board also proposed organizing a series of lectures on rehabilitation at referral hospitals as well as visits by hospital staff to al-Wafa to better understand the rehabilitation process.[156]

By 2007 al-Wafa remained the only facility providing extensive medical care—including psychosocial support and community reintegration programs—for severely disabled Palestinians in the Gaza Strip.

That professionalism defined al-Wafa above all else is also seen in the following account by the Norwegian specialist Mette Merken (who was part of a group of eight Sunnaas consultants working with al-Wafa), who was asked to discuss issues of sexuality with SCI patients and their families (and I quote her at length):

> This was a great challenge for me and I was nervous. There were men and women with SCI from El Wafa and members of CBR programs. . . . I introduced myself and when I saw everyone I realized that their story was more important than mine [Merken also suffers from SCI and is confined to a wheelchair]. They needed to be seen by me, someone in the same situation as themselves. The first person told his story, and the second and so forth. I was touched to my heart and lost for words and wished I could spend days talking to each and everyone eye to eye and in groups. Some of them ha[d] been injured for up to 25 years; they had married and become fathers after their injury, some had taken further education after their injury and one had started [his] own business. They were great role models for the newly injured and you could see it gave them all new hope in life.
>
> In the beginning the patients were talking about bladder and bowel problems, this is a big part of sexuality as I see it. A key component of sexuality is how one perceives one's body, and therefore . . . the difficulties of hygiene [involving the] bowel and bladder play a large role after an injury. . . . Then we moved on to the topic of sexuality. I was worried that the men would feel uncomfortable with me being a woman and that they would find it hard to open up. Before we started the session I asked the men if they felt comfortable talking to me about sexuality and they were very positive to my appearance. They were very open and explicit during the session and I felt very honoured and humbled by the confidence they showed me.
>
> The main topics were: How important it is for couples to communicate to each other what they have found pleasing and satisfying; It is important to experiment and discover what is satisfying; Whatever seems satisfying and pleasurable to a couple is acceptable as long as they mutually agree; Discussed the different ways to achieve an

erection and ejaculation after SCI; Fertility and sperm quality; and Different types of sexual devices.

After I had spoken to the men, I spoke to the men's spouses together with the female nurses who showed great engagement and knowledge. Each of them presented their sexual problem and we all tried to find solutions together. Here as well, erection and ejaculation was the main topic.[157]

I should also add that some of the wives of the patients with SCI participating in Merken's group were fully covered and their faces veiled.

A Concluding Note on al-Wafa

A workshop on sexuality and on different types of devices that could improve sexual performance for men and women with spinal cord injuries is not something that one would naturally associate with an Islamic or "Hamas" institution, nor with Gazans. Such were the professionalism, dedication, and willingness of the al-Wafa staff to innovate, experiment, educate, and engage the client population. How is it that Gazans—often poor, rural, or refugees and very conservative—were willing to participate in workshops on sexuality? This admittedly surprised me. Based on my experience with al-Wafa, I would say that one reason was public trust in an institution that was highly regarded for its specialized care. But I am convinced that such participation was also due to the respect with which the staff treated patients and their families. The evident dedication to care and service was a pronounced and characteristic feature of al-Wafa (and many other ISIs), its limitations notwithstanding,[158] one that clearly meant a great deal to the community.

Why was al-Wafa designated a "Hamas" institution by the Gaza "street"? As far as I could determine, it was because some of the senior medical staff, including Dr. Medhat, were Hamas members or supporters. And while Hamas as a political movement no doubt derived political capital from the good work of al-Wafa, it seems highly unlikely—in fact, it is almost impossible for me to conceive—that Hamas had any direct role in the institution's specialized programs and initiatives.[159] And even if it did (and I of course cannot absolutely say that it did not), then one could easily argue that Hamas was playing an extremely positive and progressive role. So what then does it truly mean to be a "Hamas" institution?

On a personal note, I can attest that being "Hamas" did not equate to being "anti-Jewish." Among the many other occasions on which I learned this was one exchange I had with none other than Dr. Medhat himself. One day, Dr. Medhat was driving me back to my home in the Rimal section of Gaza City. During our discussion, the issue of my religion unexpectedly arose. He naturally assumed (as had the board at the Islamic school) that I was Christian. "No, Dr. Medhat, I am not Christian, I am Jewish." A bit nervously I continued, "I hope this is not a problem for you."

He looked surprised (but not shocked) and then a little pleased. He smiled and said, "So, you are Jewish. This is good."

"Why is it good?" I asked with a tentative smile on my face.

"So you can see for yourself who we are and what we are doing." A few minutes of silence passed between us as we wove through the side streets of Gaza. Medhat then turned to me and said, "I know there are Jews who do not support what Israel is doing. *Ahlan wa sahlan* [welcome]."

Chapter 6

ISLAMIST SOCIAL INSTITUTIONS:
KEY ANALYTICAL FINDINGS

> What we learn ... is a product of the questions we ask, the connections we make, and the historical context in which we situate [Islamic political] movements.
> —Edmund Burke III[1]
>
> A person can compromise if he has a good life.
> —Ismail Abu Shanab[2]

HAMAS REGARDS Islam as a *Minhaj al-hayat*, an all-encompassing system. What this means was explained by Sheikh Abdel Fattah Dukkhan, cofounder of Hamas, in a December 13, 1996, speech for Hamas's ninth anniversary:

> Who are we, and where are we?
> We are not a charitable organization (*Jam'iyya Khairiyya*) nor a political party, nor an objectivist or positivist group that works with limited aims. We are a new spirit at the heart of *al-umma*. The Quran nourishes this spirit, and we are the new light that shines and destroys the darkness of materialism in favour of a meeting with Allah. The clear sound from the calling (*da'wa*). This light and this sound make up the prophet's mission.... If you are asked what your calling consists [of], answer: "Our calling is Islam as brought about by the prophet ... and government is a part of that [of Islam], and freedom is a necessity of its necessity. And if you are told you are calling for revolution, say that we are calling for the truth (*al-haqq*) and for peace, which we believe in. And if you are told that you are receiving help from individual persons and groups, say: We believe only in God....
> Quietly we invoke *al-da'wa* ... but it is stronger than *al-asifa* (the storm). Our *da'wa* is limited, yet it is greater than the earth's diameter. We are carrying out a mission ... with content ... our brothers believe in ... and they are just in their actions.[3]

Hence, Hamas, like Islam, is a comprehensive system embracing all aspects of social life—politics, religion, science, culture, business, and sports. In a manner that draws directly from its origins in the Muslim Brotherhood and from al-Banna's writings, Dukkhan's speech is decidedly reformist, helping Muslims return to the true Islam, which is embodied in the needs of everyday Muslim life. "We teach Islam by example, through our actions," said Ismail Abu Shanab. In this way, embracing civil society institutions has been absolutely critical for Hamas specifically and Islam in general.

In their study of Muslim politics, Eickelman and Piscatori speak of the "invention of tradition,"[4] which lies at the heart of the Islamist challenge.[5] Writing about ISIs in Egypt, Jordan, and Yemen, Janine Clark further states:

> Islamists generally regard the period of the prophet Mohammed and his first four successors as one of ideological inspiration or guidance. Islamists' appropriation of what they believe to be this tradition includes the assertion that Islam . . . is a comprehensive system encompassing all things material, spiritual, societal, individual, political and personal. The Islamist project, therefore, is an attempt to create a seemingly seamless web of religion, politics, charity, and all forms of activism. All of these realms should reinforce one another and promote public virtue and personal piety. In this invention of tradition, the concept of *da'wa* becomes central. Beyond simply proselytizing or preaching (as traditionally defined), *da'wa* becomes the very act of "activating" Islam through deed in all spheres of life.[6]

In direct opposition to the stereotype of a proselytizing recruitment process "from womb to tomb," the ethos of civic engagement within the Islamic movement in Palestine acted as a viable and powerful alternative to militancy and political violence, "a self-conscious substitute for armed action."[7] (This occurred despite the fact that Hamas had built explicitly political institutions of mobilization, notably political parties at universities.)[8] This became apparent, especially during the Oslo period, when the weakened political leadership of Hamas was explicit about its wish to avoid any confrontation with the PNA and shifted its emphasis to the social sector.[9] ISIs were not engaged in a power struggle against the "state" (i.e., the PNA) at the grassroots level. They did not seek to oppose or undermine regime control. They neither challenged the state-society relationship as it was defined in the Palestinian context nor sought greater separation of that relationship despite their linkages—direct and indirect, strong and tenuous, or none at all—to Hamas (or Islamic Jihad), the primary oppositional political movement (see below).

To the contrary, ISIs cooperated fully and in some cases worked closely with the state, a pattern found in other contexts as well. More often than not, there was a marked disconnection and separation between social (religious and cultural) and political motivations in ISI work. (Furthermore, and seldom acknowledged, there were varying degrees of animosity between certain ISI and Hamas political officials; for some there was no natural affiliation between them.) This is why, for example, there were some formal internship programs between the Islamic University in Gaza and various PNA ministries, including the Ministry of Industry (engineering students) and the Ministry of Finance (accounting students).[10]

Indeed, most ISI staff saw themselves as professionals engaged in apolitical social service and community development work. During the Oslo period ISIs were attempting to create new opportunity spaces for their clients within the myriad constraints imposed,[11] albeit with varying degrees of success. In fact, as I have already argued, through its pronounced (and pragmatic) shift in emphasis to the social sector during the Oslo period, Hamas was seeking accommodation and coexistence with dominant (secular) institutions and social arrangements and was in no way seeking to confront or overthrow them. The social sector played the primary role in this process of accommodation and coexistence (and competition), and was a de-radicalizing and even universalizing force within the movement.

In fact, as previously noted, many Hamas officials described this shift as a return to social and cultural reform, reflecting the need to rediscover Islam and its moral relevance to society in an effort to fight the "new colonization of ideas and values"[12] and catalyze social progress. Many officials also understood that in the highly factionalized environment of the Oslo period characterized by institutional erosion, people would not tolerate further political proselytization or ideological indoctrination. A key Hamas official expressed it this way in 1999: "Increasingly, Hamas represents religion and an Islamic way of life, not political violence," affirming an observation made by Amr Hamzawy in his study of moderate Egyptian Islamists that argues for a difference in Islamist political thinking between religious ideals and the form of their realization.[13]

Hence, during this time of political weakness, civic activity undertaken within the ISI infrastructure became a key means of self-preservation for Hamas by showing itself to be responsive to its constituency's basic needs and concerns, which was crucial for its survival.

Writing in 2002, I observed:

> The definition of the threats facing Palestinian society also changed. These threats were no longer confined to political or military attacks (by Israel and the P[N]A) against Palestinian resources but also included cultural aggression against Palestinian values, beliefs and practices. Defeating the occupier became a matter of cultural preservation, building a moral consensus and Islamic value system as well as political and military power. Hence the struggle was not for power per se but for defining new social arrangements and

appropriate cultural and institutional models that would meet real social needs, and do so without violence. The idea was not to create an Islamic society but one that was more Islamic, as a form of protection against all forms of aggression.[14]

By reconciling its political ideology with a desire to secure its ties to the grass roots through a shift to the sociocultural realm, Hamas tried to become culturally indigenous, revealing a certain acceptance of pluralism at both the social and political levels. The goal was accommodation by working from "the bottom to the top, not ... the top to the bottom."[15] This point is critical, for it marks a departure from other regional contexts where a separate Islamist identity was based on the creation of a new or alternative society, itself constructed on institutions challenging those of the state. This process was all but precluded by the deforming effects of the occupation and the creation of the PNA (discussed below). Similarly, there was little evidence of any direct institutionalized links to activist political groups among the ISIs examined. In fact, a common theme among ISIs was the outright rejection of violence as an acceptable response and strategy.

This in turn begs the question, What exactly was the nature of Hamas's relationship with ISIs? One theme that emerged was that whatever linkage existed between Hamas's political and social sectors was not—and never had been—organizational but rather philosophical, one of shared principles and values.[16] Beyond the findings discussed in chapter 5, notably staff membership in or support for Hamas, the relationship, if any, remained unclear. As I have argued, for various ISIs such as those in the health care and educational sectors, the specialized nature of their work made it unlikely that Hamas could have played any direct role.

Even for those ISIs engaged in more charitable and traditional activities, including *zakat*, the work was so mundane and circumscribed as to defy the direct participation of political officials. That is why I was inclined to believe those Hamas officials, both senior and junior, who admitted they had little knowledge of the ISI universe. I could never determine with absolute certainty whether Hamas's political sector had input, direct or indirect, into project work, although it is clear it benefited politically from the work of the social sector. If Hamas did play a role, it was not obstructive or manipulative but, overall, a positive contribution to individual and community development at the time. In the final analysis, however, what is most important is not whether Hamas controlled ISIs but the character and quality of ISIs' work and their role in community life.

As such, I would argue that during the Oslo period notably, the Islamic social sector acted as a brake on violence by creating a realm increasingly (and, I came to realize, largely) devoid of politics—a view that clearly runs against mainstream conceptions—helping to legitimize the social system rather than undermine it. Accordingly, the remainder of this chapter examines the nature of social Islam in Palestine, particularly the nature of Islamist mobilization and the role of the "secular versus the sacred" in social sector work.

THE NATURE OF ISLAMIST SOCIAL ACTIVISM

That Hamas is not a monolithic movement has hopefully been made clear. Rigidly defining Hamas as violent, antimodern, and radical ignores the fact that Hamas's fundamental impulse is political and nationalist, not religious, which has accounted for its pragmatism and flexibility. Similarly ignored are the other, larger dynamics of the movement that are decidedly nonviolent and civic-oriented, dynamics that reject the idea of a fixed inner logic of Islam and operate instead "on a mass level driven by the actions and concerns of ordinary Muslims."[17] As other analysts have argued, Islamic political and social movements emerge out of specific local contexts and political environments that are critical to understanding their evolution and development.[18] In the unique case of Palestine, Israel's consistent assault on Palestinian national and community existence has been the defining factor shaping Hamas's somewhat discontinuous trajectory but, as argued, not the only one.

In his exceptional study of Muslim politics, Robert Hefner argues three key points that are relevant for understanding the nature of the Islamist social project in Palestine. First, although Muslim politics are "informed by the conviction that religious scholars, the *ulama* . . . have the right and duty to make sure that all major developments in politics and society are in conformity with God's commands," this does not necessarily or automatically translate into an "imperative for theocratic rule."[19] As discussed in chapter 3, religious scholars have an important but limited role in the governing of society, and "notwithstanding certain utopian Islamisms to the contrary, real-and-existing Muslim polities are not characterized by a seamless fusion of religion and state or a dictatorship of 'clerics' over a supine civil society."[20] Indeed, in my own research many Islamist officials lectured me on the differences between Hamas, for example, and the Taliban and other extremist fundamentalist groups, whose essentialized and restricted interpretation of Islam was explicitly denounced, along with its political and social implications. However, I also found highly intolerant interpretations of Islam (particularly as it regarded social behavior), notably among individual teachers in some Islamic schools.

Many (but not all) of my respondents argued for an understanding of Islam that was broader and, as Hefner puts it, more "diffusely cultural."[21] Muslim politics are seen to operate not only on a popular level but on a more elite level, where "religious scholars respond to modern problems within the normative horizons of the *shari'a* and Islamic tradition as a whole."[22]

Second, this leads to another point made by Hefner with particular relevance for this study: the attempt to make contemporary Muslim politics more pluralist, adaptive, participatory, and democratic, a pattern seen among some of the ISIs discussed in the previous chapter. This reshaping is necessitated by the inability of the state in many parts of the Muslim world to adequately meet the social and economic needs of its constituents, who then demand alternative sources of support. Furthermore, "mass education, literacy, and a growing network of mosques and Islamic schools combined to strengthen the determination of ordinary Muslims to exercise choice and take charge of their faith,"[23] a form of "democracy in the vernacular" that underscores the importance of the grassroots level—that is, civic associations and the community itself—in the processes of pluralist participation and democratization, however incremental, however imperfect.

Third, Hefner points to the issue of mobilization: the efforts of competing groups (secular and religious) to enhance their influence by "forging pacts or alliances with influential actors and agencies in the state."[24] This follows from the first two, particularly the notion of expanded local participation. According to Hefner, "[m]obilizational initiatives like these usually begin at the local level, with efforts to bring together like-minded actors in associations dedicated to some social, religious, or welfare task," where Muslim organizations "sometimes enjoy a distinctive advantage over their secular rivals."[25] However, here the Islamic movement in Palestine has not been as successful as is commonly assumed.

Given these three factors, which I found to varying degrees in Palestine at the social level—the lack of a theocratic imperative in favor of a broader and more culturally based interpretation of Islam; the value assigned by many ISIs to a notion of civic decency that was informed by a more participatory and, for some, pluralist approach; and the problems of building alliances both among ISIs and between ISIs and secular associations—one must ask, Did Islamism in Palestine ever acquire mobilizing power within the social sector for either political or violent activity?

Islamist Mobilization: Success or Failure?

Successes

From the time I began my research in Palestine twenty-five years ago, I could never find any appreciable popular support for a political agenda based on Islam or for the creation of an Islamic state and society. There has never really been an Islamic base among Palestinians (although Hamas has always had a certain but limited ideological following), since religion never served as an organizational framework for achieving national and political goals. As Lapidus points out, "In Palestine, no unifying Muslim symbol emerged.... Islamic symbols were imperfectly related to organizational structures. They failed either to mobilize or to reflect structural conditions."[26] Hamas's successes in the 2004 and 2005 municipal elections and in the 2006 legislative elections do not contradict this finding but rather affirm it, since these victories occurred on the basis of a secular (or pragmatic) rather than religious agenda. In this regard, the election of Hamas arguably illustrated the failure of its political ideology.

Palestinians have long been secular, opposing any combination of religion and politics. I distinctly remember an interview I had with a family in the Bureij refugee camp during the first Intifada. When I entered their home and sat to begin the interview, I removed the *hijab* I was wearing. At the end, as I was preparing to leave, I put my *hijab* back on. The family patriarch approached me and said, "When we have our state, you will not have to wear that." There was no hostility in his voice, just a simple, almost gentle statement of fact. Admittedly, that was over twenty years ago, and much has changed in Gaza's political environment since then, but the general sentiment was not atypical at the time.

Yet, despite the overwhelmingly secular orientation of Palestinians, Islamic activism—as seen in the work of ISIs—has long been regarded by many Western observers as an exception because of its religious and cultural component. The prevailing assumption (as seen in the recent U.S. court decisions) is that it is natural—virtually axiomatic—for Muslims to support a political (and, inevitably, violent) agenda based on Islam; consequently, according to this logic, there is little that distinguishes the militant from the reformist since they are both part of the same egregious whole, which does not differentiate between Islamic political, social, and military institutions. Seen through this lens, clients who merely engage with ISIs are politicized, incited, and recruited into religious fanaticism ("drawn into participation ... as the result of their embeddedness in associational networks that render them 'structurally available' for protest activity"[27]) and then inexorably drawn to commit terrible acts. As Janine Clark points out, "The scholarly literature depicts Islamic associations, including their clinics, as fronts for the proselytization of the poor to Islamism. Even if this is not done directly, the mere successful provision of services is seen by many scholars as propaganda which increases the number of adherents—particularly among the poor—to the Islamist movement both in the streets and at the ballot box."[28]

As the court cases against Islamic charities in the United States have shown, the issue of recruitment has been successfully used against ISIs. Yet the Hamas leadership has long asserted (and studies have argued) the exact opposite: that Hamas separates and compartmentalizes the social, political, and military sectors in order not to jeopardize the social, given its centrality to the movement. According to the ICG, "Hamas seeks to derive prestige and political profit from social welfare activism precisely by maintaining the professionalism and integrity of such institutions rather than politicizing them. It appears to understand better than others that if schools and medical clinics developed a reputation as recruitment centres, and services were provided in exchange for support, the crown jewels of the Islamist movement would be irretrievably debased in exchange for short-term gains of dubious value."[29]

While this argument is certainly plausible, it fails to address other and, in my view, more important factors that precluded the translation of social services into a mobilized and activist constituency based on political Islam.

Perhaps a logical place to start is with a question: What did ISIs as a whole constitute, and what were they attempting to provide and create through their programmatic work? Unlike its Egyptian counterpart, the ISI sector in Palestine was not a cohesive or integrated one, intrasectorally or intersectorally. Rather, it was highly decentralized, with individual ISIs operating rather autonomously, and oriented far more to the localities they served (and in which they often resided) than to any higher, centralizing authority, social or political. Within the sector, competition and disagreement clearly existed. In the kindergartens run by the Mujamma, for example, which were closely associated with Hamas, the Islamic curriculum taught was not standardized with that of other Islamic schools run by the Jam'iyya or the House of the Book and Sunna among others but was institutionally specific. (In some cases ISIs would share aspects of their curriculum, as the House of the Book and Sunna did with the Young Women's Muslim Society, or would refer to *waqf* guidelines, but these appeared to be the exceptions.) In fact, Abu Hisham told me on more than one occasion that he considered the Mujamma in particular too political and unprepared for social work. He also revealed that various Islamic organizations had long discussed dividing and coordinating their charitable work geographically:

- Al-Jam'iyya: Jabalya and Shati camps
- Al-Salah: middle camps
- *Zakat* committee: Gaza City
- The House of the Book and Sunna and al-Rahma: Khan Younis and Rafah

These discussions ultimately failed owing to intense interorganizational competition.

The decentralized, autonomous nature of ISI operations was also expressed, to varying degrees, in institutional philosophy. As Yahya Musa, then head of the Hamas-affiliated Hizb al-Khalas Political Bureau, argued: "All Islamic parties work under the umbrella of Islam from which they all emanate. [They] start at the same point but their differences derive from their interpretation of the Quran and Hadith. The Islam implemented during Mohammed's life is different from the Islam implemented today or should be. Islam should be implemented [adapted or fashioned] according to current conditions. Other groups have a more literal interpretation and want to separate out from current reality. This is the difference between the letter of the law and the spirit of the law."[30]

For some ISI officials, this meant that community interest had to take precedence over the text; if the two conflicted, then the text had to be reinterpreted. This points to the need for flexibility in the interpretation of Islamic law that al-Banna described and the freedom from—or even rejection of—tradition if it impedes progress. In her research on Islamist women of Hamas (in Hizb al-Khalas), for example, Islah Jad found that "the text does not prohibit" was a recurrent theme in her work.[31] Hence, it was no surprise to find clear differences in philosophy and approach between the *Haj* of the HBS, Abu Hisham of the Qatar Charitable Society, Dr. Medhat of al-Wafa, and Dr. Duweiq, who was also associated with the Hebron-based al-Ahli Hospital (see below). This further reflects some important themes in the theoretical literature on Islam and civil society: that (political) authority ultimately derives legitimacy from civil society, not government, and that power depends on securing popular trust rather than religious sanction.

Furthermore, the fact that I often found myself in a position of knowing more about other ISI programs than many of my ISI interviewees strongly suggested that their orientation was proximate, often restricted to the people and places they were serving, a product of local community ties and networks, and institution based. The only apparent exceptions were specialized organizations such as al-Rahma or al-Wafa, which, by virtue of providing relatively unique services, drew nonlocal clients.

Although inter-ISI cooperation occurred, it typically concerned pragmatic bureaucratic coordination—for example, preventing the duplication of welfare benefits, since double-dipping was not uncommon (itself suggestive of a lack of ideological affiliation or loyalty among clients or the irrelevance of political ideology when it came to need).[32] Indeed, the poor would use as many facilities—Islamic and secular—as were available to them, regardless of ideological preference, and would shop around for services. Likewise, cooperation between Islamic and non-Islamic institutions was not common; when it occurred, it seemed to entail local ISIs linking more with international rather than local, secular organizations (although the latter did occur). In certain respects, and contrary to popular assumption, ISIs seemed to have had the strongest direct institutional linkages with the PNA, not with each other.

That ISI work was localized in nature was also supported by the absence of a defining vision of social, economic, or political change that might have guided programmatic initiatives in the Islamic social sector as a whole. Instead, ISI programs, like those of most Palestinian institutions, were individually determined by each ISI; typically by the director or board of directors, in accordance with the institution's mandate and the perceived needs of its constituency (and sometimes inviting beneficiary input).

With its decentralized structure and localized focus, the Islamic social sector was able to achieve certain objectives, but it failed to achieve others. On the positive side, it became a recognized (and relatively autonomous) actor within the community it served, an actor that aimed to rehabilitate the collective through a strengthened sense of neighborliness and volunteerism (which was high in ISIs[33]). The social sector inculcated a sense of community consciousness and freedom of association, particularly with regard to the functioning of civil associations, where authority was, to a marked extent, not repressive. The ISIs' strong orientation to their surrounding community meant that service delivery was often face-to-face and deeply embedded in local cultural norms that did not generally discriminate according to constituents' ideological vision or social class. In this way, many ISIs were considered tolerant and civil, even flexible. This, for example, was how Abu Hisham worked and how the *zakat* committees operated, lending a deeply human and personal dimension to the patron-client relationship—concern for the human being was clear—that was necessary and appreciated but not always sufficient for perceived program success. It was, however, one important factor that distinguished ISIs from their secular counterparts, according to many respondents, and one important way ISIs forged (rather than dictated) a social contract (of the sort al-Banna described) with the communities they served.

Because of this and possibly also because of the local orientation of staff, as noted above, ISI programs—whether traditional or developmental, successful or unsuccessful—were often perceived by clients as being part of the local human community rather than part of an Islamist ideology (whether local, regional, or international) or political party. This was particularly true of al-Ahli Hospital in Hebron, a well-known Islamic institution (affiliated with the Patients' Friends Society) serving the southern part of the West Bank. The 120-bed hospital[34] was a modern, beautiful, highly professional, and comfortable facility, employing forty doctors and approximately one hundred male and female nurses (both Islamic and secular) in 1999 (it subsequently established several clinics throughout the city). The hospital adhered to certain Islamic rules such as conservative dress for women, including the *hijab*, and segregation of the sexes. However, this did not appear to present a problem; on the contrary, it appeared to create a feeling of belonging and connectedness. When I spoke with patients and staff, there was a pronounced sense of pride in the hospital, a sense of ownership and responsibility, something that was not typical in Palestinian society.

In fact, Islamist social institutions were commonly defined (and judged) as such not by the overt practice of Islam necessarily but by the niches they worked in, the quality of their work, and the way in which they treated their clients. In this regard, the priority was service provision through organizational outreach rather than through intellectual output. Hence, Islam was not defined rigidly or literally (and not necessarily in accordance with Western stereotypes) but in a variety of ways that had more to do with the transmission of values. This allowed for the adoption of socially innovative programs where prescription, rationality, and reason—enlightened *ijtihad*—played a marked role.[35]

Another feature of ISI success was the creation of a framework and a venue within which the powerless and excluded were given what Hefner, Esposito, and Voll refer to as a certain degree of choice and participation,[36] underlining the importance of consensus (*ijma'*) and consultation (*shura*). In the Palestinian context, the capacity to choose and participate was part of an ongoing effort among ISIs to empower individuals pragmatically, notably women, creating consistent, secure, and accessible public spaces in which they could be taught how to access resources, share experiences, seek and give advice, or simply have a place where they could experience social solidarity (what the Islamic modernists referred to as the virtues of reform and self-strengthening). This gave women especially a certain sense of self-worth and satisfaction, feelings that were seldom affirmed in larger society. This may not seem like a lot, and its effects may have been limited, but in an environment as constrained and difficult as Gaza's, it was important and something the Islamic sector understood perhaps better than any other. It also helped clients understand the utility and importance of voluntary belonging, a characteristic feature of an Islamic civil society.

One powerful illustration of client inclusion was found in Gaza's al-Ihsan Association for Disabled Children, which ran kindergarten and rehabilitation programs. In January 1999, al-Ihsan started a kindergarten program for thirty-one disabled children and enlisted their mothers in its programmatic initiatives. As a condition for accepting a child into the program, al-Ihsan required the child's mother to volunteer at the institution to cook, clean, teach (if qualified), and serve as a teacher's assistant in the classroom. Mothers were also asked to share their experiences raising disabled children with one another and with the teaching staff, giving mothers a greater stake in the education of their children and empowering them as a source of information and assistance. Although this integrative process was uneven, al-Ihsan was able to create a support network for mothers who faced enormous stress at home on top of being socially ostracized because of their children.[37]

At the Jam'iyya, which ran thirty-five kindergartens throughout the Gaza Strip and considered its program to be the best, director Bahar described in great detail (although I did not myself see) several community outreach initiatives the Jam'iyya ran as part of its kindergarten program, which he considered critical to its quality: regular meetings between mothers and school officials (three "main" meetings throughout the year in addition to monthly meetings); lectures on parenting; cultural activities designed to bring mothers and their children together in an enjoyable, relaxed setting and to bring mothers, teachers, and administrators together as well; organized meetings between mothers and teachers designed to address children's problems; community meetings between school officials and parents designed to solicit their input on kindergarten activities; and invitations to parents to visit kindergarten classes and observe.[38]

Similarly the Bethlehem Charitable Society (BCS) had a program for assisting the poor by teaching them how to access the health system and receive needed services. The BCS also started a commercial kitchen and would hold training sessions for mothers on how to use the kitchen and cook in industrial batches, soliciting input from the mothers and thereby increasing their role in the cooking program as well as their chances for employment. Indeed, this policy of client inclusion created nothing less than an enlarged public domain for improved (rather than new) forms of association—e.g., counseling sessions; teacher training workshops; arts and literacy classes; parenting seminars; computer classes; reading contests; and cultural activities involving mothers and children, and mothers and teachers. Most significantly, these associational forms were accountable, honest, respectful, and (perhaps most critical of all) ordinary and coherent, providing a realm devoid of politics, ideology, and factionalism (which was ostracized at the time).

Indeed, the elements of choice and participation were important parts of an ongoing effort among ISIs to (re-)create a sense of the ordinary in an environment—characterized by Israeli occupation and PNA control—that was anything but. In this sense, I believe, many ISIs implicitly understood that what unites people is far more powerful than what divides them. This meant focusing on people's everyday concerns by embedding programs in local norms and understandings. It meant making Islam an ordinary rather than an exceptional (or violent) part of their lives. In Gaza especially, re-creating the ordinary—and interpreting the ordinary—meant normality and the factual, the attempt to carve out a prosaic realm where everyday activities could be carried out and, perhaps most distinguishing, carried out well. For some ISIs the provision of quality services also meant client dissent. And while the focus would sometimes be on dress, proper conduct, and other cultural practices, it was a realm where clients would typically expect a high(er) degree of quality, efficacy, care, accountability, and recourse no matter how mundane or complex the programmatic task. Again, performance, not the application of Islamic rules, mattered most.

In this regard, Diane Singerman observes, "The Islamist movement reshapes how people understand themselves as creators and practitioners of their world."[39] In Gaza especially, this reshaping may have assumed somewhat different dimensions than it did in Egypt or Yemen, but the principle remained the same. At its core, this reshaping strove to strengthen Gazans' sense of personal and social identity and agency, making the individual a force for positive change, to borrow from Sa'id Hawwa. Hence, while religious identity was important, it was but one of many identities needing protection and not necessarily the primary one, recalling the value of the mundane as well as the divine articulated by al-Ghannouchi.

In this sense, everyday practice was not linked to religion per se (although the need to forge a Muslim identity was important and varied in intensity among ISIs) but to clear and defined norms and standards (which did not exist in larger society, especially under the PNA) that people— both clients and staff—were expected to uphold. This, too, accounted for the almost universal and explicit emphasis on professional qualifications over political or religious conviction as a criterion for hiring ISI staff and on the provision of quality services. In fact, most interviewees indicated that there was no explicit policy against hiring Christians or people considered secular (although religious Muslims were preferred all things being equal), pointing to a certain acceptance of pluralism within ISIs.

One clear example of professionalism was the al-Anwar al Ibrahimiyya Library for Children, a project of the Islamic Charitable Society of Hebron that opened in April 1999. When I visited the library during the summer of 1999, it was a brand-new, beautiful, modern facility: clean, polished, aesthetic, air-conditioned, and inviting (with comfortable tables and chairs, marble floors, and soothing carpets). The library had 12,000 books (which had increased to 17,500 by 2008), on topics traditionally covered in school (e.g., philosophy, arts, logic, science, religion, Arabic and world literature, English language) and others (e.g., health/personal hygiene, cooking, handicrafts, international holidays, fairy tales). Stacks of books, many new, were neatly arranged by grade level. The entire library was computerized, and every borrower inputted and given a photo ID. In the first forty days, 403 people registered, most from the Hebron area. The director, Mohammed Eid Misk, told me that the library received three hundred to four hundred visitors daily, including an average of two or three delegations of children. The place was orderly and appeared to be extremely efficient. People respected the rules and behaved accordingly.

Although the library was open to the public, it targeted children aged six to eighteen. During my visit, the library was filled with boys and girls reading together at tables and sitting on floors between the stacks. The library was very much meant to serve the public in myriad ways, for example, as a venue for meetings of local library directors (secular and Islamic); as a venue for discussion forums for local school principals; and as a destination for children in (non-Islamic) summer camps.

The facility offered services unique in the Hebron area, with an emphasis on reading, computer literacy, and English language training. In addition to the main library, I saw a sixty-person-capacity meeting/study hall; a film theater; administrative offices; meeting and conference rooms; and a large room for computer training classes. The computer center was an integral part of the library. It held sixteen computers (with plans for thirty to forty), each with two seats. Four times daily, fifty-minute classes were held. Demand was high, and plans to expand to evening classes were under way. A separate room was provided for English language instruction. There were three classes for boys and three for girls, who were taught separately (with the girls attending in the evening every other day!). I sat in on one beginner-level class for high school students that used cassettes and videos from a series called "Hello America."

The library employed four people who were hired through the ICS and four male and female volunteers. The women dressed conservatively. A few of the walls held framed sayings from the Quran that related to learning and education, including one with Allah's ninety-nine names and another that said "Allah, teaches the Quran, created man and taught him knowledge." Eid Misk, who had taught high school geography for twenty-four years (eighteen of them in a secular school for girls) and with the ICS for ten years, was well known locally for his teaching skills. The enthusiasm expressed (to me) by the children and adults and the pride they derived from this facility were undeniable.

In general, the emphasis on standards and professionalism not only elevated the ISI; it elevated clients and their sense of dignity and self-worth, which was arguably more critical, given the context, than inculcation of any beliefs or identity. Hakan Yavuz, in his research on Turkey, refers to this process as the creation of new "opportunity spaces," within which "social movements can form shared identities, resist state hegemony, or change the meaning of everyday life."[40] But unlike other contexts including Turkey, the Islamists in Palestine did not have organized or explicit strategies for expanding these opportunity spaces to meaningfully restructure daily life or to produce real social or political change. Rather, their approach constituted no less than a search for meaning in a society characterized by a culture of humiliation, degradation, alienation, detachment, and exclusion. During this time especially, ISIs seized on this and were effective, even innovative at times; ultimately, they were limited by the severe political and economic constraints of the environment (see below).

The emphasis on the value and dignity of the human being and the individual's role in the renewal of Islam often meant closer personal attention for clients. And while this was framed in religious and cultural terms, it did not appear to be constrained by those terms. This is why, for example, al-Wafa could organize workshops on enhancing the sexual performance of patients with spinal cord injuries. Al-Wafa's work (and also al-Rahma's) certainly speaks to the call for making Islam more relevant to the modern requirements of the Muslim community, an approach that allows individual and collective reformulations of Islamic law according to social need and social change. This freedom from tradition points to a related feature of most ISI work: the important, if not dominant, role of nonideological factors in programmatic initiatives and in securing and maintaining a client base. The moderate Islamic discourse, as articulated by Shafiq and al-Ghannouchi, argues for the revitalization of Islamic institutions through greater openness, engagement, and compromise, emphasizing, in good part, creativity and innovation. This represents an attempt—and at times a struggle—to balance cultural and religious renewal with the need to accommodate the changing realities of life, allowing, in al-'Awwa's words, civil institutions to become critical instruments of social action. This concept can be traced back to the earliest Islamic community, which exhibited a capacity for developing and sustaining institutions to defend individual and collective rights against oppressive state mechanisms both domestic and foreign. According to El-Affendi, "[T]he strength of Muslim solidarity has manifested itself chiefly in opposing oppression, not in oppressing individuals."[41]

Although one could find individual exceptions, the majority of ISI clients I spoke with across institutions and programs indicated a range of reasons for choosing Islamic institutions, none of which were ideological: quality, better and more personal customer service, honesty, higher moral standards, courtesy, proximity, lower fees, personal connection with the staff (intimacy), referral, and accessibility. (Some people indicated that the ISI was not necessarily their first choice.) In his study of "Hamas" sports clubs, Michael Jensen writes:

> When asking the players why they had chosen to play in an Islamic sports club I got a variety of answers. To generalize there were three categories of answers. One group of players told me that they were

in the Islamic club because this club was able to fulfill their ambitions on the ground as the club offered them time to play during the matches, which was not the case in their former clubs. Other players explained their presence from a purely religious point of view, while the last group was playing there due to the proximity to their homes. From the interviews conducted it was evident that non-ideological conditions [were] of significant importance, and for a number of the interviewed it is fair to speak of a kind of consumption of clubs. They shift between clubs in order to fulfill their personal ambitions on the ground. Also of interest to point out is that not only are a number of new players coming to the club for this reason, but a significant number of players also left the club due to exactly the same reasons.[42]

Some ISI clients clearly sought services that conformed with certain Islamic practices, such as segregation of the sexes in medical facilities, properly veiled female staff, and availability of female nurses and doctors for women patients (as in al-Wafa or al-Ahli hospital). However, such expectations often and, I would argue, typically reflected conformity with cultural/social norms rather than any desire for an alternative religious model. In this regard, ISIs practiced Islam in different and somewhat inconsistent ways. Some, such as the House of the Book and the Sunna, were no doubt strict and literal in their interpretation and implementation of Islamic rules and regulations, demanding conformity from clients rather than vice versa; others, such as al-Ahli Hospital in Hebron, were clearly less so. Prayer and proper dress, while common practices even in some secular institutions (secular does not necessarily mean irreligious), were generally not rigidly imposed on clients, because to do so would have been potentially alienating.

Furthermore, ISIs were not uniquely "Islamic" in terms of their organizational structure or functions, which resembled those of any other social institutions. More often than not, there was little that distinguished ISIs as appreciably or singularly "Islamic." In fact, both clients and staff often identified an ISI as being "Islamic" more for its mission of charity and emphasis on serving the poor, stronger sense of internal solidarity and teamwork, high degree of volunteerism, and kinder, more personal manner of dealing with beneficiaries than for anything else. This "invisible process of building social capital"[43] was in part what Islamic (and Islamist) officials referred to when they spoke about their "different way" of approaching their work.

By blending religion, culture, and service with everyday life, the Islamist social sector was creating a public institutional structure that cut across cleavages of class, gender, religiosity, and setting (urban/rural), allowing people, largely the poor and marginal, to engage each other cooperatively and constructively (without concern to political affiliation), creating a sense of solidarity and strengthened sense of community. In this way, ISIs could exercise legitimate social authority that was important for the betterment of the community.

Overall, ISIs did not strongly promote a political or ideological agenda but one that was more cultural, situated within the context of shared norms and values. They engaged in what various Islamist intellectuals referred to as the moral reeducation of the individual and the articulation of a moral-ethical civilizing project. To a large extent—and in a critical departure from the Islamic political sector—social Islam was not presented (or perceived) in the language of opposition but in the language of morality, civic activity, and indigenous modernization—civility. Thus, ISI clients typically were not seeking or motivated by factional affiliation or political ideology but rather the better provision of quality services. It also should not be forgotten that ISIs had to compete with other providers such as the PNA, UNRWA, and secular NGOs, and sometimes they emerged wanting. Some clients were satisfied with ISI services while others clearly were not. The ISI universe was not perfect by any means and was subject to varying degrees of client criticism, but it did assign a clear value to the role of the individual, the importance of the community, and the value of creativity and experimentation.

Although ISIs engaged the community in the ways described above, they also placed limitations on the forms of engagement. For example, I could find no evidence that clients were actively recruited or even encouraged to join the governing bodies of ISIs or otherwise involve themselves in ISI operations (whether clients would have agreed to this is a separate issue). This is further evidence of a point already made: that ISIs were not attempting to reorganize society (or the polity) according to an Islamic model that would challenge or confront the governing authority politically or violently, creating a separate, antagonistic, and counterstatist Islamic social realm. Rather, ISIs actively cooperated with the PNA, seeking to complement "state" services and in some instances help improve them. They were clearly situated within and accommodated to the social and political status quo, where nonviolence and gradualism were prominent values.

Hence, ISIs—and Hamas—could gain greater legitimacy within, and themselves affirm the legitimacy of, the social (and political) system.[44] In this sense, there was little evidence within the Islamist social sector for what Yavuz compellingly describes as a separation of "state" and society whereby the latter sought autonomy from the former, or an "oppositional Muslimness" that called for the embrace of Islam to challenge policies of the center.[45] (Another reason Yavuz's model does not work in Palestine is because the traditional militant Kemalist secularism of the Turkish state and elites is not a factor.) Indeed, such a center arguably did not even exist in the Palestinian community. Consequently, I could find equally little evidence of a direct, organized, and systemic linkage between social/charitable work and the promulgation of violence. The notion that ISIs were used as a channeling process to socialize and recruit the perpetrators of violent acts against Israel was not plausible despite a relationship between Hamas and the ISI sector.

Failures

To what extent, therefore, did ISIs facilitate—directly or indirectly—the potential expansion of an Islamist worldview or mobilizing network, as they did in Egypt or Yemen?

Informal networks, on which Islamist movements often depend, typically arise in a context of political repression, exclusion, and marginalization that forces citizens to organize informally, forming networks that become crucial to advancing their interests and to the formation of a collective identity. These networks, in turn, generate larger group solidarities, political and otherwise. There is no doubt that, in the Palestinian context, people rely on networks because they have no rights or protection of any kind, a reality that is often ignored and misunderstood. Writing about Egypt, Singerman observes:

> Western analyses of Islamist movements often dismiss the key role played by political exclusion in the region, which obscures not only the role of networks in movements themselves but also the weight and legitimacy they carry within society at large.... As political activists in Islamist movements grow bolder and more organized, informal networks are essential for activities such as mobilizing supporters, raising funds, promoting symbolic protest, smuggling arms, hiding and feeding people, eluding the police, dispersing propaganda and organizing mass protests.[46]

Informal networks create networks of meaning—political, social, and otherwise—that given communities embrace as their own, binding people together in new, unregulated, and seemingly invisible ways.[47] This networked universe of associational life remains outside the surveillance of the state, assuming a political meaning and utility that in effect creates a parallel site of political life that connects different individuals, families, and communities to centers of power and contestation.

By aggregating the interests and demands of individuals and groups in this way, "many, though not all, of the constituents of a network know and trust each other, and these networks can be easily exploited for purposes of resisting the state and its institutions." This networked world in turn explains "the emergence and organizational power of [Islamist] movements and also the capabilities of such extreme elements as al-Qaeda in executing complicated, costly, and ultimately horrific attacks."[48] Furthermore, the activities that take place in this informal realm are technically illegal, since they take place outside an official sphere of licensing and regulation: "Networks [also] facilitate access to knowledge and resources, whether in the sense of finding the right people who can present one's case to the police or housing authorities, directing poor women and men to someone who will initiate an informal savings association on their behalf, or finding a cleric to advise young people on morality, marriage or religious observance."[49]

Although such informal networks of associational life existed in Palestine, as they did elsewhere in the region, they remained relatively opaque and inaccessible to me despite many anecdotal illustrations. For example, there were groups of committed people—some of them former employees of ISIs shut down by the PNA—who took it upon themselves to help identify those in need by collecting donations on their behalf; working through local *zakat* committees and mosques, they would distribute assistance to the poor. The Islamic committees in Gaza's refugee camps had affiliated women's groups—the majority volunteers—who worked with refugee women on a range of health and education-related issues. New volunteers typically learned about these groups and their work in the mosque and from other participants. Some societies such as the Bethlehem Charitable Society had as their director a professor of Islamic Law at al-Quds University, and no doubt this connection spawned others. The business contacts of the members and supporters of the BCS as well as other charitable institutions were no doubt important for building networks able to provide a range of services both formally and informally.

In the economic sector, networks appeared to be important for factory owners, particularly with regard to finding trustworthy employees, who often came through personal referrals or were friends of the family; employees typically came from the local neighborhood in which the factory was situated. As discussed, networks also appeared to be essential for giving Islamic businesses a certain competitive edge vis-à-vis their secular counterparts. There seemed to be some internal coordination (or informal agreement), albeit imperfect, among certain businessmen over market share for specific products in order to minimize competition and maintain, if not increase, profit margins. There also appeared to be an internal mechanism for shipping and distribution and for cost sharing or subsidization that also enhanced competitiveness.

It became increasingly clear that networks helped businesspeople maintain their position, minimize risk, and soften the impact of losses when they did occur. As argued in chapter 5, these individuals were not attempting to build an Islamic economy or alter the environment according to an Islamic economic model but trying to find a way of enhancing their leverage and competitiveness by using the networks available to them as part of the Islamic movement. The principal imperative was *economic*, not *ideological*.

In attempting to assess the political utility of these networks in Palestine and the potential for their mobilization around an Islamist political agenda, the crucial question is not whether these networks existed but how instrumental they could possibly be in an environment as small, controlled, constrained, and heavily monitored as Palestine's (particularly Gaza's), subject to a range of economic, social, political, military, and bureaucratic restrictions imposed both by Israel and the PNA. The "state" resources used against Hamas were considerable, especially during the Oslo period, and were successful in diminishing it. Many ISIs described the heavily monitored environment in which they worked, and most shunned any discussion of politics (although there could be many reasons for this). And while political, military, and bureaucratic repression against citizens (and civil society), let alone Islamists, can be found in several regional contexts, Palestinians alone must contend with the absence of sovereignty, the denial of national identity, and continued occupation.

Given their strong and intimate ties to the local community and the personal manner in which services were delivered, the potential for Islamists to use already existing social networks created around ISIs for purposes of political mobilization appeared to be considerable. Matthew Levitt argues—and officialdom in the United States believes—that through the provision of real benefits to Palestinians, ISIs have successfully recruited Palestinians to the Islamist cause, effectively buying support for Hamas and its more militant agenda. Of course, for this to happen new priorities for, and ideological dedication to, activism would have had to be created that framed activism as an obligation—moral or otherwise—"demanding self-sacrifice and unflinching commitment to the cause of religious transformation."[50] This would have required that the individual (or family) replace narrow self-interest and priorities with those of the Islamist movement generally and Hamas specifically, something that, I argue, did not occur to any appreciable degree in the Palestinian context. (It should also be noted that despite the fact that the West Bank and Gaza receive among the highest rates of foreign aid per capita in the world, "which dwarfs the funds at Hamas's disposal," support for Hamas has clearly increased over time, suggesting "that allegiance and support for the Islamic movement transcends gratitude for charitable and social services.")[51] In fact, Hamas was, for the most part, unable to translate social service into political mobilization, and there were several reasons for their failure.

First, if there is anything that is particular to Islamic movements worldwide, it is the political context in which they function. In the case of Palestine, the distinguishing factor of Palestinian life is Israel's policy of occupation and dispossession and attack on Palestinian national collective life, which has always been the primary grievance among the Palestinian people. The occupation, which is one expression of Israel's policy, has imposed the same constraints and restrictions on Islamic movements and institutions as it has on secular ones. People may reciprocate the benefits they receive from a political movement by supporting that movement—Islamist and/or non-Islamist—but this support is always mediated by the absence of sovereignty, statehood, rights, and freedom. As many Palestinians argued to me, identity creation along Islamic lines may provide a source of succor for some, but in the absence of a national identity and the rights and privileges associated with it, such an Islamic identity offers little compensation.

Alberto Melucci argues that collective action is rooted in identity construction.[52] Yet, among Palestinians as a whole, identity was fundamentally defined and consolidated by the concept of exclusion (political, economic, and social), not ideology—Islamist or otherwise. Hamas (and later Fatah) failed to understand this or assign it sufficient value. (Furthermore, under PNA rule and the divisiveness it produced, the meaning of exclusion became more confused and uncertain.) This is one reason why Hamas ultimately failed to produce, as Melucci says, "a shared moral investment in a set of issues"[53] and new, distinctive ties of solidarity based on religious or cultural practice (e.g., proper Islamic dress for women—especially veiling, segregation of the sexes in Islamic clinics, attending a school attached to a mosque, attending Quranic study classes, making the pilgrimage to Mecca) that proceed from that.

Rather, the Islamists failed the collective "we"[54] and were unable to mobilize people (politically or religiously) on a large scale based on an activist (let alone violent) interpretation of Islam. To the contrary, Hamas had to broaden its definition of Islam and "Muslimness" in order to claim and maintain as large a number of adherents as possible without alienating them at a time when Hamas's political survival was more in doubt. Indeed, during the Oslo period, the political leadership of Hamas conformed (in a manner) to Palestinians rather than demand that Palestinians conform, ideologically, to them (in stark contrast to the situation that exists today). By this I mean that Islam or what it meant to be a "sound Muslim" was broadened to incorporate a variety of cultural and political modes including support for Hamas. Rather than ideologize Islam, Hamas did the opposite—de-ideologized Islam in the name of political survival—shifting its attention to social sector work as its primary focus and widening the scope of what it meant to support Hamas.

As one senior Hamas official explained in 1999, "Everyone who is religious is Hamas and anyone who teaches Islamic values furthers Hamas's goals." Similarly, Abu Shanab explained, "those who support [the] idea [of Hamas] are Hamas supporters.... Hamas is a way of life and a belief. [Hamas members are] [p]eople who believe in Islam as a faith, a constitution and a way of life ... without membership in the [organization]."[55]

Thus, not only was Hamas unable to impose its political agenda on the majority of Palestinians; it was prevented from doing so by the occupation. The Islamist leadership offered an idiosyncratic view of Islamism that understood the central importance of secularism (not religious nationalism) in the lives of most Palestinians and pursued what Amr Hamzawy describes as the secularization of religious discourse. This is one reason why the work of the Islamist social sector was not automatically associated with an ideological, Islamist agenda, a fact that challenges the notion of an Islamist project at the social level. This also is why I found no real Islamic model being followed in any of the ISIs I encountered, let alone one that would generate some sort of vertical political loyalty despite the vertical ties that did exist. In this way, Palestinians were able, in effect, to keep political Islam at bay, challenging the facile notion that their political support could easily be purchased through the mere provision of services.

Second, it should also be noted that Hamas was never a part of a "periphery" where Yavuz's oppositional Muslimness was being articulated. Rather, Hamas was always part—and perceived itself as such—of the larger political and social order, never truly detaching itself from the "mainstream" despite its oppositional stance to the Oslo process. This partly explains why Hamas sought political and social accommodation during the Oslo period and has been open to negotiation and compromise with Israel since. It also helps explain why, in part, Hamas did not (or could not) mobilize people along a commonly constructed identity of exclusion (and why, perhaps, an alternative Islamic society never really coalesced and emerged in Palestine as it has in other contexts). Furthermore, neither Hamas nor the ISIs generally ever truly claimed to represent the Palestinian Muslim (although this has now changed) as much as they tried to crystallize a sense of Muslim identity and community consciousness.

Like other factions, Hamas could not substantively address the damaging effects of the occupation, let alone defy or end it. Unlike the situation in Egypt, where Muslim mobilizations resulted in the creation of a parallel Islamic sector where ISIs were more effective as political mobilizers (although this was not their primary role), in Palestine such mobilizations failed to occur in the same way because they had so little to offer. Put differently, Palestinians have always been united around their opposition to Israeli occupation, not around their practice or embrace of Islam.

Popular support has emanated, fundamentally, from the ability to challenge if not end the occupation, not from creating alternatives within it, which is what Hamas and Fatah have effectively tried to do, each in its own way. Because of this, the Islamists were unable for the most part to create a new Islamic identity—or position themselves as an "authentic" alternative—that would produce new meaning for people, encouraging them to replace their "old" identities and forge new solidarities.

Similarly, Hamas failed, politically and socially, to generate any real or sustained optimism about the present or the future and offered no profound change in popular consciousness. Although Hamas came to embody the spirit of Palestinian resistance (as Fatah and the PLO abandoned it), it was unable to translate the work of the social sector into broad-based political opposition. This is because the Islamists were never able to initiate a transformative social alternative—that is, a new kind of society or new forms of civic engagement inspired by Islamic ideals or by a new interpretation of Islam. In the final analysis, and despite certain important achievements at the social and political level, the Islamists (like their primary rival, Fatah) were limited in what they could offer Palestinians that could dramatically alter their adverse reality.

Third, not only was Hamas incapable of ending the occupation (and stopping Israel's attack against the Palestinian collective); Hamas did a great deal to strengthen it by incurring the wrath of the Israeli government. This is another reason why the Islamists could not mobilize popular support for political Islam or create a constituency based on Hamas's political ideology: The Islamist response to the problems facing the Palestinian community during Oslo was fundamentally no different from that of other key actors. Islam as religion, culture, or politics did not provide most Palestinians with a radically different paradigm (or, arguably, one at all) from which to view the political system, let alone articulate ways of challenging it. As Gunning points out: "though Islam informs aspects of Hamas' political, and in particular its social programme, it is only one influence and source of authority among others; and the way Islam is interpreted is influenced by the wider socio-economic and political context within which Hamas operates."[56] Prayer was not necessarily a political act, nor was participating in an Islamist social institution.

Hence, the work of the ISIs allowed Hamas to maintain an institutional structure that established a linkage of varying kinds to the grass roots and a potential source of direct (and, in my view, largely indirect) support for Hamas, but this is very different from mobilizing people into collective action in support of an activist Islamist agenda or using ISIs to underpin political or military activities.[57]

A fourth factor contributing to Hamas's inability to translate social activism into political mobilization derived from the absence of a larger, unifying framework of socioeconomic change. Several Hamas and ISI officials including Dr. Duweiq and Sheikh Yassin himself openly admitted that the Islamists and the Islamic movement as a whole had no overarching organizing social vision or program that served as a framework for institutional development or program planning (a problem afflicting the secular nationalists as well). The lack of a mobilizing vision within the Islamic sector linking social programs to a social plan—itself reflecting the absence of a centralized directive authority—revealed the absence of long-range thinking or planning at a macro level, difficult under an increasingly repressive and dislocating occupation. Rather, as argued above, ISI programs and day-to-day activities were typically the result of individual and institutional assessments of needs (as they were in secular institutions) that cannot be "conflated with other events such as protests, involving Islamists and the poor."[58]

According to Yahya Musa, "Individual institutions define their priorities according to what they think is important, according to the history of the institution and its founding fathers."[59] More commonly, the board of directors of a given ISI would set the policy framework, and the staff would shape specific programs to reflect it. Boards varied from institution to institution and could include some combination of the following: members or supporters of Hamas (or Islamic Jihad), professionals in the ISI's area of specialization or other professionals, local figures both religious and secular (although the latter were uncommon), respected community members, and other local people. As Janine Clark argues, "[w]e must break down ... various events and institutions—protests, crises, ISIs, and so forth—and examine their different agendas, locations and participants."[60]

Layered on this reality was another factor limiting the articulation of a unifying social framework within the Islamic sector: the lack of a larger social and ideological vision within society as a whole, itself a function of the conditions of occupation, particularly de-institutionalization and the increasing fragmentation and atomization of society. Consequently, within Gaza, let alone between Gaza and the West Bank, one could find a range of philosophical approaches to ISI work (from small organizations to very large ones) that resulted in a constellation of discrete programs with little or no connection to one another. Indeed, the internal shift in emphasis toward the social sector was not accompanied by the development of a new organizing model of social change (as Hroub argued), despite an emerging reorientation in social strategy that was characterized by the expansion of programmatic initiatives and examples of more creative engagement with the community. In the end few if any new institutional forms were created.

Thus, despite many excellent and expanded services and the more innovative programs of some ISIs, recipients were, in the end, given no real or greater stake in a process of genuine social change. Nor did recipients have anything additional or exceptional to lose or to fight for, which also constrained their incentive to mobilize politically around an activist Islamist agenda. This contrasts dramatically with Clark's study of Islamist women in Yemen, who, through their *da'wa* activities, actively sought to break down and rebuild society in accordance with their religious vision, pursuing a worldview that had dramatic social change as its principal goal.[61]

Fifth, Islam as a religious and political force never acquired mobilizing power among Palestinians because competing loyalties such as kinship and tribe were often too strong. People were united more by their condition (as an occupied and dispossessed nation) than by attempts to Islamize it. Not surprisingly, there were no effective mechanisms for translating grievance into collective action. One could argue that this did occur with Hamas's tangible political gains in the 2004 to 2005 municipal elections and in the 2006 legislative elections, but again, these victories were not based on a religious or ideological platform that viewed constituents as objects of mobilization but on a secular, community-oriented agenda of social and political change that constituents were demanding (see chapter 7). In effect, the vote for Hamas was actually a protest vote against Fatah for its failure to deliver on this agenda during its rule.

Hence, if an alternative domain was being created by Hamas, it was not political in the formal sense but communal in the social sense. And if mobilization was taking place, it was not occurring on the basis of political or ideological allegiance or a top-down manipulation of religious belief but rather on the foundation of local solidarities, using modes of education to create, in effect, "secular communities" rather than "sacred [or political] congregations."[62] In fact, ISIs in Palestine were best understood as community rather than as Islamic actors—as institutions whose ties to the community appeared far stronger than their ties to each other or to a larger Islamic or Islamist network. Perhaps then it might be more accurate to call the Islamic social sector in Palestine during this time a more populist social movement based on grassroots ties rather than the social ideological arm of the Islamist political movement.

Because Hamas was unable to mitigate, let alone stop, the ever-worsening Israeli occupation, it (like other groups in Palestine) was never really able to persuade people to prioritize the public good, however defined, over private self-interest. Under the PNA, of course, the "public good" was deprived of much of its meaning, particularly in light of an increasingly corrupt and mismanaged governing authority and declining economic conditions. Within this context, the ISIs' community-based efforts were all the more impressive, particularly during the early years of the second Palestinian uprising when they continued to play an important local role (chapter 7). Yet, despite these efforts, Hamas could not effectively use the politics of identity as a framework for catalyzing social (or, for that matter, large-scale political) change. For this reason, the Islamic movement never really captured the hearts and minds of most Palestinians socially or politically during the Oslo period despite Hamas's role as the primary opposition force and an important provider of social services, a pattern that began to change after the second Intifada in 2000.

Summarizing Key Findings

The Islamic movement, which Hamas dominates, has a long history of deep and sustained institutional involvement with Palestinian society, a history that predates Hamas by more than four decades. As such Islamic institutions and their ties to the Palestinian community must primarily be understood as a cultural phenomenon that found expression before Israeli occupation.

Hamas's institutional role and its close ties to the grass roots enabled the movement to undergo a process of internal transformation. This popular connection was found not only in the more traditional venues such as mosques and other religious settings but also in the educational sector, the health sector, social welfare and charitable services, sports, cultural activities, and in certain economic activities. Often what defined "Hamas" institutions as Islamic was not necessarily the overt practice of Islam or adherence to Islamic rules but the areas in which they worked and the quality of care and practice they brought to those endeavors. Islamist institutions came to be defined by their willingness to reach out to all sectors of the population, rejecting the clientelism that often characterized their secular counterparts and that Palestinians came to reject.

Contrary to the image we have in the West of narrow, indoctrinating organizations, although some certainly did exist, I found quite the opposite: institutions characterized by flexibility and openness and far greater tolerance than assumed. In fact, it was increasingly the constellation of Islamic NGOs, both Hamas-affiliated and not, that arguably were laying the foundation for civil society in Palestine more forcefully than their secular counterparts, which had become far more globalized and outward-oriented.

Thus, the dominant conceptualization of Islamic social activism in Palestine as a channel for political violence and Islamic terrorism is highly oversimplified, stereotypical, and at odds with the actual facts on the ground. In reality, this sector has been quite varied, encompassing a range of institutions and individuals who speak with diverse voices—not just one—and not always to each other. These institutions have been traditional and modern, conservative and innovative, closed to change and open to it, risk averse and risk embracing, efficient and inefficient, cooperative and territorial. Some have emphasized professionalism; others, religion. While they all have ascribed to the goal of creating a "more Islamic" way of life, their understanding of what that actually meant, and what the appropriate role of religion and politics in institutional work should be, has varied widely.

During the Oslo period, Hamas directed its attention to articulating a social agenda that emphasized collective interests, defining the social contract, as it were, in more developmental terms. Key characteristics included

- no real evidence of formal institutional links between Islamic social institutions and their political counterparts;
- no ideological preference for religion or politics over other ideologies particularly in programmatic work;
- an approach to institutional work that was not dogmatic or rigidly ideological in favor of one that advocated incrementalism, moderation, order, and stability;
- a philosophical and practical desire to do productive (versus destructive) professional work that shunned radical change;
- a philosophy that emphasized community development and civic restoration over political violence;
- no evidence of any formal attempt to impose an Islamic model of social, economic, legal, or religious behavior or create an alternative Islamic or Islamist conception of society;
- no evidence of a political battle against the ruling authority at the grassroots level;
- a desire to work legally in cooperation with, and not in opposition to, "state" authority;
- a desire to complement official services rather than challenge or otherwise attack them (and perhaps, in so doing, legitimize the social system and their role within it); that is, no attempt to create a countersociety along Islamic lines;
- a certain, albeit limited, acceptance of social and political pluralism.

Hamas's developmental agenda, which effectively aimed to redefine the contractual agreement with the Palestinian public, went beyond traditional boundaries to pursue programs and policies that (from an Islamist perspective) encouraged innovation and empowerment and growing cooperation with non-Islamic actors, although more traditional activities remained dominant. While religion certainly set the larger conceptual boundaries, it was not viewed as a form of restriction but as a form of expansion and liberation (and a source of emotional support for Hamas).

As such, Islam, increasingly, was not defined or interpreted literally or dogmatically but as a framework for pursuing a range of largely pragmatic, secular initiatives. In this sense, it could be argued that Hamas was pursuing a form of secularism from within. It was not religious or ideological purity or consistency that the Islamist social sector was pursuing overall but the implementation of good works where reason and interpretation played a critical role; civic imperatives clearly superseded political and ideological ones, and socioeconomic change was the criterion by which the Islamists were increasingly judged. Hence, community betterment and communal empowerment were the new forms of resistance; the goal was to strengthen Palestinian society, not liberate all of Palestine. More importantly, perhaps, this form of resistance shunned violence and called instead for decentralization and delegation of authority, along with greater consultation and participation in the process of decision making among the actors involved, including, at times, beneficiaries.

Islamic authenticity as it were was derived not only, or even primarily, from prayer or appropriate dress—although these remained important—but from the ability to repair from within, to heal and create rather than wound and destroy. Consequently, Islamist officials—those working within Islamic social institutions and those in the political sector—did not derive their symbolic, political, or personal capital from the degree of their religiosity or ability to inflict pain, but rather from their ability to address social needs and effect real civic change. Key measures of civic change (which were attained with varying degrees of success) were the ability to foster and strengthen linkages and connections between institutions and recipient communities; between institutions (both Islamic and other) themselves; and between recipient communities, dynamics that strengthened during the first two years of the second Intifada. This, too, accounts, at least in part, for a public discourse that became increasingly professionalized rather than Islamized (in contrast to what increasingly prevails today).

Hence, the Oslo period was crucial, not only—or even primarily—because it was then that the military wing of Hamas became almost singularly associated with horrific acts of political violence in the form of suicide bombings that killed hundreds of Israeli civilians, but also for reasons that are far less known yet at least as important: It was during the Oslo period that social and political wings of Hamas demonstrated, and to certain degrees implemented, a capacity for reexamination and accommodation, as well as reform and transformation.

There are some important lessons to highlight: Although Hamas played an important social role during the Oslo period in particular and, to varying degrees, has continued to do so since, it never really captured the hearts and minds of Palestinians on a political-ideological level despite its 2006 electoral victory. That is, if Hamas could have persuaded people to support its political and ideological agenda, the later Oslo period—characterized by the continued political failure of the secular nationalists, socioeconomic decline, and the Islamists' increasingly prominent social role—would have been the opportune time to do so (which is another reason for the importance of the Oslo period as a focal point of analysis).

Furthermore, despite its contributions to grassroots change, Hamas suffered from clear limitations—both internal and external—that ultimately precluded meaningful socioeconomic reform and, with it, the transformation of popular support into large-scale political activism let alone violent activism. This is because the majority of Palestinians have never supported an Islamic political agenda to develop an Islamic state and society. Also, Hamas institutions, despite their strengths, did not appear to form the kind of networks that could become structural mechanisms for the development of a new activist Islamic subculture, as they have in some other Muslim countries, such as Egypt. To the contrary, internal rivalries and lack of coordination kept them, in part, from doing so.

Hence, although Hamas's social support structure played a key role in building up popular support for the organization, this was not the same as mobilizing people into an activist constituency based on the political ideology of Hamas. In this, Hamas largely failed. Participating in an Islamic social institution was not automatically equated with political support, a fact some Hamas officials well understood.

At its core, Hamas's failure to translate popular grievances into collective action or tangible political gains for an Islamist agenda was due to the Israeli occupation and Hamas's inability to overcome the hardships imposed. This acted as a severe constraint on the movement and its ability to mobilize and recruit large segments of its social base. In the final analysis, Hamas had too little to offer Palestinians politically, and competing loyalties were simply too strong.

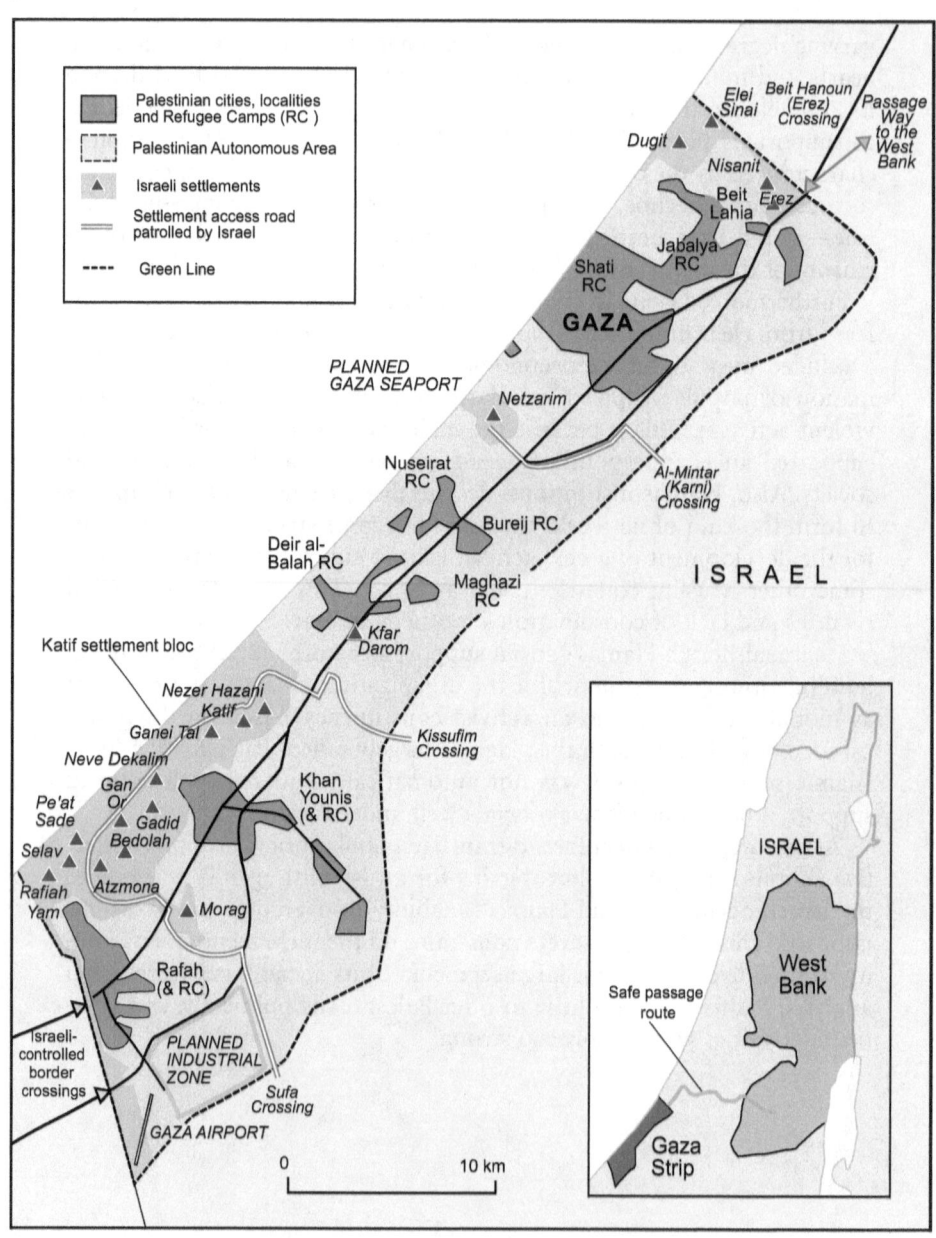

Map 2. Gaza Strip, 2002. Source: Foundation for Middle East Peace (www.fmep.org).

Chapter 7

A CHANGING ISLAMIST ORDER? FROM CIVIC EMPOWERMENT TO CIVIC REGRESSION—THE SECOND INTIFADA AND BEYOND

> The situation here is getting worse by the day. It looks like there is no normality or normal people anymore. Everything is collapsing: the economy, the health services, institutions and families, and, of course, individuals. Gaza is deprived and people are poor and apprehensive. They have no hope and feel deeply humiliated. I wanted to cry when I see them killed and when they celebrate the death of Israelis. Hamas is thriving on despair and is itself gripped by [its] own extremists. While Abbas is viewed as a collaborator with Israel, Hamas is not enthusiastically adopted by the suffering people but is seen as a victim, like all of us. In the long run there is an Armageddon waiting for all.
> —Dr. Eyad al-Sarraj, Gaza, February 2008

SINCE THE START of the second Palestinian Intifada, both Hamas and the larger Palestinian context, which the second uprising had increasingly come to define, have undergone marked changes. The second Intifada, which began in September 2000 in response to seven years of a "peace" process that not only deepened Palestinian dispossession and deprivation but strengthened Israel's occupation, reversed the dramatic changes within the Islamic movement. The militarization of the uprising by Fatah effectively marginalized the role of civil society—including both secular and Islamic institutions—in the struggle to end Israeli occupation. This contributed to the reascendance of the political/military sector as the defining and authoritative component within the secular and Islamic movements, relegating the achievements (and possibilities) of the social sector to a lesser position.

Israel's increasingly brutal and continued assault against Palestinian society and economy and the deliberate destruction of its civic institutions especially between 2000 and 2002 (and reoccupation of most West

Bank cities in June 2002) only strengthened the embrace of the military option by Palestinians including the Islamists. Despite cease-fires between Hamas and Israel in 2003 and from 2005 to 2006, the withdrawal of Israeli settlements from the Gaza Strip in August 2005, and several rounds of municipal elections between December 2004 and December 2005 that brought Hamas peacefully and democratically to local power in Gaza and the West Bank, this period was also marked by growing intrafactional and interfactional fighting that ultimately resulted in Hamas's January 2006 electoral victory and subsequent June 2007 takeover of the Gaza Strip. The latter precipitated the demise of the Palestinian unity government established in early 2007 and the division of the PNA into two parts, effectively pitting the West Bank Authority under Fatah against the Gaza-based Authority under Hamas. The political disorder that inevitably resulted has not abated; to the contrary, the specters of widening internecine violence and deepened political division appear larger, themselves amplified by large-scale economic devastation and individual ruin, especially in Gaza following Israel's three-week assault that began on December 27, 2008.

The dramatic political changes affecting Hamas since 2000 have been exhaustively examined elsewhere.[1] It is not my aim to restate what others have found but to supplement it by addressing some specific dynamics that affected Hamas and the Islamic social sector during this period. As previously argued, the period prior to the second Intifada, marked by growing ideological flexibility and greater openness to new ideas and to the role of social institutions as important instruments of social action, represented a critically important time in Hamas's history. Islamist social institutions represented structures of moderation and stability and, increasingly, creativity.

Since the second uprising (and notably in the post–January 2006 period), a critical change within the Islamist movement, and arguably one of its greatest losses, involved a shift in strategy from one that situated personal dignity and collective empowerment within a civic framework to one that increasingly located those values in militarization, authoritarianism, and violence. The social contract that the Islamists had forged with the Palestinian public years before began to weaken.

One illustration of this change is seen in policies that increasingly privilege institutions (social and otherwise) and individuals loyal to or supportive of Hamas.[2] This sort of favoritism and discrimination was, without question, largely the exception during the Oslo and early (second) Intifada periods. Similarly, since its consolidation of control over Gaza after June 2007, Hamas has shut down many Fatah NGOs in Gaza, in retaliation for attacks against Islamist institutions in the West Bank (see below). Hamas also is attempting to forcibly increase its influence among non-Islamic NGOs—both politically aligned (notably with Fatah) and nonaligned—by ensuring that its cadres be given representation within the general assemblies of these institutions. Although the Islamists have largely used the existing NGO law to actualize their demands, some NGOs have said they will close if forced to expand in this manner; others are prepared to cooperate to survive.[3]

While these policies are in large part a response to the enormous economic and political pressure to which the Hamas government has been subject and the insecurity and humiliation this creates,[4] they also represent a choice—one that Hamas once largely resisted—that embraces power over vision and particular interests over collective ones. The risk (if not already the reality) lies in the changing nature of Islamically legitimized action whereby the Islamists will be judged (and perhaps demand to be judged), not by the socioeconomic work they perform or as agents of societal change, but by the political ideology they espouse and the degree of power they command. This risk is made greater by the continued absence among Palestinians of a viable secular political alternative.

This move from more pragmatic to more absolutist behavior mirrors, and is itself a product of, the diminishing political and economic context of the Gaza Strip and West Bank not just since the 2006 establishment of the Hamas-led government but fundamentally since the beginning of the second Palestinian Intifada. One cannot understand Hamas's changing role and policy choices without understanding the larger political and socioeconomic context that shaped them.

The Second Intifada: Some Critical Features

With the Intifada—itself a response to Israel's strengthening occupation and the losses imposed by Oslo (particularly the fragmentation and cantonization of Palestinian lands in the West Bank; the demographic and economic separation of the West Bank and Gaza; and the isolation of Gaza)—the Palestinian political environment changed radically. Preexisting political arrangements were ruptured, economic conditions continued to decline, and key social structures and mediatory institutions were weakened. Within this context, the Islamist opposition, notably Hamas, reasserted itself.

The Intifada was directed primarily against Israel, but it was also a revolt against the Fatah-dominated PNA and its failure to establish viable state institutions or engage in a process of national reconstruction and democratic practice. It is critical to understand that the occupation did not mitigate during the ill-defined peace process but was *strengthened* (with the assistance of a dependent Palestinian regime and the international donor community). As such, the political reality created by Oslo of an independent, viable PNA government and president was illusory. The Oslo reality was not one of a sovereign state or institutions but of an increasingly circumscribed, weakened, and dependent administration under military occupation. The resulting arrangement was one by which Israel retained total control over the Palestinian people and their resources but relinquished all responsibility for them.

The PNA, by contrast, was given responsibility for day-to-day life (and for imposing some of the more repressive aspects of the occupation) but with limited agency and authority to manage it workably. This is why, in part, Yasir Arafat conceded to and exploited the militarization of the Intifada, which fueled the violence and the subsequent decline of Palestinian society and economy. The political and economic vacuum created by the peace process—filled during the Oslo years by growing restrictions, widening corruption, and growing bureaucratization—was replaced by violence, political paralysis, and internal disarray.

Critically, during this period, no actor, including the PNA, espoused a political program guiding its actions or a political strategy for moving forward. Political groups were mobilized around a decidedly negative agenda rather than around a positive agenda of reconstruction and rehabilitation. Tragically, Palestinian resistance and political praxis were defined by armed factions, not civic institutions. The militarization of society and the pernicious political divisions it produced contributed to violent fracture within Fatah and to varying levels of violence between Fatah and Hamas.[5]

Coupled with Israel's destruction of much of the PNA's infrastructure, particularly its security forces, and financial strangulation during this period, internal political fracture contributed to greater lawlessness, chaos, and insecurity. One dangerous phenomenon was the rapid growth of contending sources of power including militias (military and security), clans, and criminal enterprises. Militias and clans, which sometimes overlapped, also resonated strongly in a society where tribal feelings and needs for group affiliations were deeply felt at the cultural level and humiliation and alienation were the predominant experience at the political level.[6]

The resulting context was characterized by several dangerous features: the growing absence of a governing institution in Palestine able or willing to protect or defend its citizens or engage in meaningful public service or leadership in any form; the absence of due process or any real system of accountability, appeal, or justice; and the lack of economic growth or development.[7] For many if not most Palestinians, intra-Fatah violence was the greatest threat facing society by 2004 because the problem had changed from fighting the occupation to fighting one another. These trends could be seen in the strengthening of the young Fatah cadres, who sought political power through intensified militia warfare, and in the rise and widening influence of the Islamists, particularly in the granting to Islamists of veto power in political decision making (then unprecedented in the history of the Palestinian national movement) and in their loose alliance with the younger Fatah activists.

The deep fracture within the Palestinian political structure was exacerbated in April 2003 by the international community when it forced Arafat to establish a prime ministerial post. This fueled Fatah's internal power struggles and further weakened Arafat. There were now many groups within Fatah[8] with weak if any alignments vying for political power, and there were the Islamists.

Collectively, factions were not addressing liberation or reform but jockeying for raw power in an anarchic milieu. Legitimacy and immunity were derived from arms, not institutions or laws. Individual resilience was amazing, but there was no corresponding initiative on the leadership level. By 2004 the PNA had lost considerable control over Gaza, and Arafat faced perhaps his greatest challenge of the preceding decade. Hamas, no doubt satisfied by Fatah's internecine fighting, largely removed itself from this intra-Fatah violence[9] and focused instead on attacking Israel and on rising popular demands for democratic reform and public accountability.

Thus an important factor in Hamas's electoral success at the municipal and legislative levels was the fact that the Fatah structure demonstrated little if any responsibility toward its constituency, pursuing its own venal interests even at the price of growing lawlessness and disorder, which represented a reversal from the past. Hence, it was a question not only of a weak and corrupt leadership but of one that no longer wanted to fight against Israeli occupation, making itself vulnerable to Israeli and American pressure. Initiatives were being blocked at all levels, and people were terrified.[10]

Because both the PNA and Palestinian society found themselves gripped by such profound paralysis, Israel's continued attacks against them brought Palestinians to a breaking point. This explained not only Palestine's internal chaos but also the growing strength of Hamas, which represented a dramatic shift from its weakened political role in the years just prior to the second Intifada. In fact, the Intifada brought about the first significant change in the domestic balance of power since 1995–1996, when popular support for Arafat and the Oslo process was high (71 percent). Eroding support for the nationalists subsequently translated into support for the Islamists.[11]

The Changing Role of Hamas: Relations with the PNA and with Israel[12]

During the early years of the uprising, support for Hamas visibly increased.[13] The de-radicalization of Hamas during Oslo ended with the militarization of the Intifada. Hamas clearly benefited from Palestine's imploding political environment, what the late Israeli scholar Baruch Kimmerling termed the politicide of the Palestinians, particularly from Fatah's internecine struggles.[14] As Arafat's power diminished, Hamas (and other militant factions) carried out suicide bombing attacks in Israeli cities in opposition to official PNA policy. Rightly or wrongly, the PNA was held accountable for these attacks, and Israel would respond with devastating results. As the PNA weakened, Hamas's capacity to weaken it further grew to where a significant part of the Hamas leadership believed—despite Israel's assassination of several of its senior- and middle-level military officials during 2003[15]—that Hamas could fill any vacuum created by the destruction of the PNA or perhaps displace it altogether, a belief that became a reality less than three years later.

Politically, Hamas had become a powerful actor, its popular stature enhanced not only by its military actions against Israel but also by Israel's relentless assassinations of its leaders.[16] This is in part why in August 2002 the Fatah leadership had already begun negotiations with Hamas over its entry into the PLO and into more mainstream Palestinian politics.[17] (After Mahmoud Abbas became prime minister in April 2003, wresting power from Arafat—and spurred by President Bush's new Roadmap initiative—he also entered into talks with Hamas about power sharing.)[18]

Similarly, in September 2002, before Israel's siege of Arafat's compound later that month, the United States had had indirect contacts with senior Hamas officials and had apparently promised them that in exchange for their agreement to become part of a secular, democratic unity government in a new Palestinian state (a discussion that Hamas was already conducting with Fatah, and which no doubt contributed to the six-week lull in suicide bombings in 2002[19]), the United States would pressure Israeli officials to end their policy of targeted assassinations and arrests of Hamas officials. The U.S. envoy engaged in the "talks" indicated that while he could not guarantee Israeli acceptance, the United States welcomed Hamas's decision to become "a legitimate part of the political process." It was also clear that the United States endorsed Hamas-Fatah talks. Reportedly, Hamas officials were pleased by these indications that the United States would welcome Hamas's political participation.[20]

A senior U.S. diplomat put it this way: "There is a difference between Hamas and, say, the Iranian mullahs. The one tradition is nationalist and revolutionary, the other is clerical and religious. We know the difference. We know who the honest actors are. We don't happen to like Hamas tactics, but we know there's a world of difference between what they want and what, say, Mullah Omar wants."[21]

Contacts between the United States and Hamas—of which Israel was fully aware—ended when the Israeli army arrested a moderate Hamas official in Ramallah on September 9, 2002, which Hamas interpreted as a deliberate attempt by the Sharon government to undermine its exchange with the Americans. This was followed just a few days later by an Israeli attack in Rafah, which killed nine Palestinians including many civilians. On September 19, two Hamas bombs exploded, predictably and tragically, in Tel Aviv.[22] This was subsequently followed by Israel's siege of the presidential compound in Ramallah. Under U.S. pressure, Sharon ordered an end to the siege soon thereafter.

Beginning in September 2002, Hamas entered negotiations over a cease-fire,[23] although Israel's failed assassination attempt against al-Rantisi in June 2003 almost ended these negotiations. An official truce or *hudna* was declared on June 29, 2003, but the Sharon government did not accept it and continued its assassination campaign. The killing on August 9, 2003, of Hamis Abu-Salam and Faiz al-Sadar, two Hamas officials in the Askar refugee camp near Nablus, lead to the two suicide attacks at Ariel and Rosh Ha'ayin soon thereafter, breaking the June truce.[24]

According to Gideon Levy of *Ha'aretz*, "Much as Israel claims that the Palestinians are violating the truce and regrouping in order to perpetrate savage acts of terror, its pleading can't alter the facts: up until Israel renewed its assassinations campaign, there were no suicide bombings, and the two attacks [at Ariel and Rosh Ha'ayin] last week were direct responses to the Askar refugee camp slayings."[25] More attacks followed, including the killing by Hamas of twenty-two Israelis in Jerusalem on August 19, 2003. Ismail Abu Shanab was assassinated two days later on August 21, after which Hamas declared an end to the cease-fire, telling Israel it could expect "rivers of blood" in its cities.[26] Soon thereafter, on September 6, 2003, the European Union gave in to American and British pressure and adopted a resolution blacklisting the political wing of Hamas, declaring it a terrorist organization. The Israeli government immediately responded with the attempted assassination in Gaza of Sheikh Yassin, the spiritual leader of Hamas (who was later assassinated on March 22, 2004).

Suicide bombings are horrific, and the carnage perpetrated by Hamas was criminal. But the policies of the Israeli government clearly aimed to undermine any possibility of a political settlement, which would have involved compromises the government was unwilling to make, preferring instead a decisive military victory and long-term interim arrangements dictated by Israel no matter the cost. Rather than draw Hamas into a political role that would give "the Islamists a more proportional share of power in exchange for their agreement to a modified political approach"[27] and thereby encourage an internal political settlement among Palestinian factions (particularly with Fatah)—something the Sharon government vehemently opposed because it would have strengthened the Palestinian position—the Israeli government attempted to destroy the Islamists through military means and to foster continued internal political dissension.

Hence, Hamas's proposal in January 2004 of a ten-year truce in exchange for Israel's withdrawal from the West Bank, Gaza, and Jerusalem (without, admittedly, any political recognition or compromise) was ignored. Given Hamas's sensitivity to public opinion, the proposal may have signaled the beginning of a (political) shift within the organization away from the use of violence, which accomplished little and exacted enormous societal costs, reviving the tendency to political accommodation that had characterized Hamas's behavior during the Oslo period. Similarly, the proposal of a truce no doubt represented an attempt by Hamas to strengthen and secure its leadership position, perhaps in coordination with some younger, ascendant Fatah leaders—notably Marwan Barghouti, who had reached out to the Islamists before in the August 2002 negotiations.[28]

Hamas's political shift also derived from Israel's success at further weakening its military capacity (as it did during the Oslo period) through its assassination campaign and frequent raids into Palestinian towns and localities. Between 2002 and 2004, Hamas had lost almost all its original leaders in Gaza.[29] Indeed, Yassin's and al-Rantisi's assassinations in 2004—nearly one month apart—clearly undermined Hamas's military capacity to stage suicide bombings, and some Hamas officials were beginning to question their efficacy.[30] The Israeli security authorities, furthermore, had successfully thwarted many suicide bombing attempts.[31] The number of Israeli civilians killed by Palestinians (in Israel) had dropped from 184 in 2002 to 104 in 2003 to 53 in 2004 and 24 in 2005.[32] Until the July 11, 2004, bombing in Tel Aviv, the Israeli authorities were able to block every attempt at an attack inside Israel and most inside the West Bank and Gaza.[33] This signified for some observers the systematic erosion of Hamas's combat capabilities and that of Palestinian militants more generally.

Israel's policy of political assassinations arguably aimed to derail internal discussions over power sharing and efforts at cooperation. These assassinations also aimed, in part, to foment Palestinian radicalism in a manner that would justify Israel's continued occupation. Israel could argue that Palestinians can only be dealt with as militant radicals and not as people with national rights or as legitimate political actors.

While Sharon's April 2004 announcement of his intention to disengage from Gaza further encouraged a more pragmatic response by Hamas, Arafat's death in November 2004 was arguably the critical turning point. Arafat's death revealed the extent of the structural problems of the Palestinian political system. As the system had become increasingly fragmented during, but especially after, Oslo, Arafat had remained the primary source of its authenticity and defensibility. His death, therefore, amounted to a crisis of representation and legitimacy. His successors, Mahmoud Abbas in particular, had to try to relegitimize (and rehabilitate) the Palestinian political system domestically but also regionally and internationally. Domestically, Abbas attempted to do so through a series of elections: presidential in January 2005, which he won; municipal between December 2004 and December 2005; and legislative in January 2006. This attempt at relegitimization could not occur without Hamas's participation, nor could it sustain Hamas's continued opposition. Regionally and internationally, Abbas sought to revive the U.S. Roadmap initiative through renewal of the 2003 Palestinian cease-fire—offering Hamas a form of power sharing in exchange for the cessation of violence—but his dependence on Israeli and American constructive engagement and his inability to challenge Israeli unilateralism ensured failure.

Wanting to become part of the political mainstream and of the administrative structure of Gaza in the event of Israel's disengagement was vitally important to the Islamists.[34] Clearly, Hamas was no longer content to play the role of rejectionist opposition, recognizing the ineffectiveness of armed struggle in the absence of political engagement.[35] Hamas considered itself part of the political reality and was seeking longer-term political participation and modes of integration, aiming to translate popular support into institutional power. Its strategy was one of gradual political integration—itself somewhat experimental—which would allow Hamas greater legitimacy domestically and perhaps internationally by distinguishing it—as the leadership long had—from more extreme groups such as the Taliban and al-Qaeda.[36]

Hamas maintained that it had no ambitions to take over Palestinian politics—seizing power would be damaging to its credibility—and would continue to stay away from the internal fighting in Fatah, although clashes with Fatah continued, reaching a particularly acute stage in July 2005.[37] However, Hamas reiterated its call for power sharing in which it had a serious role, saying Fatah would not rule alone in Gaza. Hamas pursued what the political analyst Mouin Rabbani called a Hizballah model: legitimacy through resistance[38] and recognition and protection through political participation.[39]

In the March 2005 Cairo meeting Hamas's integration into the PLO was discussed. Fatah agreed to a Hamas proposal to allow the formation of a committee for the reform of the PLO and convinced Abbas not to disarm Hamas until the legislative elections. In return Hamas agreed to a cease-fire vis-à-vis Israel until December 2005 (which remained in effect until June 2006, when Hamas suspended it; see below) and agreed to ensure that Israel's disengagement from Gaza would not take place under Hamas gunfire. By spring 2005 Hamas was pushing harder on the issue of power sharing, particularly over the inventory of state lands.[40] Tensions increased between Hamas and Fatah over the failure to honor their agreements despite the imminence of Israel's disengagement (or, arguably, because of it).

The promise of Israeli disengagement from Gaza generated considerable internal activity, including an eighteen-point plan for Gaza known as the Barghouti document aimed at facilitating the transition of power in the Gaza Strip following Israel's withdrawal. Authored by the jailed leader of the al-Aqsa Martyrs Brigade, Marwan Barghouti, who long had a political channel open to Hamas, the plan proposed a role for the Islamists, in cooperation with the PNA, in running Gaza. Although the PNA was to be the effective governing authority, all other groups were to have real input into the administration of Gaza through their membership in a monitoring committee. In exchange, the Islamists were to cease all attacks on Israel launched from the Gaza Strip (but not West Bank). Apparently, both Hamas and Islamic Jihad responded positively in principle although not officially.

After the assassination of Yassin and al-Rantisi, the Hamas leadership was reported to have internally circulated a classified document, authored by al-Zahar and Haniyeh and titled "Document on the Approach to the Anticipated Withdrawal from the Gaza Strip," among its leadership in Gaza. Circulated on May 24, 2004, the document revealed Hamas's recognition that political participation was inevitable. In fact, the document discussed the formation of "a joint legitimate leadership" in the Gaza Strip consisting of "all the nationalistic and Islamic factions," which would share in decision making. A key point concerned the conditions under which Hamas would work with the PNA despite their ongoing conflict. The Hamas leadership made this cooperation conditional on the nature of the Israeli withdrawal: "whether it be comprehensive or partial, under agreement with the Palestinian Authority, or unilateral."[41] Not surprisingly, Hamas would have nothing to do with an agreement between the PNA and Israel that included attacks against itself. If so threatened, Hamas would "demonstrate a street presence in an active and powerful manner" and would "strive to form requisite alliances in a way that will guarantee ... that the PA makes no decisions separately."[42]

Strikingly, the document contained a directive to rank-and-file members to assume certain roles even if Hamas's official position opposed the withdrawal agreement: "In case an agreement is reached on withdrawal between Israel and the PA, we are delimiting areas in which movement members may take part—dialog with other factions; managing daily affairs in regions where withdrawal has taken place by actively participating in PA ministries and various institutions; local elections for towns and villages, professional unions and associations; participation in some of the security services of a police nature on movement affairs, criminal investigations and fire fighting." However, Hamas members would not be allowed to actively engage in elections to the Legislative Council or to leadership of the PNA, nor in any matters concerning the policy of the PNA's security services and of evacuated settlements or any agreements pertaining to them.[43]

Hamas also maintained that it would not give up its arms but said it was willing to agree "on a treatise of honor in this matter that will handle the problematic nature and complexity of arms usage for goals that are not the armed struggle."[44] The document demonstrated, in part, certain priorities and concerns. First, the Islamists were positioning themselves for possibly working with the PNA, defining the conditions for their cooperation in some form of collaborative arrangement, although it was unclear what form that cooperation would assume and what their future military policies would be. Second, the document underlined the importance of greater interaction between factions and perhaps recognized the need for a more viable strategy, domestic and "foreign." And third, it evinced a greater tolerance of the PNA and the desperate need for reform, a position the Islamists shared with other Fatah factions.

Some analysts believed that by 2004 Hamas had reached a crossroads: "Key leaders [of Hamas], determined not to be equated with Bin Laden's nihilistic terrorism and convinced they have gained considerable political strength at home, allegedly see the need for a strategic transformation that will give them the legitimacy in regional and international eyes, and given the appropriate environment, may be able to achieve it."[45] Certain Israeli security officials similarly argued that their government would ultimately have to deal with Hamas. "The IDF today understands that Hamas is also a movement like Hezbollah or ... Shas [Israel's Orthodox Sephardic party] ... [i.e., more than just a paramilitary organization], and no one really believes that it can be destroyed."[46]

Hamas at the Grass Roots: Opposing Trends over a Changing Social Agenda

Trend One: Political Strength through a Responsive Social Sector

After Yasir Arafat's death in November 2004, Palestinians found themselves in a transitional phase with a leadership that had no popular mandate to rule. Governmental institutions existed but had no legitimacy, in large part because of Arafat's attack against them and his inability to understand them. The society was characterized by what appeared to be a growing religiosity, with ordinary Palestinians turning increasingly to religion for support, solace, and solidarity. The number of persons wearing conservative dress, including women's head scarves and veils, noticeably increased. In this way, broader identities provided moral and emotional support. Islamic notions of *zakat* and assisting the poor in general and the importance of Muslims helping those in need were alive and well. Indeed, in the continued absence of viable political alternatives and forms of expression, and in light of the continued decay of those that did exist, people increasingly turned toward religion as a source of comfort, knowledge, and a sense of protectedness.

Because of this, the issue of Hamas's continued popularity, to which the organization was trying to respond, was being debated at the grassroots level in Gaza at this time (2004). My understanding, based on interviews with a range of informants, is that there were two dominant trends within the debate over the Islamists' grassroots support. First there were those who argued that despite the successful attack against its leadership structure, Hamas was proliferating from below, gaining strength and popularity largely from the services provided by its social and charitable institutions, and from the continued perception of Hamas as the only viable political faction resisting the occupation and opposing the violence and corruption of Fatah. At an NGO meeting I attended in Gaza in 2004, one woman (whose response was quite typical) told me, "We support Hamas because they take revenge for us, because they are strong and honest."

With economic and political conditions rapidly declining in the West Bank and Gaza after 2000, the shift to emergency aid was almost immediate. According to the World Bank, around 21 percent of Palestinians (650,000) were living in poverty on the eve of the second Intifada, a number that increased to 33 percent by December 2000, 46 percent by December 2001, and around 60 percent (1.9 million) by December 2002. Hence, accounting for population growth, the number of people living in poverty tripled between pre–September 2000 and December 2002.[47] By 2003, over 75 percent of Gazans were poor, as were 50 percent of West Bankers, numbers that were no doubt affected by Israel's 2002 military offensive into the West Bank.[48]

The United Nations had similar figures, with 32 percent of the population—more than one million people—receiving some form of emergency aid during the last quarter of 2000—340,000 people in the West Bank and 693,000 in the Gaza Strip.[49] The World Bank found that the "economic crisis has seriously compromised household welfare. Many families have endured long periods without work or incomes, and despite the various employment generation efforts of the PA, donors and NGOs, many are now dependent on food aid for their daily survival. Coping with the situation has meant selling assets, borrowing from families, neighbors and shopkeepers and cutting consumption, including food. In an increasing number of families, shortages are now manifesting as malnutrition.... The erratic provision of basic health, education and water services is further compromising the environment in which young Palestinians are growing up."[50]

The decline in the general well-being of the population was exacerbated by Israel's intermittent refusal to transfer Palestinian tax revenues, which greatly reduced the PNA's revenue base and, hence, its capacity to deliver basic social services. In this climate, Islamic organizations had a significant role to play, providing services that the PNA could not, or providing them more efficiently. In fact, according to the International Crisis Group (ICG), the major service providers at this time were NGOs and charitable organizations as a whole, reaching approximately 60 percent of all beneficiaries from regular and emergency programs. The second most important provider was UNRWA, whose services reached over 34 percent, followed by the PNA Ministry of Social Affairs at just 6 percent.[51]

Given the economic exigencies of the time that were causing poverty levels to rise, growing numbers of Palestinians were in need of emergency relief—especially food and cash—a form of assistance familiar to Islamic social service organizations, whose role became increasingly important. In 2001, according to the ICG, these organizations together with the *zakat* committees constituted the single largest food donor in the West Bank and Gaza after UNRWA. In fact, the four largest Islamic social welfare institutions at the time—al-Salah Islamic Association, the Gaza *zakat* committee, the Holy Land Foundation, and Hebron's Islamic Charitable Society—collectively provided food assistance to 145,450 households or 581,800 people, if the conservative estimate of four people per household is used. According to the United Nations, the *zakat* committees alone increased their food beneficiaries from 450 families prior to the Intifada to 7,000 families soon thereafter. Concentrated in the areas of greatest poverty, notably villages (since UNRWA largely served the refugee population) where it was the largest food distributor, the Islamic social welfare sector provided, directly or indirectly, 25 percent of food and cash assistance in the West Bank in 2001 and some form of assistance—emergency cash, food assistance, and medical care—to one in six Palestinians overall.[52]

In Gaza, according to the United Nations, NGOs and charitable organizations fully accounted for 87 percent of all cash contributions; of this the al-Salah Association alone accounted for 33 percent and the *zakat* committees for an additional 21 percent. (The United Nations also revealed that Islamic medical institutions were comparatively more efficient than their non-Islamic counterparts, having a larger percentage of the impoverished among their beneficiaries compared with UNRWA and the PNA.)[53] According to one UN agency, "Projects implemented by Islamic charities have been both diverse and large and have included food distribution, payment of unemployment allowances and financial support to homeless households."[54] Given the PNA's limited financial capacity, which had "been reduced to meeting the salary costs of public sector employees and operational costs of essential services ... [and] UNRWRA's chronic funding shortages and the extremely limited excess capacity of secular NGOs, the role of Islamic organizations [was] vital and, in some instances, irreplaceable."[55]

That the PNA supported the work of the Islamic social sector was clear. However, this support, both tacit and explicit, was subject to the periodic closing of Islamic social institutions, freezing of their assets, and external supervision of their governing bodies. Such measures were usually imposed after an Islamist attack inside Israel and in response to external pressure from Israel or the United States. Most of these institutions were soon able to resume operations—some officially and others not. Because the PNA was increasingly unable to fill the resulting void, Islamic institutions were more than tolerated. This further strengthened the presence of Islamic organizations in Palestinians' daily life but largely as providers, not innovators.

Furthermore, Islamist civic institutions were not engaged in activities (such as human rights, advocacy, or political reform) that exposed the PNA's deficiencies—a conscious decision on the part of the Hamas leadership, I was told. Unlike their secular civic counterparts, Islamist institutions did not challenge the PNA's work or methods but rather complemented them. In fact, during the early years of the Intifada, Islamist social institutions made a concerted effort to better coordinate their activities with the PNA and their non-Islamic counterparts. This took the typical form of information sharing about beneficiaries but also included emergency planning and sometimes the joint provision of services. While it is difficult to interpret what, if anything, this improved cooperation meant beyond the obvious, it did suggest the extension, in some form, of the Islamists' search for accommodation that defined their relations with the PNA during the Oslo period, as well as the PNA's inability and reluctance to restrict the Islamist social sector.[56] In contrast to the PNA, however, there was an international effort after 9/11 to restrict the activities of the Islamist social sector on the premise that they contributed to the political appeal and growth of Hamas, an effort at restriction that assumed draconian dimensions after January 2006.

Trend Two: Eroding Support for Hamas's Political Agenda

The other trend in the debate over the degree of popular support for the Islamists was the argument that this support was beginning to erode for two reasons. First, although Hamas had been very pragmatic vis-à-vis internal Palestinian politics, it had engaged in military policies—terrorist attacks against Israeli civilians—that proved devastating to Palestinian society. In fact, during the Oslo period, a similar phenomenon existed: Hamas's attacks inside Israel caused so much economic hardship for Palestinians that popular pressure was eventually brought to bear against Hamas to stop them, and was one factor in reducing and, for a time, ending these attacks. (However, despite Hamas's sensitivity to popular opinion, the attacks did resume for certain intervals despite the lack of popular support.)

Some observers argued that Hamas was increasingly being seen as a critical factor—perhaps the primary factor—inciting Israeli provocation, which, as stated above, contributed to Hamas's shift toward political over military action and its decision, for example, to declare a truce in June 2003, which occurred in the context of Hamas-Fatah negotiations over Hamas's future political role.[57]

Yet it is important to point out that Hamas's sensitivity to public opinion could also produce violent outcomes. In June 2006, after a dramatic rise in civilian deaths in Gaza that were blamed on Israel, Hamas suspended the 2005–2006 cease-fire largely in response to popular pressure. Salah al-Bardawil, a Hamas legislator, told an Israeli journalist that "people are calling us traitors ... and we did not want to become a new version of Fatah.... We were concerned we would lose our popularity. Therefore, we announced the resumption of the attacks."[58]

Another reason given for the growing criticism of Hamas (in 2004) was even more compelling: Hamas was increasingly perceived as politically more dishonest and socially more oppressive, a function perhaps, and in part, of its own internal weakness and the growing insularity of Palestinian society overall. For example, a disturbing phenomenon at the time concerned groups of Islamist women who would regularly attend the funerals of young men killed in suicide bombing missions in Israel. These Islamist women apparently pressured mothers and other family members not to grieve for their dead sons and brothers and derided and demeaned them for doing so. The logic was that these young men had died as martyrs in a noble cause and their deaths should be celebrated, not mourned. While I never actually spoke to family members so treated, I did speak with colleagues who had witnessed them and the negative outcomes they produced. The anger elicited from people over such issues belied, yet again, a sense of betrayal and of widening loss, a feeling perhaps that the social contract was being redefined in a manner that was unacceptable.

That Hamas was sensitive to changing popular perceptions was clear. Islamist supporters would often argue that these perceptions were wrong and were based only on the work of more extreme elements within the movement. The electoral campaigns of 2004, 2005, and 2006 provided Hamas with opportunities to channel its power to the local level when the center was clearly weak (a pattern with many precedents in the Palestinian context). These electoral campaigns enabled Hamas to appeal to the Palestinian public in a real and broader way, emphasizing (and rehabilitating?) its reputation for social and public service, efficiency, and integrity in contrast to Fatah's corruption, lawlessness, and abuses—the source of enormous public discontent and anger. And as Gunning points out, Hamas did not have to emphasize its resistance record.[59] Some municipal candidates ran on the basis of their charitable and social service work, notably women. Public opinion played a critical role in Hamas's electoral victories at the municipal and legislative levels[60] and in shaping the policies that led to those victories.

Significance of the Local and Municipal Elections: 2004–2005

The first round of local and municipal elections in the West Bank and Gaza was held in two parts: on December 23, 2004, in twenty-six districts in the West Bank and on January 27, 2005, in ten districts in the Gaza Strip. Local elections for all other districts were scheduled for May, September, and December 2005. These local elections were the first held in the occupied territories in almost thirty years; as such, they were a watershed political event that seriously and legally challenged the long-held dominance of the Fatah movement.[61] In all, Hamas did very well.

The first round was particularly significant since it "became a test of each organization's electoral capabilities and strength among the voters. The contest between Hamas and Fatah was intense, particularly in Gaza."[62] Hamas chose to highlight issues that were important to the Palestinian public, focusing on an agenda of social and political reform—which Fatah sorely lacked—in areas where Fatah was deficient and seemingly incapable of remediation.[63] Throughout the Gaza Strip and the West Bank, Hamas was able to wrest power from Fatah in many of its traditional strongholds (e.g., Nablus). Thus, in addition to its considerable social service network, Hamas found itself, by the fall of 2005, in majority control of many local councils in Gaza with access to Gaza's (and to a lesser extent the West Bank's) institutional infrastructure and attendant constituencies it had never before possessed.

As it had done with its programmatic work during Oslo, Hamas was able to identify specific and achievable developmental goals and pursue a widened form of community—and political—engagement, and was prepared to work with the Israeli civil administration if necessary. Hence, reforms were immediately implemented in several communities in Gaza and the West Bank with varying degrees of success that focused largely on infrastructural improvements long neglected by previous governments such as plans to redevelop Rafah's commercial center.[64] In March, Hamas announced that it would participate in upcoming legislative elections, which were then scheduled for July 2005. Given its success in local elections, Hamas expanded its domestic agenda in its legislative platform to include service provision (social welfare, care for the poor), economic reform (reducing unemployment, encouraging foreign investment, and free market initiatives), building a strong civil society and viable institutions, proper governance, and financial management and accountability—in short, thoroughgoing but not revolutionary change and reform.[65]

The emphasis on a secular program within parameters defined ideologically rather than on ideology (or on religiosity) itself—policies with precedent in the Oslo period—was key to Hamas's electoral victories. Not only did this allow the Islamist party to tangibly address the socioeconomic and political concerns of its constituents; it enabled Hamas to form pragmatic alliances with nonbelievers and nonsupporters including Christians, Marxists, and secularists and to pursue a broader form of civic and political engagement. (In this regard Hamas also argued that Israel's August 2005 disengagement from the Gaza Strip was a forced withdrawal due to Hamas's continued resistance, for which the organization also won public support.) In fact, religious references in Hamas's legislative electoral platform amounted to "about a page and a half out of the document's fourteen pages,"[66] pointing to a more flexible interpretation of religion—itself influenced by the extant social, economic, and political conditions also seen during the Oslo period. Not surprisingly, the majority of Hamas legislators and municipal councillors elected were professionals and community leaders with a secular as opposed to a strictly religious education, strongly underlining that socioeconomic and political factors were more important than religious ones in Hamas's overall political program and policies.[67]

Another important factor in winning grassroots support was Hamas's strong emphasis on involving people in the shaping of its election program through grassroots consultations and surveys,[68] a pattern of consultation and involvement that to varying degrees also characterized its social program during the Oslo period. In fact, Hamas's 2006 electoral platform directly speaks to the importance of involving the public in its decision-making process and in decentralizing power in the administration and implementation of its various programs.[69]

January 2006 and Beyond

By the time it had won the January 2006 legislative elections, Hamas had built up a considerable constituency who demanded redress. Continuing a pattern established during the Oslo period, Hamas demonstrated its ability to transcend its own partisan constituencies, moving beyond primordial identities toward something broader, which some in the movement articulated as citizenship—Palestinians as citizens (not subjects) with demands and constitutionally guaranteed civil rights. This is not surprising given that Hamas had always derived its legitimacy from its popular base and not from the international community, as did Fatah.[70] This constituency was able to abandon Fatah, not only because of Fatah's corruption and ineptitude, but also because it had been unable to realize its own political vision (especially after Arafat's death)—in short, because both Israel and the United States had proved Fatah so irrelevant to the fate of Palestinians. In fact, Fatah's younger guard was erased from the political map by the legislative elections.

A key challenge facing Hamas was how to deal with a victory that was larger than its support base and greater than its capabilities. Before the elections, the debate within Hamas was over the degree of its political integration—an indication that Hamas did not expect to win the elections, although Usama Hamdan, head of Hamas's Bureau of External Affairs in Beirut, stated that the senior level of Hamas did expect a victory.[71] After the elections, the debate centered on how to govern, a far greater challenge. The imperative was nothing less than a renegotiation of the status quo, moving—if desirable or possible—from partial to full integration (and not unlike the position the PLO had found itself in twenty years earlier). The goal, as articulated to me by Abu Shanab nearly seven years before, was not to defeat Israel—impossible in any case—but to deliver Palestine.[72] But how?

In April 2006, Nathan Brown of the Carnegie Endowment for International Peace issued the following assessment: "The new government is promising to focus on efficiency, clean government, and ending the disorder in Palestinian streets. Indeed, the Hamas government program says little of struggle and resistance; Islam and Islamic law are passed over in silence. But corruption is denounced three times and rule of law mentioned five times. The newly seated parliament has attracted attention for its insistence on extended prayer breaks, but the deputies themselves speak far more about transparency and economic problems than they do about the sale of alcohol or women's dress."[73]

Domestically, Hamas was pursuing a more moderate course, no doubt sensitive to the public mood and understanding that the competition with Fatah had not been completely won. The domestic arena was one in which Hamas had technocratic, organizational, and some creative expertise. This was made even more evident after Hamas assumed control over local councils in Gaza and the West Bank and improvements were subsequently implemented, many of which required coordination with Israeli officials. In this regard "Hamas did not radicalize Palestinians but Palestinians mainstreamed Hamas."[74]

Yet the obstacles were formidable. Internally, there were many issues of potential and soon to be realized conflict, some of which included Fatah's hegemony over the PNA and the security forces; power struggles between the executive (Fatah) and legislative (Hamas) branches; and Abbas's proposed reactivation of the PLO (and the Palestinian National Council) over the (Hamas-led) PNA as the primary political body empowered to negotiate on behalf of the Palestinians. Hamas's failure to form a coalition government not only meant that it had to rule alone but within an Authority of dual and opposed centers of power. Indeed, the power struggles and internecine violence (Hamas-Fatah militia violence, clan feuds) that ensued saw Fatah trying to consolidate its control over the West Bank and expand its influence in Gaza, with Hamas doing the obverse. The result was the emergence of two "increasingly antagonistic and well-armed 'fiefdoms' with competing ideological, social and political visions."[75] Tragically, no alternative to this duality or to the PNA existed.

Externally, although most of the international community accepted the election result, the United States (which had insisted on holding the elections) and the European Union did not. Hamas's political ascent only amplified its conflict with Israel, the United States, and the European Union, making its quest for legitimacy and recognition more improbable. Perhaps the greatest obstacle—itself imposed by Israel and the Quartet precisely to thwart any possibility of negotiation—was Hamas's unwillingness to honor past international agreements that called for recognition of, and negotiations with, Israel on terms imposed by Israel and the United States.

Hamas argued that recognition of the peace agreements with Israel would be equivalent to recognizing occupation, which it has steadfastly refused to do, particularly against a history of Palestinian concessions that not only failed to end Israeli occupation but deepened it. Statehood in the absence of sovereignty, which the PLO had agreed to, was an illusion. Recognition of Israel as a precondition of negotiations was criticized by none other than Efraim Halevy, the former head of Israel's Mossad intelligence service, who stated that the demand for "a priori renunciation of ideology before contact ... has never been made before either to an Arab state or to the Palestinian Liberation Organization/Fatah."[76]

Hamas voiced support for the Arab League's Beirut Declaration of March 2002, in which all Arab states including Palestine offered Israel permanent peace and normal diplomatic and economic relations in return for Israel's compliance with international law by retuning to its internationally recognized pre-1967 borders. Khaled Meshal, as chief of Hamas's Political Bureau in Damascus, as well as Hamas prime minister Ismail Haniyeh similarly confirmed the organization's willingness to accept the June 4, 1967, borders and a two-state solution should Israel withdraw from the occupied territories, a reality reaffirmed in the 2006 Palestinian Prisoners' Document, in which most major Palestinian factions had reached a consensus on a two-state solution, that is, a Palestinian state within 1967 borders including East Jerusalem and the refugee right of return.[77] Until an agreement was reached,[78] however, Hamas stated that it would solicit Palestinian, Arab, and Islamic support behind its nonrecognition of the Jewish state and the Palestinian right to resist occupation.[79]

Hamas's refusal to end armed resistance (including by other Palestinian factions) without an end to Israeli occupation remained firm in light of Israel's pursuit of unilateralism in the absence of negotiations. Other often forgotten factors impeding resolution also include Israel's continued and increasingly repressive occupation of Gaza and the West Bank, with which Hamas was ill-equipped to deal, and the refusal of Israel, the United States, and the European Union (among others) to recognize and deal with the Hamas-led government and their imposition of a sanction regime on the government (which had the support of certain Arab states). Furthermore (as stated in chapter 2), within weeks of Hamas's electoral victory, the United States was already engaged in secret talks to overthrow the Islamist government and foment greater interfactional violence,[80] signaling the West's unwillingness to tolerate an Islamic government in the region. A former political officer at the U.S. Embassy in Tel Aviv powerfully reveals:

> Hamas never called for the elections that put them in power. That was the brainstorm of Secretary Rice and her staff, who had apparently decided they could steer Palestinians into supporting the more-compliant Mahmoud Abbas ... and his Fatah Party through a marketing campaign that was to counter Hamas's growing popularity—all the while ignoring continued Israeli settlement construction, land confiscation, and cantonization in the West Bank. State Department

staffers helped finance and supervise the Fatah campaign.... An advisor working for... USAID explained to incredulous staffers at the Embassy in Tel Aviv how he would finance and direct elements of the campaign, leaving no U.S. fingerprints. USAID teams, meanwhile, struggled to implement projects for which Abbas could claim credit. Once the covert political program cemented Fatah in place, the militia Washington was building for Fatah warlord-wannabee Mohammed Dahlan would destroy Hamas militarily.... Rice was reportedly blindsided when she heard the news of Hamas's victory.... But that did not prevent a swift response. She immediately insisted that the Quartet... ban all contact with Hamas and support Israel's economic blockade of Gaza. The results of her request were mixed, but Palestinian suffering manifestly intensified. The isolation was supposed to turn angry Palestinians against an ineffective Hamas. As if such blockades had not been tried before.[81]

Hamas recognized the enormous constraints confronting it; as such, it recognized the importance of creating alliances under a common political program. From the outset, the Islamists stated their interest in forming a national coalition government with Fatah and other political factions and started a dialogue with other factions represented in the Palestinian Legislative Council to that effect.[82]

Furthermore, Hamas officials also claimed they were not averse to forming a technocratic government with none of the cabinet ministers having an explicit party affiliation. Some expressed their support for President Abbas and for eventually joining the PLO under the right conditions. Hamas was also pursuing a plan to allow the Fatah-dominated PLO to conduct the government's foreign policy while the new Hamas-led government or the PNA would concentrate on internal economic and social affairs. As such its leaders were considering handing Abbas, in his capacity as president of the PLO (not the PNA), the foreign affairs portfolio. The objective was to avoid a direct clash between Hamas and Israel and position Abbas as an intermediary.[83] While it cannot be known whether the Islamists were sincere in their intentions, it is now clear that Fatah and the West were never seriously interested in testing them.

Perhaps the most formidable constraints were economic and financial. As this book has argued, Hamas's strength and arguably the source of its greatest (productive) potential lay in the social realm, in the development and strengthening of a social/civic institutional infrastructure. The economic and financial boycott or siege subsequently imposed on the Hamas government not only damaged the economy and punished the population by cutting off desperately needed access to external (Israeli and other) markets and financial transfers (placing daunting limitations on an already hamstrung government consumed with issues of governance[84]); it had the effect of undermining precisely those sectors—that is, community-based institutions—where Hamas had consistently played a positive, more developmental, and innovative role.

For example, not long after the 2006 elections, USAID prohibited any direct contact with terrorists or terrorist groups, which included Hamas.[85] USAID partners were prohibited from meeting with ministers or other officials who were identified as Hamas, even if a "cabinet of technocrats" was formed. The United States stipulated that it would prosecute any American NGO that provided material aid to the now Hamas-led PNA, even in the form of in-kind medicines to a hospital run by the Ministry of Health.[86] In one USAID-funded NGO health program, recipients were switched away from Hamas-run Ministry of Health clinics to NGO-run clinics. In another, a major bid for a vocational and technical education program was abruptly withdrawn and was revised to focus on private rather than government-run vocational training institutes. Furthermore, most water and wastewater projects were frozen, and aid to Hamas-controlled local councils and municipalities ended. As a result, U.S.-funded agencies refused to start new initiatives or announce any new activities, especially those designed to strengthen PNA agencies or programs.[87] Instead, the donor's "development" agenda was replaced by one devoted almost entirely to relief and small-scale, labor-intensive initiatives, a pattern that had roots in the Oslo period.

With time, these constraints only deepened, becoming formal policy. Donor discomfort over the Hamas authorities in Gaza has resulted in an institutionalized policy of either withholding funding from them or being so directive about how assistance can flow, and to whom, that it has bordered on the immoral. Donor assistance, particularly from the United States, has been directed in ways that deselected whole swaths of the population.[88] USAID, for example, permits no assistance of any kind to go the Hamas-controlled Ministry of Health (MOH) in Gaza, although the ministry must urgently meet the health needs of hundreds of thousands of people. Effectively and practically, this has denied urgently needed equipment, pharmaceuticals, and disposables to anyone who ends up by design or accident in an MOH hospital or clinic.

Furthermore, U.S. government (USG) rules in the war on terror mean that an American organization working in Gaza—even if it is a conduit for European Union emergency funds—cannot contract to build, say, a reservoir in a municipality that the USG has deemed Hamas, because then the U.S. organization would be in danger of breaking OFAC (U.S. Treasury Office of Foreign Assets) rules with legal liabilities. Hence, it does not matter how much the community may need the reservoir; political imperatives supersede developmental ones. (It also should be remembered that Israel's blockade of the Gaza Strip virtually precludes the import of needed raw materials essential for development-oriented initiatives.) This has also happened in the West Bank, where, for example, an implementer may not be permitted to help with the water system in a given village because the local council is perceived as "Hamas."[89]

As economic pressures escalated and the struggle for internal political control deepened, so did factional violence. In 2006 and 2007, 407 Palestinians were killed—the vast majority in Gaza—and thousands injured as a result of internecine violence, and attacks against institutions aligned with each faction increased.[90] Human rights violations—abductions, torture, extrajudicial executions, vandalism of homes and institutions—were committed by both sides in Gaza and the West Bank.[91] Despite the short-lived establishment of a unity government brokered in Mecca in February 2007, the divisions between Hamas and Fatah had become so acute and so pernicious that by May 2007, one month before Hamas's takeover of the Gaza Strip, whole neighborhoods of Gaza City were under the control of either Hamas or Fatah; in some areas, factional control came down to individual street blocks.[92]

The conflict with Israel also intensified, given Israel's concern that Hamas's growing power and influence would spread not only in Gaza but, more important for Israel, to the West Bank. This violence was marred by continued and frightening violence largely from Israel, whose military incursions into Gaza and the West Bank continued almost daily.[93] According to the Israeli human rights group B'tselem, during the two years between January 2006 and December 2007 Israel killed 1,041 Palestinians (657 in 2006 and 384 in 2007), nearly half (480) civilians and the majority (823) from Gaza. During that same period 42 Israelis were killed by Palestinians, about 13 of them by Qassam rockets fired from Gaza.[94]

In June 2007 Hamas seized control of Gaza. The observation of a former State Department official is worth noting: "Finally, in mid-2007, faced with increasing chaos and the widely known implementation of a U.S.-backed militia, Hamas—the lawfully elected government—struck first. They routed Fatah's gangs, securing control of the entire Gaza Strip and established civil order. Its efforts stymied, the U.S. has for more than a year inflexibly backed Israel's embargo of Gaza and its collective punishment of the Strip's 1.5 million residents."[95] Clearly the political integration that Hamas had sought was denied.

Following the takeover, Israel and other key players in the international community intensified their policy of siege, isolating Hamas even more and punishing Gaza in the illusory belief that by weakening Hamas and its capacity to deliver, they would cause Gazans to cast it aside. Israel severely reduced cross-border traffic (although certain restrictions were temporarily eased after the June 19, 2008, cease-fire between Israel and Hamas went into effect), while the Ramallah-based Authority curtailed links with Gaza, preventing the normal functioning of government. At the end of August 2007, Salam Fayad announced the closing of 103 religious, educational, and charitable institutions linked to Hamas, arguing that they were operating in violation of the Non-Profit Organizations Law. Given the timing and sweeping nature of Fayad's directive, there is little doubt that it was political in basis.

In October, the PNA further dismantled what it called the Hamas charity committees in the West Bank with the aim of reforming and reorganizing these groups, since they "serve as the terror group's civilian infrastructure, and operate a network of mosques, schools, and institutions that support jailed terrorists."[96] This continued through at least December 2007.

However, time soon showed that Hamas's losses were not Fatah's gains; to the contrary, some analysts argue that Hamas gained more than it lost despite its increasingly authoritarian and repressive rule.[97] According to the International Crisis Group,

> Those intending to undermine Hamas have instead given it an assist. Persons who support current policy point out that Gazans are turning against the Islamists. There is real distress at economic hardships and anger at the Islamists' brutal behavior.... [However], [b]y boycotting the security, judicial and other government sectors ... [the] PA created a vacuum Hamas filled.... Economic punishment designed to hurt the rulers has hurt the ruled. Hamas finds ways to finance its government and can invoke the siege to justify its more ruthless practices.... Moreover, Hamas has had successes. Its new security force gradually restored order as militiamen curbed gunfire and kinsmen reduced inter-clan blood feuds. Criminal activity and mafia feuding have been sharply curbed..., Gazans blame Hamas for being unable to end the siege but also blame Israel for imposing it, the West for supporting it and Fatah for acquiescing in it. Military talk empowers Hamas's more militant, armed elements and boosts the movement's standing. Poverty and hopelessness boost the appeal of jihadi groups, particularly among under-sixteen Gazans—half the population.[98]

Impact on Islamist Social Institutions and Notions of Civism

Although the performance of the Hamas-led government has been the subject of praise (reestablishing law, order, and security) and condemnation (human rights violations in particular and refusal to release Gilad

Shalit), the fight, as it were—the nature of the resistance—became centered on power, not reform, a critical departure from the Oslo period.[99] One poignant illustration is seen in the civic institutional sector, which has become a battleground for factional power struggles and the framework for a discourse promoting the greater Islamization of society—in striking contrast to its role during Oslo.

The struggle over power affects the institutional sector in three primary ways. First, the attack as directed by the Abbas government against Islamist social institutions is clearly based on an understanding of the sector's role as the spinal cord of the movement. The Ramallah-based government aims to remove Islamic social support services and replace them, if possible, with institutional sources loyal to itself—thereby using the institutional sector to generate sustained political support for Fatah.

However, this attack against Hamas's institutional infrastructure has another, equally powerful (although, perhaps, less obvious) imperative, itself articulated to me by some Fatah activists: to diminish the sector's organizational, administrative, and managerial capacities, making it less competitive with Fatah's own and less of a mirror to Fatah's internal deficiencies and weakness. The aim, too, is to prevent the mobilization of people around a positive or productive agenda that was defined by Hamas. Hence, it was not only a matter of eliminating political competitors but of removing competent and socially productive ones.

According to Israeli security officials, the PNA successfully stepped up its attacks against Hamas's civilian infrastructure in the West Bank during the summer of 2008 and in August managed to close an additional forty-five Hamas-affiliated institutions and otherwise took over the administration of others (including some previously closed by Israel). Affected institutions included a benevolent association, charities, a cultural center, an orphanage, schools, and printing presses.[100] Clearly, it was far easier for Fatah to attack Islamist social institutions than their military counterparts.[101]

At a security coordination meeting between Israeli and Palestinian security commanders, which according to the Israeli newspaper *Yediot Ahronot* took place on September 19, 2008, Palestinian security officials revealed their plans for a violent confrontation against Hamas toward the end of 2008 just before Abbas's presidential term was set to expire (and after which Khaled Meshal declared that Abbas's government would no longer be legitimate). Majed Faraj, the head of the Fayyad government's military intelligence, apparently told his Israeli counterparts:

> Now every name of a Hamas institution you gave us is handled. You recently gave us the name[s] of 64 institutions—until today we have finished dealing with 50 of them. We closed some. In others, we

changed the management. We have also laid a hand on their funds [Israel gave the PNA numbers of 150 bank accounts that were suspected of being connected to terror organizations. The PNA closed 300 accounts].

I have two comments. First of all, once we used to think 1,000 times before entering a mosque. Today we enter every mosque when necessary. Don't understand from this that you are also permitted to enter. On the contrary: because you don't enter, we are able to. We also enter the universities, including the Islamic College in Hebron. We are doing our best. Even if we don't have a 100 percent success rate, our motivation is 100 percent.[102]

Second, the attack against social institutions has a decidedly retaliatory character, fueling political violence. Fatah attacks Hamas-linked institutions—charities, orphanages, cultural centers, printing shops, sewing workshops, and stores—in the West Bank, raiding and confiscating materials and forcing some to close,[103] and Hamas does the same to Fatah institutions in the Gaza Strip.[104] In July 2008, for example, Hamas security forces shut down 70 civil society organizations and charities linked to Fatah (reopened a month later), seized the office of the WAFA news agency run by President Abbas, banned certain newspapers, and stormed 40 other Fatah offices in response to a mysterious blast that killed a girl and five members of Hamas's armed wing on the beach in Gaza on July 25.[105]

According to the Palestinian Centre for Human Rights, Hamas attacked 152 civil society organizations—"belonging to, believed to be close to, or even not linked at all to Fatah"[106] throughout Gaza in July 2008. According to the PNA daily al-Hayat al-Jadida, Hamas also abducted 166 Fatah cadres.[107] The attacks continued in October 2008 when President Abbas deployed hundreds of troops to Hebron arresting Hamas officials and launching a "zealous operation against Hamas infrastructure," aiming their attacks at Islamic charitable associations in particular. According to Prime Minister Fayyad, this was done to bring security to the citizens of Hebron and was carried out with the approval of the Israeli authorities.[108]

Social institutions are also violated by Hamas and Fatah without provocation, as was the case when members of the pro-Hamas Islamic bloc stormed the campus of Gaza's al-Azhar University in October 2008, violating an administrative decision to freeze political activities on campus and precipitating violence with Fatah student groups.[109] These attacks also included arrest campaigns against academics, religious leaders, school principals, journalists, community figures, university students, and elected municipality officials and political supporters of one side or the other.[110] In November 2008, *al-Hayat al-Jadida* reported that Hamas declared Fatah an illegal organization in Gaza and imposed restrictions on its social and humanitarian activities. According to the paper, members of the Fatah movement were threatened with kidnapping and torture should any activities be implemented on behalf of Fatah including humanitarian activities.[111]

This factional and retaliatory behavior is further seen in a decision by the Fayyad government ordering seventy thousand PNA employees in Gaza not to report to work for the Haniyeh government or else lose their salaries (not everyone complied). This order was implemented gradually and included a series of strikes in the health and educational sectors. On August 29, 2008, for example, the Health Workers' Union in Ramallah called for a strike in the Gaza Strip protesting the decision by Gaza's Ministry of Health (MOH) to dismiss forty employees. It called for the suspension of all health services. The Hamas government claimed that the strikes were political in nature, coinciding with Ramallah's proposals to designate the Strip a "rebel territory."[112]

In eight MOH hospitals surveyed, 48 percent of health personnel were striking, including medical doctors (31 percent) and nurses (25 percent).[113] The MOH in Gaza responded by threatening the strikers with closure of their private clinics, pharmacies, and laboratories.[114] By September 22, 2008, 32 percent of all health personnel remained on strike in eight MOH hospitals: 25 percent of doctors, 29 percent of nurses, and 42 percent of other professionals. Two out of six hospitals declared emergency status, suspending all nonemergency health services, while the other six maintained full capacity even with a staff shortage.

Hamas's Internal Security forces compelled some hospital staff associated with very critical and rare specializations to return to work and closed the private clinics of striking doctors. In other cases Hamas appointed health care workers who were reportedly poorly trained and unfit for their assignments, a problem that was deepened by the rapidly eroding stocks of pharmaceuticals.[115] Hamas imposed harsh measures on community-based organizations. They were informed not to recruit or accept voluntary work from any striking health professional; a violation of this directive would result in the seizure of their organization.[116]

An analysis of the health strike by a member of the Union of Health Work Committees in Gaza clearly captures the terrible significance of the strike, particularly for the viability of civic institutions:

> The relationship between the two health ministries is still very dogmatic. The two Ministries are still giving contradictory decisions to their employees. Each Minister (Ramallah versus Gaza) reverses the decisions taken by the other side. Now, for hospitals and other

central organizations, we have two directors; one appointed by each minister and employees are divided between the two.

Employees live in a very uncertain environment and don't know to whom to report, to whom to listen and to whom to respond. This situation is dramatically affecting the ability of the MOH to deliver the services. One symbol of this is the long strike, which adversely affects the provision of services. Both ministers give priorities to their political agendas and their parties' interests [at] the price of professionalism and this is resulting in appointing the wrong people at the wrong places.... The achievements... [of] the last decade are now being dramatically erod[ed].[117]

Similar problems affected the education sector, which also went on strike on August 24, 2008. The General Union of Palestinian Teachers, which is aligned with Fatah, called on teachers to protest "arbitrary decisions" taken by the Ministry of Education in Gaza. These decisions included "transferring school directors and teachers to other schools, arresting a number of directors and teachers, attacking janitors and confiscating keys to schools."[118] Approximately 50 percent of PNA schoolteachers in Gaza were on strike by September 2, 2008. Hamas officials were able to recruit new teachers to replace the strikers, but on September 1, 80 percent of the administrative staff of al-Aqsa University joined in. By September 5, 2008, 50 percent of teachers (and 48 percent of medical workers) were on strike in Gaza.[119] By mid-November the strike had caused disruption in 381 government schools serving approximately 250,000 students.[120]

However, despite the immediate burdens imposed (and the fact that the strikes had not officially ended by early 2010), the longer-term effect of the strikes was to allow the Haniyeh government to replace thousands of public sector employees (who numbered thirty-two thousand in 2010) with Hamas members and supporters, consolidating Hamas's control over the social agenda and service delivery. Furthermore, the government had inherited a well-developed administrative apparatus that it employed with greater "coherence, effectiveness, and efficiency than had its predecessors." This was achieved in part with the help of PNA personnel who reported to work and a growing pool of university graduates among Hamas's supporters whom the government employed.[121]

The third form of attack on Islamic civil infrastructure comes from Israel and is directed at "philanthropic and social service networks"[122]—city malls, schools, charities, orphanages, soup kitchens, sewing workshops, health centers, media organizations, mosques, and municipal councils. Typically, associations considered linked or otherwise related to Hamas are raided, their offices are ransacked, and then they are arbitrarily closed.

Between 2006 and 2008, Israeli forces closed down over fifty charities in Qalqilya and Hebron, according to the United Nations.[123] In July 2008, following the February closure of the ICS (and its affiliated programs including the al-Anwar Library), 120 Israeli military vehicles stormed the city of Nablus to raid "suspicious" Palestinian associations. One place that was attacked was Nablus's shopping mall consisting of fifty shops and offices, all privately owned.[124]

Because the head of the mall's administration, Adli Yayish, was affiliated with Hamas, the mall's various owners were accused of funding Hamas and encouraging terrorism. Their stores and offices were ransacked, and some were sealed. The Israeli army commander posted notices that said, "Anyone found in this center will be considered as working on behalf of Hamas and puts himself and his properties in danger."[125] Initially the mall's ownership was to revert to Israel, but after an agreement between Israel and the PNA, the mall was reopened under PNA leadership after the PNA dismissed the mall's board of directors.[126] In a similar agreement with the Israeli authorities, the PNA reopened the ICS (and its affiliated institutions) under a Fatah-led administration that was appointed by decree. The Islamist administration of the al-Ahli Hospital also was replaced with PNA supporters. In fact, well before May 2009, Israel had "passed on the handling of the containment effort to the PA, which continues to raid Hamas-run institutions and arrest its activists."[127]

According to the Washington Institute for Near East Policy, in July 2008 Israel outlawed 36 NGOs in the West Bank considered linked to Hamas through fund-raising. PNA officials were reported to have closed 68 Hamas institutions, confiscating NIS 8.5 million. These same PNA officials also initiated a process of "replac[ing] Hamas leaders on *zakat* committee boards and audit[ing] the many NGOs that Hamas quickly—and often improperly—approved while heading the National Unity Government from March to June 2007."[128]

The use of civic institutions as a political battleground points to the growing inability of Hamas to provide social services as it once did—despite its total control over service delivery in the Gaza Strip—itself a result of the movement's primary focus on governance and political survival. Indeed, when Hamas had less support and less power among Palestinians, as it did during the Oslo period, ISIs operated more professionally and less politically, ideologically, and coercively than they have since, after Hamas gained real political power and a broader base of support.

Following Israel's December 2008 attack on Gaza (see the postscript below), the Haniyeh government pursued a more vigorous policy against NGOs in the Gaza Strip. Prior to the attack, it was mostly Fatah-affiliated institutions that were restricted or shuttered, typically in retaliation for similar measures taken against ISIs in the West Bank. Other, independent

NGOs were largely left alone. Since the end of the Israeli assault in January 2009, the Haniyeh government has required all NGOs to reregister with the Ministry of Interior and obtain prior permission for all programmatic activities. According to Yezid Sayigh,

> Again, this mirrored the new requirements applied by its PA counterpart in the West Bank; and, as there, it offered a means of political vetting. It may also have sought to limit the role of independent NGOs in the reconstruction of Gaza after Operation Cast Lead [the Israeli attack], so as to "crowd out" political competition with the government. These measures do yet amount to a sustained campaign, however: a number of NGOs that refused to comply have not suffered sanctions. It is not clear, however, if police intervention on several occasions to restore NGO premises or equipment seized by unidentified gunmen reflects the government's commitment to upholding the law, its inability to impose its will on Hamas militants, or a covert division of roles intended to intimidate independent NGOs.[129]

According to the Palestinian Centre for Human Rights in Gaza, there also have been more attacks against foreign-based and local, independent (human rights) NGOs in Gaza by unknown assailants.[130] For example, according to the United Nations, Hamas raided the offices of several NGOs including UN partner organizations, some of which were ordered to suspend their programs. Six organizations were reportedly targeted including those running care centers for women and children.[131] In the latter part of May 2010, furthermore, the Hamas Ministry of the Interior prevented a number of public activities organized by local (non-Islamic) NGOs to mark the anniversary of the *nakba* including a sit-in by the Palestinian NGO network, a workshop organized by the Independent Commission for Human Rights, and an event planned by the General Union of Palestinian Women.[132] On June 11, in violation of the Palestinian Basic Law, the Interior Ministry in Gaza issued Decision no. 48/2010, which states in part:

> All civil employees abstaining from joining their jobs in the civil service sector shall be prohibited from being affiliated to general assemblies of charitable and civil society organizations, or joining these organizations as employees or as members of their board of directors. The board of directors of any of the above-mentioned organizations shall not be approved if it includes a member who is an employee abstaining from joining his/her job in the civil service sector.[133]

Another illustration of the government's more coercive approach is seen in the way it is dealing with the delivery of desperately needed humanitarian assistance to Gaza. According to international NGOs

(INGOs), Hamas is seriously constricting the space for aid delivery. In 2010 a sophisticated and elaborate immigration facility was established near the border with Israel through which INGO officials and staff must pass before entering Gaza. While such border checks are expected, INGO officials have complained about the increasingly onerous processes they are put through by Hamas officials, including having all their official documentation opened and photocopied, including checks for vendors; periodic confiscation of equipment and attempted confiscation of monies; and demands for lists of INGO staff and dollar amounts paid to beneficiaries.[134]

INGOs are particularly concerned about one emerging problem: the growing (but as yet unrealized) demands by Hamas that foreign aid providers pay value-added taxes (VAT) to the Hamas government, which they cannot do under the rules established by the Quartet, since it would constitute an official recognition of the Islamist government—still considered illegal. According to the director of a U.S. aid organization working in Gaza with nearly thirty years of experience in the region, "We understand the need of the Hamas government to rule and be considered legitimate and we have worked hard to remain neutral and impartial so we can do our work. If Hamas demands VAT from our vendors who then demand it of us, and insist we coordinate everything with them, the INGO community will be forced to back out of Gaza bit by bit and this would be a tragedy for everyone. There is a growing lack of good faith on the part of the Hamas government and it is very worrisome. In fact, some people in Hamas have told us that they don't want us here. They tell us, God will provide."[135] This represents a critical change from the Oslo period.

Civic institutions have become legitimate political and military targets for both sides, their societal mission subsumed by factional competition, political violence, and the struggle over who will govern.[136] The growing transformation of the Islamist social sector as a site for civic reform to one of ideological conformity is further complicated by the fact that ISIs have become sites for what appears to be a broad-based initiative on the part of the Hamas government to encourage the greater Islamization of society—itself a direct response to the political challenge posed not only by Fatah but also by the steady emergence of more extreme Islamist groups in Gaza—representing perhaps the greatest change since the Oslo period.

The Rise of Salafist Groups and the Growing Islamization of Society in Gaza—ISIs as the Site of Religious Indoctrination?

For some time, Hamas has had to contend with the rise of radical, anti-Hamas Salafist groups in Gaza.[137] Small and with no direct ties to al-Qaeda, the Salafists in Gaza have strengthened over the last few years, operating independently of the Hamas leadership.[138] Salafists such as the Jund Ansar Allah (JAA) (Soldiers of the Supporters of God) refuse any form of diplomatic or political engagement or moderate interpretation of Islam in favor of violent extremism. They accuse Hamas of political and religious treason, arguing that by assuming the daily tasks of government and public service delivery (and participating in elections), Hamas has undermined its nationalistic and Islamic purity, weakening its resolve to fight Israel and to implement sharia law.[139]

For example, on May 23, 2010, approximately thirty armed and masked men attacked and set fire to an UNRWA recreation facility that was under construction at Sheikh Ajleen beach as part of UNRWA's annual summer games program for refugee children. The gunmen tied up the guard and gave him a warning letter containing three bullets for UNRWA's director John Ging. The letter read in part: "We were shocked when we heard about establishing beach locations for girls at the age of puberty and adolescence aiming to attack Muslims' honor and morality. You have to know that we will give away our blood and life but we won't let this happen and will not let you malicious people beat us. So you either leave your plans or wait for your destiny."[140] In an accompanying leaflet, the authors, who call themselves the Homeland Freemen, expressed outrage over the mixing of the sexes, particularly female teachers working in boys' schools; female students being taught to swim and dance on Gaza's beaches; and sending female students on trips to America and Europe.

Hamas's strategy for dealing with these groups has changed over time from acceptance to rejection. Initially, Hamas did not consider the Salafists a threat and even collaborated with them in the kidnapping of Gilad Shalit.[141] Today, however, any attempt to challenge Hamas's authority is met with a furious response.

One such response led to terrible clashes (that left 24 dead and 130 wounded) between the JAA and Hamas security forces on August 14, 2009, when the JAA declared an Islamic "emirate" in Rafah.[142] A particular threat is the al-Qaeda-inspired Jaljalat, "an amorphous network of armed militants believed ... to number some 2,500–3,000,"[143] including many members of the Qassam Brigades who want to return to armed resistance against Israel (other estimates place the number of adherents in the hundreds[144]). Other Salafist groups were targeted in early 2010 after being accused by the government of having joined with Fatah activists in plots against Hamas.

The challenge posed by the Salafists, which also is a product of Gaza's prolonged isolation from the outside world and continuous socioeconomic deterioration, is primarily political but one with pronounced social implications, particularly since they seek the deeper Islamization of society. According to several (non-Islamic) NGO officials interviewed in

Gaza in August 2009, the reason for Hamas's violent response in Rafah and need to assert greater if not total control over Gaza's Islamic infrastructure (e.g., schools, health clinics, *zakat* committees, mosques) is to ensure that Hamas remains the *only* representative of political and social Islam in Palestine. Hence, there is an imperative to eliminate not only political rivals but also Islamic ones. In order to "compete," as it were, and contain the dual threat posed by the Salafists, the Haniyeh government has encouraged, albeit carefully and cautiously, the greater Islamization of Gazan society through the *da'wa* arm of Hamas.[145]

Conservative female dress codes were among the first measures to be enforced. In the summer of 2009, headmasters at several government schools required young girls to wear the *hijab* and *jilbab* and sent home several girls wearing jeans. Although the Education Ministry said these policies derived from the schools and not from the government, they were implemented with government support. No individual wants to be seen as (and is no doubt fearful of) defying Islamic rules, although there were many reports in Gaza at the time that parents were desperately seeking placements for their daughters in private schools, which could not accommodate all the requests.

On July 26, Supreme Court justice Abdel Raouf al-Halabi ordered women lawyers appearing in his court to wear *hijabs* (which most do anyway). Nearly all of Gaza's 150 female attorneys challenged the ruling on the grounds that it was illegal and beyond the justice's power, forcing him to rescind his order. In this case and in some others the government retreated, but other, less public measures continued to be imposed. For example, girls have been banned from riding behind men on motor scooters; male hairdressers have been banned from women's salons; boys and girls are forbidden to sit together on beaches or dance together in public ceremonies; boys are forbidden to appear shirtless on beaches; alcoholic beverages are forbidden, and warnings exist against card playing and dating.[146] Furthermore, NGOs have been notified by the Internal Security Agency that joint activities involving girls and boys will incur an automatic fine.[147]

An internal memo from an official with a foreign-based NGO working in Gaza offers an interesting assessment of the Islamization campaign and the way the government is implementing it:

> One of my colleagues has a close relative who works in the Hamas Ministry of Education. He said that he asked his relative whether or not the new rules about new regulations regarding girls' dress codes were official or unofficial, and the relative said that—while the Ministry of Education has made no official statement to the public—the new rules are backed by the government.

> This same colleague sent his girls to school on Monday wearing jeans and headscarves. They came home yesterday and said, "Dad, we have to wear abbaya and jilbab now." They went to school today wearing conservative dress that would keep them out of trouble.... I also talked to a Palestinian journalist friend of mine who was on her way to Bashir Al Rayyis school today to interview administrators about the new policy, which has led to threats of expulsion for non-compliance. She confirmed that girls at Bashir Al Rayyis and other Gaza City girls' schools are now required to wear conservative dress. In some schools, there are signs out front that remind girls that conservative dress in now the rule.
>
> The question remains as to why the Ministry of Education won't just come out and say that they've put the new rule in place, and why they're leaving it up to schools to enforce and promote the rule on their own.[148]

The retreat from overt Islamization on the part of the government is due, in part, to Hamas's desire for international acceptance and to be seen as it once, and arguably still, sees itself: as a moderate (and politically successful) Islamic movement. A willingness to rule by religious edict also would undermine Hamas's claim to legitimacy under Palestinian civil law (which established the guidelines for the 2006 legislative elections) and would risk provoking secular-ruled Arab countries such as Egypt.[149] Yet the government's trial-and-error approach to imposing more rigid Islamic social codes reflects the strategic predicament in which it finds itself: caught between a desire for international legitimacy on the one hand and a growing embrace of militancy and Islamization on the other.[150] And the largely unrelieved siege of Gaza diminishes any possibility of meaningful change.

A Concluding Note

In the almost two decades since the Oslo process began, the quality of life in Palestine has declined markedly. The political, economic, and social possibilities of the past—both real and illusory—have since disappeared. It is striking that one theme that powerfully emerged from my interviews with members of the Islamist movement over a decade ago was the fear that Palestinians would lose an internal sense of self and purpose, resulting from the steady decline of society and itself a factor contributing to it. It seems they were not wrong. The losses are found in all areas of Palestinian life. Yet the most profound are seen in a fragmenting social order where cohesion is defined by the boundaries of the enclave and solidarity by the ability to live within it. Without the capacity to rise above the divisiveness that entraps them, to elevate discussion and action toward something larger, Palestinians will continue to experience decline in all facets of life and remain vulnerable to Israeli oppression.[151] The imperative and the challenge is primarily an internal one, for the external forces positioned against the Palestinian people, particularly in the aftermath of the assault on Gaza and the continued failure of the U.S. government to challenge Israeli policies and fairly address Palestinian grievances, will not diminish anytime soon.

The denial of society, of any collective and communal sense of being—something Hamas understood and once worked hard to provide—is the greatest threat facing Palestinians. Yet, as I have hopefully made clear, the dissolution is not Hamas's fault alone, nor is its solution Hamas's responsibility alone.

Postscript

THE DEVASTATION OF GAZA—SOME ADDITIONAL REFLECTIONS ON WHERE WE ARE NOW

> At Appomattox, the story of the war was to all intents and purposes over. At least it was over for the winners. They assimilated it as confidence, as self-respect, as an unconscious faith in the existing order of things. But for the losers, war is a different story—different from the story the winners tell, different from the story that either the most even-handed or the most polemical of the historians tell, and different from the whole idea that stories have sharp boundaries within which they are contained and concluded. The loser's story is less a thing to comprehend than a means of comprehension. It infiltrates the individual psyche as well as the collective one. It cannot allow its ingrained politics to be examined and negotiated, because it cannot allow them to be written off. Pride, identity, grief, and grievance coalesce in the story of defeat. They keep it alive; it keeps them alive.
> —*Franklin Burroughs*[1]

If men do not build, asks the poet, how shall they live?[2]

ON DECEMBER 27, 2008, Israel launched a massive assault against the Gaza Strip that killed 1,417 Palestinians—926 of whom were civilians including 313 children—in three weeks.[3] This is nearly equivalent to the number of people killed in Afghanistan during the whole of 2007.[4] In addition, 5,303 Palestinians were wounded, including 1,606 children and 828 women.[5] The total number of Israelis killed came to 10 soldiers (4 killed by friendly fire) and 3 civilians, meaning that the ratio of total Palestinians to Israelis killed was around 100:1, while the ratio of civilians killed was around 300:1.

The immediate pretext for Israel's attack was Hamas rocket fire into Israel and Israel's right to defend itself, but this does not explain the disproportionality of the Israeli attack, especially against the history of severe sanctions and attacks in the preceding months and years.[6] While no one disputes a nation's right to self-defense, the record demonstrates that Israel was the far greater aggressor.[7] This is made clear in the many human rights reports issued after the war, notably those by Amnesty International and Human Rights Watch and, most famously, the *Report of the United Nations Fact Finding Mission on the Gaza Conflict* or Goldstone Report.

The devastating assault on Gaza was not only about destroying Hamas as a political force; in fact, Hamas rockets had very little if anything to do with Israel's attack. (Furthermore, various human rights reports and IDF soldier testimonies make it clear that Israeli forces encountered little if any resistance by Hamas fighters. In fact, not a single battle was fought either in densely or sparsely populated areas for the twenty-two days of the war. According to Amnesty International, many of the Palestinians killed were not caught in crossfire but were killed in their homes while they slept or going about their daily routine.[8] And these reports were clear to point out that although Hamas, like Israel, was guilty of war crimes, it was on a far smaller scale.)

This was an attack against the Palestinian people and their continued resistance—be it by Hamas or by the people of Gaza—and their consistent refusal to accede to Israeli demands and conditions. The Israeli government argued that since all Palestinians in Gaza supported Hamas, there were no true civilians in Gaza and all attacks against them were therefore justified, including the reduction and denial of humanitarian supplies, military incursions and invasions, and the continued assassination of the Hamas leadership.

Unlike the West Bank, which has effectively been subdued by Israeli policies of land expropriation, settler expansion, territorial cantonization, demographic isolation, extrajudicial assassinations, and other forms of military control (now supported by a cooperative PNA security structure), Gaza has continued to resist and defy. This is a characteristic feature of Israel's relationship with Gaza and has been since 1967. In this regard, Israel's attack—which destroyed or partly destroyed 6,300 Palestinian homes (compared with the near-destruction of one Israeli home), 18 schools, and 30 mosques, and destroyed or damaged 280 schools and kindergartens, 1,500 factories and workshops, and nearly half of Gaza's 122 health facilities including 15 hospitals[9]—was also about pacification and sending a clear message to Palestinians in the West Bank that says Israel will not withdraw from settlements or return any lands already taken. This linkage is critically important, yet little noticed or understood.

There were other reasons for the war on Gaza. One was to enhance Israel's deterrence capacity, particularly after its defeat in Lebanon in July 2006, and to rehabilitate Israel's image as an effective ally in the American-led war against terror.[10] But most importantly, perhaps, Israel's attack came after a period of quiet in which several changes were beginning to (re)emerge: perhaps most critical was the clear indication by Hamas—from the leadership in both Damascus and Gaza—that it was seeking a settlement of the conflict along June 1967 borders, a territorial compromise that successive Israeli governments have been unwilling to make because of their desire to maintain control over the West Bank. Israel's preference for expansion over security has historically been expressed in policies that have consistently sought to delay political accommodation and compromise and eliminate the threat of political settlement, and in the "desperate fear of diplomacy."[11]

In this regard, the assault on Gaza was no different. Former Mossad director Ephraim Halevy made it clear that Israel was well aware of Hamas's willingness to reach a compromise based on a two-state solution. In December 2008, shortly before Israel attacked Gaza, Halevy told the Israeli cabinet: "The Hamas leadership has recognized that its ideological goal is not attainable and will not be in the foreseeable future. They are ready and willing to see the establishment of a Palestinian state in the temporary borders of 1967.... They know that the moment a Palestinian state is established with their cooperation, they will be obligated to change the rules of the game. They will have to adopt a path that could lead them far from their original ideological goals."[12]

Furthermore, Yuval Diskin, head of Israel's Shin Bet, insisted that Hamas was interested in renewing the relative calm with Israel, a fact fully discussed in a report issued by the Israeli Intelligence and Terrorism Information Center and released by Israel's Ministry of Foreign Affairs.[13] In fact this report stated: "The lull was sporadically violated by rocket and mortar shell fire, carried out by rogue terrorist organizations, in some instance in defiance of Hamas.... At the same time, the [Hamas] movement tried to enforce the arrangement on the other terrorist organizations and to prevent them from violating it." Diskin told the Israeli cabinet that Hamas would renew the truce if Israel lifted the siege of Gaza, stopped military attacks, and extended the truce to the West Bank.[14] In fact, all the evidence strongly suggests that if Israel's goal was truly to end Hamas rocket fire, it could have done so immediately just by easing the economic blockade of Gaza, which was Hamas's primary condition for continuing the cease-fire. This begs certain questions: Does Israel have peaceful short-term alternatives to the use of force in response to rockets from Gaza?[15] and, What is the real goal of the economic blockade?

Thus, as Norman Finkelstein argues, Israel likely feared that the Islamic movement would be regarded as a credible and legitimate negotiating partner able to extract certain meaningful concessions, which the PNA—whether under Arafat or Abbas—could not. This would enhance the standing of the Islamists—not only among Palestinians, but also within the international community. Israel would find it increasingly difficult to reject Hamas, and it would be only a matter of time before international pressure, particularly from the Europeans, would be placed on Israel to negotiate.[16] Hence Israel had to "fend off the latest threat posed by Palestinian moderation ... and [eliminate Hamas] as a legitimate negotiating partner."[17]

Furthermore, during the six-month period of the truce (June–December 2008) consensus was beginning to emerge, both among the international community and within certain sectors in Israel, for restarting a political process, engaging Hamas directly or indirectly, freezing Israeli settlement expansion, and boycotting Israeli settlement products. There were also efforts, albeit troubled, by the Egyptian government to mediate internal divisions between Hamas and Fatah and reunify the Palestinian government, a critical prerequisite to achieving any kind of workable political agreement. In fact, Israel's attack occurred just before a scheduled meeting between Fatah and Hamas in Cairo that had been aimed at political reconciliation and unification.[18]

Israel had been preparing to attack Gaza long before the June 2008 cease-fire. As Defense Minister Ehud Barak stated openly to the Israeli press in January 2009, "A two-year intensive effort that included training, amassing supplies, renewing equipment and acquainting the commanders with the necessary issues has come to fruition."[19] In fact, this training took place at the National Urban Training Center (NUTC)—a 7.4-square-mile generic city known as Baladia City—built in the Negev Desert by the U.S. Army Corps of Engineers and funded largely from U.S. military aid. Israel had been preparing its forces to fight in four theaters: Gaza, Lebanon, the West Bank, and Syria. The commander of the NUTC also commands the IDF's Gaza Division. According to the *Marine Corps Times*, Baladia City is located at the Tze'elim training base, "less than nine miles east of Rafah, a terrorist-ridden smugglers' haven that straddles the Gaza-Egyptian border, [and] naturally resembles the sandy, arid terrain of the Palestinian coastal strip."[20]

According to *Ha'aretz*, Israel negotiated the June 2008 truce only because the Israeli army needed time to prepare and had no intention of meeting the terms it had agreed to, including an easing of the economic blockade.[21] The provocation conveniently arrived on November 4, 2008, as the international community was focused on the U.S. presidential elections. Israel claimed that Hamas was digging a tunnel close to the border fence to abduct Israeli soldiers. The tunnel clearly existed, although it is debatable whether Hamas would have risked a successful truce and the possibility of political negotiations to abduct Israeli soldiers at a point when holding them would yield relatively little strategic value. According to Zvi Barel of *Ha'aretz*, "[The tunnel] was not a clear and present danger: Its existence was always known and its use could have been prevented on the Israeli side, or at least the soldiers stationed beside it removed from harm's way. It is impossible to claim that those who decided to blow up the tunnel were simply being thoughtless. The military establishment was aware of the immediate implications of the measure, as well as of the fact that the policy of 'controlled entry' into a narrow area of the Strip leads to the same place: an end to the lull. That is policy—not a tactical decision by a commander on the ground."[22]

Furthermore, it should be noted that a rocket has never been fired at Israel from the West Bank. Yet, during the period of the truce, Israel continued and indeed intensified its policies of extrajudicial killings, settler expansion, land theft, territorial cantonization, movement restrictions, home demolitions, and other measures against Palestinians in the West Bank, the control of which remains uppermost on Israel's political agenda. According to the European Union, the Israeli government is using "settlement expansion, house demolitions, discriminatory housing policies and the West Bank barrier as a way of 'actively pursuing the illegal annexation' of East Jerusalem."[23]

Israel's rejection of meaningful territorial compromise and a viable two-state solution has assumed many forms over time. One of the most damaging has been the physical and demographic separation and isolation of the West Bank and Gaza Strip, which was largely completed by 1998 during the Oslo period. Separation was designed to sever Gaza from the West Bank and East Jerusalem and, hence, from "its population, its education centres and health services, from jobs in Israel and from family members and friends."[24]

With the withdrawal of Israeli settlers from Gaza in August 2005 during Israel's disengagement, the political separation of the two territories was effectively sealed and the foundation for a Palestinian state effectively destroyed. Yet Israel retained total control, both direct and indirect, of Palestinian "land, borders, resources, water, population registry, economics, construction, education, health and medical services,"[25] in both Gaza and the West Bank. This state of affairs not only thwarted Palestinian political and economic cohesion; it also weakened the sense of national unity or community among Palestinians (where identity is now constructed by geography), and has been a critical factor in allowing Israel to isolate and control the Gaza Strip and to consolidate its control over the West Bank.

It is difficult to imagine that these measures, among others, are about peace or security. This leads to my second main point: The subjection of Gaza (and the West Bank) is not a discrete event without history or context, despite the fact that it has been portrayed that way. The December 2008 attack did not emerge in a vacuum but is a tragic though inevitable part of a far larger context of prolonged Israeli military occupation and colonization that preceded Hamas by several decades and would undeniably continue should Hamas disappear from the map tomorrow. This occupation, which is the fundamental reason underlying Palestinian resistance, is characterized by economic sanctions, closure, boycotts, and siege that have been all but forgotten. In fact, the word "occupation" is barely heard any more. The Israeli journalist Amira Hass observes: "since the creation of the PNA, Israel has treated the 'other side' as sovereign and independent—when it wants to. As if the PNA enclaves were not under occupation. Thanks to this very effective propaganda, most Israelis believe that the creation of the PNA resembles the founding of an independent state [and] an ungrateful one at that."[26]

Some Reflections on Gaza's Economy and People

The Israeli occupation has debilitated Gaza's economy and people, especially since 2005. Although economic restrictions actually increased before Hamas's electoral victory in January 2006, the deepened sanction regime and siege that was subsequently imposed and later intensified in June 2007, when Hamas seized control of Gaza, has pauperized Gazans, decimated the local economy, and, it appears, created a growing financial crisis for Hamas. Indeed, by April 2010 Israel had allowed only 73 commercial items to enter Gaza, compared with 4,000 approved products (including building materials) prior to June 2006, when the Israeli soldier Gilad Shalit was abducted.[27] A key result has been the virtual collapse of Gaza's private sector, which the December assault largely completed.[28] If there was a pronounced theme among the many Palestinians, Israelis, and internationals I have interviewed in the last four years, it was the fear of irreversible decline and irreparable damage to Gaza's society and economy.[29] Tragically, for Gazans restoration now defies comprehension.

For example, Gaza's protracted closure has resulted in the shrinking of the private sector: At least 95 percent of Gaza's industrial establishments (3,750 enterprises) were either forced to close or were destroyed between 2006 and 2010, resulting in a loss of between 100,000 and 120,000 jobs.[30] The vast restrictions on trade have also contributed to the continued erosion of Gaza's agricultural sector, which was exacerbated by the destruction of five thousand acres of agricultural land and 305 agricultural wells during the 2008 assault.[31] These losses also include the destruction of 140,965 olive trees, 136,217 citrus trees, 22,745 fruit trees, 10,365 date trees, and 8,822 other trees.[32] Furthermore, many attempts by Gazan farmers to replant the soil following the cessation of hostilities have failed owing to depletion and contamination of the water and high levels of nitrates in the soil. Gaza's agricultural sector has been further undermined by the buffer zone imposed by Israel on the Strip's northern and eastern perimeters (and by Egypt on Gaza's southern border) containing some of Gaza's most fertile land. The zone is officially 300 meters wide and 55 kilometers in length, but according to the United Nations, farmers entering within 1,000 meters of the border have sometimes been fired upon by the IDF.[33] Approximately 30–40 percent of Gaza's total agricultural land is contained in the buffer zone.[34] There should be little doubt that Gaza's agricultural economy has effectively collapsed.

Gaza's relatively productive (albeit captive) economy has been reduced to one largely dependent on public sector employment, relief aid, and smuggling, illustrating the growing informalization of the economy. Even before the war, the World Bank had already observed a redistribution of wealth from the formal private sector toward black market operators. There are many illustrations, but one that is particularly startling concerns changes to the banking sector. A few days after Gaza was declared an enemy entity in September 2007, Israel's banks announced their intention to end all direct transactions with Gaza-based banks and deal only with their parent institutions in Ramallah, West Bank. Accordingly, the Ramallah-based banks became responsible for currency transfers to their branches in the Gaza Strip. However, Israeli regulations prohibit the transfer of large amounts of currency without the preapproval of the Israeli Ministry of Defense and other Israeli security forces. Consequently, over the last two years, Gaza's formal banking sector has had serious problems in meeting the cash demands of its customers.[35] This in turn has given rise to an informal banking sector, the *hawala* banking system, which is now controlled largely by people affiliated with the Hamas-led government, making Hamas Gaza's key financial middleman. Consequently, moneychangers, who can easily generate capital, are now arguably stronger than the formal banking system in Gaza, which cannot.

Another powerful expression of Gaza's growing economic informality is its burgeoning tunnel economy, which emerged long ago in response to the siege, providing a vital lifeline for an imprisoned population. According to local economists, at least two-thirds of economic activity in Gaza was, by early 2010, devoted just to smuggling goods into (but not out of) Gaza.[36] Yet even this lifeline is threatened as Egypt, apparently assisted by U.S. government engineers, has been building an impenetrable underground steel wall along its border with Gaza in an attempt to reduce smuggling. At its completion the wall will be nine to ten kilometers long and twenty to thirty meters deep. The tunnels, which Israel has long tolerated (despite periodic attacks against them) in order to keep the siege intact, have also become an important source of income for the Hamas government and its affiliated enterprises, effectively weakening traditional and formal businesses and the re-creation of a viable business sector. In this way, the siege on Gaza has led to the slow but steady replacement of the formal business sector by a new, largely black market sector that rejects registration, regulation, or transparency and, tragically, has a vested interest in maintaining the status quo.

Gaza's economy, now incapable of sustainable productive activity, favors a desperate kind of consumption among both the poor and the rich, but it is the former who are unable to meet their needs. Despite billions in international pledges that have yet to materialize, the overwhelming majority of Gazans remain compromised. The combination of a withering private sector and stagnating economy has led to high unemployment levels, forcing the majority of people into poverty. Unemployment ranges from 31.6 percent in Gaza City to 44.1 percent in Khan Younis;[37] according to the Palestinian Chamber of Commerce, the de facto unemployment rate is closer to 65 percent.[38] A critical problem, therefore, is the lack of purchasing power. Consequently, at least 75 percent of Gaza's 1.5 million people now require humanitarian aid to meet their basic food needs, compared with around 30 percent ten years ago.

Furthermore, access to adequate amounts of food from Israel has been a critical problem and one that appears to have grown more acute after the cessation of hostilities in mid-January 2009. Internal data from September 2009 through the beginning of January 2010, for example, reveal that Israel allowed Gazans no more (and at times less) than 25 percent of needed food supplies, with levels having fallen as low as 16 percent.[39] During the last two weeks of January, these levels declined even more. Between January 16, 2010, and January 29, 2010, an average of 24.5 trucks of food and supplies per day entered Gaza, or 171.5 trucks per week. Given that the Gaza Strip requires 400 trucks of food alone *daily* to sustain the population, Israel allowed in no more than 6 percent of needed food supplies during this two-week period.[40] At the end of 2009, the Food and Agriculture Organization and World Food Programme stated: "The evidence shows that the population is being sustained at the most basic or minimum humanitarian standard."[41]

In an attempt to challenge Israel's siege of Gaza, an aid flotilla of passenger boats and cargo ships (led by a pro-Palestinian organization and a Turkish NGO) attempted to reach Gaza in late May 2010. However, the flotilla was raided by the Israeli navy in international waters and nine people were killed. The international condemnation that followed led to a decision by Israel's Security Cabinet on June 20 to adjust its policy toward Gaza. In practical effect, this meant that Israel would list only those items that are not allowed into Gaza, which are "limited to weapons and war material, including problematic dual-use items"[42] and allow, by implication, those items not listed. The cabinet also pledged to increase the capacity of current crossings to 250 trucks per day at the Kerem Shalom crossing and the equivalent of 120 truckloads of aggregates daily at the conveyor belt operating at the otherwise shuttered Karni crossing. It also promised to facilitate the entrance of construction materials for PNA-approved projects under international supervision and improve access for humanitarian cases and staff of international organizations.[43]

And while it is true that the number of consumer items (e.g., ketchup, chocolate, children's toys, spices, paper, perfume) entering Gaza has increased moderately (although still inadequate to need or to the import levels prior to the siege), the most damaging restrictions remain intact. For example, raw materials necessary for industry and manufacturing and critical for rebuilding Gaza's shattered economy remain highly restricted and will be allowed in only on a project-by-project basis (projects that the Israeli authorities will have to approve).[44] "Textiles, industrial-sized buckets of margarine, and other raw materials are still banned."[45] And even if the vast amounts of needed materials were to gain entry, most exports continue to be prohibited, precluding the resumption of normal trade and meaningful economic recovery. Furthermore and with rare exceptions, Gazans continue to be denied any freedom of movement outside the Strip. Movement of people remains limited to certain humanitarian and medical cases and international staff. In a July 2010 High Court petition submitted on behalf of a young Gazan woman wishing to travel to the West Bank to attend a master's degree program in human rights and democracy at Bir Zeit University, the state of Israel clarified:

> Regarding passage for the population, the announcement [of June 20] did not say anything about expanding the current policy, which permits entrance in humanitarian cases, with emphasis on urgent medical cases ... this decision does nothing to expand the criteria [for travel], and it certainly does not permit passage for purposes of Master's degree studies.[46]

In the summer of 2008, approximately 26,000 Gazan workers crossed into Israel daily through the Erez terminal in Northern Gaza (itself a dramatic reduction from years past). During the last week of June and first week of July 2010 an average of 95 people per day passed through Erez (travel to the West Bank is all but banned in order to ensure the separation of the two territories).[47]

A Final Comment on Hamas and Its Social Institutions

According to the *New York Times*, a senior Israeli official explained that a key goal of Israel's massive assault on Gaza was the destruction of "both aspects of Hamas—its resistance or military wing and its *dawa*, or social wing. He argued that Hamas was all of a piece ... and in a war, its instruments of political and social control were as legitimate a target as its rocket caches."[48] Affirming this position, Reserve Major-General Amiran Levin stated, "What we have to do is act systematically with the aim of punishing all the organizations that are firing the rockets and mortars, as well as the civilians who are enabling them to fire and hide." Deputy IDF Chief of Staff Dan Harel further warned, "After this operation there will not be one Hamas building left standing in Gaza," while the IDF spokesperson, Major Avital Leibowitz, stated, "Anything affiliated with Hamas is a legitimate target."[49]

This would certainly explain the massive destruction of Gaza's infrastructure, including the January 15 assault on the al-Wafa Rehabilitation Hospital, which was emblematic of the profound social loss incurred. A friend wrote: "Al-Wafa became part of the Israeli finale, as in the Lebanon war, when some of the worst acts were committed as the war was ending. A few days before the ceasefire, al-Wafa was hit by eight artillery shells, destroying the men's ward. Patients had to be discharged to their homes or other hospitals—the same day three other hospitals in Gaza City were hit."[50] Israel's aim to destroy Hamas's social and economic infrastructure also explains why the postwar reconstruction of Gaza has yet to begin and most likely will not. This is echoed in the Goldstone Report, which concludes that the invasion of Gaza constituted "a deliberately disproportionate attack designed to punish, humiliate and terrorize a civilian population, radically diminish its local economic capacity both to work and to provide for itself, and to force upon it an ever increasing sense of dependency and vulnerability."[51]

Furthermore, the Abbas government's attack against Islamist social institutions continues in the West Bank (as does the Hamas attack against Fatah's in Gaza) and is considered a critical part of a PNA strategy to undermine Hamas. In March 2010, the *Jerusalem Post* reported that over the preceding two years the PNA fired more than three hundred imams suspected of affiliation with Hamas or who had delivered lectures about Islam and sharia or provocative speeches in mosques. In addition more than one thousand schoolteachers lost their jobs, including members and supporters of Hamas, individuals with family members suspected of affiliation with Hamas, people who did not support Fatah, and those who "had become too religious" and might join Hamas (some teachers claimed they were dismissed after refusing to work as informants for certain PNA security services).[52] In August 2010 the Palestinian security services arrested six faculty members at An-Najah University in the West Bank city of Nablus because of their ties to a charity suspected of being a front for Hamas.[53] The PNA has also been successful in diminishing the flow of funding to Hamas in part by supervising charitable contributions in the West Bank and Gaza.[54]

The prolongation of the status quo and the division and isolation it produces has been extremely damaging. The need to engage Hamas at all levels remains vital, a position articulated by several analysts and negotiators including John Hume, who shared the Nobel Peace Prize for his work on the Belfast Agreement, and a group of senior intelligence officers at the U.S. Central Command (CENTCOM) in June 2010.[55] The failure to do so,[56] which has largely precluded Hamas from achieving any meaningful political outcome, forcing it inward, already can be seen in Gaza in growing tensions between Hamas's political and military wings (as well as growing divisions within each of those wings), with the latter calling for greater violence against Israel as seen in the horrible attack, at the end of August 2010, that killed four settlers—one of them a pregnant woman—in the southern Hebron hills, followed the next night by another attack near a settlement northeast of Ramallah. Tragically these attacks, which were timed to coincide with the U.S.-led peace talks between Netanyahu and Abbas in Washington in early September (and which, by excluding Hamas, will further destabilize the situation), suggest that more will follow. Emerging turf wars over the control of Gaza's increasingly lucrative, albeit informal, business sector, furthermore, have positioned the Qassam Brigades against Hamas Interior Minister Fathi Hamad and his loyalists. The growing divisions within Hamas may also have led to a resumption of clan fighting in Gaza, which had remained dormant for some time.[57] And the failure to engage is also seen in rising tensions between a variety of political factions, both old and new.[58] Perhaps most concerning is the growing prominence of the Salafist groups, a threat Hamas has tried to contain violently and through the increasing and more coercive Islamization of society, a choice the Hamas leadership once resisted.

The situation in Gaza and the West Bank is wholly unsustainable. If Palestinians continue to be denied what we demand for ourselves—an ordinary life, dignity, livelihood, protection, and a home (in short, freedom)—then violence, division, and decline will intensify. At stake is an entire generation of Palestinians. If they are lost, we shall all bear the cost.

Appendix

ISLAMIST (AND NON-ISLAMIST) SOCIAL INSTITUTIONS

AT THE TIME OF my research, some Islamist social institutions asked not to be identified and made it a condition for their participation. Hence, this list is incomplete. In some instances I provide a generic description of individual institutions.

Abu Rayya Rehabilitation Center
Al-Ahli Hospital
Al-Anwar al-Ibrahimiyya Library for Children
Al-Huda Health Clinic
Al-Ihsan Association for Disabled Children
Al-Ihsan Charitable Society
Al-Jam'iyya al-Islamiyya
Al-Mujamma al-Islami
Al-Rahma Association
Al-Salah Islamic Association
Al-Wafa Medical Rehabilitation Hospital
Bethlehem Charitable Society
Hebron Women's Union/Hebron Young Women's Club
House of the Book and the Sunna
Islamic Charitable Society
Islamic Committees, Gaza refugee camps (kindergartens, women's groups)
Islamic University in Gaza
Nuseirat Rehabilitation Center, Nuseirat refugee camp
Palestine Center for Studies and Research
Palestine Monetary Authority
Qatar Charitable Society
Society for the Care of the Handicapped
Sun Daycare Center
Various Islamist factories, wholesalers, and retail businesses
Women's Islamic Association
Young Women's Muslim Society
Zakat committees, Gaza Strip

AFTERWORD TO THE PAPERBACK EDITION

HAMAS IN A CHANGING MIDDLE EAST

> We will never forget you, Ahmed Yassin!
> —*The chant of tens of thousands of Islamists marching in solidarity with Palestine; Morocco, March 2012*[1]

IN THE PERIOD since this book was completed, there have been some momentous changes in the Middle East. The most dramatic, of course, has been the revolutions in some parts of the Arab world. If nothing else, the Arab uprisings against corrupt dictatorships demonstrate that the Arab street has not died as many analysts had long argued and that the Arab people can indeed alter the regional order (despite the political and economic problems that now attend these new regimes).[2] Yet, the profound transformations in the region did not reach Palestine or catalyze another Intifada and there are many reasons for this. At their core is the fact that toppling the regimes in Gaza and the West Bank would do nothing to liberate Palestinians, given Israel's deepening control and entrenched occupation; to the contrary, the fall of these regimes could bring about greater violence and insecurity, at least in the near term. But the regional changes produced by the "Arab Spring"—especially in Egypt now governed by the Muslim Brotherhood—have had a demonstrable impact on Palestinian politics. This is clearly seen in Gaza and in the role of the Hamas government both domestically and internationally, in the changing relationship between the internal and external leadership of Hamas, in Hamas's political vision, and in the political relationship between the Gaza Strip and West Bank.

I should state at the outset that I am only going to touch upon some of the important changes that have arisen in Gaza since the completion of this book but will not examine them in any detail, which would require several new chapters. My aim in this afterword is simply to raise some critical issues with pronounced implications for the future of Hamas, Gaza and Palestine that I shall leave others to explicate.

At the time this book ended in 2010, Hamas was politically and economically marginalized, virtually cut off from the West Bank—where its supporters were repressed by PNA and Israeli security forces—and from the region, still trying to recover from the massive damage imposed by Operation Cast Lead. Hamas, struggling with the transition from resistance movement to governing authority, was internationally and diplomatically isolated. Its widening internal divisions were mirrored by the intense divisiveness and acrimony between the Gaza government and its counterpart in the West Bank.

The destructive severing of the two territories, which had been a policy goal of the Oslo process, had long undermined the Palestinian national collective and was pursued in part to excise Gaza—the unremitting center of resistance to the occupation—from the dominant political equation. As such, Gaza long represented a political threat to Israel that went far beyond—and long preceded—Hamas. In this regard, Israel has never really known what to do with Gaza. This is why the Gaza Strip was marginalized and criminalized after Hamas's electoral victory with the imposition of a crippling closure, which has been in place since 2006. Gaza was turned into an imprisoned and impoverished enclave while the West Bank essentially dissolved into a fragmented, incoherent entity.[3]

Hamas also came under considerable popular pressure for its failures, particularly its inability to end the debilitating closure and for the additional restrictions Hamas itself has imposed on freedom of movement outside Gaza's borders (both at Erez for Palestinians wishing to enter the West Bank and at Rafah for those traveling to Egypt). Gaza's economic devastation—mediated in 2010/2011 by a short-lived and transient period of growth—acts as a key constraint on the Islamist government despite some clear achievements. Unemployment still exceeds 30 percent and could easily return to the much higher levels of the past. Around 40 percent of Gazans live in poverty, a percentage that would be higher without foreign aid and 44 percent suffer from food insecurity, meaning they cannot obtain enough food to meet their daily needs. Around ten percent of Gaza's children under five suffered from chronic malnutrition in 2010 and this problem does not appear to be improving and may in fact be deteriorating. Furthermore, between 70 to 80 percent of the population remains dependent on some form of humanitarian assistance. Consequently, Hamas finds itself on a course similar to the one that made Fatah unpopular before 2006.

Furthermore, "... some supporters saw [Hamas] as having sullied itself with the contradictions of being an Islamist movement constricted by secular governance and a resistance movement actively opposing Gaza-based attacks against Israel ... [precipitating] defections from a small but important group of militants who left to join groups more committed to upholding Islamic law and to engaging in attacks against Israel."[4]

The resulting lack of legitimacy—both domestically and internationally—was, and is—a key concern of the Hamas leadership. The incremental but steady attempt to Islamize society through the imposition of religious law (partly in response to pressures from extremist Islamist groups) further compromised the regime's legitimacy and remains a source of considerable tension within Hamas as a whole.

The Arab revolutions and Hamas's strategic shift: Some key features

The Arab revolts, notably in Egypt and Tunisia, have had a defining impact on Hamas and its policies. Perhaps the greatest change is found in ending Hamas's diplomatic isolation regionally. With the ascendency of Islamist movements to power in other countries, a critical opening was created for Hamas's external relations and the strengthening of regional alliances, potentially giving Hamas a higher profile than Fatah. The fall of the Mubarak regime and victory of the Muslim Brotherhood in Egypt, for example, meant a new and enhanced relationship between Egypt and Gaza—albeit not without its own tensions and inconsistencies—including Egypt's important role in brokering a ceasefire between Hamas and Israel ending the November 2012 conflict known as Operation Pillar of Defense, and between Hamas and Fatah over reconciliation talks.

A senior Hamas official in Gaza commented in November 2011: "Hamas is gaining throughout the region. Look at the Muslim Brotherhood in Tunisia and in Egypt and the Islamists in Libya. All of them are now the main powers on the ground. Hamas is gaining support from the Arab Spring. You cannot compare the position of Hamas in Tunisia four years ago to the position of Hamas with the An-Nahda government. After the weakening of the U.S., the Arab Spring, the failure of Abu Mazen, the internal dilemma of the Israelis, Hamas is only getting stronger and also gaining more internal support."[5] One expression of Hamas's gaining strength is a plan by the new Hamas political bureau to have its name removed from the European Union's terrorism list as part of its quest for international recognition. "European countries set only one condition to do that—avoiding martyrdom attacks inside Israel, and Hamas hasn't carried out any attack since 2004," according to Ahmed Yousef, a senior Hamas official.[6]

Turkey (whose diplomatic relations with Israel deteriorated in recent years[7]) and Qatar—both American and European allies (together with Egypt)—also engaged the Hamas government. Qatar sent government leaders and other senior officials to the Strip to break the intensified closure not long after it was imposed. During his October 2012 visit to

Gaza, for example, the Emir of Qatar, Sheik Hamad bin Khalifa al-Thani, pledged $400 million for a range of infrastructure projects including two housing complexes and three new motorways.[8]

Turkey is also investing in Gaza with a $40 million teaching hospital for Hamas's Islamic University, which now includes Turkish in its curriculum. (Furthermore, Turkey's Prime Minister Recep Tayyip Erdogan refused to delay a planned visit to Gaza in May 2013, despite public appeals by the U.S. to do so.[9]) A delegation of Arab foreign ministers led by Nabil Elaraby, the Secretary General of the Arab League, visited Gaza during Israel's November 2012 assault, as did delegations from Egypt, Tunisia, and Turkey in an expression of solidarity. Head of the Political Bureau Khaled Meshal visited various countries including Tunisia, Morocco and Iran as did Gaza's Prime Minister Ismail Haniyeh and Gaza's Foreign Minister, Mahmoud al-Zahar. In this regard the November conflict, like Operation Cast Lead before it, was also a test of Israel's changing position in the region as it was Egypt's.

A new page was even turned in Gaza's relations with Jordan, which is undergoing its own domestic turmoil as relations between King Abdullah and his (non-Palestinian) constituents become strained. Jordan was formerly home to Hamas's external leadership who were forced to leave Amman for Damascus in 1999. In January 2012, Khaled Meshal and other members of Hamas's political bureau, accompanied by the crown prince of Qatar, Sheik Tamim bin Hamad al-Thani, visited Jordan to meet with King Abdullah II. Qatar played a key role in reconciling the two sides. According to the *New York Times*, "Jordan wants to restore relations with Hamas [without harming its relationship with Fatah, Israel or the US] ... because the group is an offshoot of the Muslim Brotherhood, whose Islamist allies are forming new governments around the Arab world, and because Jordan wants to remain an influential go-between in the region, especially in the Israeli-Palestinian conflict."[10] At least half (if not more) of Jordan's 6.5 million people are of Palestinian origin, including around two million Palestinian refugees (who comprise around 30 percent of the population). Many of them have great regard for Meshal and see him as a popular leader capable of revitalizing the nationalist movement.

Meshal's decision to leave Syria in early 2012 in the wake of the Assad regime's brutal response to popular opposition and relocate to Qatar (while other officials moved elsewhere, including Egypt) was also critical in creating and widening regional channels, especially to Turkey and the Gulf, and beyond.[11] The Syrian regime's horrific crackdown on its own people compelled a strategic reassessment by Hamas that was painful given Assad's longstanding support for the Islamist movement. However, Hamas's ties to the Muslim Brotherhood, Sunni Arabs overall, and to Syria's popular majority[12] were more compelling. Meshal's defection, furthermore, worsened relations with Iran (which is rumored to have suspended its financial support) although it appears that neither side is interested in completely severing relations (particularly as ties between Islamic Jihad and Iran appear to be growing stronger). A political analyst in Gaza, Talal Okal observed that although "Hamas, as a pragmatic movement, cannot abandon the Iran-Syria alliance altogether . . . [it] is no longer interested in being considered part of it."[13] (Hamas's ties with Hezbollah in Lebanon remain intact despite their differences over Syria.)

Hence, since its withdrawal from Syria, various analysts argue that Hamas can no longer be thought of as an Iranian proxy—further enhancing its status in the region and potentially, some Hamas leaders apparently hope, within the West, where attitudes toward Islamist regimes in the region are shifting toward greater exchange.[14] Yet there are signs of internal divisions within Hamas over Iran, with the Gaza-based leadership more interested in maintaining closer relations for clearly strategic reasons. According to a Hamas leader in Gaza:

> All of the speculation about Hamas abandoning Iran is silly. Who else is going to supply Hamas with weapons and training? Qatar? Turkey? Iran is the only option. And the Iranians understand that Hamas is a valuable bridgehead for them in the Sunni world, so they are not going to complain about Hamas having closer ties with other countries, even if they are in conflict with those countries concerning Syria. More important, Iran understands that Hamas is the most crucial element in the fight against Israel. Especially at this time of escalation with Israel, it knows that it cannot afford to lose Hamas.[15]

Khaled Hroub, an expert on Hamas, further states, "With newly emerging governments in the post-Arab-Spring era, many of them Islamist, Hamas wants to be hosted and embraced and have offices in these countries, so they want to establish a distance from the old Hamas. This will make it easier for countries like Egypt and Tunisia to deal with them, without having problems with the Americans and the West."[16]

The quest for greater international legitimacy as pursued by Hamas's external leadership, distancing themselves from the "old Hamas," as it were, has exposed the considerable tensions and contradictions—arguably at their height—with the internal leadership based in the Gaza Strip. One acute expression of these differences is seen in the fact that while the outside leadership increasingly views isolation as a "big burden"[17] and is pursuing wider regional and international relationships with the assistance of Qatar—due in part to the insecurity they felt after abandoning their Syrian patron—the inside leadership is far more concerned with intensifying its control over the Gaza Strip and solidifying its domestic position in a territory within which they feel reasonably secure.

This suggests two important changes. First, whereas the outside leadership (together, it appears, with the Hamas leadership in the West Bank) wants to make Palestine part of the Arab world and thereby legitimize the Palestinian cause (which has receded for the time being from political view) given the ascendency of Islamists to power in Egypt and the West's growing rapprochement with Islamists in general, the inside leadership appears more focused on a Muslim Spring not an Arab Spring, believing that the Muslim world will ultimately rescue them.

In September 2011, a Hamas minister in Gaza stated: "Sixty years ago Palestinians were part of the *umma* ... then they became part of the Arab region, then the Palestinian question, then the Palestinian Authority. But everything has changed after the Arab Spring, or, in my opinion, the Islamic Spring. In Iraq, Afghanistan, Iran, even Europe, we're talking about a strategic, historic shift in the world ... After ten years, you will see that the Palestinians are part of this world. Abu Mazen and his project will be part of history."[18]

Second, there is an interesting reversal in roles: whereas the Gaza-based leadership was once more conciliatory than its Damascus-based counterpart, currently Gaza's leaders are more intransigent and inflexible, unwilling to bend to any policy decision that may compromise their control over the Strip such as the possibility of reconciliation.[19] Indeed, with regard to reconciliation, the Palestinian scholar Salim Tamari argued that Meshal is now considered "a non-repressive force calling for reconciliation with Abbas, and Haniyeh and Zahar are more hardline ... calling Abbas a traitor."[20]

The reconciliation issue further reveals the depth of the division and areas of friction between the inside and outside leaderships. The failure of Egyptian-brokered reconciliation talks lies in both Gaza and Ramallah and in the continued inability and unwillingness of both sides to articulate a common political vision that would force compromises neither side wants to make. Fatah is unwilling to reconcile because they would lose their privileges and if the PNA collapses and a national government is formed they fear losing popular support. Another factor influencing Fatah's position is the fear that as long as Hamas remains on the list of terrorist organizations, any reconciliation with the Islamist government would further jeopardize the PNA's desperately needed funding especially from the U.S.[21]

Hamas, in turn, fears the extension of Fatah control over Gaza and a significant loss of power. Yet a further complication is found within Hamas itself, between an external leadership that seeks reconciliation because it believes unity will enhance their legitimacy regionally, bring them greater control of the PLO and give them a stronger position in the national movement, and an indigenous leadership (and military wing) that has resisted it despite consistent and overwhelming popular support for this initiative among Gazans (and West Bankers).[22] A critical component is security. "For many Hamas leaders in Gaza, the notion that they would have to compromise in the Strip while security cooperation continued between Israel and the PA is particularly unacceptable."[23]

Nathan Brown makes an additional point: "[R]econciliation would have to allow Hamas to come out of hibernation in the West Bank. An Israeli leadership that has successfully bottled Hamas up in Gaza and a Palestinian leadership in Ramallah that has rooted Hamas out of Palestinian institutions over the past five years will hesitate to allow Hamas to come out into the open there. Of course, their own past efforts to destroy Hamas can be likened to that of someone trying so desperately to remove a stain from an article of clothing that he only sets it more permanently within the fabric."[24]

The tension between the two leaderships is also seen in debates over the movement's future strategy particularly with regard to resistance. In a 2011 meeting with Prime Minister Abbas, Meshal endorsed a policy change from armed struggle to non-violent popular protests, accepting for the first time since the establishment of Hamas to turn away from armed resistance as a strategic choice. This change in strategy, an attempt no doubt to link the Palestinian struggle with those in Egypt, Tunisia and Libya and more closely align Hamas's strategy with populist movements in the region, angered the Gaza leadership who insisted that armed struggle remain a critical part of Hamas's political vision.[25] (Similar tensions exist within Fatah between those political cadres calling for negotiations and those calling for military resistance.)

It should also be noted that if Hamas enjoyed any modicum of success—as they would define it—in its November 2012 conflict with Israel,[26] it was in creating a greater balance of terror with Israel given Hamas's more sophisticated arsenal of weapons, which can now reach Israeli cities (and also in the fact that there was no ground invasion by Israeli forces). During the ten months before the November attack, for example, over 500 projectiles (rockets and mortars) hit Israel. They included a "higher percentage of rockets, which travel farther [and] are a more significant military and political threat. In parallel Hamas acquired Grad [multiple rocket launchers] and anti-tank missiles (as did Islamic Jihad) and, for the first time, smuggled in and developed long-range missiles (Fajr-5 and M-75), putting a wider swathe of Israel within its range."[27]

While Hamas has not renounced the use of violence nor will it in the foreseeable future, some (non-Islamist) analysts in Gaza and the West Bank believe that is has accepted non-violent resistance as a form of popular struggle.²⁸ An Israeli analyst, Alon Ben David, who is the senior defense correspondent for Israel's Channel 10, similarly observes:

> For the first time since Operation "Pillar of Defense," Israel targeted [and killed in an April 30 airstrike] a single terrorist in the Gaza strip. Hitam al-Mashal was an expert in the manufacture of rockets, who worked as a freelancer for several of the radical organizations in the Gaza Strip... Hamas did not respond [to al-Mashal's targeted assassination]. But that was not all. Immediately after the event, Hamas warned the other organizations that anyone who dares to fire rockets at Israel would be arrested at once. No less intriguing is that as of now, Hamas has still avoided restocking its arsenal of [Fajr and Grad] rockets.²⁹

As one prominent Gaza-based analyst concluded, "the Arab Spring has changed [the way Hamas appears] in the eyes of the world—from a resistance movement only to a political [as well as] resistance movement."³⁰

Khaled Meshal's visit to the Gaza Strip in December 2012 was his first since his family fled their home in the West Bank 45 years before. His visit followed the November assault, which Hamas felt it had won, encouraging him to return. (It also marked the 25th anniversary of the start of the first Intifada and the founding of Hamas). Orchestrated by Egypt, Turkey, and Qatar, Meshal's return was no doubt bolstered by Hamas's improved status in the region after the Arab Spring. Among other objectives, it signaled an attempt to bridge some of the differences—which remain largely unresolved—with the internal leadership, perhaps moving toward a united leadership with Meshal as the head of Hamas overseeing its transformation into a conventional political actor able to negotiate with regional powers and perhaps at some future point, with Israel. Meshal also pointed to the need for reconciliation with Fatah, whose comparatively small presence at the rally was nonetheless important.

Yet some of Meshal's statements to the tens (and, according to Hamas, hundreds) of thousands of people who came to hear him (including around 1,000 foreign visitors among whom were delegations from Qatar, Egypt, Turkey, Bahrain and Malaysia³¹) stood in striking contrast to his more pragmatic and conciliatory position on ending the occupation and acceptance, in effect, of a two-state arrangement based on 1967 borders. Meshal, appearing defiant and unyielding, stated,

> Palestine is ours, from the river to the sea and from the south to the north. There will be no concession on an inch of the land. We will never recognize the legitimacy of the Israeli occupation and therefore there is no legitimacy for Israel, no matter how long it will take ... The state will come from resistance, not negotiation ... We don't

fight Jews because they are Jews. We fight the Zionists because they are conquerors and we will continue to fight anyone who takes our land and our holy places . . . We fight those who fight us, who attack us, who besiege us, who attack our holy places and our land. . . . We will free Jerusalem inch by inch, stone by stone.[32]

He further stated that Palestinian refugees and their descendants would eventually return to their ancestral homes in what is now Israel. As part of his promise to free Palestinian prisoners held in Israeli jails, Meshal also hinted that more Israeli soldiers could be kidnapped: "We will not rest until we liberate the prisoners. The way we freed some of the prisoners in the past is the way we will use to free the remaining prisoners."[33]

However, according to the political analyst Ali Abunimah, there was another passage in Meshal's speech that was also important and more consistent with his previous statements about Hamas's openness to political negotiations over armed resistance:

Resistance for us is a means and not an end. I am speaking to the whole world through the media. If the world finds a means, without resistance or bloodshed, to return Palestine and Jerusalem to us, and the right of return, and to end the Zionist occupation then we welcome it. We tried you [the world] for 64 years and you have done nothing. So if we resort to resistance do not blame us. If we found another way without war we would have seized it, but the history of nations shows that there is no victory or liberation without resistance, without battles, without sacrifice.[34]

While some (non-Islamist) Palestinian analysts argued that Meshal's speech was no more than an attempt to win over his audience, especially against the highly emotional backdrop of his first visit to Gaza, the Netanyahu government quickly seized on it, arguing that the speech "exposed the true face" of Israel's enemies, making it clear that Hamas has no intention of compromising with Israel, which it seeks only to destroy.[35]

A potentially more significant and revealing event came in April 2013 in Cairo, when Meshal was reelected to a fourth term as the head of Hamas's political bureau (with strong support from Qatar) and Haniyeh was elected his deputy. At that same election, al-Zahar, who is known for his hardline and rejectionist positions (strongly opposing any resolution with Fatah and any move away from armed struggle against Israel), was not elected to be part of the political bureau, the body that sets policy for Hamas, and was "de facto removed from its institutions and leadership," making it clear that Meshal is now the more powerful force.[36] According to the Israeli analyst and reporter (for Israel's Channels 1 and 10) Shlomi Eldar, who has covered the Gaza Strip for two decades:

[T]wo significant facts emerge from the election results and the makeup of Hamas' new political bureau:

- The first is that Meshaal, who only a year ago said he was "weary," succeeded in ousting his opposition from the political bureau and strengthening the exiled external Hamas, whose leaders had fled Damascus. He was able to do that at the expense of the Gaza leadership, which in the past had greater impact on the decision-making process.
- The second is that the movement's activists endorsed the champions of pragmatism, while pushing aside the hard-liners who were opposed to reconciliation with Fatah and a new popular struggle instead of an armed one.

It can therefore be said that Meshaal received a clear mandate to solidify Hamas as a political movement that seeks international recognition. The road is still fraught with obstacles. That being the case, there is one fact that can nonetheless be highlighted: Hamas is no longer the movement that encouraged and even initiated suicide bombings and the killing of civilians. Rather, this is a movement that has come to the realization that terror will bring it nothing but doom. This is what Meshaal understood already five years ago. What is interesting is that even the members of the Majlis al-Shura [Shura Council], who appoint the political bureau, have also come to that realization.[37]

While it would be premature to draw any definitive conclusions at this point, certain questions are worth asking: Does the election of Meshal and Haniyeh and the ousting of al-Zahar suggest some internal organizational changes based on new regional alliances and strategic calculations? Does Meshal's reelection signal a desire for greater moderation and pragmatism within Hamas as Eldar suggests (which includes the leadership's efforts to have Hamas removed from the EU's list of terrorist organizations), particularly as it regards a changing and volatile Middle East that Meshal, with his extensive regional contacts, may be best positioned to engage?

An interesting and related aside is the observation by a highly respected (non-Islamist) political analyst in Gaza: "Whenever Abu Mazen speaks, he loses. Everyone [is seeking] a new partner to lead the Palestinian people and Hamas is the only [actor] that works to [fill] this role while all other factions, including Fatah . . . lack a clear strategy and vision. . . Hamas has a clear political program [with] growing support not in Gaza and the West Bank but in the Arab and Islamic world."[38] Indeed, the Hamas leadership seems to understand that despite the willingness, albeit uncertain, of the EU and U.S. to engage other Islamists including the Muslim Brotherhood government in Cairo, they will be slow to engage Hamas which is one reason why "Hamas today is almost entirely focused on its Arab hinterland."[39]

The internal tensions—which are not new or restricted to the internal and external leaderships and the West Bank and Gaza but also include the political and the military wings and the religious leadership—themselves reflect, an ideological struggle currently being waged within Islamic political movements generally and the Muslim Brotherhood specifically between those who seek greater openness and those who advocate for greater restriction.[40] Hamas still claims to be a wasati or "centrist" movement, a term used by Islamists "to communicate their responsiveness to the interests of the public rather than their devotion to the strictest version of religious teachings."[41] The current struggle within Hamas and its varied constituencies over the validity of this claim can only be resolved by Palestinians themselves through promised elections that have yet to be held, elections which arguably face problems even greater than those impeding reconciliation.[42]

Changing regional relationships: Shifting the focus to Gaza and Egypt's unclear role

That the regional environment has opened up to Hamas is undeniable. Meshal's return to Gaza, as stated above, was facilitated by regional powers, notably Qatar, which clearly view him as the legitimate leader of Hamas. Perhaps more importantly, Meshal was brought back as a national leader not as the leader of a political faction, suggesting an elevation in Gaza's status (and a demotion of the West Bank's) regionally from factional enclave to nationalist base. Indeed, many in the West Bank believe that Qatar's support for Hamas and Gaza is an attempt to undermine Fatah and the Palestinian Authority in the West Bank, deepening the divide between the two territories. One example was a Hamas demand that Abbas arrest those individuals responsible for burning an effigy of the Emir of Qatar in the city of Tulkaram.

These events illustrate an important emerging trend in the post-revolution period: the shift in focus of certain Arab states away from the Fatah-led authority in the West Bank, where it has been particularly since the January 2006 election, to the Hamas-led authority in the Gaza Strip. This is seen in funding levels from Qatar and Saudi Arabia, for example, which are increasing, relatively, for Gaza and decreasing similarly for the West Bank (underlined by the slow decline of Fatah) and in the fact that Qatar has played a central role in strengthening Hamas's ties with

Arab and certain European countries.[43] This shift, furthermore, may be reflected in Israeli strategy as well. Speaking after Operation Pillar of Defense, one Israeli official observed: "Intended or not, one of the upshots of the war is that the central Palestinian address increasingly will be viewed as Gaza and the central player as Hamas. Abbas was the single most significant political casualty of the operation."[44]

Yet, Hamas's strengthened relationship with Qatar is not inviolate, with detractors in Gaza as well (and among Palestinians generally) who maintain that their relationship "is not a convergence of political positions . . . but a Qatari dominance at all levels, which is part of the country's goal to impose its vision on the Arab system [facilitated by the toppling of longstanding Arab dictatorships] to draw a new map of the Middle East, where Qatar can play a major role."[45] Furthermore, Hamas officials powerfully criticized Qatar for its support "of the principle of mutually agreed land swaps with Israel, rather than full Israeli withdrawal to the pre-1967 borders,"[46] which followed an April 2013 meeting between Arab League officials and the U.S. Secretary of State. The Arab League decision was denounced by all Palestinian factions as a dangerous and unacceptable compromise, tantamount to legitimizing occupation and the presence of major Israeli settlement blocs on Arab land.

Egypt is another critical factor for both Hamas and Fatah.[47] The removal of Mubarak from power represented the loss of a critical patron for Abbas and the Palestinian Authority in the West Bank as well as for Israel. Mubarak's Egypt clearly "collaborated with Israel in trying to weaken and isolate Hamas"[48] and was instrumental in facilitating occupation's repressive regime in the Gaza Strip. Yet Israel, not wanting to jeopardize its ties with Egypt, has made it clear that while it will deal directly with the Muslim Brotherhood in Egypt, it will not deal directly (i.e., officially) with Hamas although the two actors have long dealt with each other over a number of administrative and bureaucratic issues and even over security concerns.[49] In August 2012, a senior Israeli security official acknowledged, "we have a de facto working relationship with the de facto power on the ground."[50]

For Hamas, Egypt's status has changed significantly despite the growing difficulties and tensions between them. Egypt is considered a friendly government with which Hamas has direct contacts on many levels, although their relationship remains unclear, particularly as expected Egyptian support has not always materialized, including during Operation Pillar of Defense when the "Egyptians demanded that Hamas halt all military actions against Israel."[51] It is beyond the scope of this discussion to examine the increasingly complex relationship between Hamas and Egypt but one area of growing concern that reveals some of the tensions between them is the underground tunnel trade, a vital economic lifeline for Gaza that emerged several years ago in response to Israel's damaging closure.⁵² The tunnel trade has allowed Hamas to consolidate its hold on the territory, circumvent U.S.-led international financial restrictions, and in, effect, build its own economic system.⁵³ This is no doubt one reason why the Ramallah PNA has called on the Egyptian government to destroy all the tunnels.⁵⁴

Following the August 5, 2012 terrorist attack in the Sinai that resulted in the death of 16 Egyptian soldiers—an event that strained Egypt-Hamas relations, as some in Egypt believed Hamas was responsible—the tunnel trade came under increasing threat. In response the Egyptian army destroyed 120 tunnels, around 10 percent of the total number, and temporarily closed the Rafah crossing. Hamas then proposed a free trade zone on the border as an alternative to the tunnel trade, and the free movement of goods and people through the Rafah crossing all year round (balancing Gaza's humanitarian needs with Egypt's security needs), which Egyptian President Morsi rejected under increasing pressure from the security establishment.⁵⁵ Both these proposals present some potential problems for Egypt.

First, a free trade zone (FTZ) with Hamas would not be viewed favorably by the U.S. or Israel, two countries Egypt needs to renegotiate its Qualifying Industrial Zones agreement.⁵⁶ The political and legal consequences of a free trade zone with the Haniyeh government may not be worth the price of closing the tunnels.⁵⁷ And the last thing Morsi wants is for Gaza to become a part of Egypt, which is what a FTZ would effectively facilitate, demonstrating that political Islam does not always translate ideologically and will be superseded by the imperatives of realpolitik.

Second, allowing the transfer of goods through Rafah is problematic, given the terms of the November 2005 Agreement on Movement and Access (AMA)—signed by Israel and the PNA—which stipulated (among other things) that the Rafah crossing was not to be used for commercial trade, which had to pass through Israeli crossing points. Changing Rafah's status in the way Hamas proposes would effectively abrogate the AMA, opening Egypt up to legal challenges and "potentially allowing Israel to claim that there is no further need for it to keep its own crossings to Gaza open and that it can no longer be deemed the occupier of the territory under international humanitarian law (since it would no longer control all of Gaza's external borders)."⁵⁸ This argument was long used by the Mubarak government to defend its refusal to challenge the Gaza closure. According to an Egyptian diplomat opening Rafah to goods would also mean "ending totally our relationship with Abbas; deepening the division between the West Bank and Gaza; and being remembered in history as the ones who connected Gaza to Egypt, thereby ending once and for all the notion of a Palestinian state."⁵⁹

By September 2012, the Rafah crossing had reopened to people and processed 42,916 individuals traveling in both directions (however, the monthly numbers of people using the crossing reached 51,665 in July 2012 and dropped to 33,596 in February 2013).[60] Interestingly, some critics contend: "Eased travel restrictions at the Rafah crossing bolstered Gaza's leaders' ability to raise funds and conduct diplomacy on their own, even as the loss of a headquarters in Damascus reduced the external leadership's ability to do the same, and the release and return to Gaza of senior military figures with less connection to the outside leadership as part of the Shalit prisoner exchange [in October and December 2011] purportedly lessened its control over the military wing."[61]

On December 29, 2012, the Egyptian authorities allowed the entry of building materials into Gaza via the Rafah crossing. These materials, donated by Qatar as part of its $400 million aid package for Gaza's reconstruction, were said to be the first such shipment to cross through Rafah since June 2007. The Egyptian authorities stated, however, that this change in policy did not portend Rafah's full opening to commercial goods[62] or even a marked change towards the tunnel industry. (In mid-May 2013, seven Egyptian soldiers and policemen were abducted in northern Sinai by hardline Islamist groups—and released a few days later—in what turned out to be an internal Egyptian issue. The Egyptian government responded by closing and subsequently re-opening the Rafah crossing—by now, an established pattern—over concerns that the abducted individuals might be taken into Gaza.[63])

On February 3, 2013 (and perhaps earlier), stunned Hamas officials and local tunnel operators accused Egypt of renewed and intensified attacks against the tunnel economy, this time by flooding the border tunnels with sewage water, an act targeting tunnels transporting weapons and militants to the unstable Sinai Peninsula. Gaza's tunnel operators reportedly shot at Egyptian soldiers, which prompted further reprisals. The tunnel flooding was justified as part of a ceasefire agreement to terminate all cross-border violence between Israel and Gaza following the November 2012 conflict.[64] It also targeted tunnels transporting commercial goods including "all of the strip's fuel needs and much of its material for building."[65] In fact, the Egyptians even "forbade Hamas to import subsidized Egyptian oil from El Arish as an alternative to the oil that Gaza bought from Israel," which Hamas could then sell at a considerable profit.[66] The tunnel flooding is part of a campaign by Egypt to restrict tunnel activity that actually began in August 2012.

This has created great uncertainty and anxiety in Gaza (and in Hamas's finances), threatening to throw thousands of people out of work. According to Osama Kheil, the speaker of the union of Palestinian contractors, "Both contractors and citizens are worried because Egypt plans to shut down smuggling tunnels and there isn't a clear mechanism for the shipment of construction material into Gaza once tunnels are completely shut down."[67]

The intensified campaign against the tunnel enterprise occurred in response to a court case in Cairo brought by people who fear that the Gaza Strip is a national security risk for Egypt, particularly after the rise of the Muslim Brotherhood in Egypt and its still undefined relationship with Hamas. According to *The Economist*, "One reason for the Egyptians' hostility to Hamas is that they are worried that jihadist militants making mayhem in the Sinai desert may co-operate with like-minded people in Gaza. Gleeful Israeli soldiers say that their co-ordination with their Egyptian counterparts at the border is better than under Hosni Mubarak's old regime."[68]

A political analyst in Gaza pointed out another concern raised in September 2012: "Morsi said [that] Washington is asking Egypt to honor its treaty with Israel... [He said that] Washington should also live up to its own Camp David commitment to Palestinian self-rule. Morsi spoke nothing about [an] independent state. As he told Egypt TV two days ago ... [he] used the term self-rule."[69]

The hope of Hamas for an economic and political gateway to Egypt has turned to disillusion and future prospects remain uncertain to say the least. Egyptian support is clearly not a given. As an advisor to Abbas stated, "Hamas believed Egypt is changing. Now Hamas realizes five things will never change in Egypt: the army, the intelligence services, the foreign ministry, the pyramids and the Nile."[70] Rather, according to local sources in Gaza, official contacts between the Hamas and Egyptian governments have focused on the need to mitigate tensions between them, which have not abated since the killing of the soldiers in the Sinai. These tensions appear to center on two issues both tied to Egypt's need (shared by Israel and Gaza) to secure stability in the Sinai[71]: the fear of Hamas interference in internal Egyptian affairs—a critical concern of the security establishment—and the need for Hamas to focus greater attention on politics over military activities (i.e., the smuggling of militants and weapons. A particular Egyptian concern centers on Hamas's relationship with Bedouin smugglers). In a March 2013 meeting in Gaza "the Egyptian Ambassador asked Hamas [officials] not to intervene in the internal politics of Egypt and to work hard to be neutral,"[72] even, apparently, as it concerns Egypt's relationship with Israel.

In April 2013, for example, two rockets fired from the Sinai close to the border with Israel, hit the Israeli city of Eilat in addition to some other incidents of rocket fire against Israeli civilian areas.[73] The extremist Islamic group, Majlis Shura al-Mujaddin, took responsibility, further testing the relationship between Egypt, Hamas and Israel. Yet, "[e]very time a rocket was launched, Hamas' internal security forces were quick to arrest anyone they thought might have been involved."[74] In this regard, argues Ben David, Egypt's assault against the tunnels sent a strong message to Hamas. Under Khaled Meshal's leadership abroad, Hamas "decided unanimously to stop firing at Israel and to focus instead on what it called 'the project,' i.e., the expansion of its rule in Gaza to the West Bank."[75]

Hamas and Fatah: Competition or Convergence?

On January 4, 2013, a massive rally was held in Gaza City to mark the 48th anniversary of the founding of Fatah (and the beginning of the Palestinian revolution). At first, the Hamas authorities refused to allow the rally to take place and then conceded under pressure from Egypt, Turkey, and Qatar, believing that it would not draw many people. Conservative estimates placed the number of participants at 250,000–350,000 while others claimed as many as 1,000,000 (which would represent over half the population). This rally was significant for a number of reasons. The large turnout could be understood as a kind of referendum for Hamas (whether Hamas understood it in these terms is unclear), showing that it can no longer claim to rule by consensus or be a mainstream movement and that a majority of Gazans do not necessarily support them, diminishing the possibility of a political state of their own.

The rally was also a signal to Fatah and the Palestinian Authority in Ramallah, demonstrating that Gaza cannot be ignored and continues to play a central role in the nationalist cause. In a personal communication with the author, one Fatah official cautioned that his political party "must be careful not to interpret [the rally] as support." As a political independent in Gaza noted, "People came to the Fatah rally spontaneously and not as a result of Fatah leaders' efforts. This is due to many reasons like the forced absence of the Fatah movement . . . for more than five years; salaries for more than seventy thousand employees; [and the fact that] leftists were heavily [re]presented in the rally. [M]any sectors of Gaza society . . . came in defiance [of] Hamas and its government."[76]

The largely peaceful nature of the rally also demonstrates Hamas's ability to lead and provide security states the same local observer, a notable achievement of the Hamas regime overall. The problems that did arise during the rally derived from internal Fatah disputes, not from any attempt by Hamas to silence protesters (although the Islamist government has not been tolerant of public political demonstrations, which it construes as a denial of its legitimacy[77]). As such, "Hamas is no longer number two but competing with Fatah to be number one."[78] Yet others claimed that both Hamas and Fatah have deeply alienated their own constituencies and the massive turnout was one of very few ways available to demonstrate the lack of popular support.

It cannot be denied that Hamas's position vis-à-vis Fatah is changing—both domestically and regionally. While it remains too early to predict what these changes will look like and how much popular support they will generate, their evolution represents a critical departure from the past. However, there are also some interesting points of convergence between Hamas and Fatah (despite Hamas's aversion to any comparison with Fatah) with their own set of implications for the future that are certainly worth noting.

For example, in order to end the November 2012 hostilities, Hamas had to reach a political agreement with Israel brokered by Egypt. Although the specific terms of the ceasefire were not disclosed, Hamas claimed victory particularly with regard to Israel's decision to ease some onerous economic restrictions and to end attacks, incursions and assassinations against Gaza. Yet the terms imposed on Hamas, namely that Hamas stop rocket and military attacks along the border fence, have placed Hamas in a position not dissimilar from that of Fatah. In May 2013, IDF Gaza Division Commander Brigadier General Micky Edelstein confirmed that Hamas is working to stop rocket attacks from Gaza into southern Israel. Towards this end Hamas replaced policemen at the border areas with fighters from its Qassam Brigades.[79] In that same month Hamas policemen broke up an anti-Israeli protest in Gaza and confiscated 100 rockets and other weapons from the al-Aqsa Martyrs Brigade, the military wing of Fatah.[80]

Furthermore, "Hamas was actually quite zealous about enforcing a state of calm in the security "perimeter" along the Israeli border . . . The IDF prevented anyone from entering that zone, including local farmers. Now, however, it was Hamas itself that barred civilians from getting within 100 meters of the fence and its own armed forces from coming within 500 meters of it."[81] Thus, Hamas now guards its borders for Israel (and Egypt) as does Fatah in the West Bank. In this regard there is arguably little difference between the two governments as both are dominated by a security agenda. (Their actions also point to a possible shift within Hamas away from armed resistance toward political resistance as discussed above.)

Similarly revealing is Hamas's support for Abbas's November 2012 UN initiative seeking to upgrade the status of Palestinians in the UN from a non-member observer entity to a non-member observer state, possibly creating the basis for some future rapprochement. The Islamist government supported the initiative, in part, because it would reinsert the Palestinian issue into the international agenda, itself suggestive of its desire for greater popular legitimacy.[82] Yet, with their support for the UN initiative, Hamas's external leadership effectively adopted Fatah's political program, notably, a state on June 4, 1967, borders with East Jerusalem as its capital (Meshal's December 2012 speech notwithstanding) if the Palestinian people accept it in a referendum. In this way, one high level Fatah official argued, "Hamas reached the same political point more or less as Fatah but in a much shorter period of time. Hamas is now part of the Palestinian national movement."[83]

Hamas's Political Versus Social Agenda: The Source of Greatest Tension?

The obstacles to reconciliation and unity are very political and deeply institutionalized and entrenched. Yet, talks are scheduled to resume in Cairo in 2013 and there is some basis for discussion. Despite the acrimony between Hamas and Fatah, which is not to be underestimated, the political differences between them may not be the source of greatest tension within Hamas. Rather, the source of greatest tension may reside in the internal struggle between a larger political agenda (supported by Meshal and his supporters both outside and inside Gaza and the West Bank) that is becoming more pragmatic and seeking greater diplomatic openings internationally and with the West, and a social agenda—largely imposed, it appears, by more hardline elements in the Gaza leadership—that is becoming more religious and restrictive, designed in part to secure Hamas's hold on the territory (and counterbalance accusations that Hamas is slowly normalizing its relationship with Israel politically and economically), but deepening the polarizing Islamization policies described in this book. This struggle—expressed culturally and reflected regionally—also resides between Islamists and secularists.

This social agenda includes a new law enacted only by Hamas parliamentarians and published on April 1, 2013, that will segregate girls and boys older than nine years in Gaza's schools beginning in the fall. Although such segregation has long existed in Gaza (and the West Bank) by fourth grade generally due to cultural norms, it has not been legislated. The law will also apply to UNRWA schools and private (including Christian) schools where classes are mixed through high school, and will further bar male teachers from working in girls' schools. Hamas similarly has issued bans on Western clothing and hairstyles, going as far as forcibly shaving the heads of young men—which is unusual since women are typically targeted—who look too "western."[84] This followed a cultural campaign begun last year barring clothing stores from displaying lingerie, short skirts and dresses in front windows. Another policy in March 2013 prohibited women and girls from taking part in a marathon organized by UNRWA, which resulted in the marathon's cancellation while another requires female students at Al-Aqsa University to dress in traditional Islamic attire.[85]

It appears that the leadership in Gaza intends to continue their measured but steady campaign to impose a religious agenda on social behavior and it may be a factor affecting Hamas's ability to successfully pursue broader diplomatic engagements going forward (and perhaps an instrument the internal leadership will attempt to use against their external counterpart), further testing an already difficult and by some accounts, fractious relationship between the two leaderships. An important factor will be the degree to which restriction and conservatism are allowed to proceed unchallenged within Hamas given competing and increasingly opposed agendas.

Some Critical Points Regarding Gaza's Declining Economy

The many political challenges currently confronting Hamas are further shaped by an economic context that is extremely adverse and according to the World Bank, "resemble[s] no other in the world."[86] Gaza is a stark example of how economic factors can limit and shape political change (and vice versa).[87] Gaza is an urban economy that relies heavily on "intensive trade, communication and movement of people."[88] Yet since 2005 at least, the Gaza Strip has been effectively isolated from the rest of the world, allowing Hamas to solidify its control over an increasingly unviable economy. According to the World Bank "the private sector, especially in Gaza, has been devastated by the economic restrictions imposed by the GOI [Government of Israel]. As a result, foreign aid has provided the base for recent growth."[89]

In a subsequent report, the World Bank further argued, "Despite some easing of movement within the West Bank in previous years, and increased imports to Gaza, including for internationally funded projects, the current system put in place by the GOI . . . remains the major impediment preventing the Palestinian economy from reaching its full potential."[90] Hence, the Strip's highly underproductive and consumer-driven economy is dangerously dependent on a number of factors including (but not limited to) foreign assistance, black market (tunnel) trade, and public sector and UNRWA salaries, a situation that is clearly untenable over the longer-term.

There is no doubt that the economy has declined dramatically despite some impressive GDP growth rates in 2010 and 2011, which do not reflect a recovering economy, particularly given the profound constraints that remain on the productive sectors and the almost complete termination of Gaza's export trade. Indeed despite robust growth in output and employment in the private sector in 2011 especially, the level of unemployment among Gazans remained among the world's highest.

The UN predicts that in the year 2020, the population of the Gaza Strip (which they estimated at 1.64 million in 2012) will grow by 30 percent or approximately 500,000 people, reaching 2.13 million (and 2.76 million by 2028). Over half are children and nearly 70 percent are refugees living in an area of 365 square kilometers or 140 square miles. In just eight years, therefore, Gaza's population density, already among the highest in the world, will increase by nearly 30 percent from 4,505 to 5,835 people per square kilometer.[91]

The urbanization rate is projected to remain very high, reaching 95.5 percent by 2015[92] and underlines Gaza's extreme dependence on access to the outside world, given its need to trade goods and services (and secure workforce mobility) in order to grow. Self-sufficiency in a number of sectors is no longer an option in Gaza. Some economists estimate that it will take decades to return Gaza economically to where it was just years ago, a position that was already deeply compromised. This continuing and worsening tragedy palpably threatens the physical and psychological wellbeing of nearly 1.7 million people, the majority of whom are children.

A Concluding Note

Gaza cannot be solved simply; neither can Hamas. Regional and domestic dynamics are shifting and unpredictable. The challenges—both internal and external—facing Hamas are complicated and will shape not only Gaza's future but Palestine's. Fundamentally, Gaza's political and economic viability depends on several factors. Perhaps foremost among them is the immediate lifting of the disastrous closure. Another is the direct engagement by Israel and the West—whose policies have done a great deal to entrench the occupation—of the Hamas government as a vital political actor in Palestinian politics and in Israeli-Palestinian relations. It should not be forgotten that there was a time not that long ago when the PLO and Fatah were vilified, arguably more intensely than Hamas is today. A further challenge confronting the West is working to end the damaging separation of the territories by facilitating rather than thwarting—as has long been the case—political reconciliation between Hamas and Fatah. In this regard, U.S. Secretary of State Kerry's envisioned economic investment plan for the West Bank represents yet another initiative that will only deepen Palestine's internal divisions.[93]

There can be no resolution to the conflict without Gaza and there can be no Gaza without including Hamas. In short, what is needed is a new point of departure, a new strategic alternative not just for Gaza but for all Palestinians and Israelis. Without a new approach the resulting vacuum will be filled by greater uncertainty and insecurity for both peoples. And finally, the continued isolation of Gaza's very young, very dense population under a deepening stranglehold is indefensible and immoral and it must finally be brought to an end.

Sara Roy
Cambridge, MA
May 2013

EPILOGUE

THE COUP AGAINST THE ISLAMIST GOVERNMENT IN EGYPT—EMERGING NEW DYNAMICS AND THEIR IMPLICATIONS FOR HAMAS

> If those who ousted Morsi believe that they were continuing the January 25 Revolution, the issue of Gaza is the test they will be put to.
> —*Nouhad al-Sheikh Khalil*[1]

WITHIN A FEW weeks of completing the afterword, the Islamist government of Mohammed Morsi was overthrown in a coup by the Egyptian military. Key Muslim Brotherhood figures were arrested including President Morsi himself who, at the time of this writing, remains in detention. While the future is unclear and impossible to predict, regional dynamics are again shifting in dramatic new ways. These changes have short- and long-term implications for Hamas and for the people of Gaza that require some brief comment.

CHANGING DYNAMICS: EXTERNAL

The Arab revolutions that brought Islamists to power in Egypt and Tunisia represented a marked geopolitical shift in the region, one that had a clear impact on Hamas's external relations. Hamas abandoned Syria and distanced itself from Iran and Hezbollah in favor of closer ties with Egypt, Qatar, and Turkey, believing that these new political and economic relationships would not only compensate for the loss of their strategic ally in Damascus and for the reduction in funding from Iran,[2] widening their regional and possibly, international reach, but would also support Hamas in expanding its control over the West Bank.

After President Morsi's election and subsequent ouster, Hamas finds itself in a relatively weaker, more isolated position with Turkey and Qatar, arguably, its only allies, according to some observers. Yet both these countries are undergoing internal changes of their own, introducing further (political and financial) uncertainties into their relationship with Hamas. Turkey is experiencing a growing and increasingly violent domestic crisis over the religious-secular divide and issues of free speech and dissent. Qatar has a new leadership with the transfer of power from the Emir, Sheikh Hamad bin Khalifia Al Thani to his son Crown Prince Sheikh Tamim bin Hamad Al Thani, which could have particular implications for Meshal and his agenda. According to Daoud Khuttab, the change of leadership "is said to be the result of a yet undeclared policy to moderate Qatar's foreign policy."[3]

Hamas's relationship with Egypt will remain vital but is presently extremely tense. According to reports, there has been little communication between Hamas officials and their Egyptian counterparts since the coup. More tunnels than ever before have been closed or destroyed because of fears over the smuggling of weapons and fighters to an eroding and violent Sinai. The number of people allowed to cross via Rafah has fallen dramatically, and Hamas officials are reportedly banned from entering Egypt.

"During Morsi's one-year rule, Hamas bore the blame for many of his blunders and had attained massive losses in the Egyptian public opinion," according to Mohamed Goma'a of Cairo's Al-Ahram Center for Political and Strategic Studies.[4] Since the coup especially, the Egyptian media has been inciting hatred against Hamas and Palestinians with accusations of all kinds including the alleged infiltration of 7,000 Hamas militants to support the Morsi regime (which both Egyptian and Hamas officials denied).[5] Hamas was also accused of direct involvement in Morsi's January 28, 2011 escape from the Wadi El-Natroun Prison. In fact, on June 23, 2013, an Egyptian court found that members of the Muslim Brotherhood had plotted with Hamas (and Hezbollah) to attack the prison, which "set free 34 high-level Brotherhood members," including Morsi himself, an attack that also led to the escape of "thousands of prisoners who are a danger to society."[6] Other reports claimed that Hamas sent its fighters to kill Egyptian soldiers and civilians in the Sinai (which has become particularly lawless since the coup), and that leaders of the Egyptian Muslim Brotherhood fled to Gaza after the coup in order to organize activities in support of Morsi.[7] (In response to the latter, the Hamas government closed two media outlets in Gaza, *Al-Arabiya* and *Ma'an*, which published this accusation and, more recently, has been monitoring social media for anti-Hamas opinions and planned demonstrations.[8])

A number of complaints against Hamas are pending in the Egyptian courts based on the claim that it interferes in Egypt's internal affairs with some commentators consequently calling on the Egyptian military to attack the Gaza Strip.[9] One individual on Egyptian television attempted to defame Morsi by claiming that he is originally Palestinian.[10] Furthermore, on August 3, 2013 a top Egyptian court formally detained Morsi accusing him of collaborating with Hamas to escape prison; destroy prison records; attack police stations; and intentionally kill and abduct police officers and prisoners during the 2011 uprising; and espionage."[11]

It should not be forgotten that despite their obvious ties, the relationship between Hamas and the Morsi government was often difficult, characterized by ongoing strain and dispute as seen in the tunnel closures, which, by some accounts, were more draconian under Morsi than Mubarak. Morsi also refused to allow official trade through the Rafah crossing and rejected a free trade zone between Egypt and the Gaza Strip. Furthermore, Morsi upheld Egypt's 1979 peace treaty with Israel. According to Ibrahim Barzak, a noted journalist and analyst based in Gaza, "The 1979 treaty has been a critical component of Israeli security, allowing the military to divert resources to volatile fronts with Syria, Lebanon, and the Palestinians. Israeli officials say security cooperation between the two militaries has remained strong during the Morsi era and even during the past few days of unrest."[12] Hence, it is not unreasonable to suggest that the ideological and political ties between the Morsi government and Hamas have been "exaggerated for political reasons, a way of undermining the Brotherhood."[13]

Many Egyptians (and Israelis) believe that Hamas is largely responsible for the rapidly increasing instability in the strategic Sinai Peninsula, a critical security issue for Egypt that long preceded the coup. Hamas has consistently denied involvement. According to one report, the Northern Sinai "has become a war zone with almost daily attacks on [Egyptian] military and police camps, checkpoints, airports and the obvious targeting of Christians."[14] By one account, there are 30,000 Egyptian troops in the peninsula.[15] Sinai's Jihadi militants who appear to have no organizational links to the Muslim Brotherhood, claim that the attacks will stop if Morsi is reinstated because they consider the coup against him as a coup against Islam.[16] On July 11, 2013 the Egyptian army killed dozens of armed men and carried out massive arrests; reportedly 32 Hamas fighters were among those arrested.[17] On July 27, 2013 the Egyptian army launched Operation Desert Storm in the North Sinai, a 48-hour operation aimed at crushing the 500 (or more) Islamist extremists believed to be operating there.[18] Of particular concern to Hamas is an incident that occurred on July 12 when Egyptian attack helicopters—with Israeli permission—flew over southern Gaza (Rafah and Khan Younis) as part of the Sinai assault, the first time that Egyptian military aircraft flew over the Gaza Strip since the June 1967 war. Some observers interpreted this as a warning to Hamas to prevent the movement of militants into the Sinai.[19] On August 9, 2013, Israel also launched a drone strike in the northern Sinai, killing five suspected Islamic militants, and destroyed a rocket launcher.[20]

With Morsi removed from power and Hamas's increasing regional isolation, some observers speculate that Israel may also be less concerned about attacking Gaza since it no longer has to worry about harming its relationship with an Islamist government in Cairo. In fact, the Israeli Ambassador in Cairo stated that the people of Israel look upon General Abdul-Fattah al-Sisi, the man who orchestrated the coup, as a "national hero for all Jews."[21] However, while an Israeli attack against Gaza cannot be ruled out (which some encourage as a way of crippling Hamas given its weakened position[22]), the need for Israel to maintain stability inside the Strip, given the insecure situation in the Sinai, may be of greater immediate importance (see below).

Changing dynamics: internal

The contraction of Hamas's regional position and relatively greater isolation, particularly with regard to Egypt, has amplified the sense of siege in Gaza in palpable ways. In addition to the loss and/or decline of economic support from Syria, Iran, and likely Qatar, Hamas and Gaza must contend with heightened restrictions from the new Egyptian regime. For example, after the fall of the Morsi government, the tunnel trade became extremely vulnerable to closure, particularly as the Egyptian authorities intensified the targeting of the tunnels "as part of a drive to regain control of the vast Sinai desert, whose population is hostile to Cairo."[23] In July 2013, in an unparalleled move, the Egyptian government closed or destroyed around 80 percent of the tunnels, dealing a devastating blow to Gaza's fragile economy. The Egyptian navy also imposed "unprecedented limits on access to Egyptian waters by Gaza's fishing fleet, which is already suffering from the debilitating effects of similar Israeli restrictions."[24] Gazans consider the border restrictions implemented by the current Egyptian regime "tougher than any enforced by Morsi's pro-Western, [anti-Hamas] predecessor, Hosni Mubarak,"[25] (whose restrictions remained largely in place) while some in Hamas fear that Egypt's crackdown is part of a campaign against the Muslim Brotherhood, including inside Gaza.[26]

Consequently, from around the middle of June to the middle of July 2013, the Gaza Strip lost around $225 million due to the decline of imports, namely fuel and construction materials (which likely includes direct losses to the Hamas government of millions of dollars in tax revenue on tunnel products[27]). By early August 2013, the loss reportedly increased to a quarter of a billion dollars.[28] As a result, 20,000 construction workers lost their jobs.[29] According to an official with Gaza's Ministry of the Economy, during the third week in July, 50,000 laborers who depended directly and indirectly on the construction sector were newly unemployed.[30]

Furthermore, the shortages in fuel necessitated rationing by the Hamas government with priority given to hospitals (whose fuel reserves had dropped to 20 percent), power plants, and water facilities.[31] Gaza's Ministry of Health estimates that the average daily need of the health sector is 500,000 liters of fuel.[32] The prolonged absence of fuel would create an economic and political crisis, if not chaos in Gaza, which is undoubtedly one reason why the Israeli government sent in 165 fuel tankers during the last three weeks of July in response to requests from Gaza (and despite the fact that Israeli fuel is three times the price of the Egyptian fuel supplied through the tunnels).[33]

The movement of people via the Rafah crossing was similarly impacted. Towards the end of July 2013, such travel was restricted to patients with medical referrals from Gaza's Health ministry and to foreigners including Palestinians holding foreign passports. Hamas officials were prohibited from leaving Gaza and aid missions were unable to enter given deteriorating security conditions in the Sinai.[34] Since Morsi's ouster, the hours of operation at the Rafah crossing have been reduced from nine to four and the number of daily passengers decreased from about 1,000 to 150 (with around 10,000 people waiting to leave Gaza).[35] These conditions, among others, have led to comparisons between the post-coup situation in Gaza and Israel's intensified closure of 2007 (still in effect but with certain modifications), which has undermined Gaza's economy. However, the risk is not Gaza's alone, but Egypt's (and Israel's) as well; if conditions become too onerous, Gazans may erupt as they did in January 2008 when as many as half of the population poured across the border into Egyptian territory after Hamas members tore down part of the border wall.[36]

Politically, the chasm between Hamas and Fatah may have widened even further. First, President Abbas "congratulated the Egyptian army on its removal of Morsi, saying it had prevented Egypt's "slide towards an unknown fate."[37] In a similar vein, a Fatah official stated, "Now it's Gaza's turn to get rid of the Muslim Brotherhood branch. The dark era of political Islam has ended. The era of hypocrisy and lies has ended and Gaza will soon witness its own revolution against Hamas."[38] Although the possibility of overthrowing the Hamas regime is extremely unlikely given the absence of support from its military and security services, which would respond to such a challenge with violent force, the Hamas government may be compelled, over time, to redirect its focus from the international Muslim Brotherhood to the domestic political arena. In the words of Nazir Majali, a political analyst, "Today, Hamas must realize that the road to Ramallah is shorter than the road to Cairo or Doha."[39]

Second, Hamas published documents that they say reveal the involvement of Fatah and the Palestinian Authority in the Egyptian media's incitement campaign against Hamas. The documents apparently reveal that Fatah has a special committee or department headed by President Abbas, whose job it is to demonize Hamas and the Gaza Strip in the eyes of the Egyptian public. One such document, a letter, states that the goal of this newly formed "department is to develop ways to embarrass Hamas and link the group to the events in Egypt."[40] Hamas argues that the collusion between the PNA and the Egyptian media produced false claims that Hamas and its military wing were responsible for the military attacks in the Sinai and for the killing of the 16 Egyptian soldiers in 2012, among other accusations including involvement with Salafist parties.[41]

Perhaps the most serious struggle facing the movement may reside within Hamas itself "between its politically pragmatic, reformist tendency led by the politburo chief Khaled Meshal, and a hardline military-oriented wing inside Gaza"[42] most likely led by Mahmoud al-Zahar who maintained close ties to Iran. According to Shlomi Eldar,

> Zahar's supporters and admirers never reconciled with the idea that a leader of the movement who sacrificed two of his sons would be so humiliated by "that gang of bootlickers," the derisive term they use to describe Meshaal's confidantes and supporters. It turns out that even in a movement whose leaders attempt to conceal their disagreements and give a false impression of unity, ardent political struggles are an inseparable part of the game. Zahar was humiliated when he was left out, but he waited on the sidelines, ready to spring as soon as the leader who orchestrated his removal, and anyone who participated in it for that matter, afforded him an opportunity. That opportunity came sooner than he expected. Over the past few months, all the traditional allies that Hamas depended on disappeared, one after the other, while Meshaal and the other leaders of the movement watched in stunned silence. . . . His supporters are quite happy . . . When they watch how Zahar is becoming more and more powerful by the day, they are convinced that God himself is intervening.[43]

Eldar further points out that because of his continuing ties with Iran, al-Zahar has successfully managed to secure large sums of money from Tehran while Hamas's traditional sources of funding are evaporating:

> With the money that he was able to raise, Zahar established a camp of supporters who are gradually emerging as a significant opposition to the faction that deposed him from the movement's supreme leadership council. While Meshaal and the other heads of the Hamas political bureau, Hamas Prime Minister in Gaza

Ismail Haniyeh and deputy head of the Hamas political bureau Mousa Abu Marzouk, are banging their heads against the wall, trying to find money to fund the movement's activities and offer financial support to the people of the Gaza Strip, the deposed doctor is building up his stature, especially among the Izz ad-Din al-Qassam Brigades, the military wing of the movement.[44]

Concluding thoughts

There is little doubt that Hamas is currently in a sensitive and relatively uncertain position, which has been compared to, or at least reminds Palestinians of, Yassir Arafat's support of Iraq's Saddam Hussein during the 1990 Gulf War. His support of the Iraqi President against the Gulf States cost the Palestinians dearly, a cost they continue to incur. "This is exactly what Hamas supporters are saying, in whispers, to Fatah supporters in any discussion about Hamas's political alliances in the region."[45]

Yet, despite Hamas's relatively weakened position regionally and the internal tensions and shifting alliances within it, Hamas appears to be in firm control of the Gaza Strip; as such, it remains a crucial and requisite player in the Israeli-Palestinian conflict and in its resolution. This is one reason (among many) why the 2013 U.S.-led peace negotiations under Secretary of State John Kerry will fail—they exclude Hamas, undermining Meshal's reformist wing, and Gaza. Furthermore, as the political analyst Geoffrey Aronson argues, despite their antipathy toward each other and despite the fact that "Israel certainly remains committed to maintaining Gaza on a diet that keeps it just on the side of economic functionality," both Israel and Hamas have a vested interest in maintaining the status quo in Gaza. "[I]n a time of great uncertainty, [the Israeli government] has no interest in toppling "the devil it knows" in Gaza [while] Hamas . . . knows that . . . raison d'etat [state interest] favors practical cooperation with the Zionist entity on its main project—consolidating its power, authority and well-being in Gaza."[46] And as it has been argued "[t]his ability to cooperate, as well as to fight, has been a prominent feature of the relationship [between Israel and Hamas] since Israel's evacuation of settlements and its army from Gaza in September 2005."[47] Increasing back channel contacts between Hamas and official representatives of Britain and France (among other European countries), furthermore, attest to the continued and perceived importance of Hamas's role in national politics.[48]

The relationship between Egypt and the Gaza Strip is central and it has been historically. Political life in Gaza cannot be isolated from political events in Cairo: Gaza shares a border with Egypt and important cultural ties. Egypt brokered a Palestinian unity agreement and a ceasefire between Hamas and Israel. It has long provided a primary gateway for Palestinians to the outside world and a vital economic lifeline, troubled though it may be. According to Hani Habeeb, a Gaza-based political analyst, "Gaza represents an issue of national security for Egypt and that will never change. Sooner or later (Egypt's) new leadership will have to engage with Gaza's rulers"[49] and Gaza's rulers will have to engage with their Egyptian counterparts. Hamas's longstanding relationship with Syria, for example, suggests that it can and will participate in strategic relationships outside the Muslim Brotherhood. In fact, according to Mousa Abu Marzouk, Hamas's deputy chief of the political bureau who lives in Cairo, Hamas had established contacts with the Egyptian opposition long before the July coup and he claims that official relations between Hamas and Egypt remain unbroken.[50]

There also are indications that Hamas is slowly repositioning itself vis-à-vis Iran. Not only is al-Zahar pursuing stronger relations with Tehran, so, too, are other senior Hamas officials. Repairing relations with Iran is one immediate way of dealing with the increasing isolation, financial distress (and threat?) in which Hamas now finds itself post-Morsi. Senior Hamas official Ahmad Youssef admitted that the movement has been engaged in meetings with Hezbollah and Iran, two actors which no doubt recognize that Hamas still occupies a critical position in the Israeli-Palestinian struggle. Consequently, both Iran and Hezbollah are "keen to see Hamas remain in the fold of 'resistance,' at least in terms of rhetoric" especially as Hamas's military wing appears, for the moment at least, to be ascending in power and profile relative to the declining fortunes of its civilian leadership under Meshal.[51]

Mousa Abu Marzouk and one other senior Hamas official met with Iranian officials in the presence of Hezbollah representatives at the Iranian embassy in Beirut in June 2013 "in which the strategic relations between the movement and Iran were discussed."[52] The meetings reportedly produced the following outcomes: restoration of Iranian aid to Hamas albeit below previous levels; creating direct channels of communication between Hamas and Hezbollah (despite reports of growing divisions between them) with particular attention on keeping the Palestinian refugee camps out of the growing Sunni-Shia tension in Lebanon; and preparation for a leadership meeting between Hamas and Hezbollah.[53]

Other signs that Hamas is attempting to restore its relations with Iran are found inside Gaza. In late July 2013, Hamas met with other groups at an Islamic Jihad office to plan activities for International Quds Day, "a day of solidarity with Jerusalem that Ayatollah Ruhollah Khomeini instituted when he came to power in Iran in 1979 and which falls on the last Friday of Ramadan."[54] Typically, only Islamic Jihad observed the day by demonstrating in Gaza. Additionally, the Islamic Jihad had "allocated 3,000 Iranian-financed food packages to Hamas for distribution to needy families on its lists,"[55] which had become necessary due to the Egyptian assault on the tunnel trade.

While it is still not possible to predict what Hamas's future strategic and internal alliances will be nor is it clear how the ongoing political struggles in Egypt will be resolved, Morsi's overthrow presents issues that certainly go beyond Hamas and Egypt; prominent among them are the future of the Muslim Brotherhood and political Islam in the entire region. The Egyptian coup sent a terrible message to Islamists saying they never will be allowed to succeed in elections,[56] democratic practices and secularism will inevitably miscarry and backfire, and the U.S. especially colluded with the counterrevolution. These beliefs have no doubt been deepened by the failure of key Western governments and human rights organizations to publicly condemn the killing by Egyptian security forces of at least 120 Morsi supporters at a sit-in in Cairo on July 27, 2013 in what was called the "worst state-led massacre in the country since the fall of Hosni Mubarak."[57] In the words of an Islamist protester in Cairo: "Many of the youth now say, 'No more ballot boxes.' We used to believe in the caliphate. The international community said we should go with ballot boxes, so we followed that path. But then they flip the ballot boxes over on us. . . If ballot boxes don't bring righteousness, we will all go back to demanding a caliphate."[58]

On August 14, 2013, Egyptian security forces stormed two pro-Morsi sit-ins in Nahda Square and the Rabbah al-Adawiya Mosque, "firing weapons, bulldozing tents and beating and arresting protesters in raids that . . . caused heavy casualties"[59] with hundreds dead and thousands injured. This attack, striking for its ferocity, was condemned by the U.S., but no sanctions were imposed on the Egyptian authorities, likely destroying whatever faith there was in a "new American relationship with the Islamic world."[60] According to Emad Shahin, a professor of political science at the American University in Cairo, "This is the beginning of a systematic crackdown on the Muslim Brotherhood, other Islamists and other opponents of a military coup."[61] A month-long state of emergency and nighttime curfew were also imposed.

Intensifying the sense of betrayal among Islamists is the following observation: "It's not just an anti-Islamist shift [taking place in Egypt] but elements of the revolutionary leftists and liberals who had once allied with the Islamists against the old regime now allying with old regime against the Islamists."[62] Not only are the more moderate voices within the Islamist movement discredited and marginalized, there may be less, if any, perceived need among the hardline elements to cooperate or compromise over other regional conflicts, including the Israeli-Palestinian conflict, arguing instead for their own solidification.

It is unlikely that the military coup in Egypt will diminish political Islam as a force and ideology in the region as it remains a highly organized and relevant political movement in many countries despite various military attempts to suppress it, including Algeria in 1991, Gaza in 2006 and 2007,[63] and, perhaps, Egypt in 2013. As such—and as this book has argued—political Islam must be constructively engaged.

Yet, there is considerable potential for political disorder including in the Gaza Strip. While predictions of Hamas's demise are surely premature, the situation in Gaza is increasingly tenuous, particularly in light of a rapidly eroding economy, deepening isolation, and the worsening crisis in Egypt. For Gaza (like the region overall) and the various political actors within it—both Islamist and non-Islamist—this is not a moment of consolidation, but fragmentation. A great deal is at stake, not least of which is the future of the Gaza Strip.

Cambridge, MA
August 2013

NOTES

Prologue

1. Albert Hourani, "Islamic History, Middle Eastern History, Modern History," in Malcolm Kerr, ed., *Islamic Studies: A Tradition and Its Problems* (Malibu, CA: Undena Publications, 1980), pp. 9 and 10.
2. All names have been changed to protect interviewees' identities.
3. See Sara Roy, "Introduction," in *Failing Peace: Gaza and the Palestinian-Israeli Conflict* (London: Pluto Press, 2007), pp. 3–4.

Chapter 1
Introduction: Structure, Arguments, and Conceptual Framework

1. "The President—Executive Order 12947—Prohibiting Transactions with Terrorists Who Threaten to Disrupt the Middle East Peace Process, Part IX," *Federal Register*, vol. 60, no. 16, January 25, 1995, www.treas.gov/offices/enforcement/ofac/legal/eo/12947.pdf. Also see Clyde Mark and Kenneth Katzman, *Hamas and Palestinian Islamic Jihad: Recent Developments, Source of Support and Implications for U.S. Policy* (Washington, DC: Congressional Research Service, Library of Congress, 1994); and Office of Public Affairs, "U.S. Designates Five Charities Funding Hamas and Six Senior Hamas Leaders as Terrorist Entities," JS-672, United States Department of the Treasury, August 22, 2003, http://www.ustreas.gov/press/releases/js672.htm.
2. James Brooke and Elaine Sciolino, "U.S. Muslims Say Their Aid Pays for Charity, Not Terror—Bread or Bullets: Money for Hamas," *New York Times*, August 16, 1995. Also see Danny Rubinstein, "The New Message of Hamas," *Ha'aretz*, February 10, 1993, translated by Israel Shahak in *From the Hebrew Press*, March 1993.
3. Office of the Press Secretary, White House, "President Announces Progress on Financial Fight against Terror: Remarks by the President on Financial Fight against Terror, the Rose Garden," December 4, 2001, www.whitehouse.gov/news/releases/2001/12/print/20011204-8.html.
4. United States District Court for the Northern District of Texas, Dallas Division, *United States of America versus Holy Land Foundation, Et Al.*, Number 3: 04-240-G, July 25, 2007, vol. 2, Transcript of Trial Before the Honorable A. Joe Fish, p. 163.
5. Ibid., p. 154.
6. United States Department of the Treasury, Press Room, "Treasury Designates Al-Salah Society Key Support Node for Hamas," August 7, 2007, HP-531.
7. Ibid.
8. Ibid. "In late 2002, an official of the Al-Salah Society in Gaza was the principal leader of Hamas military wing structure in the Al-Maghazi refugee camp

in Gaza. The founder and former director of the Al-Salah Society's Al-Maghazi branch reportedly also operated as a member of the Hamas military wing structure in Al-Maghazi, participated in weapons deals, and served as a liaison to the rest of the Hamas structure in Al-Maghazi. At least four other Hamas military wing members in the Al-Maghazi refugee camp in Gaza were tied to the Al-Salah Society."

9. Adam Entous, "US-Backed Campaign against Hamas Expands to Charities," Reuters, August 20, 2007, www.alertnet.org/db/crisisprofiles/IP_CON.htm?v=at_a_glance>conflict.

10. Ibid.

11. Karin Laub, "Abbas Shuts Hamas Charities in the West Bank," Associated Press, December 3, 2007.

12. Christian Peacemaker Teams—Hebron, "International NGOs Rally to Rescue Hebron Orphans," press release, May 10, 2008, http://www.hebronorphans.blogspot.org.

13. International Crisis Group, *Islamic Social Welfare Activism in the Occupied Palestinian Territories: A Legitimate Target?* ICG Report no. 13 (Brussels: ICG, April 2, 2003), p. 2.

14. Ibid.

15. Janine A. Clark, *Islam, Charity, and Activism: Middle Class Networks and Social Welfare in Egypt, Jordan and Yemen* (Bloomington: Indiana University Press, 2004), p. 43, makes this point.

16. This argument is often made in the literature. This is the core argument of Matthew Levitt's book, *Hamas: Politics, Charity, and Terrorism in the Service of Jihad* (New Haven, CT, and Washington, DC: Yale University Press in cooperation with the Washington Institute for Near East Policy, 2006). For an interesting discussion of civil society and the Islamist movement in Egypt see Sami Zubaida, "Islam, the State and Democracy: Contrasting Conceptions of Society in Egypt," *Middle East Report* 179 (November–December 1992), pp. 2–10; and Mustapha K. al-Sayyid, "A Civil Society in Egypt," *Middle East Journal* 47 (Spring 1993), pp. 228–242.

17. See, for example, Sara Roy, *The Gaza Strip: The Political Economy of De-development* (Washington, DC: Institute for Palestine Studies, 1995, 2001).

18. Sara Roy, "Beyond Hamas: Islamic Activism in the Gaza Strip," *Harvard Middle Eastern and Islamic Review* 2 (Fall 1995).

19. During the Oslo period, there were Islamic institutions that claimed to be independent of Hamas or other Islamist groups. Whether this claim was genuine was difficult to determine; however, some institutions attempted to dissociate themselves politically, a trend that seemed to evaporate completely once the second Intifada began in 2000.

20. See, for example, the excellent studies by Janine A. Clark (2004); Lara Deeb, *The Enchanted Modern: Gender and Public Piety in Shi'i Lebanon* (Princeton, NJ: Princeton University Press, 2006); Quintan Wiktorowicz, ed., *Islamic Activism: A Social Movement Theory Approach* (Bloomington: Indiana University Press, 2004); idem, *The Management of Islamic Activism: Salafis, the Muslim Brotherhood and State Power in Jordan* (Albany: State University of New York Press, 2001); Carrie Rosefsky Wickham, *Mobilizing Islam: Religion, Activism,*

and Political Activism in Egypt (New York: Columbia University Press, 2002); Diane Singerman, *Avenues of Participation: Family, Politics, and Networks in Urban Quarters of Cairo* (Princeton, NJ: Princeton University Press, 1995); Jenny White, *Islamist Mobilization in Turkey: A Study in Vernacular Politics* (Seattle: University of Washington Press, 2002); and Sheila Carapico, *Civil Society in Yemen: The Political Economy of Activism in Modern Arabia* (Cambridge: Cambridge University Press, 1998).

21. In the decade since, I have made various trips to the Gaza Strip and West Bank.

22. See Azzam Tamimi, *La Vanguardia Dossier*, special issue on the Palestinians, October/December 2003.

23. See Khaled Hroub, "A 'New Hamas' through Its New Documents," *Journal of Palestine Studies* 35 (Summer 2006), pp. 6–27; Mouin Rabbani, "A Hamas Perspective on the Movement's Evolving Role: An Interview with Khalid Mishal, Part II," *Journal of Palestine Studies* 37 (Summer 2008), pp. 59–81; and Jerome Slater, "A Perfect Moral Catastrophe: Just War Philosophy and the Israeli Attack on Gaza," *Tikkun* (March–April 2009). Also see "Interviews from Gaza," *Middle East Policy*, December 2002; Seumas Milne, "Too Late for Two States?" *The Guardian*, January 24, 2004; International Crisis Group (ICG), *Dealing with Hamas*, ICG Report no. 21, Amman/Brussels, January 26, 2004; and Shaul Mishal, "The Pragmatic Dimension of the Palestinian Hamas: A Network Perspective," *Armed Forces & Society* 29 (Summer 2003).

24. Taghreed el-Khodary and Ethan Bronner, "Addressing U.S., Hamas Says It Grounded Rockets," *New York Times*, May 5, 2009; and "Transcript: Interview with Khaled Meshal of Hamas," *New York Times*, May 5, 2009, nytimes.com.

25. "Transcript: Interview with Khaled Meshal" (May 5, 2009).

26. Earlier works include Wolfgang Freund, *Looking into Hamas and Other Constituents of the Palestinian-Israeli Confrontation* (Frankfurt: Peter Lang, 2002); Jean-Francois Legrain, "Vers une Palestine Islamique?" *L'Arabisant* 35 (2001); Khaled Hroub, *Hamas: Political Thought and Practice* (Washington, DC: Institute for Palestine Studies, 2000); Shaul Mishal and Avraham Sela, *The Palestinian Hamas: Vision, Violence and Coexistence* (New York: Columbia University Press, 2000); Graham Usher, "What Kind of Nation? The Rise of Hamas in the Occupied Territories," in idem, ed., *Dispatches from Palestine: The Rise and Fall of the Oslo Peace Process* (London: Pluto Press, 1999); Andrea Nusse, *Muslim Palestine: The Ideology of Hamas* (Amsterdam: Harwood Academic Publishers, 1998); Beverly Milton-Edwards, *Islamic Politics in Palestine* (London: I. B. Tauris, 1996); Meir Litvak, *The Islamization of Palestinian Identity: The Case of Hamas* (Tel Aviv: Moshe Dayan Center for Middle Eastern and African Studies, Tel Aviv University, 1996); Laura Guazzone, ed., *The Islamist Dilemma—the Political Role of Islamist Movements in the Contemporary Arab World* (Reading, PA: Ithaca Press, 1995); Ziad Abu-Amr, *Islamic Fundamentalism in the West Bank and Gaza: Muslim Brotherhood and Islamic Jihad* (Bloomington: Indiana University Press, 1994); Hisham Ahmad, *Hamas: From Religious Salvation to Political Transformation—the Rise of Hamas in Palestinian Society* (Jerusalem: Passia, 1994); Ziad Abu-Amr, "Hamas: A Historical and Political Background," *Journal of Palestine Studies* 22 (Summer 1993); Michel Jubran and Laura Drake,

"The Islamic Fundamentalist Movement in the West Bank and Gaza Strip," *Middle East Policy* 2, no. 2 (1993); Ahmad Rashad, "Hamas: Palestinian Politics with an Islamic Hue," Occasional Paper no. 2 (Springfield, VA: United Association for Studies and Research, December 1993); and Jean-Francois Legrain, "A Defining Moment: Palestinian Islamic Fundamentalism," in James Piscatori, ed., *Islamic Fundamentalisms and the Gulf Crisis* (Chicago: American Academy of Arts and Sciences, 1991). More recent additions include Helga Baumgarten, *Hamas: From the Palestinian Resistance into the Government* (Munich: Diederichs, 2006); Khaled Hroub, *Hamas: A Beginner's Guide* (London: Pluto Press, 2006); Matthew Levitt (2006); Carmen Lopez Alonso, *Hamas: La Marcha Hacia El Poder* (Madrid: Catarata, 2007); Zaki Chehab, *Inside Hamas: The Untold Story of the Militant Islamic Movement* (New York: Nation Books, 2007); Joseph Croitoru, *Hamas: Der Islamische Kampf um Palastina* [Hamas: The Islamic Struggle for Palestine] (Munich: C. H. Beck, 2007); Azzam Tamimi, *Hamas: A History from Within* (Northampton, MA: Olive Branch Press, 2007); Jeroen Gunning, *Hamas in Politics: Democracy, Religion, Violence* (New York: Columbia University Press, 2008); Michael Irving Jensen, *The Political Ideology of Hamas: A Grassroots Perspective* (London: I. B. Tauris, 2009); and Paola Caridi, *Hamas: From Resistance to Government?* (Jerusalem: Palestinian Academic Society for the Study of International Affairs [PASSIA], 2010).

27. Hroub (2000), p. 234.

28. Levitt (2006) makes this argument the focus of his book.

29. Scholarship revisiting the history of the Mandate period argues that Islamic themes were more important in the Palestinian struggle against Zionism than was allowed during the ascendancy of the PLO and Fatah (which also used certain Islamic themes despite its overall secular thrust). For example, Al-Hajj Amin al-Husayni and other ulama issued a major fatwa forbidding the sale of land to Jews.

30. Augustus Richard Norton, "Introduction," in Augustus Richard Norton, ed., *Civil Society in the Middle East*, vol. 2 (Leiden and New York: E. J. Brill, 1996), p. 10.

31. Loren Lybarger, *Identity and Religion in Palestine: The Struggle between Islamism and Secularism in the Occupied Territories* (Princeton, NJ: Princeton University Press, 2007), p. xv.

32. Cited in Jeroen Gunning, "Re-Thinking Western Constructs of Islamism: Pluralism, Democracy and the Theory and Praxis of the Islamic Movement in the Gaza Strip" (PhD Thesis, Centre for Middle Eastern and Islamic Studies, University of Durham, 2000).

CHAPTER 2
A BRIEF HISTORY OF HAMAS AND THE ISLAMIC MOVEMENT IN PALESTINE

1. See, for example, Michael Irving Jensen, *The Political Ideology of Hamas: A Grassroots Perspective* (London: I. B. Tauris, 2009); Jeroen Gunning, *Hamas in Politics: Democracy, Religion, Violence* (New York: Columbia University Press, 2008); Khaled Hroub, *Hamas: Political Thought and Practice* (Washington, DC:

Institute for Palestine Studies, 2000); idem, *Hamas: A Beginner's Guide* (London: Pluto Press, 2006); Shaul Mishal and Avraham Sela, *The Palestinian Hamas: Vision, Violence and Coexistence* (New York, NY: Columbia University Press, 2000, 2006); Zaki Chehab, *Inside Hamas: The Untold Story of the Militant Islamic Movement* (New York: Nation Books, 2007); Azzam Tamimi, *Hamas: A History from Within* (Northampton, MA: Olive Branch Press, 2007) ; Matthew Levitt, *Hamas: Politics, Charity, and Terrorism in the Service of Jihad* (New Haven, CT, and Washington, DC: Yale University Press in cooperation with the Washington Institute for Near East Policy, 2006); Beverly Milton-Edwards, *Islamic Politics in Palestine* (London: I. B. Tauris, 1996); and Ziad Abu-Amr, *Islamic Fundamentalism in the West Bank and Gaza: Muslim Brotherhood and Islamic Jihad* (Bloomington: Indiana University Press, 1994).

2. Hroub (2000), pp. 11–41.
3. Ibid., p. 6.
4. This section is derived from the following sources: Ziad Abu-Amr, "Shaykh Ahmad Yasin and the Origins of Hamas, " in R. Scott Appleby, ed., *Spokesmen for the Despised: Fundamentalist Leaders of the Middle East* (Chicago: University of Chicago Press, 1997), pp. 225–256; Abu-Amr (1994); Hroub (2000); Mishal and Sela (2000); Milton-Edwards (1996); International Crisis Group (ICG), *Dealing with Hamas*, ICG Report no. 21 (Amman/Brussels: ICG, January 26, 2004); and Tamimi (2007). Individual points will be referenced as needed.
5. Sami Zubaida, "The Quest for the Islamic State: Islamic Fundamentalism in Egypt and Iran," in Lionel Caplan, ed., *Studies in Religious Fundamentalism* (London: Macmillan, 1987), pp. 34–35; and Richard P. Mitchell, *The Society of Muslim Brothers*, 2nd edition (New York: Oxford University Press, 1993), pp. 211–212.
6. Tamimi (2007), p. 4.
7. Ibid., p. 5.
8. Mitchell (1993), p. 328.
9. ICG (January 26, 2004), pp. 4–5; Hroub (2000), pp. 19–23; and Abu-Amr (1994), pp. 1–10.
10. Hroub (2000), p. 23.
11. The Brotherhood also engaged in armed struggle against Israel during its four-month occupation of the Gaza Strip in 1956 and 1957. Abu-Amr (1994), p. 9.
12. Ibid., p. 8; and Hroub (2000), p. 23.
13. Glenn E. Robinson, "Hamas as Social Movement," in Quintan Wiktorowicz, ed., *Islamic Activism: A Social Movement Theory Approach* (Bloomington: Indiana University Press, 2004), p. 120.
14. Milton-Edwards (1996), p. 76.
15. Hroub (2000), p. 27.
16. Ibid., p. 28.
17. Abu-Amr (1994), p. 11.
18. Milton-Edwards (1996), p. 93.
19. Ibid.
20. Ibid, pp. 74 and 80. Israel's control of Jerusalem, however, did act as a catalyst in defining, over time, a Palestinian Islamic response.

21. Ibid., p. 85.
22. Abu-Amr (1994), p. 15.
23. Emile Sahliyeh, *In Search of Leadership—West Bank Politics since 1967* (Washington, DC: Brookings Institution, 1988), p. 144.
24. Robinson (2004), p. 119.
25. Graham Usher, *Dispatches from Palestine: The Rise and Fall of the Oslo Peace Process* (London: Pluto Press, 1999), p. 19. Also see Abu-Amr (1994), p. 35.
26. For an important study of the Islamic Jihad, see Meir Hatina, *Islam and Salvation in Palestine: The Islamic Jihad Movement* (Tel Aviv: The Moshe Dayan Center for Middle Eastern and African Studies, University of Tel Aviv, 2001).
27. Abu-Amr (1997), p. 239.
28. ICG (January 26, 2004), p. 6.
29. Hroub (2000), p. 33.
30. Robinson (2004) argues that the internal changes in the Brotherhood derived from divisions along class and ideological lines between the old elite of the Muslim Brothers and a newly emerging middle stratum of activists. As such, the formation of Hamas represented a coup against the older leadership of the Muslim Brotherhood by the younger, activist stratum, who reorganized the movement, giving it a new agenda.
31. Shaul Mishal, "The Pragmatic Dimension of the Palestinian Hamas: A Network Perspective," *Armed Forces & Society* 29 (Summer 2003), p. 575 (article, pp. 569–589).
32. Robinson (2004), p. 123.
33. Ibid., pp. 121–122.
34. Jeroen Gunning, "Peace with Hamas? The Transforming Potential of Political Participation," *International Affairs* 80 (March 2004), pp. 246–247.
35. Mishal (2003), p. 575. See Abu-Amr (1997), pp. 235–238.
36. See my work, *The Gaza Strip Survey* (Jerusalem: West Bank Data Base Project and Jerusalem Post Press, 1986).
37. Interview with Ismail Abu Shanab, Gaza City, July 1999. Also see Gunning (2004), pp. 246–247.
38. For example, when Hamas called strike days—typically on days the UNLU did not—the population honored them, especially in Gaza, where support for the organization appeared greater than in the West Bank.
39. Milton-Edwards (1996), pp. 149–152.
40. Mishal and Sela (2000), p. 56.
41. Article 11 of the Hamas charter states that "the land of Palestine is an Islamic land [*waqf*] entrusted to the Muslim generations until Judgment Day. No one may renounce all or even part of it. No Arab state nor all Arab states combined, no king or president nor all kings and presidents, and no organization nor all organizations, Palestinian or Arab, have the right to dispose of it or relinquish or cede any part of it, because Palestine is Islamic land that has been entrusted to generations of Muslims until the Day of Judgment. Who, after all, has the right to act on behalf of Muslim generations until the Day of Judgment?" Hroub (2000), p. 273. Hamas's leaflets at the time express this view in political, violent, and sometimes racist language. See Hroub (2000), appendix, p. 275; and Mishal and

Sela (2000), pp. 51–53. Also see Islamic Resistance Movement (Hamas), "Introductory Memorandum," in Hroub (2000), pp. 292–301.

42. Mishal and Sela (2000), p. 54.

43. Hroub (2000), p. 76.

44. Ibid., pp. 69–86, and 204–208; Abu-Amr (1994), pp. 75–76; and Mishal (2003), pp. 577–578.

45. Kobi Ben-Simhon, "Israel Could Have Made Peace with Hamas under Yassin," *Ha'aretz*, April 18, 2009, www.haaretz.com/hasen/spages/1078849.html.

46. Milton-Edwards (1996), pp. 152–153. For Sheikh Yassin's account of his own arrest and interrogation, see Tamimi (2007), pp. 58–59.

47. ICG (January 26, 2004), p. 7.

48. Interview with Ismail Abu Shanab, Gaza, February 1999.

49. Musa Abu Marzuq, who was based in Springfield, Virginia, was a key player in the restructuring and later became head of Hamas's Political Bureau until his arrest.

50. Mishal and Sela (2000), pp. 58–59 and 156. When compared with the Fatah-PLO relationship, Hamas's outside leaders appeared to have less power over the inside Hamas leaders and Islamist social institutions.

51. See Sara Roy, "Gaza: New Dynamics of Civic Disintegration," in idem, *Failing Peace: Gaza and the Palestinian-Israeli Conflict* (London: Pluto Press, 2007), p. 73.

52. For example, the director of the UN Relief and Works Agency (UNRWA) in Gaza at the time, Klaus Worm, admitted that he sometimes relied on Hamas to distribute needed monies and supplies to the refugee population. Abu-Amr (1994), p. 70, also describes the important role Hamas leaders played in mediating social disputes (with no personal payments), which undermined the authority not only of the occupation but also of the PLO and nationalist institutions.

53. Chehab (2007), pp. 42–43. There does not appear to be any consensus on when exactly the Qassam Brigades were established and operationalized. Even Chehab contradicts himself by saying they became operational in 1991 (p. 43) and on January 1, 1992 (p. 67).

54. In July 1992, Fatah and Hamas engaged in street battles that killed three and injured more than one hundred people.

55. ICG (January 26, 2004), p. 8.

56. Some of the material in this section was first published in Sara Roy, "Hamas and the Transformation(s) of Political Islam in Palestine," *Current History*, January 2003, pp. 13–20. Reprinted with permission.

57. Milton-Edwards (1996), p. 163.

58. Mishal and Sela (2000), p. 69.

59. Ibid., p. 101.

60. Ibid.

61. Mishal (2003), p. 579.

62. The term "controlled violence" is taken from Mishal and Sela (2000), pp. 49–82 and p. 68.

63. Hamas's political leadership consistently argued that they had limited if any control over the military wing.

64. Mishal and Sela (2000), p. 73.
65. Ibid., pp. 73–74.
66. Ibid., pp. 132–138.
67. See an internal Hamas document from July 1992 translated in Mishal and Sela (2000), p. 129.
68. Imad Faluji, who was then editor in chief of *al-Watan*, a Hamas publication, ran as an independent.
69. Graham Usher, "Arafat's Opening," *New Statesman and Society* 8, no. 82 (December 1, 1995), p. 25.
70. Chehab (2007) provides an interesting history of Ayyash, pp. 54–59.
71. The first point, unlike the second, was not explicitly made but was strongly implied in interviews with senior Hamas leaders, notably the late Ismail Abu Shanab and Ismail Haniyeh, Gaza, summer 1999.
72. ICG (January 26, 2004), p. 9.
73. Mishal and Sela (2000), p. 80.
74. For some insight into Hamas's political strategy at the time, see a memo prepared by the Hamas Political Bureau, "The Islamic Resistance Movement (Hamas)," June 2000. Cited in Tamimi (2007), pp. 271–283.
75. Interview, Usama Hamdan, Beirut, February 2010.
76. Robert Malley and Henry Siegman, "The Hamas Factor," *International Herald Tribune*, December 27, 2006.
77. The Israeli Information Center for Human Rights in the Occupied Territories (B'tselem), *Statistics*, www.btselem.org/english/statistics/casualties.
78. Malley and Siegman (December 27, 2006).
79. Although little reported in the U.S. press at the time, the factional violence that erupted in mid-May 2007 began over a conflict involving the refusal of Fatah forces to transfer to Hamas forces monies collected at the Karni crossing point (for commercial goods), which they were mandated to do by law.
80. Palestinian Centre for Human Rights, "Gaza Drowns in Blood Because of the Conflict between Fatah and Hamas Movements," press release, June 12, 2007.
81. Palestinian Centre for Human Rights, "PCHR Publishes 'Black Days in the Absence of Justice: Report on Bloody Fighting in the Gaza Strip from 7 to 14 June 2007,'" Gaza Strip, October 2007.
82. Alvaro de Soto, *End of Mission Report, May 2007, Under Secretary General, UN Special Coordinator for the Middle East Peace Process and Personal Representative of the Secretary General to the Palestine Liberation Organization and the Palestinian Authority, Envoy to the Quartet*. United Nations, May 2007.
83. Rory McCarthy and Ian Williams, "UN Was Pummeled into Submission, Says Outgoing Middle East Envoy," *The Guardian*, June 13, 2007, www.guardian.co.uk/israel/Story/0.2101630.00.html.
84. de Soto (2007), p. 21, para. 56.
85. Conflicts Forum, "Elliot Abrams' Uncivil War," *Conflicts Forum Reports*, January 7, 2007. Also see Mark Perry and Paul Woodward, "Document Details 'U.S.' Plan to Sink Hamas, *Asia Times*, May 16, 2007; and Jonathan Steele, "Hamas Acted on a Very Real Fear of a US-Sponsored Coup," *The Guardian*, June 22, 2007. Also see Kathleen Christison, "Thoughts on the Attempted

Murder of Palestine: The Siren Song of Elliot Abrams," *Counterpunch*, July 26, 2007, www.counterpunch.org/christison07262007.html; and Norman Olsen, "An Inside Story of How the US Magnified Palestinian Suffering," *Christian Science Monitor*, January 12, 2009.

86. Adam Entous, "After Gaza, Some Question Who Was Overthrowing Whom," Reuters, June 17, 2007.

87. Steele (June 22, 2007).

88. David Rose, "The Gaza Bombshell," *Vanity Fair*, April 2008.

89. Ibid.; and Conflicts Forum (January 7, 2007). Also see Amira Hass, "Growing Bitterness in Gaza," *Ha'aretz*, February 9, 2007. The Presidential Guard protected Fatah's top officials, border crossings, and strategic areas in the Gaza Strip.

90. Conflicts Forum (January 7, 2007).

91. Steele (June 22, 2007); and Rose (2008).

92. Steele (June 22, 2007).

93. According to Rose (2008), five hundred fighters—Fatah's National Security Forces—were trained in Egypt and arrived in Gaza in mid-May with weapons and vehicles.

94. Danny Rubinstein, "Analysis: Re-occupation of Gaza—Is It the Only Way Out?" *Ha'aretz*, June 13, 2007.

95. Eli Lake, "Hamas Takes Over Gaza Security Services," *New York Sun*, June 15, 2007. Also see "'It Will Be a Hot Summer,' Interview with Fatah's Intelligence Coordinator," *Speigel Online*, June 18, 2007.

96. Yizhak Benhorin, "State Department Spokesperson Confirms That US Will Continue Program to Train PA's presidential guard, although Training Would Likely Move from Gaza to West Bank," *Israel News*, June 15, 2007, www.ynetnews.com/articles/0,7340,L-3413190,00.html.

97. See Danny Rubinstein, "Occupation Under the Guise of Self-government," *Ha'aretz*, June 13, 2007.

98. Tony Karon, "The 8 Fallacies of Bush's Abbastan Plan," http://tonykaron.com, June 20, 2007.

99. Steele (June 22, 2007).

100. Peter Beraumont and Mitchell Prothero, "How Hamas Turned on Palestine's 'Traitors,'" *The Observer*, June 17, 2007.

101. Palestinian Centre for Human Rights, "No Alternative to Political Dialogue: PCHR's Position towards the Current Crisis in the Gaza Strip and the Palestinian National Authority," press release, June 18, 2007.

102. "Abbas to Alter Voting Laws to Exclude Hamas," International Middle East Media Center, July 27, 2007, www.imemc.org.

103. See Adam Entous, "Abbas Exceeded Powers in Sacking Government," Arab News and Reuters, July 9, 2007; and Palestinian Centre for Human Rights, "Presidential Decree Destroys the Judicial Authority and the Civil Life and Militarizes the Society," press release, July 10, 2007.

104. "Israeli Authorities to Provide up to $1 Billion for President Abbas to Fight Hamas," Ma'an News Agency, June 23, 2007.

105. Isabel Kershner and Steven Erlanger, "Palestinian Split Deepens, with Government in Chaos," *New York Times*, June 15, 2007.

106. "Economics for the 21st Century," Missing Links, June 18, 2007, http://arablinks.blogspot.com. Also see Joshua Mitnick, "US Starts Aid Projects to Boost Palestinian Economy," *Washington Times*, August 2, 2007.

107. E-mail correspondence, Gaza, June 18, 2007.

108. E-mail correspondence, Gaza, June 18, 2007.

109. E-mail correspondence, Gaza, June 19, 2007.

110. See Elizabeth Freed, *Fatah and Hamas Human Rights Violations in the Palestinian Occupied Territories from June 2007 to October 2007*, Palestinian Human Rights Monitoring Group, 2007; and Hussein Ibish, "Sense, Nonsense and Strategy in the New Palestinian Political Landscape," Issue Paper, American Task Force on Palestine, September 7, 2007.

111. Freed (2007); and Palestinian Centre for Human Rights, "PCHR Is Concerned over Measures Taken by Dismissed Government towards Gaza Municipality," press release, December 6, 2007; and idem, "Human Rights Organizations Condemn the Takeover of the Civilian Courts Compound," press release, December 6, 2007.

112. Karin Laub, "Disagreements in Hamas Camps Laid Bare," Associated Press, October 22, 2007.

113. See the statement by Ahmed Yousef, "Engage with Hamas," *Washington Post*, June 20, 2007. Yousef is the senior political adviser to Ismail Haniyeh, the Hamas prime minister whom Abbas dismissed. Also see Loren Lybarger, "Hamas May Become Victim of Own Success: Isolating Group Further Serves No One's Interest," *San Francisco Chronicle*, June 24, 2007.

114. See Alastair Crooke, "Our Second Biggest Mistake in the Middle East," *London Review of Books* 29, July 5, 2007; and Chris Patten, "To Avert Disaster, Stop Isolating Hamas," *Financial Times*, July 28, 2010.

115. A confidential document I am not at liberty to identify.

116. Ibid.

Chapter 3
Islamist Conceptions of Civil Society

1. For example, see Augustus Richard Norton, ed., *Civil Society in the Middle East*, 2 vols. (Leiden and New York: E. J. Brill, 1995, 1996); Edward Shils, "The Virtue of Civil Society," *Government and Opposition* 26 (Winter 1991), pp. 3–20; John Keane, *Democracy and Civil Society* (London: Verso, 1988); Ernest Gellner, *Conditions of Liberty: Civil Society and Its Rivals* (London: Hamish Hamilton, 1994); Dankwart Rustow, "Transitions to Democracy," *Comparative Politics* 2, no. 3 (April 1970), pp. 337–363; Ghassan Salame, ed., *Democracy without Democrats: The Renewal of Politics in the Muslim World* (London: I. B. Tauris, 1994); Larry Diamond, "Toward Democratic Consolidation," *Journal of Democracy* 5 (July 1994), pp. 4–17; John A. Hall, ed., *Civil Society: Theory, History, Comparison* (Cambridge: Polity Press, 1995); Iliya F. Harik, "Pluralism in the Arab World," *Journal of Democracy* 5 (July 1994), pp. 43–56; and Amy Hawthorne, *Middle Eastern Democracy: Is Civil Society the Answer?* Carnegie Papers no. 44, Carnegie Endowment for International Peace, March 2004.

2. Azzam S. Tamimi, *Rachid Ghannouchi: A Democrat within Islamism* (Oxford: Oxford University Press, 2001), p. 127. Also see idem, *Civil Society in Islamic Political Thought*, Institute of Islamic Political Thought, January 21, 2005, www.ii-pt.com/web/papers/civil.htm. With regard to the imposition of Western concepts in a Middle Eastern context, see Albert Hourani, *Arabic Thought in the Liberal Age, 1798–1939*, 3rd edition (Cambridge: Cambridge University Press, 1983).

3. Amr Hamzawy, "Normative Dimensions of Contemporary Arab Debates on Civil Society," in Amr Hamzawy, ed., *Civil Society in the Middle East*, Nahost-Studein 4 (Berlin: Verlag Hans Schiler, 2002), pp. 11–12.

4. For example, see John Ehrenberg, *Civil Society: The Critical History of an Idea* (New York: New York University Press, 1999); Adam B. Seligman, *The Idea of Civil Society* (New York: Free Press, 1992); Robert W. Hefner, ed., *Democratic Civility: The History and Cross-cultural Possibility of a Modern Political Ideal* (New Brunswick, NJ: Transaction Publishers, 1998); and John Keane, *Civil Society: Old Images, New Visions* (Stanford, CA: Stanford University Press, 1998).

5. See Ernest Gellner (1994); Bernard Lewis, *The Shaping of the Modern Middle East* (New York: Oxford University Press, 1994); Daniel Lerner, *The Passing of Traditional Society: Modernizing the Middle East* (Glencoe, IL: Free Press, 1958); and Nawaf Salam, *Civil Society in the Arab World: The Historical and Political Dimensions*, Occasional Publications 3, Islamic Legal Studies Program, Harvard Law School, Cambridge, MA, October 2002.

6. There are those who argue in the affirmative based on the important and often critical socioeconomic work that Islamist groups such as Hamas or Hizballah do, while others maintain that their violence (and hence intolerance) precludes for them any role in civil society.

7. Ahmad S. Moussalli, "Modern Islamic Fundamentalist Discourses on Civil Society, Pluralism and Democracy," in Augustus Richard Norton, ed., *Civil Society in the Middle East*, vol. 1 (Leiden and New York: E. J. Brill, 1995), pp. 80–81. I consider this article (pp. 79–119) one of the best and most succinct on the topic. Also see Mansoor Moaddel and Kamran Talattof, *Contemporary Debates in Islam: An Anthology of Modernist and Fundamentalist Thought* (New York: St. Martin's Press, 2000); Meir Hatina, *Identity Politics in the Middle East: Liberal Thought and Islamist Challenge in Egypt* (London: Tauris Academic Studies, 2007); and Egbert Harmsen, *Islam, Civil Society and Social Work: Muslim Voluntary Welfare Associations in Jordan between Patronage and Empowerment* (Amsterdam: Amsterdam University Press, 2008).

8. Gudrun Kramer, "Islamist Notions of Democracy," *Middle East Report*, no. 183 (July–August 1993), p. 4. Also see, John L. Esposito and James P. Piscatori, "Democratization and Islam," *Middle East Journal* 45 (Summer 1991), pp. 427–440.

9. Moussalli (1995), p. 106.

10. Hatina (2007), p. 156. For a different view see Bassam Tibi, *The Challenge of Fundamentalism: Political Islam in the New World Disorder* (Berkeley: University of California Press, 1998), pp. 159–164.

11. Moussalli (1995), p. 80.

12. Muhammad Abduh, "Quranic Exegesis," (*Tafsir al-Quran al-Hakim*) *al-Manar* 8, no. 24 (February 10, 1906), pp. 921–930, in Moaddel and Talattof (2000), pp. 41–42.

13. John O. Voll, *Islam, Continuity and Change in the Modern World*, 2nd edition (Syracuse, NY: Syracuse University Press, 1994), p. 12.

14. Salam (October 2002), p. 8.

15. Tamimi (2001), p. 129.

16. See Jonathan P. Berkey, *The Formation of Islam: Religion and Society in the Near East, 600–1800* (Cambridge: Cambridge University Press, 2003), pp. 64–69; and R. B. Serjeant, "The Sunnah Jami'ah, Pacts with the Yathrib Jews, and the Tahrim of Yathrib: Analysis and Translation of the Documents Comprised in the So-Called 'Constitution of Medina,'" *Bulletin of the School of Oriental and African Studies* 41, no. 1 (1978), pp. 1–42.

17. Moussalli (1995), pp. 87–88.

18. See Michael Cook, *Commanding Right and Forbidding Wrong in Islamic Thought* (Cambridge: Cambridge University Press, 2000), p. xi and 585–596.

19. Michael Irving Jensen, "Islamism and Civil Society in the Gaza Strip," in Ahmad S. Moussalli, ed., *Islamic Fundamentalism: Myths and Realities* (Ithaca, NY: Ithaca Press, 1998), p. 198.

20. Salam (October 2002), pp. 6–7.

21. Moussalli (1995), p. 87.

22. See, for example, Muhammad Salim El-Aw[w]a, *On the Political System of the Islamic State* (Indianapolis: American Trust Publications, 1980).

23. Tamimi (2001), p. 134.

24. See Harmsen (2008), p. 48; Nazih Ayubi, *Political Islam: Religion and Politics in the Arab World* (London: Routledge, 2004), p. 179; Ilya Harik, "Democratic Thought in the Arab World: An Alternative to the Patron State," in Charles E. Butterworth and I. William Zartman, eds., *Between the State and Islam* (Cambridge: Cambridge University Press, 2001), p. 145 (pp. 134–157); and Michaelle Browers, *Democracy and Civil Society in Arab Political Thought: Transcultural Possibilities* (Syracuse, NY: Syracuse University Press, 2006), pp. 99–110.

25. Hamzawy (2002), p. 28

26. Dina Rizk Khoury, *State and Provincial Society in the Ottoman Empire: Mosul, 1540–1834* (Cambridge: Cambridge University Press, 1997), p. 13 (see pp. 11–13).

27. Salam (October 2002), pp. 6–7. Also see Nawaf Salam, "The Emergence of Citizenship in Islamdom," *Arab Law Quarterly* 12 (1997), pp. 125–147; Claude Cahen, "Reflexions sur le waqf ancien," in *Studia Islamica* 14 (1961), pp. 37–56; Mohammed Arkoun, "Religion et societe d'apres l'exemple de l'Islam," *Studia Islamica* 55 (1982), pp. 5–59; Benjamin Braude and Bernard Lewis, eds., *Christians and Jews in the Ottoman Empire: The Functioning of a Plural Society* (New York: Holmes and Meier Publishers, 1982); and Nikki R. Keddie, ed., *Scholars, Saints and Sufis: Muslim Religious Institutions in the Middle East since 1500* (Berkeley: University of California Press, 1972).

28. Keddie (1972), pp. 1–2.

29. Ibid., p. 2.

30. Moussalli (1995), p. 84.

31. Amr Hamzawy, "Exploring Theoretical and Programmatic Changes in Contemporary Islamist Discourse: The Journal Al-Manar al-Jadid," in Azza

Karam, ed., *Transnational Political Islam: Religion, Ideology and Power* (London: Pluto Press, 2004), p. 131.

32. Munir Shafiq, "Secularism and the Arab-Muslim Condition," in John L. Esposito and Azzam Tamimi, eds., *Islam and Secularism in the Middle East* (New York: New York University Press, 2000), pp. 146 and 147. Shafiq states that the ulama led many uprisings over the last two hundred years and forged truces that prevailed for most of the period.

33. Hatina (2007), p. 174.

34. See Muhammad Qasim Zaman, *The Ulama in Contemporary Islam: Custodians of Change* (Princeton, NJ: Princeton University Press, 2007), pp. 1–16 and 144–180; Meir Hatina, "Between Harmony and Dissent: Ulama and Nationalist Movements," in Moshe Gammer, ed., *Community, Identity and the State: Comparing Africa, Eurasia, Latin America and the Middle East* (London: Routledge, 2004), pp. 117–131; idem, "Historical Legacy and the Challenge of Modernity in the Middle East: The Case of al-Azhar in Egypt," *The Muslim World* 93 (January 2003), pp. 51–68; and idem, "The Ulama and the Cult of Death in Palestine," *Israel Affairs* 12 (Winter 2006), pp. 29–51.

35. Shafiq in Esposito and Tamimi (2000), p. 147.

36. Moussalli (1995) p. 85.

37. Tamimi (2001), p. 125.

38. Ibid., p. 133.

39. Hamzawy (2002), p. 30.

40. Hamzawy (2004), p. 131. Also see Ira M. Lapidus, "The Separation of State and Religion in the Development of Early Islamic Society," *International Journal of Middle East Studies* 6 (October 1975), pp. 363–385.

41. Hatina (2007), p. 3.

42. Shafiq in Esposito and Tamimi (2000), p. 148.

43. Hamzawy (2004), p. 131; and Hatina (2007), pp. 220–221n3. Also see Meir Hatina, ed., *Guardians of the Faith in Modern Times: 'Ulamma' in the Middle East* (Leiden and Boston: E. J. Brill, 2009); and Zaman (2007).

44. Hamzawy (2002), p. 37.

45. Salam (October 2002), p. 9.

46. For a discussion of the distorting impact of colonialism on civil society in Tunisia, see Rachid Al-Ghannouchi, "Secularism in the Arab Maghreb," in Esposito and Tamimi (2000), pp. 97–111. In fact, the Islamist activist Kamal Habib feels that Qutb's beliefs concerning the use of violence were formulated during a specific phase of Islamic history—Nasserism and its degrading and repression of Islam. Hamzawy (2004), p. 134.

47. Al-Qaradawi has sanctioned suicide bombing attacks in Israel, Iraq, and other lands considered occupied; has recommended female circumcision; and approves the execution of homosexuals. He also holds moderate views on certain issues such as "allowing men and women to study together, endorsing Muslim participation in Western democracies, and condemning al-Qaeda style attacks such as 9/11." See Samuel Helfont, *Islam and Islamism Today: The Case of Yusuf Al-Qaradawi*, Foreign Policy Research Institute, January 12, 2010. He also argues that extremist religious practices, while allowed in Islam, may not be imposed

on others, and addresses defects in religious extremism. See Yusif al-Qaradawi, "Extremism," in Charles Kurzman, ed., *Liberal Islam: A Sourcebook* (New York: Oxford University Press, 1998), pp. 196–204.

48. Hamzawy (2004), p. 139; and Helfont (January 12, 2010).

49. Hamzawy (2004), p. 139. Al-Qaradawi accepts the need for revising religious judgments, which he considers necessary in an age of rapid and great transformations (p. 138).

50. Ibid.

51. See the collection of primary source documents (translated into English) in Moaddel and Talattof, particularly Ali Abd al-Raziq, "The Unity of Religion and Arabs," *al-Islam waUsul al Hukm* (Islam and the Fundamentals of Authority), Cairo, 1925, pp. 81–89, in Moaddel and Talattof (2000), pp. 95–100.

52. For an excellent discussion of Hamas's political philosophy see Jeroen Gunning, *Hamas in Politics: Democracy, Religion, Violence* (New York: Columbia University Press, 2008), pp. 55–94.

53. Hatina (2007), pp. 138–157.

54. Kramer (1993), p. 6.

55. Helfont (January 12, 2010).

56. Moussalli (1995), p. 88.

57. Hamzawy (2004), p. 121. Also see Kramer (1993), pp. 2–8.

58. Voll (1994), p. 23.

59. Also see Voll (1994), pp. 21–23 and pp. 289–374.

60. Richard P. Mitchell, *The Society of the Muslim Brothers*, 2nd edition (New York: Oxford University Press, 1993), pp. 232–294, makes this clear as does Kramer (1993), pp. 5–6. In this regard also see Loren Lybarger, *Identity and Religion in Palestine: The Struggle between Islamism and Secularism in the Occupied Territories* (Princeton, NJ: Princeton University Press, 2007).

61. Kramer (1993), p. 4. Also see Roxanne Euben, *Enemy in the Mirror: Islamic Fundamentalism and the Limits of Modern Rationalism* (Princeton, NJ: Princeton University Press, 1999); and Roxanne Euben and Muhammad Qasim Zaman, *Princeton Readings in Islamist Thought: Texts and Contexts from al-Banna to Bin Laden* (Princeton, NJ: Princeton University Press, 2009).

62. Sayyid Qutb, *Islam and Universal Peace* (Plainfield, IN: American Trust Publications, 1993), p. 53. Also see Mitchell (1993), p. 239; and Sayyid Qutb, *Social Justice in Islam*, translated from the Arabic by John B. Hardie (Washington, DC: American Council of Learned Societies, 1953); and William E. Shepard, *Sayyid Qutb and Islamic Activism: A Translation and Critical Analysis of Social Justice in Islam* (Leiden: E .J. Brill, 1996).

63. Mitchell (1993), p. 243.

64. Moussalli (1995), pp. 91–93.

65. Sayyid Qutb, *Milestones*, English translation (Cedar Rapids, IA: Unity Publishing, 1981), p. 36.

66. Ibid., pp. 94–95 and 33–36; and Gunning (2008), p. 69.

67. Gunning (2008), pp. 64–65. Qutb's writings provided a source for Hamas's political philosophy with regard to the importance of submitting to sharia in order to achieve personal freedom (although Hamas's views depart from those of

Qutb in other ways). To be free means to submit oneself to God's will and to do as one wishes in a divine contract that is both religious and social.

68. Qutb (1993), p. 73.
69. Qutb (1981), pp. 80–84 and 45–51.
70. Moussalli (1995), p. 92.
71. Concomitantly, this separatist, sectarian discourse seeks to create purely Islamic communities as articulated, for example, by Shukri Mustafa, an Egyptian and founder of the Society of Muslims; and Salih Sirriyyah, a Jordanian who founded the Society of Mohammed's Youth and the Islamic Liberation Organization. They reject all societies, systems, ideologies, institutions, legislative processes, and ways of life that are not based on Islam and its principal texts. See Gilles Kepel, *Jihad: The Trail of Political Islam* (Cambridge, MA: Harvard University Press, 2002), pp. 84–85; John O. Voll, "Fundamentalism in the Sunni Arab World: Egypt and the Sudan," in Martin E. Marty and R. Scott Appleby, ed., *Fundamentalisms Observed* (Chicago: University of Chicago Press, 1994), pp. 382–384; and Geneive Abdo, *No God but God: Egypt and the Triumph of Islam* (New York: Oxford University Press, 2002), pp. 54–55.
72. See Harmsen (2008), pp. 45–66.
73. Moussalli (1995), p. 100.
74. Abdelwahab El-Affendi, "Rationality of Politics and Politics of Rationality: Democratisation and the Influence of Islamic Religious Traditions," in Esposito and Tamimi (2000), pp. 156 and 166. Also see Sana Abed-Kotob, "The Accommodationists Speak: Goals and Strategies of the Muslim Brotherhood in Egypt," *International Journal of Middle East Studies* 27 (August 1995): pp. 321–339; Tim Niblock, "Islamic Movements and Sudan's Political Coherence, " in Herve Bleuchot, Christian Delmet, and Derek Hopwood, eds., *Sudan: History, Identity, Ideology* (Reading, PA: Ithaca Press, 1991), pp. 253–268; Glenn Robinson, "Can Islamists Be Democrats? The Case of Jordan," *Middle East Journal* 51 (Summer 1997), pp. 373–387; Olivier Roy, *The Failure of Political Islam* (Cambridge, MA: Harvard University Press, 1994); Robert W. Hefner, *Civil Islam: Muslims and Democratization in Indonesia* (Princeton, NJ: Princeton University Press, 2000); and Emmanuel Sivan, "Eavesdropping on Radical Islam," *Middle East Quarterly* 2 (March 1995): pp. 13–24.
75. Nikki R. Keddie, *Sayyid Jamal ad-Din "al-Afghani": A Political Biography* (Berkeley: University of California Press, 1972), p. 2; Voll, *Fudamentalism in the Sunni Arab World* (1994), pp. 355–356; and Charles C. Adams, *Islam and Modernism in Egypt: A Study of the Modern Reform Movement Inaugurated by Muhammad 'Abduh* (London: Oxford University Press, 1933).
76. Nikki R. Keddie, *An Islamic Response to Imperialism: Political and Religious Writings of Sayyid Jamal ad-Din "al-Afghani"* (Berkeley: University of California Press, 1983), p. xiii. See pp. xiii–xxii.
77. Keddie (1972), p. 1. See also pp. 271–334.
78. Hamzawy (2004), p. 125. Also see the seminal work by Malcolm H. Kerr, *Islamic Reform: The Political and Legal Theories of Muhammad 'Abduh and Rashid Rida* (Berkeley: University of California Press, 1966); Keddie (1972); Keddie (1983); Hourani (1983); and Roy Mottahedeh, *The Mantle of the Prophet:*

Religion and Politics in Iran (Oxford: Oneworld Publications, 2000). For another view of Abduh see Elie Kedourie, *Afghani and 'Abduh: An Essay on Religious Unbelief and Political Activism in Modern Islam* (London: Routledge, 2008; originally published in 1966).

79. Gunning (2008), pp. 57–61. He also writes that Hamas advocates a form of government consisting of an executive, legislative, and judicial branch (and checks and balances). A *shura* council would be the source of legislative power, and its members would be elected in regular elections open to all citizens including non-Muslims, communists, and secular Muslims. However, there is disagreement over the rights of non-Muslims.

80. Mitchell (1993), p. 234. Also see Brynjar Lia, *The Society of Muslim Brothers in Egypt: The Rise of an Islamic Mass Movement, 1928–1942* (Reading, UK: Ithaca Press, 1998).

81. Mitchell (1993), p. 325.
82. Ibid., p. 238.
83. Ibid.
84. Ibid., p. 239.
85. Ibid.
86. Ibid., p. 247.
87. Ibid., pp. 232–233.
88. Shafiq in Esposito and Tamimi (2000), p. 145.
89. Gunning (2008), p. 67.
90. Ibid.
91. Ibid., p. 72.
92. Ibid., p. 60.
93. Ibid., p. 67.
94. Ibid., p. 63.
95. Ibid., p. 65.
96. Shafiq in Esposito and Tamimi (2000), p. 145.
97. Kramer (1993), p. 7. She goes on to say that within their thinking, however, there is reluctance to allow for unlimited freedom of speech particularly as it regards religious indifference, blasphemy, and heresy, and there can be no toleration of the enemies of Islam. In this regard, Moussalli (1995), pp. 108–113, discusses Hasan al-Turabi, a leading Islamist thinker who argued that having one public opinion leads to "halting the progress of life." (p. 111).

98. Gunning (2008), p. 119.

99. Hatina (2007), p. 178. Also see Joel Beinin and Joe Stork, eds., *Political Islam: Essays from Middle East Report* (London: I. B. Tauris, 1997).

100. However, all agreed that once an Islamic state was established and agreed to by the majority, no party should be allowed to undermine the Islamic nature of the state. Gunning (2008), p. 59.

101. For many in Hamas a communist party would be allowed in an Islamic state as long as it does not preach atheism. Gunning (2008), p. 88.

102. Al-Ghannouchi in Espositio and Tamimi (2000), p. 114 and pp. 112–115.

103. Rachid al-Ghannouchi, "Participation in Non-Islamic Government," in Kurzman (1998), pp. 89–95.

104. Ibid., p. 92.

105. For a detailed examination of Hawwa's thought see Itzchak Wiesman, "Saʻid Hawwa and Islamic Revivalism in Bathist Syria," *Studia Islamica* 85 (1997), pp. 131–154; and idem, Saʻid Hawwa—the Making of a Radical Muslim Thinker in Modern Syria," *Middle Eastern Studies* 29 (October 1993), pp. 601–623.

106. Moussalli (1995), p. 105.

107. Kramer (1993), p. 7; and Hatina (2007), p. 145.

108. Hatina (2007), p. 140.

109. Ibid., p. 143. See Michael I. Jensen, *The Political Ideology of Hamas: A Grassroots Perspective* (London: I. B. Tauris, 2009), p. 58.

110. Hamzawy (2004), p. 140.

111. Ibid., pp. 140–141.

112. Hatina (2007), p. 179.

113. Asghar Schirazi, "The Debate on Civil Society in Iran," in Hamzawy (2002) p. 62. Hatina (2007), p. 179, also states that the Islamist perception of civil society calls for the autonomy of social institutions.

114. El-Affendi in Esposito and Tamimi (2000), p. 168.

115. Moussalli (1995), p. 118.

CHAPTER 4
THE EVOLUTION OF ISLAMIST SOCIAL INSTITUTIONS IN THE GAZA STRIP: BEFORE AND DURING OSLO (A SOCIOPOLITICAL HISTORY)

1. International Crisis Group, *Islamic Social Welfare Activism in the Occupied Palestinian Territories: A Legitimate Target?* ICG Report no. 13 (Brussels: ICG, April 2, 2003), p. 4.

2. Beverly Milton-Edwards, *Islamic Politics in Palestine* (London: I. B. Tauris, 1996), pp. 73–102.

3. Ibid., p. 102.

4. Ibid.

5. Ibid., p. 101.

6. Azzam Tamimi, *Hamas: A History from Within* (Northampton, MA: Olive Branch Press, 2007), pp. 36–37.

7. Others included Khalil Koka, Sheikh Salah Shehada, Dr. Mohammad Siam Fadel Khaled Zabout, Ibrahim Abu Salem, and Ahmad al-Alami. Milton-Edwards (1996), p. 126.

8. Ibid., p. 127.

9. Ibid., p. 125.

10. Shaul Mishal and Avraham Sela, *The Palestinian Hamas: Vision, Violence and Coexistence* (New York: Columbia University Press, 2000), p. 20 and 18–24.

11. Tamimi (2007), p. 38.

12. Milton-Edwards (1996), p. 102. See Michael Irving Jensen, *The Political Ideology of Hamas: A Grassroots Perspective* (London: I. B. Tauris, 2009).

13. Ziad Abu-Amr, *Islamic Fundamentalism in the West Bank and Gaza: Muslim Brotherhood and Islamic Jihad* (Bloomington: Indiana University Press, 1994), p. 15.

14. Mishal and Sela (2000), p. 19.
15. Ibid., p. 20.
16. Milton-Edwards (1996), p. 102.
17. Mishal and Sela (2000), 20.
18. Michael Irving Jensen, "Islamism and Civil Society in the Gaza Strip," in Ahmad S. Moussalli, ed., *Islamic Fundamentalism: Myths and Realities* (Ithaca, NY: Ithaca Press, 1998), p. 201. Jensen cites, as the original source, al-Jam'iyya al-Islamiyya, *Qanun asasi* (Gaza, 1976), which was not available to the author. Abraham is called *hanif allah* in the Quran. This is typically translated as "friend of God" and refers to his monotheism as being a form of the true religion later embodied in Islam.
19. Mishal and Sela (2000), p. 20.
20. Jeroen Gunning, "Re-Thinking Western Constructs of Islamism: Pluralism, Democracy and the Theory and Praxis of the Islamic Movement in the Gaza Strip" (PhD Thesis, Centre for Middle Eastern and Islamic Studies, University of Durham, 2000), p. 39.
21. Mishal and Sela (2000), p. 19.
22. Abu-Amr (1994), p. 16. The Mujamma and the Department of Islamic Endowments struggled over control of the mosques, in which the latter prevailed.
23. Mishal and Sela (2000), pp. 19 and 20.
24. Gunning (2000), pp. 113–141, argues that the (sometimes violent) history of the IUG was dichotomized and distorted by Western and pro-PLO sources and was far more complex and nuanced than presented. The Islamists, he argues, are simply depicted as antinationalist and antidemocratic, trying to impose Islam on "an otherwise secularly inclined university." This, according to Gunning, is rewriting history. "Such rewriting appears to be part of the dichotomisation process that both PLO and Western authors are tempted to engage in, justifying secularist actions against Islamists by depicting the latter as usurpers and outsiders" (p. 140). Also see Gunning's chapter 5, "Socio-Political Violence: The Hijab Campaign in Gaza," pp. 142–169, for a similar argument. He shows that although Hamas was accused of orchestrating the campaign, the evidence suggests otherwise. Also see Jensen (2009), pp. 97–139.
25. Mishal and Sela (2000), pp. 23–25; and Tamimi (2007), pp. 39–42.
26. Abu-Amr (1994), p. 17.
27. See, for example, the study of the Islamic Jihad by Meir Hatina, *Islam and Salvation in Palestine: The Islamic Jihad Movement* (Tel Aviv: Moshe Dayan Center for Middle Eastern and African Studies, Tel Aviv University, 2001); Milton-Edwards (1996), pp. 116–121; Tamimi (2007), pp. 43–44; and Emmanuel Sivan, *Radical Islam: Medieval Theology and Modern Politics* (New Haven, CT: Yale University Press, 1990).
28. Milton-Edwards (1996), p. 111.
29. Ibid., p. 106.
30. See Tamimi (2007), pp. 44–50.
31. Gunning (2000) indicates that the "s" is the first consonant of "Islami," p. 41, n. 20.
32. Khaled Hroub, *Hamas: Political Thought and Practice* (Washington, DC: Institute for Palestine Studies, 2000), p. 239.

33. Mishal and Sela (2000), p. 37. Also see Gunning (2000) and Jensen (1998).
34. Hroub (2000), pp. 276–277.
35. Sara Roy, "Beyond Hamas: Islamic Activism in the Gaza Strip," *Harvard Middle Eastern and Islamic Review* 2 (Fall 1995), pp. 1–39. The information in this section is derived from this article. Reprinted with permission.
36. Given a conservative average of six people per family, there were approximately 6,700 families in Nuseirat camp at the time. Hence, to cover the whole camp, each volunteer would have had to work with 22 families, which is not inconceivable.
37. See Sara Roy, "Hamas and the Transformation(s) of Political Islam in Palestine," *Current History*, January 2003, pp. 14–17 (reprinted with permission); and Sara Roy, "Professionalization versus Politics: The Transformation of Islamic NGOs in Palestine," *Middle East Report* 214 (Spring 2000), pp. 24–27, in which some of the findings described herein were first presented.
38. Jensen (2009), p. 33, found the same.
39. Roy (2000), "Professionalization versus Politics," p. 25.
40. Ismail Abu Shanab indicated that privileging the social as well as other sectors of Hamas was a function of existing circumstances. See Wolfgang Freund, *Looking into Hamas and Other Constituents of the Palestinian-Israeli Confrontation* (Frankfurt: Peter Lang, 2002), p. 34.
41. It is also important to reiterate that the core impulse within Hamas has always been political, not religious; indeed, religion has never dominated politics among Palestinian Islamists, a fact accounting for their pragmatism and flexibility. For another interesting account of a similar phenomenon among Islamists in Egypt, see Augustus Richard Norton, "Thwarted Politics: The Case of Egypt's Hizb al-Wasat," in Robert W. Hefner, ed., *Remaking Muslim Politics: Pluralism, Contestation, Democratization* (Princeton, NJ: Princeton University Press, 2005), pp. 133–160. Also see Meir Hatina, *Identity Politics in the Middle East: Liberal Thought and Islamic Challenge in Egypt* (London: Tauris Academic Studies, 2007), pp. 158–172; idem, "The 'Other Islam': The Egyptian Wasat Party," *Critique: Critical Middle Eastern Studies* 14 (Summer 2005), pp. 171–184; Robert W. Hefner, "Introduction: Modernity and the Remaking of Muslim Politics," in Robert W. Hefner, ed., *Remaking Muslim Politics: Pluralism, Contestation, Democratization* (Princeton, NJ: Princeton University Press, 2005), pp. 1–36; and Jenny B. White, "The End of Islamism? Turkey's Muslimhood Model," in Robert W. Hefner, ed., *Remaking Muslim Politics: Pluralism, Contestation, Democratization* (Princeton, NJ: Princeton University Press, 2005), pp. 87–111. Tim Niblock's study, "Islamic Movements and Sudan's Political Coherence," in Herve Bleuchot, Christian Delmet, and Derek Hopwood, eds., *Sudan: History, Identity, Ideology* (Reading, PA: Ithaca Press, 1991), is also relevant.
42. See Jeroen Gunning, *Hamas in Politics: Democracy, Religion, Violence* (New York: Columbia University Press, 2008), p. 85 (also see pp. 85–88). He points out the tension between Hamas's commitment to a popular mandate (even if it goes against specific political positions such as the establishment of an Islamic state) and the need to implement God's law.
43. It should be noted that even the language used had changed somewhat, from singular political references to Hamas or Islamic Jihad to the more benign

use of the religious/cultural referent "Muslim Brothers." Ironically, those individuals in Gaza who today identify themselves as Muslim Brothers espouse an ideology more extreme than that of Hamas.

44. Roy (January 2003), p. 16. By 1999–2000, approximately 10 percent to 40 percent of all social institutions in the West Bank and Gaza were Islamic, according to official and private sources.

45. The Portland Trust, *Palestinian Economic Bulletin*, issue 32, May 2009, www.portlandtrust.org; and "Hamas Hangs On," *The Economist*, April 3, 2010.

46. Shaul Mishal, "The Pragmatic Dimension of the Palestinian Hamas: A Network Perspective," *Armed Forces & Society* 29 (Summer 2003), p. 579, states, "although Hamas propaganda continued to discredit and delegitimize the PA's leadership, Hamas was careful not to alienate the rank and file within the PA administration."

47. Amr Hamzawy, "Exploring Theoretical and Programmatic Changes in Contemporary Islamist Discourse: The Journal Al-Manar al-Jadid," in Azza Karam, ed., *Transnational Political Islam: Religion, Ideology and Power* (London: Pluto Press, 2004), p. 137; and idem, *Civil Society in the Middle East*, Nahost-Studein 4 (Berlin: Verlag Hans Schiler, 2003), pp. 7–46.

48. Mishal and Sela (2000), p. 111.

49. Hroub (2000), pp. 241–242.

50. Mishal and Sela (2000), p. 120.

51. This also may have been a way for Hamas's domestic political leadership in Palestine to strengthen its position vis-à-vis the external leadership, given the ongoing tensions between them.

52. Gunning (2008), p. 87.

53. Mishal and Sela (2000), p. 126.

Chapter 5
Islamist Social Institutions: Creating a Descriptive Context

1. Eric Hoffer, *The True Believer: Thought on the Nature of Mass Movements* (New York: Harper and Row, 1951), p. 39.

2. Gretel C. Kovach, "U.S. Wins Convictions in Retrial of Terrorism-Financing Case," *New York Times*, November 25, 2008. For a complete list of unindicted coconspirators and/or joint venturers (which include some of the ISIs and individuals in my sample) see United States District Court for the Northern District of Texas, Dallas Division, *United States of America versus Holy Land Foundation, Et Al.*, Number 3:04-240-G, Attachment A. In this regard see "The Terrorist Financing Operations Section," testimony of John S. Pistole, Assistant Director, Counterterrorism Division, FBI, before the House Committee on Financial Services, Subcommittee on Oversight and Investigations, Federal Bureau of Investigation, September 24, 2003, http://www.fbi.gov/congress/congress03/pistole092403.htm; and Palestine Children's Relief Fund, *US Treasury Antiterrorist Financing Guidelines: Voluntary Best Practices for U.S.-Based Charities*, 2009, http://www.pcrf.net/?page_id=1804.

3. Matthew Levitt, "Financial Setbacks for Hamas," Policy Watch no. 1436 (Washington, DC: The Washington Institute for Near East Policy, December 3, 2008).

4. Kovach (November 25, 2008). Also see Jeroen Gunning, "Terrorism, Charities and Diasporas: Contrasting the Fundraising Practices of Hamas and al Qaeda among Muslims in Europe," in Thomas J. Biersteker and Sue E. Eckert, eds., *Countering the Financing of Terrorism* (London: Routledge, 2008), pp. 93–125; and "The Terrorist Financing Operations Section," testimony of John S. Pistole (September 24, 2003).

5. It should be noted that HLF CEO Shukri Abu Baker's brother, Jamal Issa, is the head of Hamas operations in Yemen. Ghassan Elashi, HLF chairman and cofounder, is related by marriage to a key Hamas official, Mousa Abu Marzook. Cofounder Mohammad El-Mezain is a cousin of Abu Marzook. HLF fund-raiser Mufid Abdulqader is the brother of Khaled Meshal.

6. See, for example, Daniel Nasaw, "Leaders of Muslim Charity in U.S. Found Guilty of Providing Funds to Hamas," *The Guardian*, November 24, 2008, www.guardian.co.uk; "U.S. Charity Guilty of Funding Hamas," *Al Jazeera*, November 24, 2008, http://english.aljazeera.net/news/americas/2008/11/20081124212126642596.html; "Editorial: U.S.' Conflict with Reality," *Arab News* (Jeddah), November 26, 2008; and Jason Trahan, "Closing Arguments to Begin in Holy Land Foundation Terrorism Financing Case," *Dallas Morning News*, November 10, 2008.

7. Kovach (November 25, 2008). For a list of designated charities see United States Department of Treasury, Office of Terrorism and Financial Intelligence, *Key Issues: Protecting Charitable Organizations, Additional Background Information on Charities Designated Under Executive Order 13224*, August 21, 2007, http://www.ustreas.gov/offices/enforcement/key-issues/protecting/charities_execorder_13224; and idem, *Key Issues: Protecting Charitable Organizations: Designated Charities and Potential Fundraising Front Organizations for FTOs (listed by affiliation and designation date)*, February 21, 2006, http://www.ustreas.gov/offices/enforcement/key-issues/protecting/fto.shtml.

8. Trahan (November 10, 2008).

9. "Hamas Backers Jailed in Texas," *BBC News*, May 28, 2009, http://news.bbc.co.uk/go/pr/fr/-/2/hi/americas/8071113.stm; "US Moves to Counter Palestinian Democracy: US Muslim Charity Leaders Get 65 Years in Jail for Financing Democratically Elected Hamas," *Middle East On Line*, May 28, 2009, www.middle-east-online.com/english/?id=32347; and Stephen Lendman, "Targeting Muslim Charities in America," thepeoplesvoice.org, November 23, 2009.

10. United States Department of the Treasury, Office of Terrorism and Financial Intelligence, *Key Issues: Union of Good (Saudi Arabia)*, February 3, 2009, http://www.ustreas.gov/offices/enforcement/key-issues/protecting/union-of-good.shtml.

11. Intelligence and Terrorism Information Center, "The war on financing terrorism: Defense Minister Ehud Barak signed an order outlawing 36 global 'Union of Good' Islamic funds ... ," Israel Intelligence Heritage & Commemoration Center (IICC), July 8, 2008. See the appendix for the actual order signed by

Defense Minister Ehud Barak. Also see Israel Ministry of Foreign Affairs, "Defense Minister Signs Order Banning Hamas-Affiliated Charitable Organizations," July 7, 2008; United States Department of the Treasury, "Treasury Designates the Union of Good," press release, November 12, 2008, http://www.ustreas.gov/press/releases/hp1267.htm; and Steve Merley, *The Union of Good: INTERPAL and the U.K. Member Organizations*, The NEFA Foundation, March 23, 2009.

12. Intelligence and Terrorism Information Center (July 8, 2008).

13. Merley (March 23, 2009), p. 8.

14. Intelligence and Terrorism Information Center (July 8, 2008).

15. Levitt (December 3, 2008).

16. Marc Perelman, "Charities Held Liable for Cast to Terror Group's Social Service Arm," *Jewish Daily Forward*, December 11, 2008; and Steve Emerson, "Court Upholds $156 Million Judgment against Hamas Supporters," *Family Security Matters*, December 5, 2008, www.familysecuritymatters.org. Also see Levitt (December 3, 2008).

17. "Faith, Hate and Charity: Transcript," PANORAMA, *BBC News*, July 30, 2006. For an alternative view see Jonathan Benthall, "The Overreaction against Islamic Charities," *ISIM Review* 20 (Autumn 2007), pp. 6–7.

18. In June 2010, the U.S. Supreme Court went even further when it effectively criminalized nonviolent speech by upholding a federal law making it a crime to provide "material support" to groups designated as terrorist by the U.S. government even when that support is directed toward peaceful ends (as it was in this case: training members of a designated group in techniques designed to peacefully resolve conflicts, "equating such actions with trafficking in weapons.") (The issue of funding was not before the Court.) According to the Supreme Court, providing material support—which now includes lawful, nonviolent activities such as advocating for human rights and peace, political advocacy, distributing literature, and providing aid to a designated terrorist group—is a crime punishable by fifteen years in prison because it strengthens the image of the group and thereby legitimizes it. Because this ruling also criminalizes direct contact with members of a designated group, scholars such as myself could be imprisoned for up to fifteen years for conducting research of the kind presented in this book. See David D. Cole, *Advocacy Is Not a Gun*, Center for Constitutional Rights, June 22, 2010, who writes, "[F]or the first time ever, the Supreme Court has ruled that the First Amendment permits the criminalization of pure speech advocating lawful, nonviolent activity"; Adam Liptak, "Justices Uphold a Ban on Aiding Terror Groups," *New York Times*, June 22, 2010; "A Bruise on the First Amendment," *New York Times*, June 22, 2010; Joshua Holland, "How Easy Is It for Peaceful People to Violate the Patriot Act?" AlterNet, July 10, 2010, www.truthout.org/criminalizing-peacemaking61229; and Supreme Court of the United States, *Holder, Attorney General et al versus Humanitarian Law Project et al*, No. 08-1498, argued February 23, 2010–decided June 21, 2010.

19. The common definition of an orphan is a child who has no father. Beyond that, individual ISIs will expand that definition to include children without any parents, or whose families have no stable income, etc.

20. Sara Roy, "Professionalization versus Politics: The Transformation of Islamic NGOs in Palestine," *Middle East Report* 214 (Spring 2000), pp. 25–26.

21. Interviews in Gaza and Ramallah, summer 1999.

22. International Crisis Group, *Islamic Social Welfare Activism in the Occupied Palestinian Territories: A Legitimate Target?* ICG Report no. 13 (Amman/Brussels: ICG, April 2, 2003), p. 11.

23. Ibid., pp. 7–9. Also see Haim Malka, "Hamas: Resistance and Transformation of Palestinian Society," in Jon B. Alterman and Karin von Hippel, eds., *Understanding Islamic Charities* (Washington, DC: Center for Strategic and International Studies Press, 2007), p. 105.

24. Glenn E. Robinson, "Hamas as Social Movement," in Quintan Wiktorowicz, ed., *Islamic Activism: A Social Movement Theory Approach* (Bloomington: Indiana University Press, 2004), pp. 112–139.

25. Interviews with Ismail Abu Shanab, spring 1999 and Ismail Haniyeh, Gaza City, summer 1999. Other typologies, for example, could be sources of funding, volunteer versus paid staff, size, single site versus multibranch, target audience.

26. ICG (April 2, 2003), p. 8.

27. Although some of these organizations still exist, I refer to them all in the past tense here because this information was collected some years ago and even those organizations that still exist have no doubt evolved. Data in this section were obtained primarily during the spring and summer of 1999.

28. These officials were almost always from the Ministry of Social Affairs.

29. ICG (April 2, 2003), p. 8.

30. Here the ICG (ibid., n. 45) cites the PNA's *Palestinian Poverty Report* (1998) and an unpublished study by UNESCO and OCHA titled, "Food and Cash Assistance Programmes, October 2000–August 2001: A Brief Overview."

31. ICG (April 2, 2003), p. 8.

32. Documentation with lists of items provided by the *zakat* for the needy, Gaza and Rafah, summer 1999.

33. Interview, Mohammed Majdaloun, director, orphans' program, *zakat* committee, Gaza, summer 1999.

34. Interview, Nizar Ramadan, al-Ihsan Charitable Society, Hebron, summer 1999.

35. United States Department of the Treasury, "Treasury Designates Al-Salah Society Key Support Node for Hamas," August 2007, www.ustreas.gov/press/releases/hp531.htm; and Mohammed Abu Asaker, "Islamic Movements and Micropolitics of Development," draft, American University, Washington, DC, 2006.

36. For a description of current programs see www.alsalah.org.

37. Even if donors stopped paying when children reached age fifteen, other children in the same family were probably receiving the same kind of assistance, ensuring, to the extent possible, that the family was not left destitute.

38. The illiterate would sign with their fingerprint, a common practice across ISIs.

39. Interview, Ahmad al-Kurd, al-Salah Islamic Association, Deir al-Balah, summer 1999.

40. Areas covered by the Gaza branch included Sejaia, Sabra, Darraj, and Tuffah. Names have been changed.

41. Abu Hisham indicated that the Qatar Charitable Society gave al-Salah funds to support 112 disabled children.

42. It was through Abu Hisham that I got access to al-Salah.
43. Meeting with Alya and other social workers, al-Salah Islamic Association, Deir al-Balah, summer 1999.
44. By 2006, the number of needy families served by al-Salah had increased to 1,200.
45. Recipients, largely refugees, were divided as follows: Middle Camps 16%; Jabalia 17%; Khan Younis 20%; Rafah 12%; Gaza City and Beach Camp 35%.
46. Interview, Ahmad al-Kurd, Deir al-Balah, Gaza Strip, summer 1999.
47. Al-Salah had a traditional women's training program in two of its camps: two centers for embroidery and sewing in Deir al-Balah and al-Maghazi camps. Women's activities in all these institutions were very traditional, with some more progressive variations on the theme. There was a six-month training program for twenty women in each center at a cost of NIS 100 and free for those in need.
48. Interview with Ahmad al-Kurd and two members of his staff, Deir al-Balah, Gaza Strip, summer 1999.
49. Abu Asaker (2006).
50. Dr. al-Lu'lu', Director, al-Huda health clinic, Gaza, summer 1999.
51. Abu Asaker (2006).
52. Ibid.
53. Al-Huda also ran a series of twelve kindergartens throughout the Gaza Strip that I did not see.
54. The choice of the word "illegitimate" was that of my respondents at al-Rahma, not mine. They included the director, Ahmad al-Zahar, and two members of the board of directors, Mr. Zaza and Mr. Abu Nasser Kujuk. I also spoke more informally with some of the staff, and these interviews and site visits took place in the spring and summer of 1999. Also see Mariam Hamed, "Gaza: Cases of Abandoned Children on the Rise," Palestinenote.com, February 7, 2010.
55. Hamed (February 7, 2010). Also see "Illegitimate Orphans in Gaza on the Rise: Report," www.alarabiya.net, 20 October 20, 2008.
56. Interview, Ahmad al-Zahar, director, al-Rahma Association, spring 1999.
57. Ibid.
58. More recent accounts describe a somewhat different process, claiming that once the child is received, the Ministry of Health is contacted to issue a birth certificate with fake parents' names. They also claim that children will be placed with families when they are seven years old. See, for example, Hamed (February 7, 2010); and "Illegitimate Orphans in Gaza on the Rise" (October 20, 2008).
59. Interview, Mr. Abu Nasser Kujuk, al-Rahma Association, summer 1999.
60. I was given conflicting accounts about this point.
61. I wanted to meet with adoptive families but was told by officials at al-Rahma that my visit would be an invasion of their privacy, something that I, as an adoptive parent myself, fully understood. There was a promise by al-Rahma to inquire with individual families whether I could visit, but nothing ever materialized, and I decided not to pursue it.
62. Al-Rahma also had the "Poor Palestinian Child" kit, which consisted of a school uniform, backpack, and school supplies for one year for one hundred children.

63. I sit on ANERA's Advisory Council although I did not at the time of this research.

64. These words, in English, were often used by al-Zahar and members of the board.

65. See Roy (Spring 2000), p. 26.

66. Interview, Dr. Aziz Duweiq, An-Najah University, Nablus, West Bank, summer 1999. Dr. Duweiq was a key figure in the Islamist movement locally and regionally.

67. Interview, Ahmad Bahar, Director, Jam'iyya al-Islamiyya, Gaza, summer 1999.

68. This was the case at the al-Ihsan Association for Disabled Children in Sejaija, Gaza, headed by Ahmad Hijazi, who was affiliated with the Islamic Jihad.

69. Ahmad al-Kurd, al-Salah Islamic Association, Deir al-Balah, Gaza, summer 1999; and other interviews with officials in both institutions (and in other ISIs) in the spring and summer of 1999.

70. Interview, Dr. Aziz Duweiq, An-Najah University, Nablus, West Bank, summer 1999.

71. Interviews, Iffat Jabari, Hebron, summer 1999. Although Jabari never told me this herself, she apparently was a member of the Islamic Jihad, not Hamas. The HWU was also known as the Hebron Young Women's Club.

72. Jeroen Gunning, *Hamas in Politics: Democracy, Religion, Violence* (New York: Columbia University Press, 2008), p. 169.

73. Interview, Iffat Jabari, Hebron, summer 1999.

74. Interview, Ismail Abu Shanab, Gaza, spring 1999.

75. *Zakat* committees were made accountable to the Ministry of Religious Affairs, which apparently audited their finances weekly. ICG (April 2, 2003), p, 10.

76. Interview, Fathi Darwish, deputy minister, Ministry of NGOs, Ramallah, West Bank, summer 1999.

77. Interview, Younis Abu Nada, director of NGOs, Ministry of the Interior, Gaza, summer 1999.

78. ICG (April 2, 2003), p. 10.

79. Ibid.

80. Interviews with a variety of ISI officials in Gaza and the West Bank reiterated this point, spring and summer 1999.

81. Sara Roy, "Hamas and the Transformation(s) of Political Islam in Palestine," *Current History* (January 2003), p. 19.

82. As stated earlier, for example, in order to provide supplementary services, Islamic clinics would remain open after government clinics closed.

83. Official, Ministry of Interior, Gaza, summer 1999.

84. Gunning (2008), p. 104.

85. The Israel Security Agency claims that in 2007 approximately $120,000,000 was transferred to Hamas in the West Bank and Gaza "to finance terrorist organization activity, about 30% of which was earmarked for financing Hamas's *da'wah*." Intelligence and Terrorism Information Center (July 8, 2008).

86. Anna Field, "Hizbollah Admits Full Support for Hamas," *Financial Times*, May 13, 2009.

87. ICG (April 2, 2003), p. 12. Also see Jeroen Gunning, "Terrorism, Charities and Diasporas: Contrasting the Fundraising Practices of Hamas and al Qaeda among Muslims in Europe," in Biersteker and Eckert (2007), pp. 93–125; and Michael Irving Jensen, *The Political Ideology of Hamas: A Grassroots Perspective* (London: I. B. Tauris, 2009), pp. 29–32.

88. Helga Baumgarten, "Hamas and the Challenge of Democratic Transformation in Palestine," Lecture, The Middle East Seminar, Harvard University, October 4, 2007; and idem, *Hamas—Der Politische Islam in Paleastina* (Munich: Heinrich Hugendubel Verlag, 2006).

89. Council on Foreign Relations, *Hamas*, January 7, 2009, www.cfr.org/publication/8968.

90. In 2003, the U.S. government claimed Hamas's annual budget to be at least $50 million. See "The Terrorist Financing Operations Section," testimony of John S. Pistole (September 24, 2003).

91. ICG (April 2, 2003), p. 13.

92. I had the opportunity to meet with other officials of the al-Jam'iyya and had a better exchange. Jensen (2009), pp. 29–30 had the same experience.

93. Gunning (2008), p. 115.

94. Interview, Nizar Ramadan, al-Ihsan Charitable Society, Hebron, summer 1999.

95. Site visits, spring and summer 1999.

96. ICG (April 2, 2003), p. 12.

97. Ibid.

98. Interviews, Bethlehem Charitable Society, Bethlehem, West Bank, spring 1999.

99. ICG (April 2, 2003), pp. 18–20. Also see Gunning in Biersteker and Eckert (2007), pp. 93–125.

100. Interview with Mohammed Shama, al-Mujamma, Gaza, summer 1999.

101. ICG (April 2, 2003), pp. 10–11.

102. ICG (April 2, 2003), p. 18.

103. This was not a question I could often ask, because when I did, respondents would immediately get defensive, angry, or exasperated, and the interview would soon end. It was seldom my sense that people were trying to conceal anything; rather they were clearly annoyed, insulted, and even bored by the question, and the fact that I had asked it suggested to them that my agenda was political, not professional. Therefore, I stopped asking the question except in those situations where I felt I could elicit a meaningful response.

104. Interview, Abu Oweida, al-Mujamma kindergarten, Khan Younis, Gaza, summer 1999.

105. Gunning (2008), p. 115, n. 8.

106. Malka (2007), p. 105.

107. Interview, Ismail Abu Shanab, Gaza, summer 1999.

108. Interview, Nizar Ramadan, al-Ihsan Charitable Society, Hebron, summer 1999.

109. Interview, Sayyid Abu Mussameh, Rafah, Gaza, summer 1999.

110. Interview, Mahmoud al-Zahar, Gaza, summer 1999.

111. Ibid.

112. Interview, Sayyid Abu Mussameh, Rafah, Gaza, summer 1999.
113. Interview, Mohammed el-Hindi, Palestine Center for Studies and Research, Gaza, summer 1999.
114. Ibid.
115. Interview, Sayyid Abu Mussameh, Rafah, Gaza, summer 1999.
116. The then head of the PNA police in the West Bank, Jabril Rajoub, gave the al-Ihsan Charitable Society US $10,000 toward the salaries of ten rehabilitation teachers working at the Society.
117. The interviews and site visits to the Islamic economic institutions described in this section were carried out during the summer of 1999, all in the Gaza Strip.
118. I have changed all the names, as I promised I would.
119. One title I saw was "How to Collect Zakat."
120. It may have been that some of these firms received subsidies from sources within the Islamic movement—something I could not substantiate—which would have made it possible for them to lower their prices and increase their competitiveness.
121. I am also including factories I was told about but did not visit.
122. Such discussions took place during my interviews and seemed totally genuine.
123. This was also true of Islamic banks, which were first and foremost financial institutions with no political affiliations whatsoever, according to a senior official at the Palestine Monetary Authority, Halim Badran. Interview, Palestine Monetary Authority, West Bank, summer 1999. In 1999 there were four Islamic banks in the occupied territories: the al-Aqsa Bank, the Arab Islamic Bank, the Palestine Islamic Bank, and the Cairo-Amman Bank with an Islamic window. Badran argued that these banks, like the others in Palestine, were highly regulated by the PNA and were strictly professional institutions. That economic and financial interests superseded religious or political ones was also seen with the Islamic investment house Beit al-Mal (House of Money). The Beit al-Mal apparently enjoyed high rates of investment early in the Oslo process when many believed peace was possible. Land prices rose dramatically, and many investors enjoyed high returns. However, as political and economic conditions declined, people began withdrawing their funds, strongly suggesting that economics, not politics or religion, was the principal factor behind the decision to invest. Despite repeated attempts to get an interview with officials at the Beit al-Mal in the West Bank, I was unsuccessful.
124. David Henley, MD, "Report: al-Wafa Medical Rehabilitation Hospital, Gaza-Palestine," Consultation Visit, Uppsala, Sweden, November 15–20, 1999, p. 3. This was the case until 2004, when a new rehabilitation center in Gaza opened, the Palestinian Center for Human Perseverance, Fatah Rehabilitation Hospital.
125. Ibid.; and interview with Dr. Medhat, al-Wafa, summer 1999.
126. Henley (November 15–20, 1999), pp. 6–8.
127. Dr. David Henley and Marianne Holth, "Report: al-Wafa Medical Rehabilitation Hospital, Gaza-Palestine—Recommendations for Capacity Building for al-Wafa Medical Rehabilitation Hospital, Consultation Visit, June 13–18, 2004," June 19, 2004, internal report, p. 2.

128. Henley (November 15–20, 1999), table 3, p. 6.

129. Ibid., p. 2. Furthermore (p. 10–11), the records and filing systems were good: "There are special, detailed records for the medical assessment, as well as the initial evaluation forms for physiotherapy, occupational therapy and psychosocial data. Records exist for establishing a cognitive rehab profile. There are records for following the doctor's care plan, physiotherapy treatment, occupational therapy treatment, nursing care and special dietary recommendations. Detailed and well formulated discharge summaries, in English, exist for all patients. There is also statistical data available concerning admissions, diagnosis, length of stay and out-patient visits."

130. Diakonia/NAD-Sunnaas Rehabilitation Hospital and al-Wafa Medical Rehabilitation Hospital, "Seminar Sharm el-Sheikh 2006: Establishing a structure for a follow-up programme at al-Wafa Medical Rehabilitation Hospital," internal document, 2006, pp. 3–4.

131. Henley (November 15–20, 1999), pp. 6–7.

132. Ibid., pp. 5–6.

133. Henley and Holth (June 19, 2004), p. 2.

134. This was the case with adults as well.

135. Henley (November 15–20, 1999), p. 6.

136. Henley and Holth (June 19. 2004), p. 3.

137. Diakonia/NAD-Sunnaas ... , "Seminar Sharm el-Sheikh" (2006), pp. 15–17. Also see Diakonia/NAD-Sunnaas Rehabilitation Hospital, "Seminar/Workshop on: Traumatic Brain Injury, Quality Development Project, 2006," September 12–16, 2006, Amman, Jordan.

138. Diakonia/NAD-Sunnaas ... , "Seminar Sharm el-Sheikh" (2006), p. 3.

139. Henley (November 15–20, 1999), p. 8.

140. See Bjorn Erik Bogstad et al., "Sunnaas Rehabilitation Hospital, Norway & El Wafa Medical Rehabilitation Hospital, Gaza," Report from First Phase of Implementation—May/June 2005, Quality Development Project, internal document, Sunnaas Rehabilitation Hospital, Norway. The report identified some areas that needed further development including goal setting between staff and patient; regular meetings for the SCI team; absence of timetables for patients; no systematic follow-up for patients. Also see Diakonia/NAD-Sunnaas ... , "Seminar Sharm el-Sheikh" (2006); and Diakonia/NAD-Sunnaas Rehabilitation Hospital, "Seminar/Workshop on: Traumatic Brain Injury" (2006).

141. Henley (November 15–20, 1999), p. 9.

142. Interview, Dr. Medhat, al-Wafa, summer 1999. Confirmed in ibid.

143. Henley (November 15–20, 1999), p. 9; and Sunnaas Rehabilitation Hospital–Palestinian Rehabilitation Centres (in cooperation with the Norwegian Association for the Disabled), "Report on First Visit May 2003," internal document, Nesodden, Norway, October 2003, p. 7.

144. Henley (November 15–20, 1999), p. 9.

145. Palestinian Rehabilitation Centres (October 2003), p. 7.

146. Bogstad et al. (May/June 2005), p. 25.

147. Henley (November 15–20, 1999), p. 9.

148. However, there was no available orthopedic workshop. Simple hand splints were made by the occupational therapist.

149. Palestinian Rehabilitation Centres (October 2003), p. 7; Bogstad et al. (May/June 2005); and Diakonia/NAD-Sunnaas ..., "Seminar Sharm el-Sheikh" (2006).

150. Diakonia/NAD-Sunnaas ..., "Seminar Sharm el-Sheikh" (2006).

151. Follow-up of inpatients has remained a key objective of al-Wafa's collaboration with the Sunnaas Rehabilitation Hospital through to the present.

152. Henley and Holth, (June 19, 2004), p. 3.

153. Palestinian Rehabilitation Centres (October 2003), pp. 7–8.

154. Henley and Holth (June 19, 2004), p. 2.

155. Palestinian Rehabilitation Centres (October 2003), p. 8.

156. Henley and Holth (June 19, 2004), p. 4.

157. Bogstad et al. (May/June 2005), pp. 21–22.

158. In a 1999 evaluation report, the author concluded that al-Wafa was "carrying out exceptionally good work, despite all its limitations and the complexities of the patients being treated there. No doubt this degree of success has to do with the many hard working, dedicated and knowledgeable staff members. There is, however, much to be done towards developing good rehabilitation services, improved competence and sustainability." See Henley (November 15–20, 1999), p. 14.

159. In earlier writings on the subject, I concluded that al-Wafa's decision to send some of its staff to Israeli institutions for training most likely could not have been made without the approval of the Hamas leadership. While I cannot rule out this possibility, I now feel it may not have been required.

CHAPTER 6
ISLAMIST SOCIAL INSTITUTIONS: KEY ANALYTICAL FINDINGS

1. Edmund Burke III, "Islam and Social Movements: Methodological Reflections," in Edmund Burke III and Ira M. Lapidus, eds., *Islam, Politics, and Social Movements* (Berkeley: University of California Press, 1988), p. 25.

2. Interview with author, Gaza, summer 1999. Also cited by Gunning (2008), p. 237. See note 35.

3. Michael Irving Jensen, *The Political Ideology of Hamas: A Grassroots Perspective* (London: I. B. Tauris, 2009), pp. 55–56. I did not have access to the original Arabic.

4. Dale Eickelman and James Piscatori, *Muslim Politics* (Princeton, NJ: Princeton University Press, 1996), pp. 22–45.

5. Janine Clark, "Social Movement Theory and Patron-Clientelism: Islamic Social Institutions and the Middle Class in Egypt, Jordan, and Yemen," *Comparative Political Studies* 37, no. 8 (October 2004), p. 948.

6. Ibid.

7. International Crisis Group (ICG), *Islamic Social Welfare Activism in the Occupied Palestinian Territories: A Legitimate Target?* ICG Report no. 13. (Amman/Brussels: ICG, April 2, 2003), p. 29.

8. In addition, Hamas used mosques in this way as well. Glenn Robinson further notes that during the Oslo period Hamas founded the Supreme Council

for Islamic Information in order to disseminate its perspectives in Palestine. See Glenn E. Robinson, "Hamas as Social Movement," in Quintan Wiktorowicz, ed., *Islamic Activism: A Social Movement Theory Approach* (Bloomington: Indiana University Press, 2004), p. 129.

9. Although I heard this from a number of officials, one of the most explicit was Sayyid Abu Mussameh, the former head of the political wing of Hamas. Interview, Rafah, summer 1999. Abu Mussameh headed Hamas when Yassin was in jail and was editor of *Al-Watan*, the first Islamic newspaper. I should also note that during our first interview he taped me, something I had never before and have never since encountered!

10. Interviews with officials at the Islamic University, Gaza, summer 1999.

11. Here I refer to constraints imposed by Israel, the PNA, and by the Islamic/st movement itself.

12. Interview, Abu Mussameh, Rafah, summer 1999.

13. See Amr Hamzawy, "Exploring Theoretical and Programmatic Changes in Contemporary Islamist Discourse: The Journal Al-Manar al-Jadid," in Azza Karam, ed., *Transnational Political Islam: Religion, Ideology and Power* (London: Pluto Press, 2004), pp. 120–146. Also idem, "The Key to Arab Reform: Moderate Islamists," Policy Brief 40, Carnegie Endowment for International Peace, August 2005.

14. Sara Roy, "Hamas and the Transformation(s) of Political Islam in Palestine," *Current History* (January 2003), p. 15.

15. Interview, Abu Mussameh, Rafah, summer 1999.

16. This was argued in similar ways by Mohammed el-Hindi, Ismail Abu Shanab, Mahmoud al-Zahar, and Dr. Aziz Duweiq.

17. Robert W. Hefner, "Introduction: Modernity and the Remaking of Muslim Politics," in Robert W. Hefner, ed., *Remaking Muslim Politics: Pluralism, Contestation, Democratization* (Princeton, NJ: Princeton University Press, 2005), p. 6.

18. For example, see Soheir Morsy, "Islamic Clinics in Egypt: The Cultural Elaboration of Biomedical Hegemony," *Medical Anthropology Quarterly* 2, no. 4 (December 1988), pp. 355–369; Diane Singerman, *Avenues of Participation: Family, Politics, and Networks in Urban Quarters of Cairo* (Princeton, NJ: Princeton University Press, 1995); Janine A. Clark, "Democratization and Social Islam: A Case Study of the Islamic Health Clinics in Cairo," in Rex Brynen, Bahghat Korany, and Paul Noble, eds., *Political Liberalization and Democratization in the Arab World*, vol. 1 (Boulder, CO: Lynne Rienner, 1995), pp. 167–186; Eickelman and Piscatori (1996); Sheila Carapico, *Civil Society in Yemen: The Political Economy of Activism in Modern Arabia* (Cambridge: Cambridge University Press, 1998); Denis J. Sullivan and Sana Abed-Kotob, *Islam in Contemporary Egypt: Civil Society versus the State* (Boulder, CO: Lynne Rienner, 1999); Quintan Wiktorowicz, *The Management of Islamic Activism: Salafis, the Muslim Brotherhood and State Power in Jordan* (Albany: State University of New York Press, 2001); Jenny B. White, *Islamist Mobilization in Turkey: A Study in Vernacular Politics* (Seattle: University of Washington Press, 2002); Carrie Rosefsky Wickham, *Mobilizing Islam: Religion, Activism, and Political Change in Egypt* (New York: Columbia University Press, 2002); Janine A. Clark, *Islam, Charity, and Activism: Middle Class Networks and Social Welfare in Egypt, Jordan and*

Yemen (Bloomington: Indiana University Press, 2004); Quintan Wiktorowicz, ed., *Islamic Activism: A Social Movement Theory Approach* (Bloomington: Indiana University Press, 2004); and Lara Deeb, *An Enchanted Modern: Gender and Public Piety in Shi'i Lebanon* (Princeton, NJ: Princeton University Press, 2006).

19. Hefner (2005), p. 5.
20. Ibid., p. 6.
21. Ibid.
22. Ibid.
23. Ibid., p. 9.
24. Ibid.
25. Ibid., pp. 9–10.
26. Ira M. Lapidus, "Islamic Political Movements: Patterns of Historical Change," in Burke and Lapidus (1988), p. 15.
27. Doug McAdam, "Culture and Social Movements," in Enrique Larana, Hank Johnston, and Joseph R. Gusfeild, eds., *New Social Movements: From Ideology to Identity* (Philadelphia: Temple University Press, 1994), pp. 36–37.
28. Clark (2004), p. 43. Also see Augustus Richard Norton, "Introduction," in Augustus Richard Norton, ed., *Civil Society in the Middle East*, vol. 1 (Leiden and New York: E. J. Brill, 1995); and Sami Zubaida, "Islam, the State and Democracy: Contrasting Conceptions of Society in Egypt," *Middle East Report* 179 (November–December 1992), pp. 2–10.
29. ICG (April 2, 2003), p. 21.
30. Interview, Yahya Musa, director, Hizb al-Khalas Political Bureau, Gaza City, summer 1999. Hizb al-Khalas was a legally authorized political branch of Hamas that operated during the 1990s (other affiliates included various ISIs and the Islamic Bloc student organizations). It was formed to separate the political sector of Hamas from other sectors. It weakened and became insignificant in recent years.
31. Islah Jad, "Between Religion and Secularism: Islamist Women of Hamas," in Fereshteh Nouraie-Simone, ed., *On Shifting Ground: Muslim Women in the Global Era* (New York: City University of New York, 2005), p. 184. Women figured prominently in the leadership of Hizb al-Khalas in the 1990s.
32. This phenomenon has been documented by other researchers. This was also the case with some people I interviewed who had given their money to an Islamic institution, Beit al-Mal, which invested in commercial real estate, commercial enterprises, and urban development.
33. Several PNA officials I interviewed openly expressed disdain for the concept of volunteerism, seeing little value in it, while others recognized that the comparatively low levels of volunteerism within many secular institutions placed them at a disadvantage vis-à-vis ISIs.
34. When I visited the hospital in 1999, it contained 120 beds with plans to expand it to 305. Doctors on staff included one neurosurgeon, three orthopedic surgeons, one urologic surgeon, three general surgeons, and three anesthesiologists. Departments, facilities, and services included outpatient and inpatient, fluoroscopy, CT scans, X-rays, nuclear medicine, mammography, a pharmacy, a computer center, a laboratory (the largest in the West Bank or Gaza), a blood bank, physiotherapy, a burns center, an internal medicine ward, a cardiac care unit, an

intensive care unit, an ob-gyn unit, a recovery room, laparoscopy, urothroscopy, an induction room, imaging, and a sterilization room.

35. Jeroen Gunning, *Hamas in Politics: Democracy, Religion, Violence* (New York: Columbia University Press, 2008), p. 170.

36. Hefner (2005); and John L. Esposito and John O. Voll, *Makers of Contemporary Islam* (New York: Oxford University Press, 2001).

37. Interview, Ahmed Hijazi, al-Ihsan Association, Sejaia, Gaza, summer 1999.

38. Interview, Ahmad Bahar, al-Jam'iyya al-Islamiyya, Gaza, summer 1999.

39. Diane Singerman, "The Networked World of Islamist Social Movements," in Wiktorowicz (2004), p. 151.

40. M. Hakan Yavuz, "Opportunity Spaces, Identity, and Islamic Meaning in Turkey," in Wiktorowicz (2004), p. 272.

41. Abdelwahab El-Affendi, "Rationality of Politics and Politics of Rationality: Democratisation and the Influence of Islamic Religious Traditions," in John Esposito and Azzam Tamimi, eds., *Islam and Secularism in the Middle East* (New York: New York University Press, 2000), p. 167.

42. Michael Irving Jensen, "Youth, Moral[ity] and Islamism: Spending Your Leisure Time with Hamas in Palestine," draft, 2003; and idem (2009), pp. 61–95.

43. Clark (2004), p. 37. In this regard also see Wiktorowicz (2001).

44. Clark (2004), p. 157. In this regard see Morsy (1988) and Wiktorowicz (2001), who reach similar conclusions.

45. Yavuz (2004), p. 273.

46. Singerman (2004), p. 156.

47. See Clark (1995, 2004); Wiktorowicz (2001); Singerman (1995); and Wickham (2002).

48. Singerman (2004), p. 144.

49. Ibid., p. 156.

50. Wickham (2002), p. 151.

51. Haim Malka, "Hamas: Resistance and Transformation of Palestinian Society," in Jon B. Alterman and Karin von Hippel, eds., *Understanding Islamic Charities* (Washington, DC: Center for Strategic and International Studies Press, 2007), p. 110.

52. Alberto Melucci, "The Process of Collective Identity," in Hank Johnston and Bert Klandermans, eds., *Social Movements and Culture* (Minneapolis: University of Minnesota Press, 1995), pp. 41–63; idem, "The New Social Movements: A Theoretical Approach," *Social Science Information* 19, no. 2 (1980), pp. 199–226; and idem, "A Strange Kind of Newness: What's "New" in New Social Movements?" in Larana, Johnston, and Gusfield (1994), eds., pp. 101–130.

53. Singerman (2004), p. 153.

54. See Carrie Rosefsky Wickham, "Interests, Ideas, and Islamist Outreach in Egypt," in Wiktorowicz (2004), pp. 231–249, for an alternative outcome.

55. Wolfgang Freund, *Looking into Hamas and Other Constituents of the Palestinian-Israeli Confrontation* (Frankfurt: Peter Lang, 2002), pp. 36 and 39.

56. Gunning (2008), p. 167.

57. See Helga Baumgarten, *Hamas—Der Politische Islam in Paleastina* (Munich: Heinrich Hugendubel Verlag, 2006), pp. 132–133; and Jonathan Benthall,

The Palestinian Zakat Committees 1993–2007 and Their Contested Interpretations, PSIO Occasional Paper 1/2008 (Geneva: Graduate Institute of International and Development Studies, 2008), both cited in Emanuel Schaublin, *The West Bank Zakat Committees (1977–2009) in the Local Context*, CCDP Working Paper (Geneva: Centre on Conflict, Development and Peacebuilding, the Graduate Institute, 2009), pp. 12–13.

58. Clark (2004), p. 156.

59. Interview, Yahya Musa, director, Hizb al-Khalas Political Bureau, Gaza, summer 1999.

60. Clark (2004), p. 156.

61. Janine A. Clark, "Islamist Women in Yemen: Informal Nodes of Activism," in Wiktorowicz (2004), pp. 164–184.

62. I borrow these terms from Jenny B. White and her seminal study of Turkey, *Islamist Mobilization in Turkey* (2002), p. 268.

Chapter 7
A Changing Islamist Order? From Civic Empowerment to Civic Regression—the Second Intifada and Beyond

1. Sources on Hamas have been provided in other chapters. Of particular note are Azzam Tamimi, *Hamas: A History from Within* (Northampton, MA: Olive Branch Press, 2007); and Jeroen Gunning, *Hamas in Politics: Democracy, Religion, Violence* (New York: Columbia University Press, 2008).

2. See International Crisis Group (ICG), *After Mecca: Engaging Hamas* (Amman/Jerusalem/Brussels: ICG, February 28, 2007), p. 8.

3. Interviews with officials of the donor community, spring 2008.

4. The attack by both Israel and the Abbas-led government in the West Bank against Islamic charities and social institutions is one example.

5. Looking at the patterns of interfactional violence during the 2004–2006 election period, Gunning (2008), p. 183, observes that "much of the violence between Hamas and Fatah is driven by clan loyalties and the logic of vendettas." Also see Israeli Information Center for Human Rights in the Occupied Territories (B'tselem), *Severe Human Rights Violations in Intra-Palestinian Clashes*, www.btselem.org/English/Inter_Palestinian_Violations.

6. See International Crisis Group (ICG), *Inside Gaza: The Challenge of Clans and Families* (Gaza/Jerusalem/Brussels: ICG, December 20, 2007).

7. International Crisis Group (ICG), *Enter Hamas: The Challenges of Political Integration* (Amman/Brussels: ICG, January 18, 2006), p. 12, n. 82. On the eve of Israel's 2005 disengagement from Gaza, the Palestinian Centre for Policy and Survey Research reported that for the first time since the occupation began, unemployment was ranked as the most critical issue for Palestinians, superseding the Israeli occupation.

8. They included major factions within Fatah (PLO hard-liners outside the occupied territories); Arafat's inner circle (e.g., Nabil Shaath, Hani al-Hasan); the so-called moderates (Abu Mazen, Abu Ala, Mohammed Dahlan); the so-called

grassroots radicals (Tanzim, a grassroots Fatah organization on the West Bank; Al-Aqsa Brigades linked to Tanzim and military wing of Fatah); and at least fourteen security services within Fatah.

9. However, sometimes Hamas would get involved in internal Fatah power struggles. For example, in mid-July 2004 following the violence in Gaza, Hamas Political Bureau head Khalid Meshal telephoned Arafat emphasizing the need for national unity and reform, which was interpreted as a slap to Mohammad Dahlan, whom the Islamists hated.

10. See Beverly Milton-Edwards and Alastair Crooke, "Elusive Ingredient: Hamas and the Peace Process," *Journal of Palestine Studies* 33 (Summer 2004), pp. 41–42. Also see Gideon Levy, "The Generation That Doesn't Know Joseph," *Ha'aretz*, August 10, 2003.

11. Center for Policy and Survey Research, *The Mitchell Report, Cease Fire, and Return to Negotiations; Intifada-Armed Confrontations; Chances for Reconciliation; and, Internal Palestinian Conditions*, Public Opinion Poll no. 2, July 5–9, 2001, Ramallah; and idem, *Palestinians Support the Ceasefire, Negotiations, and Reconciliation between the Two Peoples but a Majority Opposes Arrests and Believe That Armed Confrontations Have Helped Achieve National Rights*, Public Opinion Poll no. 3, December 19–24, 2001, Ramallah.

12. Some data in this section first appeared in Sara Roy, "Hamas and the Transformation(s) of Political Islam in Palestine," *Current History* (January 2003), pp. 13–20, reprinted with permission; and Sara Roy, "Religious Nationalism and the Palestinian-Israeli Conflict: Examining Hamas and the Possibility of Reform," *Chicago Journal of International Law* 5, (Summer 2004), pp. 251–270, reprinted with permission.

13. Center for Policy and Survey Research (no. 10) indicates that between July 2000 and July 2001 support for Fatah dropped from 37 to 29 percent and increased for Hamas from 17 to 27 percent.

14. Baruch Kimmerling, *Politicide: Ariel Sharon's War against the Palestinians* (London: Verso, 2003).

15. International Institute for Counter Terrorism (ICT), *Breakdown of Fatalities: 27 September 2000 through 1 January 2005* (Herzliya: ICT, 2005), http://www.ict.il/casualties_project/stats_page.cfm>; and idem, *Database: Incidents*, http://www.instituteforcounterterrorism.org/apage/10583.php>.

16. Gunning (2008), pp. 225 and 228, fig. 4.

17. See Beverly Milton-Edwards and Alastair Crooke, "Waving, Not Drowning: Strategic Dimensions of Ceasefires and Islamic Movements," *Security Dialogue* 35 (September 2004), pp. 302–303.

18. "Abbas Offering Hamas a Spot in Government," *Jerusalem Post*, June 19, 2003.

19. The absence of suicide bombings inside Israel is often referred to by media and government alike as a period of quiet. Yet, during this six-week "lull," at least eighty Palestinians were killed. A similar period of "quiet" between October and December 2003 left over one hundred Palestinians dead.

20. Mark Perry, "Israeli Offensive Disrupts US-Hamas Contacts," *Palestine Report*, October 9, 2002.

21. Ibid.

22. There are other examples of Hamas-PNA cease-fires undermined by Israeli attacks. See Alex Fishman, "A Dangerous Liquidation," *Yediot Achronot*, November 25, 2001.

23. Milton-Edwards and Crooke, "Waving, Not Drowning" (September 2004), pp. 302–303. There were several reasons for this: the need to ensure Hamas's strengthened political position (and avoid political marginalization) and respond to the possibility of real power sharing offered by Fatah; a dramatic change in public opinion supporting a mutual cease-fire that began in November 2002 and remained high through 2003; and a weakening military capacity that was further compromised by Israel's policy of targeting the Hamas political leadership involved with planning suicide attacks.

24. According to several Israeli and U.S. officials, neither the internal nor the external Hamas leadership ordered the attack, which was a rogue operation that took the Hamas leadership by surprise. International Crisis Group (ICG), *Dealing with Hamas*, ICG Report no. 21 (Amman/Brussels: ICG, January 26, 2004), pp. 26–27. Also see Tanya Reinhart, "The Complex Art of the Simulation of Peace," *Borderlands e-journal* 4, no. 1 (2005).

25. Gideon Levy, "Israel Endangers Jewish Lives," *Ha'aretz*, August 17, 2003.

26. Shlomo Shamir et al., "Hamas Ends Hudna after Assassination," *Ha'aretz*, August 22, 2003.

27. ICG (January 26, 2004), p. 23. Original source: Alastair Crooke and Beverly Milton-Edwards, "Missed Opportunity? Hamas, Ceasefires, and the Future of the Israeli-Palestinian Conflict," *The World Today*, December 2003.

28. Reuters, "Hamas Proposes 10-Year Truce for Israeli Pullback," *Ha'aretz*, January 26, 2004.

29. "Stymied Intifada Bombers Turn to Politics," *Jane's Islamic Affairs Analyst*, August 2, 2004.

30. Milton-Edwards and Crooke, "Waving, Not Drowning" (September 2004), pp. 303–304. Also see Khaled Hroub, "Hamas after Shaykh Yasin and Rantisi," *Journal of Palestine Studies* 33 (Summer 2004), pp. 21–38.

31. "Stymied Intifada Bombers Turn to Politics," (August 2, 2004).

32. Israeli Information Center for Human Rights in the Occupied Territories (B'tselem), *Statistics: Israeli Civilians Killed by Palestinians in Israel*, www.btselem.org/english/Statistics/Casualties_Data.asp?Category=6&region=ISRAEL. Ten Israelis were killed in 2006.

33. For example, in Nablus, 60 would-be bombers were arrested through August 2004. The Israeli authorities stated that the numbers of wanted men in Nablus declined from 300 to 160, indicating that militants who were captured or assassinated were not being replaced.

34. The continued combination of weakening military capabilities, popular exasperation, and political opportunity (in addition to declining regional support from the Gulf states, Syria, and Iran following the U.S. invasion of Iraq and Afghanistan, and the strategic reassessments that this necessitated) resulted in a renewed emphasis on political over military engagement that aimed to position Hamas as a legitimate political actor.

35. This pattern also was seen among other groups such as the al-Aqsa Martyrs Brigade, which demanded internal reforms (e.g., an end to corruption, free

and fair elections within Fatah and in future legislative elections, separation of powers between the PNA and PLO).

36. ICG (January 18, 2006), pp. 1–6. for a discussion of integration in Hamas's thinking.

37. See Graham Usher, "The New Hamas: Between Resistance and Participation," *al-Ahram Weekly*, August 21, 2005.

38. In fact Hamas was able to own disengagement as vindication of its attacks against Israel, mirroring Israel's forced withdrawal from southern Lebanon in May 2000. Mahmoud al-Zahar said of the disengagement: "Hamas said that resistance is the solution and events have proved it was correct. No one can claim the withdrawal was a unilateral step and a gift from Sharon. It was a crushing defeat to the dignity of the Jewish State." Draft of a paper by Helga Baumgarten on Hamas; original citation, *Asharq al-Awsat*, August 12, 2005.

39. Mouin Rabbani, "The Hamas Paradigm: National, Regional, and International Repercussions," lecture, Middle East Forum, Harvard University, April 26, 2006, Cambridge, MA.

40. During the 2004–2006 electoral period, Hamas engaged in several different tracks of negotiations: private discussions with Fatah on halting attacks against Israeli civilians in which Hamas promised restraint but not a cease-fire; discussions with the Egyptians over the possibility of a cease-fire prior to Israel's disengagement, which did occur in March 2005 and lasted through June 2006; and talks between factions on reaching an agreement over power sharing in Gaza after disengagement. The 2005 cease-fire was called a *tahdi'a* (calming) or period of calm and was unilaterally imposed. It was concluded among all major Palestinian organizations (except some smaller Fatah factions). Israel never reciprocated the initiative in word or deed. This was meant to contrast it with the failed June 2003 cease-fire, which was called a *hudna* or long-term truce.

41. Arnon Regular, "Gaza: Hamas Policy Document on 'Unilateral Disengagement,'" *Ha'aretz*, August 15, 2004.

42. Ibid.

43. Ibid.

44. Ibid. Regarding its struggle against Israel, Hamas maintained the right to resist the occupation outside Gaza so long as it continued. In this regard, Hamas emphasized that withdrawal from Gaza was not the end of the process.

45. ICG (January 26, 2004), p. 23.

46. Ibid.

47. World Bank, *Twenty-Seven Months—Intifada, Closures and Palestinian Economic Crisis: An Assessment* (Jerusalem, May 2003), p. 31.

48. Ibid.

49. Riccardo Bocco, Matthias Brunner, and Jamil Rabah, *International and Local Aid during the Second Intifada, an Analysis of Palestinian Public Opinion in the West Bank and the Gaza Strip (October 2000–February 2001)—Final Report* (Geneva: Graduate Institute of Development Studies, University of Geneva, March 2001), p. 27.

50. World Bank (May 2003), p. 30. Also see Pal Sletten and Jon Pedersen, *Coping with Conflict: Palestinian Communities Two Years into the Intifada*, Fafo Report 408 (FAFO, 2003).

51. See the International Crisis Group (ICG), *Islamic Social Welfare Activism in the Occupied Palestinian Territories: A Legitimate Target?* ICG Report no. 13 (Amman/Brussels: ICG, April 2, 2003), p. 15. It cites UNSCO-OCHA, "Food and Cash Assistance Programmes October 2000–August 2001: A Brief Overview," unpublished manuscript.

52. ICG (April 2, 2003), pp. 15–17. World Bank (May 2003), p. 51, cites some of these statistics. Also see Riccardo Bocco, Matthias Brunner, and Jami Rabah, *International and Local Aid during the Second Intifada: An Analysis of Palestinian Public Opinion in the West Bank and the Gaza Strip on Their Living Conditions (Mid-June–31 October 2001)* (Geneva: Graduate Institute of Development Studies, University of Geneva, 2001).

53. ICG (April 2, 3003), p. 16.

54. United Nations, *Humanitarian Plan of Action 2003—Occupied Palestinian Territory* (New York and Geneva: Office for the Coordination of Humanitarian Affairs, November 2002), p. 18.

55. ICG (April 2, 2003), p. 17. However, it should also be stated that the literature is not unanimous on the relative importance and impact of ISIs vis-à-vis other providers (UNRWA, PNA, and other NGOs). See Bocco, Brunner, and Rabah (March 2001); and Riccardo Bocco, Matthias Brunner, Isabelle Daneels, Jalal Husseini, Frederic Lapeyre, and Jamil Rabah, *Palestinian Public Perceptions on Their Living Conditions*, Report 6 (Geneva: Graduate Institute of Development Studies, University of Geneva, October 2003).

56. ICG (April 2, 2003), p. 16; and Roy (January 2003), p. 19.

57. Gunning (2008), p. 156, indicates that the June 2003 cease-fire was "influenced by shifts in the public mood as evidenced by its canvassing public opinion prior to the declaration."

58. Ibid., p. 239.

59. Ibid., p. 178.

60. See Menachem Klein, "Hamas in Power," *Middle East Journal* 61 (Summer 2007): pp. 442–459.

61. National Democratic Institute (NDI), *Report on Palestinian Elections for Local Councils: Round One* (Washington, DC: NDI, 2005), p. 9.

62. Ibid.

63. See Meir Litvak, "Hamas's Victory in Municipal Elections," *Tel Aviv Notes*, no. 156, December 26, 2005. Hamas, by contrast, did not have a clear position on Israel and the peace process.

64. ICG (January 18, 2006), pp. 10–11.

65. Other areas included administrative reform and fighting corruption; legislative policy and judicial reform; public liberties and citizen rights; social policy (e.g., personal status law); cultural and media policy; women, children, and the family; youth; housing; health; agriculture; economic, fiscal, and monetary policy; and transport. See Khaled Hroub, "A 'New Hamas' through Its New Documents," *Journal of Palestine Studies* 35 (Summer 2006), pp. 6–27 (notably 23–24); and Azzam Tamimi, "Appendix VI: Hamas Election Manifesto for the Legislative Elections Held on 25 January 2006," in idem, *Hamas: Unwritten Chapters* (London: Hurst and Company, 2007), pp. 274–294.

66. Hroub (Summer 2006), p, 13.

67. Gunning (2008), pp. 178–182 and 192, furthermore states that other important factors shaping Hamas's program were the exposure to higher education among the Hamas leadership and the increasing heterogenization of Hamas's membership.

68. Ibid., p. 146.

69. In the section on "administrative reform and fighting corruption," Hamas stated that it would "embrace decentralization and delegation of power and participation in decision making." See Tamimi, "Appendix VI" (2007), p. 279, and Hroub (Summer 2006), p. 11.

70. See Khalid Mishal, "We Will Not Sell Our People or Principles for Foreign Aid," *The Guardian*, January 31, 2006; and Alistair Crooke, "The Rise of Hamas: Hamas and Fatah Radicals Will Transform Palestinian Politics," *Prospect*, February 2006.

71. Interview, Usama Hamdan, Beirut, February 2010.

72. Interview, Gaza, summer 1999.

73. Nathan J. Brown, "Hamas in Power," Carnegie Endowment for International Peace, April 13, 2006, www.carnegieendowment.org/t/70241/27063/42793/0/. Also see Beverly Milton-Edwards, "Prepared for Power: Hamas, Governance and Conflict," *Civil Wars* 7 (2005), pp. 311–329.

74. This was told to me by a Palestinian academic whose name, regretfully, I cannot remember and did not note.

75. Luke Baker, "Rival 'Fiefdoms' Eclipsing Dream of Palestinian State," *Alternet News*, October 11, 2006, www.alternet.org/thenews/newdesk/LO42496884.htm; and Amira Hass, "Not an Internal Palestinian Matter," *Ha'aretz*, October 4, 2006. It should be noted that the 132-member Palestinian Legislative Council (PLC), which Hamas dominates, has not convened since Hamas's electoral victory owing to a Fatah boycott.

76. Ali Abunimah, "Shifting Attitudes toward Hamas," Palestine Center Information Brief 160 (Washington, DC: Palestine Center, March 11, 2008). Also see Ran HaCohen, "Israel Says 'No,'" *Antiwar.com*, February 19, 2008, www.antiwar.com/hacohen. Halevy further argued that Hamas is "more credible and effective as a political force" than Fatah, having pulled off three coups under extremely adverse conditions: winning the 2006 legislative elections, preempting a Fatah plan to take control of Gaza from Hamas in 2007, and withstanding the sanction regime imposed by the West.

77. "Meshal Signals Readiness to Accept 1967 Borders—Look at the Program on the Table," *The Daily Star*, April 4, 2008; "Interview with Khaled Mesh'al in Damascus," *Al Hayat*, October 2006; and Amira Hass, "Haniyeh: Hamas Would Accept State under 1967 Borders," *Ha'aretz*, November 11, 2008. According to Haniyeh, Israel rejected the offer, which was not canceled by Hamas but suspended. The five factions signing the Prisoners' Document included Fatah, Hamas, Islamic Jihad, Popular Front for the Liberation of Palestine (PFLP), and the Democratic Front for the Liberation of Palestine (DFLP). Also see Dror Ze'evi, "My Talks with Hamas: Israeli Leaders Should at Least Consider Hamas Proposals for Long-Term Ceasefire," *Israel Opinion*, January 23, 2008; and Mouin Rabbani, "A Hamas Perspective on the Movement's Evolving Role: An Interview with Khalid Mishal: Part II," *Journal of Palestine Studies* 37 (Summer 2008), p. 80.

78. Patrick Seale, "Will Obama Talk to Hamas?" *Agence Global*, December 15, 2008, http://www.agenceglobal.com/article.asp?id=1835.

79. In November 2008, it was revealed that soon after Hamas's electoral victory Ismail Haniyeh wanted to initiate a dialogue between Hamas and President Bush, writing: "We are so concerned about stability and security in the area that we don't mind having a Palestinian state in the 1967 borders and offering a truce for many years. We are not warmongers, we are peace makers and we call on the American government to have direct negotiations with the elected government." Washington did not reply. See Barak Ravid, "In 2006 Letter to Bush, Haniyeh Offered Compromise with Israel," *Ha'aretz*, November 14, 2008.

80. See Joseph Massad, "The (Anti-) Palestinian Authority," *al-Ahram Weekly*, June 16, 2006, http://weekly.ahram.org.eg/2006/799/op11.htm; and David Rose, "The Gaza Bombshell," *Vanity Fair*, April 2008.

81. Norman H. Olsen and Matthew N. Olsen, "An Inside Story of How the US Magnified Palestinian Suffering," *Christian Science Monitor*, January 12, 2009, www.csmonitor.com/2009/0112/p09s01-coop.html.

82. Islamic Jihad was the only faction to say no point-blank but also stated that it would not be an obstacle to forming a government.

83. This was particularly interesting since it was originally agreed in the Oslo Accords that the PNA would handle only domestic affairs and the PLO would be responsible for foreign affairs. Arafat changed that in order to concentrate power in himself, and Hamas claimed it wanted to return to the original format, signifying, albeit tacitly, a certain willingness to work within the Oslo framework. The Portfolio of Security Affairs was contentious since Hamas had always been excluded from the Palestinian security forces, long under Fatah's hegemony. There was talk of dividing control over the security forces between the president (Fatah) and the Ministry of Interior (Hamas). However, the Qassam Brigades would remain a separate force—neither dismantled nor folded into the Authority's police force—in order to continue fighting the occupation. There were also calls for a united Palestinian army under the PNA's authority within which all militias would be organized.

84. See "PA Officials Have Fewer Powers than a Swiss Local Council—UN Body," *The Daily Star*, September 9, 2008.

85. Soon after the January 2006 elections the U.S. administration was asking for the return of $50 million of direct aid to the PNA. Congress introduced HR4681—the Palestinian Anti-Terrorism Act of 2006, which designated the occupied territories as a "terrorist sanctuary"; placed aid to Palestinian NGOs in the same category as aid to the Palestinian Authority; subtracted from America's contribution to the United Nations the amount allocated to Palestinian issues and rights, including monies allocated to UN specialized agencies such as UNICEF, WHO, and FAO (although this did not include UNRWA); ended all Palestinian diplomatic representation in the United States; and ended all funding to the PNA through the US vote in the World Bank. See http://thomas.loc.gov/cgi-bin/bdquery/z?d109:h.r.4681l and www.govtrack.us/congress/bill.xpd?bill=h109-4681.

86. There was a similarly dramatic about face with respect to ribbon cuttings and other public relations events; these once obligatory exercises were strictly avoided if they had any remote connection to the Hamas-led PNA.

87. Interviews with USAID officials based in the Middle East and with officials of NGOs receiving USAID monies, summer 2006 and spring 2007.

88. EU programs are relatively less restrictive. The diminished presence of internationals has also had a regressive impact socially.

89. Interviews with international development professionals who asked not to be identified, Jerusalem, 2007 and 2008.

90. Israeli Information Center for Human Rights in the Occupied Territories (B'tselem), *Severe Human Rights Violations in Intra-Palestinian Clashes;* and idem, *Statistics*, www.btselem.org/english/statistics/casualties. In 2008, eighteen Palestinians were killed by other Palestinians. Also see, for example, the reports of the Palestinian Centre for Human Rights (PCHR) in Gaza: PCHR, "Internal Palestinian Fighting Continues . . . ," Gaza, January 29, 2007; "Attacks on Public Institutions Continue: Over the past two days, scores of armed Palestinians have carried out attacks on Al-Aqsa University in Khan Yunis, Al-Karama Military Hospital in Khan Yunis and the Electric Power Station located in the centre of the Gaza Strip," Gaza, March 13, 2006; "Gaza Strip Witnesses a New Wave of Security Chaos Incidents," Gaza, March 30, 2006; "Attacks on Public Institutions Continue: Gunmen Storm the New Abasan District Court in Khan Yunis," Gaza, April 11, 2006; "Further Deterioration of Security Chaos in the Gaza Strip: 3 Kidnappings Reported and a Member of the Preventive Security Service Injured," Gaza, April 19, 2006; and "Attacks on Public Institutions Continue—Palestinian Gunmen Attack the Municipalities of Nablus and Bani Suheila," Gaza, April 23, 2006.

91. Human Rights Watch, *Internal Fight: Palestinian Abuses in Gaza and the West Bank* (New York, 2008).

92. Visit by the author to Gaza City, May 2007. Also see Sami Abdel-Shafi, "We Are Being Suffocated," *The Guardian*, February 10, 2007.

93. See Amira Hass, "The Fear in Gaza," *Ha'aretz*, October 8, 2006.

94. Israeli Information Center for Human Rights in the Occupied Territories (B'tselem), *Statistics*. In June 2006, Hamas kidnapped the Israeli soldier Gilad Shalit, who is still in captivity.

95. Olsen and Olsen (January 12, 2009).

96. "PA Dismantles Hamas 'Charities,'" Arutz Sheva/IsraelNationalNews.com, October 19, 2007.

97. For example see "Reassessing the Strategy on Hamas," Bitterlemons.org, March 31, 2008, www.bitterlemons.org; Nicholas D. Kristof, "Strengthening Extremists," *New York Times*, June 19, 2008; Rami G. Khouri, "Hamas Grows Stronger," *Agence Global*, March 19, 2008, www.agenceglobal.com; Taghreed El-Khodary, "Life in Gaza Today," interview, *Middle East Progress*, June 17, 2008; Ethan Bronner, "Poll Shows Most Palestinians Favor Violence over Talks," *New York Times*, March 19, 2008; Daoud Kuttab, "Whether Anyone Admits It or Not, Hamas Appears to Have Won," *The Daily Star*, September 3, 2008; International Crisis Group (ICG), *Ruling Palestine I: Gaza under Hamas* (Jerusalem: ICG, March 19, 2008); Intelligence and Terrorism Information Center at the Israel Intelligence Heritage & Commemoration Center (IICC), "Since Hamas took over the Gaza Strip, it has intensified its activities to impose an Islamic

social code. Hamas is careful not to represent it as a step toward establishing a radical Islamic state. The process is just beginning but indicates an increase in the Islamization of the Gaza Strip," August 31, 2007; and Jonathan Schanzer, "The Talibanization of Gaza: A Liability for the Muslim Brotherhood," *Current Trends in Islamist Ideology* 9, Hudson Institute, August 19, 2009.

98. ICG (March 19, 2008), executive summary. Also see "Hamas-Israel Escalation," bitterlemons.org, February 18, 2008, edition 7, www.bitterlemons.org; and "Hamas Arrests More Journalists in Gaza," October 14, 2008, http://www.menassat.com.

99. Given the scope of this chapter, I shall not address the relationship between Hamas (the party and resistance movement) and the Haniyeh government, and the sometimes subtle differences in the way each approaches other societal actors. Suffice it to say that both the movement's agenda and the government's policies are largely aligned along most issues.

100. ICG (March 19, 2008), executive summary. Also, Karin Laub, "Abbas Shuts Hamas Charities in West Bank," Associated Press, December 3, 2007.

101. Avi Issacharoff and Amos Harel, "Israeli Security Officials Laud PA Crackdown on Hamas," *Ha'aretz*, September 7, 2008.

102. Nahum Barnea, "Talking to Palestinians," *Yediot Ahronot*, September 19, 2008 (translation from the Hebrew original). Also see Palestinian Centre for Human Rights (PCHR), *General Intelligence Service raids Hebron Office of PLC Member Samira al-Halaiqa*, Gaza, September 23, 2008. Samira al-Halaiqa is a member of the Palestinian Legislative Council for the Hamas Change and Reform Bloc in Hebron.

103. Palestinian Centre for Human Rights (PCHR), "PCHR Condemns Attacks on Civil Society Organizations and the Continued Arrests against Hamas Members in the West Bank," Gaza, August 10, 2008; Agence France Presse, "Fatah Shuts Down West Bank Charity Linked to Hamas," *The Daily Star*, August 21, 2008; and Voice of America, "Palestinian Forces Shut Down Hamas-Linked Charities, Shops," August 9, 2008.

104. For example, see Board of Directors, Sharek Youth Forum, "Sharek Youth Forum in Palestine Condemns the Assault against Civil Society Organizations and the Assault on Its Main Office in the Gaza Strip by Masked Militants Claiming to Be from the Ezzedine Al-Qassam Brigades," Gaza, July 30, 2008; Palestinian Centre for Human Rights (PCHR), "'El-Ata Charitable Society' Burned in Beit Hanoun, Gaza," April 11, 2007; idem, "Explosive Device Detonated in Yabous Benevolent Society and Rafah Service Club in Southern Gaza," Gaza, July 13, 2008; and idem, "PCHR Condemns Campaign of Arrests against Hamas Supporters in the West Bank," Gaza, October 29, 2008.

105. "Hamas Seizes Abbas-Run News Agency," *ABC News*, July 27, 2008; and "Hamas Reopens 70 Civil Organizations in Gaza," August 25, 2008, www.chinaview.cn.

106. Palestinian Centre for Human Rights (PCHR), "PCHR Gravely Concerned over the Deterioration of the Human Rights Situation in the Occupied Palestinian Territory," Gaza, July 30, 2008. Hamas also launched a campaign against the Hilles clan, one of Gaza's most powerful and allied with Fatah. This

was significant because the Hilles clan was a key Fatah stronghold in Gaza; with its undoing and coupled with the attack against Fatah-linked civic institutions, Hamas weakened Fatah's capacity to mobilize in Gaza. However, violence between the Hamas security forces and other clans continued over issues that were not necessarily political but social—that is, criminal activity.

107. "Hamas Abducts 166 Fateh Cadres and Closes 42 Associations, Confiscates Governorate and Political Offices in Gaza Strip," *al-Hayat al-Jadida*, July 27, 2008.

108. Ali Waked, "Palestinian Forces in Hebron Say Hamas Caught 'In the Crosshairs,' *YNET news*, www.ynetnews.com/articles/0,7340,L-3614547,00.html.

109. Palestinian Centre for Human Rights (PCHR), "PCHR Calls for Keeping Universities and Educational Institutions out of the Ongoing Power Struggle," Gaza, April 1, 2008; idem, "PCHR Condemns Violence at al-Azhar University in Gaza," Gaza, August 25, 2008; and idem, "PCHR Condemns Eruption of Violence at Gaza City's al-Azhar University," Gaza, October 19, 2008.

110. Palestinian Centre for Human Rights (July 30, 2008).

111. As reported in Palestinian Media Watch, "Hamas Forbids Fatah to 'Bring Flowers to the Sick'"; Fatah Declared 'Illegal Organization' by Hamas in Gaza," *Bulletin*, November 25, 2008, www.pmw.or.il.

112. "Haniya Looking for Direct Assistance to Gaza," Palestine News Network; and Doctors Without Borders, "Occupied Palestinian Territories: Politics Cannot Be More Important Than Patients," press release, Jerusalem, September 3, 2008.

113. Ma'an News Agency, "UN Report: 50% of Teachers and 48% of Medical Workers on Strike," September 5, 2008, www.maannews.net/en/index.php?opr=ShowDetails&ID=31756; and Ali Waked, "Gaza Strip: Hamas Disperses Teachers' Strike," ynetnews.com, September 6, 2008.

114. United Nations Office for the Coordination of Humanitarian Affairs, *Protection of Civilians Weekly Report 27 August–2 September 2008* (East Jerusalem: UNOCHA, September 4, 2008).

115. Ma'an News Agency, "Israeli Journalist Speaks to Palestinians in Ramallah after Spending Three Weeks in Gaza," December 7, 2008; internal document of an international NGO that asked not be identified, Jerusalem, September 18, 2008; and World Health Organization, "Gaza Health Workers Strike—WHO Update 7 October 2008," Jerusalem, October 7, 2008.

116. Internal document of an international NGO that asked not be identified, Jerusalem, September 18, 2008.

117. Ibid.

118. Palestinian Centre for Human Rights (PCHR), "PCHR Calls for Schools to Be Allowed to Operate without Destructive Political Conflicts," Gaza, August 25, 2008.

119. Ma'an News Agency, "UN Report...." (September 5, 2008).

120. Save the Children, "Child Rights Fact Sheet," November 17, 2008, Jerusalem.

121. Yezid Sayigh, "Hamas Rule in Gaza: Three Years On," Middle East Brief 41, Crown Center for Middle East Studies, Brandeis University, March 2010, p. 3.

122. Amos Harel, "PA forces working to root out Hamas, Hezbollah agents," *Ha'aretz*, May 5, 2009, www.haaretz.com/hasen/spages/1083173.html.

123. Michael Sfard, "Welcome to Year 41," *Ha'aretz*, June 4, 2008; and Haitham Sabbagh, "Video and Photos: Israeli Army Raids and Loots Hebron Orphanage Home to 110 Girls," May 13, 2008, www.hebronorphans.blogspot.com; "International NGOs Rally to Rescue Hebron Orphans," www.hebronorphans.blogspot.org.

124. Palestine Monitor, "The Israeli Siege on Nablus: The Mall Must Fall?" July 17, 2008, www.palestinemonitor.org/spip/spip.php?article 529; Gideon Levy, "The General of Onions and Garlic," *Ha'aretz*, July 13, 2008; and Gush Shalom, "Orphans and Widows," advertisement, *Ha'artez*, July 11, 2008.

125. Palestine Monitor (July 17, 2008); Khaled Amayreh, "Israel Attacks Charities, Orphanages," *Al-Ahram Weekly*, August 1, 2008; and Missionary International Service News Agency (MISNA), "Israel Targets Charities Also Amid Widespread Silence, an Account from Nablus," July 31, 2008, www.reliefweb.int/rw/rwb.nsf/db900sid/MUMA-7H596Q?OpenDocument&vc=3&emid=ACOS-635PFR.

126. Palestine Monitor (July 17, 2008); and Issacharoff and Harel (September 7, 2008). In this regard, see Yaakov Katz, "Israel Allows Transfer of Rifles, Bullets to the PA," Israel.jpost.com, September 5, 2008.

127. Harel (May 5, 2009).

128. Matthew Levitt, "Financial Setbacks for Hamas," Policy Watch no. 1436 (Washington, DC: The Washington Institute for Near East Policy, December 3, 2008).

129. Sayigh (March 2010), pp. 3–4.

130. Ma'an News Agency, "Attack on Gaza-Based NGOs Condemned," December 13, 2009.

131. "UN Official Voices Deep Concern as Hamas Raids Offices of Aid Agencies," *UN News*, June 3, 2010, www.un.org/apps/news/story.asp?NewsID=34903; Associated Press, "Masked Assailants Vandalise UN Summer Camp in Gaza," *Ha'aretz*, June 28, 2010, www.haaretz.com/news/international/masked-assailants-vandalize-un-summer-camp-in-gaza-1.298749; and Palestinian Center for Human Rights, "PCHR Condemns Continued Campaign against Non-Governmental Organizations," press release, June 15, 2010.

132. Palestinian Center for Human Rights, "PCHR Condemns Unjustified Intervention into Public Freedoms and Prevention of Public and Private Meetings by Ministry of Interior in Gaza," press release, May 25, 2010.

133. Palestinian Center for Human Rights, "PCHR Demands Minister of the Interior and National Security Retract Decision No. 48/2010 Concerning Civilians Abstaining from Joining Their Jobs in the Civil Service Sector," Gaza, August 9, 2010.

134. Phone interview, NGO official, Jerusalem, March 2010. Also see Ulrike Putz, "International Donations Not Always Welcome in Gaza," *Spiegel Online*, June 4, 2010, www.spiegel.de/international/world/0,1518,698766,00.html.

135. Phone interview, NGO official, Jerusalem, March 2010.

136. For a similar finding, see Jacob Hoigilt, *Raising Extremists? Islamism and Education in the Palestinian Territories* (Oslo: FAFO, 2010).

137. See Khaled Hroub, "Salafi Formations in Palestine: The Limits of a De-Palestinised Milieu," in Roel Meijer, ed., *Global Salafism: Islam's New Religious Movement* (New York: Columbia University Press, 2009), pp. 221–243; Yoram Cohen, "Jihadist Groups in Gaza: A Developing Threat," Policy Watch no. 1449 (Washington, DC: Washington Institute for Near East Policy, January 5, 2009); and Yoram Cohen, Matthew Levitt, and Becca Wasser, "Deterred but Determined: Salafi-Jihadi Groups in the Palestinian Arena," Policy Focus no. 99 (Washington, DC: Washington Institute for Near East Policy, January 2010).

138. Cohen (January 5, 2009).

139. Sayigh (March 2010), p. 4; and Ulrike Putz, "Salafi Jihadists in Gaza: 'Compared to Us, Hamas Is Islamism Lite,'" *Spiegel Online*, July 18, 2008.

140. United Nations Relief and Works Agency, translated leaflet, Gaza, May 19, 2010.

141. Cohen (January 5, 2009).

142. Laurent Zecchini, "Dans la bande de Gaza, des combats opposent la police du Hamas a des salafistes," *Le Monde*, August 16–17, 2009; and Association of International Development Agencies, *Urgent Briefing Document: 14 August Clashes: Analysis, Implications, & Recommendations* (Jerusalem: AIDA, 2010).

143. Sayigh (March 2010), p. 4. Also see Hroub (2009); "Hamas Arrests the Most Prominent Leader of Salafi Groups in Gaza," *al-Quds al-Arabi* (London), February 11, 2010; Roi Kais, "Report: Al-Qaeda-Linked Groups Reject Hamas Proposal," ynetnews.com, October 2, 2009; and Cohen, Levitt, and Wasser (January 2010).

144. Associated Press, "Ultraconservative Jihadists Challenge Hamas Rule in Gaza," *Ha'aretz*, February 13, 2010, www.haaretz.com/news/ultraconservative-jihadists-challenge-hamas-rule-in-gaza-1.263254.

145. It should be noted that various practices were introduced soon after the June 2007 takeover, such as providing Quranic classes in prisons and rewarding police officers with an automatic promotion for memorizing the Quran. See Sayigh (March 2010).

146. Daniel Williams, "Hamas Bans Women Dancers, Scooter Riders in Gaza Push," Bloomberg.com, November 30, 2009; Rory McCarthy, "Hamas Patrols Beaches in Gaza to Enforce Conservative Dress Code," *The Guardian*, October 18, 2009; Palestinian Centre for Human Rights, "PCHR Condemns Police's Prevention of Show in Gaza City," press release, Gaza, April 25, 2010; idem, "PCHR Condemns Restrictions Imposed by the Two Governments in the Gaza Strip and West Bank on Activities Organized by Hizb Ut Tahrir," Gaza, July 14, 2010; and Nidal al Mughrabi, "Gazans Debate Hamas 'Islamisation' Signals," Reuters, August 3, 2009. Also see Thanassis Cambanis, "Islamism Has Won Hearts and Minds across the Middle East. It Also Offers a BA," *Boston Globe/boston.com*, February 28, 2010.

147. Sayigh (March 2010), p. 5.

148. Internal memo dated August 25, 2009, Gaza.

149. Williams (November 30, 2009).

150. This has led to speculation that the two attacks (May and June 2010) by masked gunmen against UNRWA's summer camps in Gaza—Hamas's main

competitor in running summer camps—may have had the tacit approval of Hamas if not direct participation. See International Crisis Group (ICG), *Round Two in Gaza* (Gaza City/Ramallah/Brussels: ICG, September 11, 2008; Intelligence and Terrorism Information Center at the Israel Intelligence Heritage & Commemoration Center (IICC) (August 31, 2007); and idem, "Yet another step in the establishment of a totalitarian 'Islamic Emirate' in the Gaza Strip: the Hamas administration announces that it is now drawing a new bill imposing also shari'ah-based penal codes on the Gaza Strip," November 13, 2008.

151. One seemingly successful attempt to overcome such divisions is found in a Palestinian national strategy document, announced in August 2008, in the making of which representatives of various political factions successfully strategized about Palestine's political future. See Palestine Strategy Group, *Regaining the Initiative* (Ramallah, August 27, 2008).

Postscript
The Devastation of Gaza—Some Additional Reflections on Where We Are Now

1. "Lost Causes and Gallantry: Johnny Reb and the Shadow of Sir Walter," *American Scholar*, September 22, 2003.
2. Cited in Maxwell Taylor Kennedy, ed., *Make Gentle the Life of This World: The Vision of Robert F. Kennedy* (New York: Harcourt Brace, 1998), p. 97.
3. Palestinian Centre for Human Rights, "Confirmed Figures Reveal the True Extent of the Destruction Inflicted upon the Gaza Strip," Gaza, March 12, 2009; idem, "PCHR Contests Distortion of Gaza Strip Death Toll," Gaza, March 26, 2009; and Sagi Or, "How Many Palestinians Were Killed?," *Ha'aretz*, March 19, 2009. Also see Gideon Levy, "The IDF Has No Mercy for the Children in Gaza Nursery Schools," *Ha'aretz*, January 15, 2009. Levy also reports that since 2000, the Israeli army has "killed nearly 5,000 Palestinians, at least half of them innocent civilians, nearly 1,000 of them children and teenagers." Israel put the number of dead at just over 1,000.
4. In 2007, 1,523 people were killed in Afghanistan. See Dexter Filkins, "Civilians' Deaths in Afghanistan Soared in 2008, a U.N. Survey Says," *New York Times*, February 18, 2009.
5. Physicians for Human Rights—Israel and Dan Magen, "'Ill Morals': Grave Violations of the Right to Health during the Israeli Assault on Gaza," Israel, March 2009, p. 9.
6. Jeff Halper, *Israel in Gaza: A Critical Reframing* (Israel Committee against Home Demolitions, January 2009).
7. Israeli Information Center for Human Rights in the Occupied Territories (B'Tselem), *Human Rights in the Occupied Territories: 2008 Annual Report* (Jerusalem, 2008); and Norman G. Finkelstein, "Gaza: The Last Jewish War," manuscript, April 2009, pp. 1–2.
8. Norman G. Finkelstein, *This Time We Went Too Far: Truth & Consequences of the Gaza Invasion* (New York.: OR Books, 2010), p. 87.

9. Ibid., pp. 60–61, 63, 70.

10. Norman G. Finkelstein (April 2009) powerfully makes this argument in "Gaza: The Last Jewish War," and (2010) *This Time We Went Too Far*. For a different interpretation, see Jim Zanotti et al., *Israel and Hamas: Conflict in Gaza (2008–2009)*, CRS Report for Congress, Congressional Research Service 7-5700, www.crs.gov, January 15, 2009.

11. Noam Chomsky, "'Exterminate the Brutes': Gaza 2009," Chomsky.info, January 19, 2009. For a compelling examination of this preference see Zeev Maoz, *Defending the Holy Land: A Critical Analysis of Israel's Security and Foreign Policy* (Ann Arbor: University of Michigan Press, 2006).

12. Johann Hari, "The True Story behind This War Is Not the One Israel Is Telling," *The Independent*, December 29, 2008.

13. Intelligence and Terrorism Information Center at the Israel Intelligence Heritage & Commemoration Center (IICC), "The Six Months of the Lull Arrangement," December 2008. Diskin said, "Make no mistake, Hamas is interested in maintaining the truce." See Gareth Porter, "Israel Rejected Hamas Cease-Fire Offer in December," Antiwar.com, January 10, 2009.

14. "Hamas Wants Better Terms for Truce," *Jerusalem Post*, December 21, 2008.

15. Chomsky (January 19, 2009).

16. Norman Finkelstein, "Foiling another Palestinian 'Peace Offensive,'" *Counterpunch*, January 28, 2009, www.counterpunch.com/finkelstein01282009.html; and Finkelstein (2010), where he makes this argument.

17. Ibid., and Finkelstein (April 2009), pp. 13 and 16. He also points out that this was a strategy used by Israel before. In order to thwart Yasir Arafat's "peace offensive" in the early 1980s, Israel embarked on the 1982 Lebanon War. Quoting Avner Yaniv, Finkelstein writes, the "raison d'etre of the entire operation" was "destroying the PLO as a political force capable of claiming a Palestinian state on the West Bank." See Avner Yaniv, *Dilemmas of Security: Politics, Strategy and the Israeli Experience in Lebanon* (New York: Oxford University Press, 1987).

18. See the piece I coauthored with Augustus Richard Norton, "End Game in the Gaza War, Parts I, II & III," icga.blogspot.com/2009/01/end-game-in-gaza-war-part-i.html.

19. Roni Sofer, "Olmert: Gaza Op Goals Yet to Be Obtained," *ynetnews.com*, January 8, 2009.

20. Barbara Opall Rome, "Marines to Train at New Israeli Combat Center," *Marine Corps Times*, June 25, 2007, www.marinecorpstimes.com/news/2007/06/marine_israel_combattraining_070624. Also see idem, "Israel Upgrades Training Center Capabilities: Offers Fixed Exportable, Force-on-Force Drills," *DefenseNews*, December 1, 2008, www.defensenews.com/story.php?i=3844091.

21. Barak Ravid, "Disinformation, Secrecy, and Lies: How the Gaza Offensive Came About," *Ha'aretz*, December 28, 2008. Also see Uri Avnery, "The Calculations behind Israel's Slaughter of Palestinians in Gaza," January 2, 2009, www.redress.cc/palestine/uavnery20080102; and, in an interview on January 4, 2009, with the *al-Jazeera News*, Yuval Steinitz, a Likud MK, admitted that Israel had been planning to execute the operation "for eight or nine months."

22. Zvi Barel, "Crushing the Tahadiyeh," *Ha'aretz*, November 16, 2008.

23. Rory McCarthy, "Israel Annexing East Jerusalem, Says EU," *The Guardian*, March 7, 2009.

24. Amira Hass, "Return to Gaza," *London Review of Books*, February 26, 2009.

25. Ibid.

26. Ibid.

27. "Hamas Hangs On," *The Economist*, March 31, 2010. Amira Hass, "Israel Bans Books, Music and Clothes from Entering Gaza," *Ha'aretz*, May 17, 2009, reported 30–40 items.

28. Sara Roy, "If Gaza Falls . . . ," *London Review of Books*, January 1, 2009.

29. There are many reports and studies describing this. See, for example, United Nations Office for the Coordination of Humanitarian Affairs, *Gaza Humanitarian Situation Report—the Impact of the Blockade on the Gaza Strip: A Human Dignity Crisis* (Jerusalem: OCHA, December 15, 2008); United Nations Relief and Works Agency, *Prolonged Crisis in the Occupied Palestinian Territory: Socio-Economic Developments in 2007, Report No. 3* (Gaza: UNRWA, July 2008); World Bank, *Palestinian Economic Prospects: Aid, Access and Reform* (Washington, DC: World Bank, September 22, 2008); and Catholic Agency for Overseas Development, Amnesty International, Christian Aid, et al., *The Gaza Strip: A Humanitarian Implosion* (Jerusalem 2008).

30. This section is drawn from Sara Roy, "Gaza: Treading on Shards," *The Nation* (online), February 17, 2010, reprinted with permission.

31. These figures were provided by the Union of Agricultural Work Committees, Gaza, January 2010; and personal correspondence with Desmond Travers, January 2010.

32. Ibid.

33. United Nations Office for the Coordination of Humanitarian Affairs (UNOCHA), *Locked In: The Humanitarian Impact of Two Years of Blockade on the Gaza Strip* (Jerusalem: UNOCHA, August 2009), p. 8.

34. Save the Children UK, "Fact Sheet: Gaza Buffer Zone," October 2009. Also see Husam Zomlot, *The Politics of International Post-Conflict Interventions: Palestine between Peacebuilding, State-building and Back to Reconstruction* (Belfer Center for International Affairs, Kennedy School of Government, Harvard University, December 2009).

35. Omar Shaban, "The Shortage of Israeli Shekels in the Gaza Strip," Palthink, Gaza, September 27, 2008, http://www.palthink.org/en/Economy/46.html.

36. This proportion could not be verified with any hard data and may be overstated. However, the tunnel economy is undeniably a dominant feature of the local economy.

37. World Food Programme (WFP), Food and Agriculture Organization (FAO), and the Palestinian Central Bureau of Statistics (PCBS), "Gaza Socio-Economic and Food Security (SEFSec) Survey," October 1, 2009, Powerpoint presentation.

38. Stephen Lendeman, "ICRC: Israel Traps Gazans in Deprivation and Despair," January 10, 2010, http://www.globalresearch.ca/index.php?context=va&aid=14393; and Cooperation Internationale pour le Developpement et la Solidarite (CIDSE), *Gaza: Dignity under Siege; Voices from behind the Blockade* 18 (Brussels: November 18, 2009), pp. 10–11.

39. Internal documents, international NGOs, Jerusalem, September 2009 – January 2, 2010.

40. Internal document, international donor government, Jerusalem, February 2010.

41. Food and Agriculture Organization (FAO) and World Food Programme (WFP), "Socio-Economic and Food Security (SEFSec) Survey Report 2—Gaza Strip," November 2009, p. 6.

42. State of Israel, *The Civilian Policy toward the Gaza Strip* (Tel Aviv: Coordinator of Government Activities in the Territories, Ministry of Defense, 2010).

43. Legal Center for Freedom of Movement (GISHA), "Unraveling the Closure of Gaza: What Has and Hasn't Changed since the Cabinet Decision and What Are the Implications?" information sheet, Tel Aviv, July 7, 2010.

44. State of Israel (2010).

45. GISHA (July 7, 2010).

46. Ibid.; and GISHA, "Excerpt of State's Response in HCJ 4906/10 Fatma Sharif v. Defense Ministry," July 6, 2010, unofficial translation.

47. GISHA (July 7, 2010).

48. Cited in Chomsky (January 19, 2009).

49. Finkelstein (April 2009), p. 9; and idem (January 28, 2009). Original sources: "Israeli General Says Hamas Must Not Be the Only Target in Gaza," IDF Radio, Tel Aviv, in Hebrew 0600 gmt, December 26, 2008, BBC Monitoring Middle East; Tova Dadon, "Deputy Chief of Staff: Worst Still Ahead," December 29, 2009, www.ynetnews.com/articles/0,7340.L-36466558,00.html; and www.btselem.org/English/Gaza_Strip/20081231_Gaza_Letter_to_Mazuz.asp. Also see "Israel: Does the Army Target Civilians?" *The Week* 9, issue 406 (April 2009), p. 14.

50. E-mail correspondence, January 30, 2009. Also see World Health Organization, "Health Situation in Gaza—19–20 January 2009," www.who.iht/hac/crises/international/wbgs/sitreps/gaza_19_20jan2009/en/index.html; and Aleem Maqbool, "Gaza Hospital Bears Heavy Strain," February 3, 2009, *BBC News*, http://news.bbc.co.uk.

51. Finkelstein (2010), p. 128.

52. Khaled Abu Toameh, "PA Purges Hamas-Linked Educators," *Jerusalem Post*, March 29, 2010.

53. Matthew Kalman, "6 Faculty Members at a Palestinian University Are Arrested for Suspected Hamas Ties," *The Chronicle of Higher Education*, August 4, 2010.

54. Hilary L. Krieger, "PA Making Bold Bid to Curb Hamas Funds," *Jerusalem Post*, April 9, 2010.

55. Ali Abunimah, "Hamas, the I.R.A. and Us," *New York Times*, August 29, 2010; Mark Perry, "CENTCOM Thinks Outside the Box on Hamas and Hezbollah," ForeignPolicy.com, June 30, 2010; and Rami G. Khouri, "Beyond Islamists," *Agence Global*, July 5, 2010. Also see Henry Siegman, "US Hamas Policy Blocks Middle East Peace," Noref Report 8 (Oslo: Norwegian Peacebuilding Centre, September 2010); and Nicholas Pelham, "Hamas Back Out of Its Box," *Middle East Report Online*, September 2, 2010, www.merip.org/mero/mero090210.html.

56. This includes Egypt, which has severed ties with Hamas, obstructed Iranian foreign aid from reaching Gaza, and barred senior Hamas officials from traveling into or out of the Strip.

57. *The Economist* (March 31, 2010).

58. See, for example, Yoram Cohen, Matthew Levitt, and Becca Wasser, "Deterred but Determined: Salafi-Jihadi Groups in the Palestinian Arena," Policy Focus no. 99 (Washington, DC: Washington Institute for Near East Policy, 2010).

Afterword
Hamas in a Changing Middle East

1. International Crisis Group (ICG), *Light at the End of the Tunnels? Hamas and the Arab Uprisings*, Middle East Report no. 129, August 14, 2012, Gaza City/Cairo/Jerusalem/Ramallah/Brussels, p. 2.

2. Salim Tamari, "Why there was no Arab Spring in Palestine," Lecture, Center for Middle Eastern Studies, Harvard University, March 13, 2013. Also see Jean-Pierre Filiu, *The Arab Revolution: Ten Lessons from the Democratic Uprising* (New York: Oxford University Press, 2011).

3. See Sara Roy, "Reconceptualizing the Israeli-Palestinian Conflict: Key Paradigm Shifts," *Journal of Palestine Studies*, Volume XLI, No. 3 (Spring 2012), p. 74 and pp. 71–91.

4. ICG (August 14, 2012), p. i.

5. Ibid, p. 27, fn. 216.

6. "Hamas to ask EU to remove it from terrorism list," *The Jerusalem Post*, www.jpost.com/Middle-East/Hamas-to-ask-EU-to-remove-it-from-terrorism-list-310567, April 21, 2013.

7. The deterioration in diplomatic relations followed the Gaza Freedom Flotilla incident on May 31, 2010, in which eight Turkish nationals were killed by Israeli forces aboard the Turkish ship, *Mavi Marmara*. The U.S. has encouraged Turkish-Israeli reconciliation, and during President Obama's visit to Israel in March 2013, Israeli Prime Minister Netanyahu phoned Turkish Prime Minister Erdogan and apologized on behalf of his nation, which Erdogan accepted.

8. Jodi Rudoren, "Qatar's Emir Visits Gaza, Pledging $400 Million to Hamas," *New York Times*, www.nytimes.com/2012/10/24/world/middleeast/pledging-400-million-qatari-emir-makes-historic-visit-to-gaza-strip.html?_r=0, October 23, 2012. However, Qatar will not provide military aid given that it hosts critical U.S. military bases. Adnan Abu Amer, "Hamas Ties to Qatar Have Cost," *Al-Monitor*, www.al-monitor.com/pulse/originals/2013/04/hamas-qatar-relationship-independence.html, April 22, 2013.

9. "Turkish PM Erdogan rules out postponing Gaza visit," *Hurriyet Daily News*, www.hurriyetdailynews.com/PrintNews.aspx?PageID=383&NID=45461, April 23, 2013. Erdogan will need Egyptian permission to visit Gaza and it is unclear whether it will be given.

10. Stephen Farrell, "Hamas Leader Takes Rare Trip to Jordan," *New York Times*, January 29, 2012. Also see Geoffrey Aronson, "The Return of the

Jordanian Option for Palestine," *Al-Monitor*, www.al-monitor.com/pulse/originals/2013/05/jordan-option-palestine-israel-peace-process.html, May 9, 2013.

11. See ICG (August 14, 2012), pp. 7–10 for a more detailed discussion.

12. Ibid, pp. 5–14. Also see, David Kennar, "We Are Not Fanatic Killers," *Foreign Policy*, www.foreignpolicy.com/articles/2013/05/14/exclusive_interview_khaled_meshaal_hamas_syria_israel_gaza, May 22, 2013.

13. Abeer Ayyoub, "Hamas Maintains Ties With Iran Despite Difference Over Syria," *Al Monitor*, www.al-monitor.com/pulse/originals/2013/01/hamas-iran-ties.html, January 25, 2013.

14. See Shlomi Eldar, "Is Hamas Considering Recognition of Israel?" *Al-Monitor*, www.al-monitor.com/pulse/originals/2013/03/hamas-considers-recognizing-israel-in-its-1967-borders.html, March 11, 2013. Also see ICG (August 14, 2012), pp. 10–13 for a detailed discussion of Hamas-Iran relations.

15. See ICG (August 14, 2012), p. 13.

16. Farrell (January 29, 2012).

17. Harriet Sherwood, "Arab Spring uprisings reveal rift in Hamas over conflict tactics," *The Guardian*, www.guardian.co.uk/world/2012/jan/06/arab-spring-hamas-rift-gaza, January 6, 2012.

18. ICG (August 14, 2012), pp. 37.

19. For an excellent discussion of conditions in Gaza since Hamas's takeover, see Nathan Brown, *Gaza Five Years On: Hamas Settles In*, Carnegie Endowment for International Peace, carnegieendowment.org/2012/06/11/gaza-five-years-on-hamas-settles-in/birb, June 11, 2012.

20. Tamari (March 13, 2013).

21. Eldar (March 11, 2013). Also see Aronson (May 9, 2013).

22. See, for example, "Poll: 90.9% of Palestinians Believe Hamas and Fatah Should Reach Reconciliation Deal," *Algemeiner*, www.algemeiner.com/2013/04/10/poll-90-9-of-palestinians-believe-hamas-and-fatah-should-reach-reconciliation-deal, April 10, 2013.

23. ICG (August 14, 2012), p. 31.

24. Nathan Brown, "The Long Road to a Moderate Hamas," *New Republic*, www.newrepublic.com/blog/plank/110277/the-long-road-moderate-hamas#, November 18, 2012.

25. Sherwood (January 6, 2012).

26. The November conflict was precipitated by Israel's assassination of Hamas's military commander, Ahmed Jabari.

27. International Crisis Group (ICG), *Israel and Hamas: Fire and Ceasefire in a New Middle East*, Middle East Report no. 133, November 22, 2012, p. 8.

28. Hamas must contend with its military wing as well as other more militant Islamic factions who oppose any engagement with the West.

29. Alon Ben David, "Hamas Enforces Quiet Border With Israel," *Al-Monitor*, www.al-monitor.com/pulse/originals/2013/05/hamas-enforces-a-quiet-border-with-israel.html, May 3, 2013.

30. Email correspondence, April 2013. Also see Kennar (May 22, 2013).

31. Abeer Ayyoub and Harriet Sherwood, "Tens of thousands celebrate Hamas 'victory' rally as exiled leader returns," *The Guardian*, www.guardian.co.uk/

world/2012/dec/08/hamas-gaza-palestine-khaled-meshaal-israel, December 8, 2012.

32. Ibid; Ali Abunimah, "UK's Observer adds "kill Jews" to Hamas leader Khaled Meshal's Gaza speech when he did not say it," *Occupied Palestine Blog*, electronicintifada.net/blogs/ali-abunimah/uks-observer-adds-kill-jews-hamas-leader-khaled-meshals-gaza-speech-when-he-did, December 9, 2012; and Steven Erlanger, "Leader Celebrates Founding of Hamas With Defiant Speech," *New York Times*, December 8, 2012. Also see Barak Ravid, "Netanyahu: Palestinians have no intention of compromising with Israel," *Haaretz*, www.haaretz.com/news/diplomacy-defense/netanyahu-palestinians-have-no-intention-of-compromising-with-israel.premium-1.483625, December 9, 2012.

33. Ayyoub and Sherwood (December 8, 2012); and Erlanger (December 8, 2012).

34. Abunimah (December 9, 2012).

35. Ravid (December 9, 2012).

36. Shlomi Eldar, "Exclusive: Al-Zahar, Meshaal's Rival, Out of Hamas Leadership," *Al-Monitor*, www.al-monitor.com/pulse/originals/2013/04/al-zahar-hamas-political-bureau.html, April 3, 2013.

37. Ibid.

38. Email correspondence, January 2013. In this regard, see Wasseem El-Sarraj, "Why Hamas," *The Cairo Review of Global Affairs*, www.aucegypt.edu/gapp/cairoreview/pages/articleDetails.aspx?aid=274, December 16, 2012.

39. ICG (August 14, 2012), p. 38.

40. See Wadah Khanfar, "Key Strategic Trends for the Middle East in 2013," *Huffington Post World*, www.huffingtonpost.com/wadah-khanfar/middle-east-trends_b_2421755.html, January 6, 2013.

41. Brown (November 18, 2012). Also see Raymond Baker, *Islam Without Fear: Egypt and the New Islamists* (Cambridge, MA: Harvard University Press, 2003).

42. For a discussion of these problems see Brown (June 11, 2012).

43. Hazem Balousha, "Hamas' Relationship with Qatar Widens Rift With West Bank," *Al-Monitor*, www.al-monitor.com/pulse/iw/contents/articles/opinion/2013/04/hamas-relationship-qatar-widens-rift-west-bank-fatah.html, April 10, 2013; and "A Special Meeting with Mr. Osama Hamdan entitled "Hamas in the International Context," *Pal-Think for Strategic Studies*, palthink.org/en/?p=898, January 28, 2013.

44. ICG (November 22, 2012), p. 11. Also see Amira Hass, "At Ramallah protest, Hamas' green overcomes Fatah's yellow," *Haaretz*, www.haaretz.com/news/middle-east/at-ramallah-protest-hamas-green-overcomes-fatah-s-yellow.premium-1.478486, November 16, 2012.

45. Balousha (April 10, 2013). Also see Abu Amer (April 22, 2013); and Alistair Dawber, "Hamas rebuffs renewed Israel-Palestinian peace initiative from Arab League," *The Independent*, www.independent.co.uk/news/world/middle-east/hamas-rebuffs-renewed-israelpalestinian-peace-initiative-from-arab-league-8603369.html, May 3, 2013.

46. Mohammed Sullman, "Hamas Slams Qatar, Arab League on Peace Plan," *Al-Monitor*, www.al-monitor.com/pulse/originals/2013/05/hamas-qatar-arab-peace-initiative.html, May 7, 2013; and Ron Kampeas, "Why Qatar? Why Now? And What About Hamas?" *Haaretz*, www.haaretz.com/news/middle-east/oil-rich-qatar-pushing-to-make-its-name-as-a-mideast-peace-broker-1.519935, May 10, 2013.

47. For a detailed discussion see Sara Roy, "Introduction--De-development Completed: Making Gaza Unviable," in Sara Roy, *The Gaza Strip: The Political Economy of De-development*, Third Edition (Washington, DC: Institute for Palestine Studies, 2013, Forthcoming). Parts of this section are drawn from this Introduction.

48. Joel Beinin, "The Israeli-Palestinian Conflict and the Arab Awakening," *Middle East Research and Information Project*, www.merip.org/mero/mero080111, August 1, 2011.

49. "Hamas on the defensive," *The Economist*, March 9, 2013, writes with regard to the Sinai, "Hamas's security forces have begun acting on Israeli intelligence passed via Egypt about wayward militants planning attacks, say Western officials."

50. ICG (August 14, 2012), p. 38, fn. 283.

51. Ben David (May 3, 2013). Also see "Senior Hamas officials denied entry to Egypt," Ma'an News Agency, www.maannews.net/eng/ViewDetails.aspx?ID=592382, May 10, 2013.

52. Security in the Sinai, itself often related to the tunnel trade, is another key area of concern between Hamas and Egypt with security chiefs from both meeting on a regular basis to deal with increasing violations.

53. Nicolas Pelham, "Gaza's Tunnel Phenomenon: The Unintended Dynamics of Israel's Siege," *Journal of Palestine Studies*, Volume XLI, no. 4 (Summer 2012), p. 21.

54. "Frustrated Hamas seeks light at the end of Egyptian tunnel," Reuters, ca.reuters.com/article/newsOne/idCABRE87C0IC20120813, August 13, 2012.

55. ICG (November 22, 2012), p. 16; Omar Shaban, *Hamas and Morsi: Not So Easy Between Brothers*, Carnegie Middle East Center, Carnegie Endowment for International Peace, carnegie-mec.org/2012/10/01/hamas-and-morsi-not-so-easy-between-brothers/f0z6, October 1, 2012; Reuters (August 13, 2012); and "Hamas to close tunnels if Egypt will open border," *The Jerusalem Post*, www.jpost.com/Middle-East/Hamas-Will-close-tunnels-if-Egypt-opens-crossing-313892, May 21, 2013.

56. Shaban (October 1, 2012). According to QIZEGYPT, www.qizegypt.gov.eg/About_QIZ.aspx, "Qualifying Industrial Zones (QIZ) are designated geographic areas, within Egypt, that enjoy a duty free status with the United States. Companies located within such zones are granted duty free access to the US markets, provided that they satisfy the agreed upon Israeli component, as per the predefined rules of origin." For a discussion of the domestic constraints on Morsi in this regard see ICG (November 22, 2012), pp. 12–17.

57. Ibid; and "A building boom," *The Economist*, August 18, 2012.

58. Ibid, Shaban. Israel, too, has arguably abrogated the AMA.

59. ICG (August 14, 2012), p. 36, fn. 269. Also see ICG (November 22, 2012), p. 15.

60. GISHA, *Movement of people through Rafah crossing* (Tel Aviv: Legal Center for Freedom of Movement, 2013), www.gisha.org/graph.asp?lang_id=en&p_id=1235.

61. ICG (August 14, 2012), pp. 33–34.

62. "Egypt lets building materials cross its border into Gaza," Reuters, www.reuters.com/article/2012/12/29/us-israel-palestinians-egypt-rafah-idUS-BRE8BS08V20121229, December 29, 2012.

63. In response to the kidnapping Hamas increased patrols at the border, closing all tunnels except those used for building materials and gasoline, in order to prevent the smuggling of the hostages into Gaza. Elhanan Miller, "Hamas shuts tunnels to keep kidnappers from sneaking in," *The Times of Israel*, www.timesofisrael.com/hamas-shuts-tunnels-to-keep-kidnappers-from-sneaking-in, May 21, 2013.

64. "Building material skyrockets as Egypt targets Gaza tunnels," Ma'an News Agency, www.maannews.net/eng/ViewDetails.aspx?ID=570635, March 2, 2013; and *The Economist* (March 9, 2013).

65. *The Economist* (March 9, 2013). One Egyptian military official involved with the flooding of the tunnels stated that "large quantities of goods" such as steel, cement, flour, sugar, fruit and computers were also confiscated. See Ibrahim Barzak, "Hamas Accuses Egypt of flooding Gaza tunnels," *Associated Press*, news.yahoo.com/hamas-accuses-egypt-flooding-gaza-tunnels-132142173.html, February 19, 2013. Barzak states that 250 tunnels are operational employing 2,000 people.

66. Ben David (May 3, 2013).

67. Ma'an News Agency (March 2, 2013).

68. *The Economist* (March 9, 2013).

69. Email correspondence, September 2012.

70. ICG (August 14, 2012), p. 36, fn. 271.

71. See Nicolas Pelham, *Sinai: The Buffer Erodes*, Chatham House, London, September 2012; and Nicolas Pelham, "In Sinai: The Uprising of the Bedouin," *The New York Review of Books*, December 6, 2012.

72. Email correspondence, March 2013.

73. "Egypt: Missiles on Eilat launched near border," *Ynetnews.com*, www.ynetnews.com/articles/0,7340,L-4369274,00.html, April 18, 2013; and "IDF source: Hamas working to stop Gaza rockets," *Jerusalem Post*, www.jpost.com/LandedPages/PrintArticle.aspx?id=311977, May 3, 2013.

74. Ben David (May 3, 2013).

75. Ibid.

76. Email correspondence, January 2013. Also see Talal Awkal, "Gaza Rally for Fatah Unites Palestinians," *Al-Monitor*, www.al-monitor.com/pulse/politics/2013/01/gaza-rally-for-fatahs-birthday-unites-palestinians.html, January 8, 2013.

77. Amira Hass, "Who has a tighter iron fist, Hamas or Israel? It's hard to tell," *Haaretz*, www.haaretz.com/news/features/who-has-a-tighter-iron-fist-hamas-or

-israel-it-s-hard-to-tell.premium-1.476889, November 12, 2012. Hass further indicated that "the day after the demonstration, the Hamas government issued an apology and promised that the Interior Ministry would appoint a committee to investigate . . ."; and "Hamas apologizes after police beat female activists," Ma'an News Agency, maannews.net/eng/Print.aspx?ID=534706, November 8, 2012. Also see Human Rights Watch, "Gaza: Stop Suppressing Peaceful Protests," www.hrw.org/news/2011/03/19/gaza-stop-suppressing-peaceful-protests, March 19, 2011.

78. Email correspondence, January 2013.

79. *Jerusalem Post* (May 3, 2013). Also see David Barnett, "Hamas and Salafi jihadists at odds over rocket fire from Gaza into Israel," *The Long War Journal*, www.longwarjournal.org/threat-matrix/archives/2013/05/hamas_and_salafi_jihadists_at.php, May 11, 2913.

80. "Hamas police break up anti-Israel protest," *YNET news.com*, www.ynetnews.com/articles/0,7340,L-4377455,00.html, May 7, 2013; and Khaled Abu Toameh, "Hamas confiscates rockets from Fatah's armed wing," *The Jerusalem Post*, www.jpost.com/Middle-East/Hamas-confiscates-rockets-from-Fatahs-armed-wing-313627, May 19, 2013.

81. Ben David (May 3, 2013).

82. See ICG (August 14, 2012), p. 21, fn. 166; and Sara Roy, "Reconfiguring Palestine: A Way Forward?" in Antony Loewenstein and Ahmed Moor (eds.), *After Zionism: One State for Israel and Palestine* (London: Saqi Books, 2012), p. 53.

83. Telephone correspondence, March 2013.

84. Abeer Ayyoub, "Hamas segregates Gaza schools by gender," *Al Jazeera*, m.aljazeera.com/story/20134711112489892, April 11, 2013; Reuters, "Hamas law promotes gender segregation in Gaza schools," www.reuters.com/article/2013/04/01/us-palestinians-hamas-schools-idUSBRE93009920130401, April 1, 2013; "Hamas ban on Western garments, hair styles criticized in Gaza," *Xinhua*, english.peopledaily.com.cn/90777/8196453.html, April 7, 2013; and Hugh Naylor, "Human rights groups attack Hamas for head-shaving incidents," *The National*, www.thenational.ae/news/world/middle-east/human-rights-groups-attack-hamas-for-head-shaving-incidents, May 5, 2013. Some of these incidents may be political, directed at people with Fatah affiliations or who publicly criticize the authorities. See Lena Odgaard, "Gaza Rappers Persevere Despite Hamas Ban," *Al-Monitor*, www.al-monitor.com/pulse/originals/2013/05/gaza-rapper-hamas-youth-islamization.html, May 21, 2013.

85. Fares Akram, "Gaza Marathon Canceled After Women Are Barred From Participating," *New York Times*, www.nytimes.com/2013/03/06/world/middleeast/gaza-marathon-canceled-after-women-are-barred-from-participating.html?_r=0, March 5, 2013; Elior Levy, "Radicalization in Gaza: Female students required to wear Muslim garb," *YNetnews.com*, www.ynetnews.com/articles/0,7340,L-4341398,00.html, May 2, 2013; and Abeer Ayoub, "Hamas Pushes Islamization of Gaza," *Al-Monitor*, www.al-monitor.com/pulse/originals/2013/02/hamas-islamization-gaza.html, February 4, 2013. A related issue is Asmaa al-Ghoul, "Gaza's Academics Face Censorship in Classroom," *Al-Monitor*, www.

al-monitor.com/pulse/originals/2013/04/gaza-academics-universities-increasing-restrictions.html, April 23, 2013. Also of relevance is David D. Kirkpatrick and Mayy El-Sheikh, "Muslim Brotherhood's Statement on Women Stirs Liberals' Fears," *New York Times*, March 15, 2013.

86. The World Bank, *Coping with Conflict: Poverty and Inclusion in the West Bank and Gaza* (Gaza and Washington: The World Bank Group, 2011), p. 1.

87. For a detailed discussion of this fact and the Gaza Strip economy generally, see Roy (2013, Forthcoming).

88. Office of the United Nations Special Coordinator for the Middle East Peace Process (UNSCO), *Gaza in 2020: A liveable place? A report by the United Nations Country Team in the occupied Palestinian territory*, Jerusalem, August 2012, p. 2.

89. The World Bank, *Towards Economic Sustainability of a Future Palestinian State: Promoting Private Sector-Led Growth (West Bank and Gaza)*, April 2012, p. 87.

90. The World Bank, *Fiscal Crisis, Economic Prospects: The Imperative for Economic Cohesion in the Palestinian Territories, Economic Monitoring Report to the Ad Hoc Liaison Committee*, Washington, DC, September 23, 2012, p. 11.

91. UNSCO (August 2012), pp. 8–9.

92. Ibid, p. 9.

93. Michael R. Gordon and Jodi Rudoren, "Trying to Revive Mideast Talks, Kerry Pushes Investment Plan for West Bank," *New York Times*, May 27, 2013.

EPILOGUE

THE COUP AGAINST THE ISLAMIST GOVERNMENT IN EGYPT—EMERGING NEW DYNAMICS AND THEIR IMPLICATIONS FOR HAMAS

1. Asmaa Al-Ghoul, "Tamarod Comes to Palestine," *Al-Monitor*, July 11, 2013, http://www.al-monitor.com/pulse/originals/2013/07/hamas-tamarod-palestine-gaza-egypt.html.

2. The exact amount of Iranian funding allocated to, and withdrawn from, Hamas is difficult to determine with any accuracy.

3. Daoud Kuttab, "Hamas, First Victim of Egypt Revolt," *Al-Monitor*, July 3, 2013, http://www.al-monitor.com/pulse/originals/2013/07/hamas-egypt-morsi-june30-muslim-brotherhood.html.

4. Dahlia Kholaif, "Morsi's downfall hammers Hamas," *Al Jazeera*, July 10, 2013, http://www.aljazeera.com/indepth/features/2013/07/2013710113757741999.html; and Shlomi Eldar, "Hamas Isolated After Coup in Egypt," *Al-Monitor*, July 4, 2013, http://www.al-monitor.com/pulse/fa/contents/articles/opinion/2013/07/fall-egyptian-brotherhood-trouble-hamas.html.

5. Kuttab (July 3, 2013).

6. "Foreign groups implicated in Morsi jailbreak," *Al Jazeera*, June 23, 2013, http://www.aljazeera.com/news/africa/2013/06/201362310172950482.html. Also see, Osama Al Sharif, "How Hamas Lost Egypt," *The Jordan Times*, July 16, 2013, http://jordantimes.com/how-hamas-lost-egypt.

7. Khaled Abu Toameh, "Hamas: Fatah, PA responsible for Gaza media campaign against Islam," *The Jerusalem Post*, July 30, 2013, http://www.jpost.com/Breaking-News/Hamas-Fatah-PA-responsible-for-Gaza-media-campaign-against-Islam-321545.

8. Roy Greenslade, "Hamas orders closure of Gaza media outlets," *Greenslade Blog, The Guardian*, July 29, 2013, http://www.theguardian.com/media/greenslade/2013/jul/29/hamas-gaza.

9. Roi Kais, "Egyptians protest against Hamas," *Ynetnews.com*, June 19, 2013, http://www.ynetnews.com/articles/0,7340,L-4394514,00.html; and Haidar Eid, "Why is the Egyptian Regime Demonizing Palestinians?" *Al Shabaka*, August 2013, http://al-shabaka.org/node/638.

10. Asmaa Al-Ghoul, "Is Egypt Media Inciting Hatred Against Palestinians?" *Al-Monitor*, July 17, 2013, http://www.al-monitor.com/pulse/originals/2013/07/egypt-media-incitement-palestinians.html.

11. El-Sayed Gamaledine, "Updated: Egypt court orders Morsi detention over Hamas collaboration," *Ahram Online*, July 26, 2013, http://english.ahram.org.eg/News/77419.aspx; Samer Al-Atrush, "Mass demos across Egypt after Morsi detained," Agence France Presse, July 26, 2013, http://www.google.com/hostednews/afp/article/ALeqM5hDplXvWXE2l4bNGYl7aSJduYCKcA?hl=en&docId=CNG.4b1ca761fbb484a4817129ebb819c9b7.531; and Agence France Presse, "Hamas denounces Egypt over Morsi detention as clashes break out in Cairo," *Hurriyet Daily News*, August 5, 2013, http://www.hurriyetdailynews.com/hamas-denounces-egypt-over-morsi-detention-as-clashes-break-out-in-cairo-.aspx?pageID=238&nid=51450.

12. Ibrahim Barzak, "Egyptian turmoil jolts Gaza's Hamas rulers," *The Daily Star*, July 6, 2013, http://www.dailystar.com.lb/News/Middle-East/2013/Jul-06/222715-egyptian-turmoil-jolts-gazas-hamas-rulers.ashx#axzz2b2OmCRBv.

13. Kholaif (July 10, 2013).

14. Mohamed Fadel Fahmy, "The Jihadist Threat in Egypt's Sinai," *Al-Monitor*, July 22, 2013, http://www.al-monitor.com/pulse/originals/2013/07/jihad-threat-egypt-sinai.html.

15. "Report: 30,000 Egyptian troops in Sinai," *Ynetnews.com*, July 19, 2013, http://www.ynetnews.com/articles/0,7340,L-4407144,00.html.

16. Mohamed Fadel Fahmy (July 22, 2013). In fact many of these Jihadist groups "blamed Morsi for being too soft on his commitment to the project for an Islamic Egypt based on strict Sharia."

17. Jack Khoury, "Egyptian army killed dozens of Hamas fighters in Sinai, report says," *Haaretz*, July 11, 2013, http://www.haaretz.com/news/middle-east/1.535170. Israel must give Egypt permission to operate militarily in the Sinai.

18. Adiv Sterman and Lazar Berman, "Egyptian military launches major Sinai offensive," *The Times of Israel*, July 27, 2013, http://www.timesofisrael.com/egyptian-military-launches-major-sinai-offensive. Other reports place the number at 1,000.

19. The Israeli Air Force maintains constant surveillance over the Strip. Ibrahim Barzak and Mohammed Daraghmeh, "Egypt imposes toughest Gaza restrictions

in Years," *ABC News*, July 24, 2013, http://abcnews.go.com/International/wireStory/egypt-imposes-toughest-gaza-restrictions-years-19763258 and http://www.npr.org/templates/story/story.php?storyId=205210779; "Egyptian attack helicopter flies over Gaza for first time since 1967," *World Tribune.com*, July 14, 2013, http://www.worldtribune.com/2013/07/14/egyptian-attack-helicopter-flies-over-gaza-for-first-time-since-1967; Chana Ya'ar, "First Time Since 6-Day War: Egypt Helicopter Over Gaza," *Arutz Sheva*, July 17, 2013, http://www.israelnationalnews.com/News/News.aspx/170001#.UgE6t-DKSf4; Khaled Abu Toameh, "Hamas: Egypt trying to restore rule over Gaza," *The Jerusalem Post*, July 23, 2013, http://www.jpost.com/Middle-East/Hamas-Egypt-is-trying-to-restore-sovereignty-over-Gaza-320825; and "Hamas welcomes Iran's approach to restore ties: official," *Global Times*, July 25, 2013, http://www.globaltimes.cn/content/798980.shtml#.UgE4CeDKSf4.

20. "Egyptian officials: Israeli drone strike kills 5 Islamic militants in Sinai Peninsula, *The Washington Post*, August 9, 2013, http://www.washingtonpost.com/world/middle_east/egyptian-officials-israeli-drone-strike-kills-5-suspected-islamic-jihadists-inside-egypt/2013/08/09/d2fd7bb0-0109-11e3-8294-0ee5075b840d_story.html.

21. "Israeli ambassador calls Al-Sisi a "national hero for all Jews," *Middle East Monitor*, July 19, 2013, http://www.middleeastmonitor.com/news/middle-east/6617-israeli-ambassador-calls-al-sisi-a-qnational-hero-for-all-jewsq.

22. For an example of this position see, Jonathan Schanzer, "Strangling Hamas," *ForeignPolicy.com*, July 22, 2013, http://www.foreignpolicy.com/articles/2013/07/22/strangling_hamas_palestine_gaza_islamists. In response see Benedetta Berti, "Hurting Hamas helps it," *ForeignPolicy.com*, July 26, 2013, http://mideast.foreignpolicy.com/posts/2013/07/26/hurting_hamas_helps_it.

23. Harriet Sherwood and Hazem Balousha, "Palestinians in Gaza feel the Egypt effect as smuggling tunnels close," *The Guardian*, July 19, 2013, http://www.theguardian.com/world/2013/jul/19/palestinians-gaza-city-smuggling-tunnels.

24. Geoffrey Aronson, "Egyptian Crisis Reduces Friction Between Israel and Hamas," *Al-Monitor*, August 2, 2013, http://www.al-monitor.com/pulse/originals/2013/08/egyptian-crisis-reduces-friction-between-israel-and-hamas.html.

25. Barzak and Daraghmeh (July 24, 2013).

26. Ibid; and "Egypt's new rulers virtually seal Gaza as part of campaign against the Muslim Brotherhood," *The Washington Post*, July 24, 2013. Also see "Hamas official lambasts new Egyptian regime," *The Daily Star*, July 14, 2013, http://www.dailystar.com.lb/News/Middle-East/2013/Jul-14/223628-hamas-leader-lambasts-new-egyptian-regime.ashx#axzz2b2OmCRBv.

27. Ibid, Barzak and Daraghmeh.

28. Aronson (August 2, 2013).

29. Sherwood and Balousha (July 19, 2013).

30. Fares Akram, "Gaza's Economy Suffers From Egyptian Military's Crackdown," *The New York Times*, July 24, 2013, http://www.nytimes.com/2013/07/25/world/middleeast/gazas-economy-suffers-from-egyptian-crackdown.html?_r=0; and Amira Hass, "Egypt crisis sets off economic and humanitarian Gaza chain reaction," *Haaretz*, July 9, 2013, http://www.haaretz.com/news/middle-east/.premium-1.534853.

31. Sherwood and Baloushsa (July 19, 2013).

32. Asmaa al-Ghoul, "Fuel Crisis Threatens Gaza After Egypt Border Closure," *Al-Monitor*, July 8, 2013, http://www.al-monitor.com/pulse/originals/2013/07/gaza-fuel-crisis-egypt-unrest.html.

33. Aronson (August 2, 2013).

34. Akram (July 24, 2013).

35. Barzak and Daraghmeh (July 24, 2013); and "Hamas warns of a 'humanitarian crisis' if Rafah crossing to Gaza is not re-opened," *Ahram Online*, August 1, 2013, http://english.ahram.org.eg/News/77971.aspx. As of this writing, the PLO has not responded to the pressures imposed on Gaza by the Egyptian authorities.

36. Kholaif (July 10, 2013). Haidar Eid (August 2013) writes, "[Former Egyptian Foreign Minister Ahmed] Aboul Gheit went so far as to threaten to break the legs of the Palestinians of Gaza if they 'encroached on Egypt's national security' after they breached the border wall with Egypt, seeking to buy medicines and other necessary supplies in Al-Arish City."

37. Harriet Sherwood et al, "Egypt's upheaval makes waves across region," *The Guardian*, July 12, 2013, http://www.theguardian.com/world/2013/jul/12/egypt-upheaval-region-mohamed-morsi?CMP=twt_gu.

38. Khaled Abu Toameh, "Fatah calls on Palestinians to overthrow Hamas in wake of Morsi's fall," *The Jerusalem Post*, July 4, 2013, http://www.jpost.com/Middle-East/Fatah-calls-on-Palestinians-to-overthrow-Hamas-in-wake-of-Morsis-fall-318792.

39. Naela Khalil, "Fatah Official Urges Hamas to Abandon Muslim Brotherhood," *Al-Monitor*, July 11, 2013, http://www.al-monitor.com/pulse/originals/2013/07/fatah-hamas-muslim-brotherhood-egypt.html.

40. "Hamas shames Fatah on demonization of Palestinians in Egypt," *Middle East Monitor*, July 31, 2013, http://www.middleeastmonitor.com/news/middle-east/6738-hamas-shames-fatah-on-demonisation-of-palestinians-in-egypt.

41. "Fatah leader colluded with Egyptian media against Hamas," *Middle East Monitor*, July 29, 2013, http://www.middleeastmonitor.com/news/africa/6712-fatah-leader-colluded-with-egyptian-media-against-hamas; and "Hamas: Docs expose Fatah campaign in Egypt," Ma'an News Agency, July 31, 2013, http://www.maannews.net/eng/ViewDetails.aspx?ID=618095.

42. Sherwood et al (July 12, 2013).

43. Shlomi Eldar, "Exclusive: Zahar Rebuilds Ties Between Hamas and Iran," *Al-Monitor*, July 15, 2013, http://www.al-monitor.com/pulse/fa/contents/articles/opinion/2013/07/al-zahar-ties-hamas-iran.html.

44. Ibid.

45. Khalil (July 11, 2013).

46. Aronson (August 2, 2013).

47. Ibid.

48. Al Sharif (July 16, 2013).

49. Reuters, "Hamas Badly Shaken by Egypt Coup," *The Jewish Daily Forward*, July 8, 2013, http://forward.com/articles/180038/hamas-badly-shaken-by-egypt-coup/?p=all.

50. Agence France Presse, "Morsi Ouster in Egypt crushes Hamas dreams: analysts," *Foxnews.com*, July 6, 2013, http://www.foxnews.com/world/2013/07/06/morsi-ouster-in-egypt-crushes-hamas-dreams-analysts; and "Hamas insists relations with Cairo remain intact," *Middle East Monitor*, July 25, 2013, http://www.middleeastmonitor.com/news/africa/6674-hamas-insists-relations-with-cairo-remain-in-tact.

51. "Fortunes in flux," *The Daily Star*, August 3, 2013, http://www.dailystar.com.lb/Opinion/Editorial/2013/Aug-03/226088-fortunes-in-flux.ashx#axzz2b2OmCRBv.

52. "Hamas rekindles ties with Iran and Hezbollah," *Al Bawaba English*, July 30, 2013, http://www.albawaba.com/news/hamas-rekindles-ties-iran-and-hezbollah-510488. Also see "Report: Hamas, Iran secretly met in Beirut to talk truce," *The Jerusalem Post*, July 28, 2013, http://www.jpost.com/Diplomacy-and-Politics/Report-Hamas-Iran-secretly-met-in-Beirut-to-talk-truce-321260.

53. Ibid, *Al Bawaba English*. Also see Kareem Shaheen, "Hamas will adjust to Egypt, retain Hezbollah ties," *The Daily Star*, July 20, 2013, http://www.dailystar.com.lb/News/Politics/2013/Jul-20/224371-hamas-will-adjust-to-egypt-retain-hezbollah-ties.ashx#axzz2b2OmCRBv.

54. Fares Akram, "In Gaza, Iran finds an Ally More Agreeable Than Hamas," *The New York Times*, July 31, 2013, http://www.nytimes.com/2013/08/01/world/middleeast/in-gaza-iran-finds-a-closer-ally-than-hamas.html?_r=0.

55. Ibid.

56. Paul Schemm, "Egypt: Military's Overthrow of Mohammed Morsi Shakes Islamists in the Region," *Huffington Post/World*, July 7, 2013, http://www.huffingtonpost.com/2013/07/07/egypt-islamists_n_3558853.html, who further writes, citing a Jihadist website: "Secularism has shown its ugly face to those who were blind, and the mask of democracy has fallen in the struggle between right and wrong," said Sheik Zahran Alloush, a commander of the Islam Brigade. "As the mujahedeen leaders say, we chose ammunition boxes over ballot boxes." Also see Jeffrey D. Sachs, "Bring Back Egypt's Elected Government," *Project Syndicate*, July 15, 2013, http://www.project-syndicate.org/commentary/democracy-in-egypt-requires-reinstating-mohamed-morsi-by-jeffrey-d--sachs.

57. Patrick Kingsley, "At least 120 Morsi supporters reported killed in Egypt clashes," *The Guardian*, July 27, 2013, http://www.theguardian.com/world/2013/jul/27/morsi-supporters-killed-egypt-cairo. Also see Eric Schmitt, "White House Muted in Response to New Mass Killing of Egyptian Protesters," *The New York Times*, July 29, 2013.

58. Robert F. Worth, "Egyptian Islamists Sit In, Seethe, Preach and Wait," *The New York Times*, July 29, 2013. He quotes another protester echoing the same sentiment: "What is strange is that we followed the democratic game very well. We joined the elections, we did what they wanted us to. Then we're faced with military force... Game over."

59. Abigail Hauslohner, "Egyptian security forces storm protesters' camps," *The Washington Post*, August 14, 2013, http://www.washingtonpost.com/world/egyptian-security-forces-move-against-protesters-camps/2013/08/14/bc079750-04a7-11e3-9259-e2aafe5a5f84_story.html.

60. Mark Landler and Michael R. Gordon, "U.S. Condemns Crackdown but Announces No Policy Shift," *The New York Times*, August 15, 2013.

61. David D. Kirkpatrick, "Hundreds of Egyptians Killed in Government Raids; Emergency Declared as Sectarian Violence Spreads," *The New York Times*, August 15, 2013.

62. Schemm (July 7, 2013).

63. Ibid.

SELECTED BIBLIOGRAPHY

"Abbas to Alter Voting Laws to Exclude Hamas." *International Middle East Media Center*, July 27, 2007.

Abdel-Shafi, Sami. "We Are Being Suffocated." *The Guardian*, February 10, 2007.

Abed-Kotob, Sana. "The Accommodationists Speak: Goals and Strategies of the Muslim Brotherhood in Egypt." *International Journal of Middle East Studies* 27, 1995.

Abu-Amr, Ziad. "Hamas: A Historical and Political Background." *Journal of Palestine Studies* 22, Summer 1993.

Abu-Amr, Ziad. *Islamic Fundamentalism in the West Bank and Gaza: Muslim Brotherhood and Islamic Jihad*. Bloomington: Indiana University Press, 1994.

Abu-Amr, Ziad. "Shaykh Ahmad Yasin and the Origins of Hamas," in R. Scott Appleby, ed., *Spokesmen for the Despised: Fundamentalist Leaders of the Middle East*. Chicago: University of Chicago Press, 1997.

Abu Manneh, Bashir. "In Palestine, a Dream Deferred." *The Nation*, December 18, 2006.

"Abu Marzouk: Israel Allowed PA Security Plan to Finish What It Failed to Do." The Palestinian Information Center, October 28, 2008.

Abu Toameh, Khaled. "PA to Purge Hamas-Controlled Councils." *The Jerusalem Post*, December 3, 2008.

Abu Zayd, Karen. "Palestine Refugees: Exile, Isolation and Prospects." Edward Said Lecture, Princeton University, May 6, 2008.

Abunimah, Ali. "Shifting Attitudes toward Hamas." Palestine Center Information Brief 160. Washington, DC: Palestine Center, March 11, 2008.

Abunimah, Ali. "Hamas, the I.R.A. and Us." *New York Times*, August 29, 2010.

Affendi, Abdelwahab El-. "Rationality of Politics and Politics of Rationality: Democratisation and the Influence of Islamic Religious Traditions," in John L. Esposito and Azzam Tamimi, eds., *Islam and Secularism in the Middle East*. New York: New York University Press, 2000.

Afifeh, Wisam. "Has Hamas Succeeded in Combining Government with Resistance?" *Filasteen Al Muslima* 28, no. 1, January 2010.

Agence France Presse. "Fatah Shuts Down West Bank Charity Linked to Hamas." *The Daily Star*, August 21, 2008.

Ahmad, Hisham. *Hamas: From Religious Salvation to Political Transformation—the Rise of Hamas in Palestinian Society*. Jerusalem: Palestinian Academic Society for the Study of International Affairs, 1994.

Alexander, Justin. "Conflict, Closure and Human Security in Gaza." Oxford Research Group, Consultative draft, July 22, 2007.

Almeghari, Rami. "Haniya of Hamas: The Tahdiya Did Not Serve Palestinians." International Middle East Media Center, December 14, 2008.

Alonso, Carmen Lopez. *Hamas: La Marcha Hacia El Poder*. Madrid: Catarata, 2007.

Alterman, Jon B., and Karin von Hippel, eds. *Understanding Islamic Charities.* Washington, DC: Center for Strategic and International Studies Press, 2007.

Amayreh, Khaled. "Israel Attacks Charities, Orphanages." *Al-Ahram Weekly*, August 1, 2008.

American Near East Refugee Aid (ANERA). "The Separation Wall in Jayyous Village." Report submitted to the United States Agency for International Development (USAID). Jerusalem, November 20, 2002.

Anderson, Lisa. *The State and Social Transformation in Tunisia and Libya, 1830–1980.* Princeton, NJ: Princeton University Press, 1986.

Andoni, Lamis. "Deeds Speak Louder Than Words." *The Washington Quarterly*, Spring 2002.

Arkoun, Mohammed. "Religion et societe d'apres l'exemple de l'Islam." *Studia Islamica 55*, 1982.

Aw[w]a, Muhammad Salim el-. *On the Political System of the Islamic State.* Indianapolis: American Trust Publications, 1980.

Ayubi, Nazih. *Political Islam: Religion and Politics in the Arab World.* London: Routledge, 2004.

Baker, Raymond. *Islam without Fear: Egypt and the New Islamists.* Cambridge, MA: Harvard University Press, 2003.

Barghouti, Iyad. "Islamist Movements in Historical Palestine," in Abdel Salam Sidahmed and Anoushiravan Ehteshami, eds., *Islamic Fundamentalism.* Boulder, CO: Westview Press, 1996.

Barnea, Nahum. "Talking to Palestinians." Translated from the original Hebrew. *Yedioth Ahronoth*, September 19, 2008.

Baumgarten, Helga. *Hamas: From the Palestinian Resistance into the Government.* Munich: Diederichs, 2006.

Baumgarten, Helga. "Hamas and the Challenge of Democratic Transformation in Palestine." Lecture. The Middle East Seminar, Harvard University, October 4, 2007.

Beinin, Joel, and Joe Stork, eds. *Political Islam: Essays from Middle East Report.* London: I. B. Tauris, 1997.

Bennet, James. "Palestinians in Nablus Fed Up with Crime Posing as Jihad." *New York Times*, July 19, 2003.

Ben-Simhon, Kobi. "Israel Could Have Made Peace with Hamas under Yassin." *Ha'aretz*, April 18, 2009.

Benthall, Jonathan. "The Overreaction against Islamic Charities." *ISIM Bulletin.* Leiden: Institute for the Study of Islam in the Modern World, Autumn 2007.

Beraumont, Peter, and Mitchell Prothero. "How Hamas Turned on Palestine's 'Traitors.'" *The Observer*, June 17, 2007.

Beres, Louis Rene. "On Hamas 'Freedom Fighters': The View from International Law." *Midstream 50*, January 2004.

Berkey, Jonathan P. *The Formation of Islam: Religion and Society in the Near East, 600–1800.* Cambridge: Cambridge University Press, 2003.

Binder, Leonard. *Islamic Liberalism: A Critique of Development Ideologies.* Chicago: Chicago University Press, 1988.

"Blame Arafat: The Struggle for Palestinian Power." *Jane's Foreign Report*, February 18, 2004.

Board of Directors, Sharek Youth Forum. "Sharek Youth Forum in Palestine Condemns the Assault against Civil Society Organizations and the Assault on Its Main Office in the Gaza Strip by Masked Militants Claiming to Be from the Ezzedine Al-Qassam Brigades." Gaza, July 30, 2008.

Bocco, Riccardo, Matthias Brunner, Isabelle Daneels, Jalal Husseini, Frederic Lapeyre, and Jamil Rabah. *Palestinian Public Perceptions on Their Living Conditions*. Report 6. Geneva: Graduate Institute of Development Studies, University of Geneva, October 2003.

Brooke, James, and Elaine Sciolino. "U.S. Muslims Say Their Aid Pays for Charity, Not Terror—Bread or Bullets: Money for Hamas." *New York Times*, August 16, 1995.

Browers, Michaelle. *Democracy and Civil Society in Arab Political Thought: Transcultural Possibilities*. Syracuse, NY: Syracuse University Press, 2006.

Brown, Nathan J. *Palestinian Politics after the Oslo Accords: Resuming Arab Palestine*. Berkeley: University of California Press, 2003.

Brown, Nathan J. "Hamas in Power." Carnegie Endowment for International Peace, April 13, 2006.

Brown, Nathan J. "The Green Elephant in the Room: Dealing with the Hamas Party-State in Gaza." *Web Commentary*. Carnegie Endowment for International Peace. June 2009.

Brown, Nathan J. "Palestine: The Schism Deepens." *Web Commentary*. Carnegie Endowment for International Peace. August 2009.

Buck, Tobias. "Attacks Devastate Basic Infrastructure." *Financial Times*, January 9, 2009.

Burgat, Francois. *Face to Face with Political Islam*. London: I. B. Tauris, 2003.

Cahen, Claude. "Reflexions sur le waqf ancien." *Studia Islamica* 14, 1961.

Camus, Albert. *Resistance, Rebellion and Death*. New York: Knopf, 1960.

Carapico, Sheila. *Civil Society in Yemen: The Political Economy of Activism in Modern Arabia*. Cambridge: Cambridge University Press, 1998.

CARE. "Gaza Strip Faces a Distinct Humanitarian Emergency." *Report*, January 3, 2003.

Challand, Benoit. "A *Nahda* of Charitable Organizations? Health Service Provision and the Politics of Aid in Palestine." *International Journal of Middle East Studies* 40, May 2008.

Chehab, Zaki. *Inside Hamas: The Untold Story of the Militant Islamic Movement*. New York: Nation Books, 2007.

Chomsky, Noam. "'Exterminate All the Brutes': Gaza 2009." Chomsky.info, January 19, 2009.

Christian Peacemaker Teams—Hebron. "International NGOs Rally to Rescue Hebron Orphans." Press release, May 10, 2008, http://www.hebronorphans.blogspot.org.

Christison, Kathleen. "Thoughts on the Attempted Murder of Palestine: The Siren Song of Elliot Abrams." *Counterpunch*, July 26, 2007, www.counterpunch.org/christison07262007.html.

Clark, Janine A. *Islam, Charity, and Activism: Middle Class Networks and Social Welfare in Egypt, Jordan and Yemen*. Bloomington: Indiana University Press, 2004.

Cohen, Amit. "Break the Taboo and Talk." *Ma'ariv*, February 29, 2008 (Hebrew print edition, translation by Israel News Today).

Cohen, Yoram. "Jihadist Groups in Gaza: A Developing Threat." Policy Watch no. 1449. Washington, DC: Washington Institute for Near East Policy, January 5, 2009.

Cohen, Yoram, Matthew Levitt, and Becca Wasser. "Deterred but Determined: Salafi-Jihadi Groups in the Palestinian Arena." Policy Focus no. 99. Washington, DC: Washington Institute for Near East Policy, January 2010.

"Comprehensive List of Terrorists and Groups Identified under Executive Order 13224." www.state.gov/s/ct/rls/fs/2002/12327.htm.

Conflicts Forum. "Elliot Abrams' Uncivil War." *Conflicts Forum Reports*, January 7, 2007.

Cook, Michael. *Commanding Right and Forbidding Wrong in Islamic Thought*. Cambridge: Cambridge University Press, 2000.

Cooke, Miriam, and Bruce B. Lawrence, eds. *Muslim Networks: From Hajj to Hip Hop*. Chapel Hill: University of North Carolina Press, 2005.

Council on Foreign Relations. *Hamas*. January 7, 2009, www.cfr.org/publication/8968.

Crenshaw, Martha. "The Causes of Terrorism." *Comparative Politics* 13, July 1981.

Crenshaw, Martha. "Thoughts on Relating Terrorism to Historical Contexts," in Martha Crenshaw, ed., *Terrorism in Context*. University Park: Pennsylvania State University, 1995.

Croitoru, Joseph. *Hamas: Der Islamische Kampf um Palastina* [Hamas: The Islamic Struggle for Palestine]. Munich: C. H. Beck, 2007.

Crooke, Alistair. "The Rise of Hamas: Hamas and Fatah Radicals Will Transform Palestinian Politics." *Prospect*, February 2006.

Crooke, Alistair. "Our Second Biggest Mistake in the Middle East." *London Review of Books* 29, July 5, 2007.

de Soto, Alvaro. *End of Mission Report*. United Nations, May 2007.

Deeb, Lara. *An Enchanted Modern: Gender and Public Piety in Shi'i Lebanon*. Princeton, NJ: Princeton University Press, 2006.

Della Porta, Donatella, ed. *Social Movements and Violence: Participation in Underground Organizations*. London: JAI Press, 1992.

Diamond, Larry. "Rethinking Civil Society: Toward Democratic Consolidation." *Journal of Democracy* 5, July 1994.

Diani, Mario. "The Concept of Social Movement." *Sociological Review* 40, February 1992.

Eickelman, Dale, and James Piscatori. *Muslim Politics*. Princeton, NJ: Princeton University Press, 1996.

Ellis, Marc E. *O, Jerusalem: The Contested Future of the Jewish Covenant*. Minneapolis: Fortress Press, 1999.

Entous, Adam. "US-Backed Campaign against Hamas Expands to Charities." Reuters, August 20, 2007, www.alertnet.org/db/crisisprofiles/IP_CON.htm?v=at_a_glance>conflict.

Erlanger, Steven. "West Bank Boys Dig a Living in Settler Trash." *New York Times*, September 2, 2007.

Erlanger, Steven, and Isabel Kershner. "With Pressure Put on Hamas, Gaza Is Cut Off." *New York Times*, July 10, 2007.

Esposito, John, ed. *Voices of Resurgent Islam*. New York: Oxford University Press, 1983.

Espositio, John. *The Islamic Threat: Myth or Reality?* 3rd edition. New York: Oxford University Press, 1999.

Esposito, John L., and James P. Piscatori. "Democratization and Islam." *Middle East Journal* 45, Summer 1991.

Esposito, John L., and John O. Voll. *Makers of Contemporary Islam*. New York: Oxford University Press, 2001.

Euben, Roxanne. *Enemy in the Mirror: Islamic Fundamentalism and the Limits of Modern Rationalism*. Princeton, NJ: Princeton University Press, 1999.

Fafo Institute for Applied International Studies. *Life in the Gaza Strip Six Weeks after the Armed Conflict 27 Dec 2008–17 January 2009: Evidence from a Household Sample Survey—a Summary*. Oslo, Norway, n.d.

Field, Anna. "Hizbollah Admits Full Support for Hamas." *Financial Times*, May 13, 2009.

Finkelstein, Norman G. *Image and Reality of the Israel-Palestine Conflict*. 2nd edition. London: Verso, 2003.

Finkelstein, Norman G. "Seeing Through the Lies: The Facts about Hamas and the War on Gaza." *Counterpunch*, January 13, 2009.

Finkelstein, Norman G. "Foiling Another Palestinian 'Peace Offensive.'" *Counterpunch*, January 28, 2009.

Finkelstein, Norman G. *This Time We Went Too Far: Truth and Consequences of the Gaza Invasion*. New York: OR Books, 2010.

Fishman, Alex. "A Dangerous Liquidation." *Yediot Achronot*, November 25, 2001.

"Former Peace Negotiators Urge World to Engage with Hamas." *Ha'aretz*, February 26, 2009.

Foundation for Middle East Peace. "Sharon Government's Separation Plan Defines Palestine's Provisional Borders." *Report on Israeli Settlement*, July–August 2003.

Francis, David R. "What Aid Cutoff to Hamas Would Mean." *Christian Science Monitor*, February 27, 2006.

Freed, Elizabeth. *Fatah and Hamas Human Rights Violations in the Palestinian Occupied Territories from June 2007 to October 2007*. Palestinian Human Rights Monitoring Group, 2007.

Freund, Wolfgang. *Looking into Hamas and Other Constituents of the Palestinian-Israeli Confrontation*. Frankfurt: Peter Lang, 2002.

Frisch, Hillel. "Has the Israeli-Palestinian Conflict Become Islamic? Fatah, Islam and the al-Aqsa Martyrs' Brigades." *Terrorism and Political Violence* 17, October 2005.

Gaess, Roger. "Interviews from Gaza: What Hamas Wants," *Middle East Policy* 9, December 2002.

Gannouchi, Rachid al-. "Secularism in the Arab Maghreb," in John L. Esposito and Azzam Tamimi, eds., *Islam and Secularism in the Middle East*. New York: New York University Press, 2000.

Giacaman, George. "In the Throes of Oslo: Palestinian Society, Civil Society and the Future," in George Giacaman and Dag Lonning, eds., *After Oslo: New Realities, Old Problems*. London: Pluto Press, 1998.

Gisha: Legal Center for Freedom of Movement. *Commercial Closure: Deleting Gaza's Economy from the Map*. Tel Aviv, July 2007.

Gisha: Legal Center for Freedom of Movement. *Unraveling the Closure of Gaza: What Has and Hasn't Changed since the Cabinet Decision and What Are the Implications?* Tel Aviv, July 7, 2010.

Gordon, Neve. *Occupation*. Berkeley: University of California Press, 2008.

Guazzone, Laura, ed. *The Islamist Dilemma—the Political Role of Islamist Movements in the Contemporary Arab World*. Reading, UK: Ithaca Press, 1995.

Gunning, Jeroen. "Re-Thinking Western Constructs of Islamism: Pluralism, Democracy and the Theory and Praxis of the Islamic Movement in the Gaza Strip." PhD Thesis, Centre for Middle Eastern and Islamic Studies, University of Durham, 2000.

Gunning, Jeroen. "Peace with Hamas? The Transforming Potential of Political Participation." *International Affairs* 80, March 2004.

Gunning, Jeroen. "Terrorism, Charities and Diasporas: Contrasting the Fundraising Practices of Hamas and al Qaeda among Muslims in Europe," in Thomas J. Biersteker and Sue E. Eckert, eds., *Countering the Financing of Terrorism*. London: Routledge, 2008.

Gunning, Jeroen. *Hamas in Politics: Democracy, Religion, Violence*. New York: Columbia University Press, 2008.

Hafez, Mohammed, and Quintan Wiktorowicz. "Violence as Contention in the Egyptian Islamic Movement," in Quintan Wiktorowicz, ed., *Islamic Activism: A Social Movement Theory Approach*. Bloomington: Indiana University Press, 2004.

Halliday, Fred. *Islam and the Myth of Confrontation: Religion and Politics in the Middle East*. London: I. B. Tauris, 1996.

Halper, Jeff. *Israel in Gaza: A Critical Reframing*. Israel Committee against Home Demolitions, January 2009.

"Hamas Arrests the Most Prominent Leader of Salafi Groups in Gaza." *al-Quds al-Arabi* (London), February 11, 2010.

"Hamas Lays Out Truce Conditions." *BBC News*, March 12, 2008.

Hamas Political Bureau. *The Islamic Resistance Movement (Hamas)*, June 2000.

"Hamas Reopens 70 Civil Organizations in Gaza." August 25, 2008, www.chinaview.cn.

"Hamas Seizes Abbas-Run News Agency." *ABC News*, July 27, 2008.

Hammami, Rema. "From Immodesty to Collaboration: Hamas, the Women's Movement, and National Identity in the Intifada," in Joel Beinin and Joe Stork, eds., *Political Islam: Essays from the Middle East*. Berkeley: University of California Press, 1997.

Hammami, Rema. "Palestinian NGOs since Oslo: From NGP Politics to Social Movements?" *Middle East Report* 214, Spring 2000.

Hamzawy, Amr. "Normative Dimensions of Contemporary Arab Debates on Civil Society," in Amr Hamzawy, ed., *Civil Society in the Middle East*. Nahost-Studein 4. Berlin: Verlag Hans Schiler, 2002.

Hamzawy, Amr. "Exploring Theoretical and Programmatic Changes in Contemporary Islamist Discourse: The Journal Al-Manar al-Jadid," in Azza Karam, ed., *Transnational Political Islam: Religion, Ideology and Power*. London: Pluto Press, 2004.
Hansen, Peter. "Hungry in Gaza." *The Guardian*, March 5, 2003.
Harel, Amos. "IDF Probe: Cannot Defend Destruction of Gaza Homes." *Ha'aretz*, February 15, 2009.
Harik, Iliya F. "Pluralism in the Arab World." *Journal of Democracy* 5, July 1994.
Harik, Iliya. "Democratic Thought in the Arab World: An Alternative to the Patron State," in Charles E. Butterworth and I. William Zartman, eds., *Between the State and Islam*. Cambridge: Cambridge University Press, 2001.
Harmsen, Egbert. *Islam, Civil Society and Social Work: Muslim Voluntary Welfare Associations in Jordan between Patronage and Empowerment*. Amsterdam: Amsterdam University Press, 2008.
Hass, Amira. *Drinking the Sea at Gaza: Days and Nights in a Land under Siege*. New York: Metropolitan Books, 1999.
Hass, Amira. "The Real Disaster Is Closure." *Ha'aretz*, May 21, 2002.
Hass, Amira. "Growing Bitterness in Gaza." *Ha'aretz*, February 9, 2007.
Hass, Amira. "Haniyeh: Hamas Would Accept State under 1967 Borders." *Ha'aretz*, November 11, 2008.
Hass, Amira. "Return to Gaza." *London Review of Books*, February 26, 2009.
Hass, Amira. "Israel Bans Books, Music and Clothes from Entering Gaza." *Ha'aretz*, May 17, 2009.
Hatina, Meir. *Islam and Salvation in Palestine: The Islamic Jihad Movement*. Tel Aviv: Moshe Dayan Center for Middle Eastern and African Studies, Tel Aviv University, 2001.
Hatina, Meir. "Historical Legacy and the Challenge of Modernity in the Middle East: The Case of al-Azhar in Egypt." *The Muslim World* 93, 2003.
Hatina, Meir. "Between Harmony and Dissent: Ulama and Nationalist Movements," in Moshe Gammer, ed., *Community, Identity and the State: Comparing Africa, Eurasia, Latin America and the Middle East*. London: Routledge, 2004.
Hatina, Meir. "The 'Other Islam': The Egyptian Wasat Party." *Critique: Critical Middle Eastern Studies* 14, Summer 2005.
Hatina, Meir. "The Ulama and the Cult of Death in Palestine." *Israel Affairs* 12, Winter 2006.
Hatina, Meir. *Identity Politics in the Middle East: Liberal Thought and Islamic Challenge in Egypt*. London: Tauris Academic Studies, 2007.
Hatina, Meir, ed. *Guardians of the Faith in Modern Times: 'Ulamma' in the Middle East*. Leiden and Boston: E. J. Brill, 2008.
Hawthorne, Amy. "Middle Eastern Democracy: Is Civil Society the Answer?" Carnegie Papers no. 44, Carnegie Endowment for International Peace, March 2004.
Haykel, Bernard. *Revival and Reform in Islam: The Legacy of Muhammad al-Shawkani*. Cambridge: Cambridge University Press, 2003.
Hefner, Robert W., ed. *Democratic Civility: The History and Cross-cultural Possibility of a Modern Political Ideal*. New Brunswick, NJ: Transaction Publishers, 1998.

Hefner, Robert W. *Civil Islam: Muslims and Democratization in Indonesia.* Princeton, NJ: Princeton University Press, 2000.

Hefner, Robert W. "Introduction: Modernity and the Remaking of Muslim Politics," in Robert W. Hefner, ed., *Remaking Muslim Politics: Pluralism, Contestation, Democratization.* Princeton, NJ: Princeton University Press, 2005.

Helmont, Samuel. "Islam and Islamism Today: The Case of Yusuf Al-Qaradawi." Foreign Policy Research Institute, January 12, 2010, www.fpri.org.

Herzog, Michael. "The Hamas Conundrum." *Foreign Affairs,* February 2010.

Hever, Shir. *The Political Economy of Israel's Occupation: Beyond Mere Exploitation.* London: Pluto Press, 2010.

Hilal, Jamal. "Hamas's Rise as Charted in the Polls, 1994–2005." *Journal of Palestine Studies* 35, Spring 2006.

Hill, Allan G. "Demographic and Health Prospects in the Occupied Palestinian Territory (oPt)." Harvard School of Public Health, Cambridge, MA, 2007.

Hoffer, Eric. *The True Believer: Thought on the Nature of Mass Movements.* New York: Harper and Row, 1951.

Hoigilt, Jacob. *Raising Extremists? Islamism and Education in the Palestinian Territories.* Oslo: FAFO, 2010.

Holt, Maria. "Palestinian Women and the Contemporary Islamist Movement." *Encounters: Journal of Inter-Cultural Perspectives* 3, March 1997.

Hourani, Albert. *Arabic Thought in the Liberal Age, 1798–1939.* 3rd edition. Cambridge: Cambridge University Press, 1983.

Hroub, Khaled. *Hamas: Political Thought and Practice.* Washington, DC: Institute for Palestine Studies, 2000.

Hroub, Khaled. "Hamas after Shaykh Yasin and Rantisi." *Journal of Palestine Studies* 33, Summer 2004.

Hroub, Khaled. *Hamas: A Beginner's Guide.* London: Pluto Press, 2006.

Hroub, Khaled. "A 'New Hamas' through Its New Documents." *Journal of Palestine Studies* 35, Summer 2006.

Hroub, Khaled. "Hamas's Path to Reinvention." OpenDemocracy.net/conflict-middle_east_politics/hamas_3982.jsp, October 9, 2006.

Hroub, Khaled. "Salafi Formations in Palestine: The Limits of a De-Palestinised Milieu," in Roel Meijer, ed., *Global Salafism: Islam's New Religious Movement.* New York: Columbia University Press, 2009.

Humanitarian Task Force for Emergency Needs. "Minutes of Meeting" Internal document, Jerusalem, October 18, 2001.

Hunter, Shireen. "The Rise of Islamist Movements and the Western Response: Clash of Civilizations or Clash of Interests," in Laura Guazzone, ed., *The Islamist Dilemma: The Political Role of Islamist Movements in the Contemporary Arab World.* Reading, UK: Ithaca Press, 1995.

Independent Catholic News. "Caritas Reports on Desperate Plight of 6,000 Palestinians Trapped at Border Crossing," July 20, 2007. www.indcatholicnews.com/trap325.html.

Intelligence and Terrorism Information Center at the Israel Intelligence Heritage & Commemoration Center (IICC). "'Charity' and Palestinian Terrorism—Spotlight on Hamas-Run Islamic Al-Tadhamun 'Charitable Society' in Nablus." Special Information Bulletin, 2005. www.intelligence.org.il.

Intelligence and Terrorism Information Center at the Israel Intelligence Heritage & Commemoration Center (IICC). "Since Hamas took over the Gaza Strip, it has intensified its activities to impose an Islamic social code. Hamas is careful not to represent it as a step toward establishing a radical Islamic state. The process is just beginning but indicates an increase in the Islamization of the Gaza Strip." August 31, 2007.
Intelligence and Terrorism Information Center at the Israel Intelligence Heritage & Commemoration Center (IICC). "Yet another step in the establishment of a totalitarian "Islamic Emirate" in the Gaza Strip: the Hamas administration announces that it is now drawing a new bill imposing also shari'ah-based penal codes on the Gaza Strip." November 13, 2008.
Intelligence and Terrorism Information Center at the Israel Intelligence Heritage & Commemoration Center (IICC). "The Six Months of the Lull Arrangement." December 2008, www.mfa.il.org.
International Crisis Group (ICG). *Islamic Social Welfare Activism in the Occupied Palestinian Territories: A Legitimate Target?* ICG Report no. 13. Amman/Brussels: ICG, April 2, 2003.
International Crisis Group (ICG). *Dealing with Hamas.* ICG Report no. 21. Amman/Brussels: ICG, January 26, 2004.
International Crisis Group (ICG). *Enter Hamas: The Challenges of Political Integration.* Amman/Brussels: ICG, January 18, 2006.
International Crisis Group (ICG). *After Mecca: Engaging Hamas.* Amman/Jerusalem/Brussels: ICG, February 28, 2007.
International Crisis Group (ICG). *Ruling Palestine I: Gaza under Hamas.* Jerusalem: ICG, March 19, 2008.
International Crisis Group (ICG). *Round Two in Gaza.* Gaza City/Ramallah/Brussels: ICG, September 11, 2008.
International Crisis Group (ICG). *Palestine Divided.* Brussels: ICG, December 17, 2008.
International Institute for Counter Terrorism. *Breakdown of Fatalities: 27 September 2000 through 1 January 2005.* Herzliya: ICT, 2005.
International Institute for Counter Terrorism. *Database: Incidents.* Herzliya: ICT. 2005.
International Institute for Counter-Terrorism. *Database: Incidents.* Herzliya: ICT, n.d.
"Interview with Khaled Mesh'al in Damascus." *Al Hayat*, October 2006.
"Interviews from Gaza." *Middle East Policy*, December 2002.
Israeli Information Center for Human Rights in the Occupied Territories—B'tselem. *Behind the Barrier: Human Rights Violations as a Result of Israel's Separation Barrier.* Jerusalem, April 2003.
Israeli Information Center for Human Rights in the Occupied Territories—B'tselem. *Ground to a Halt: Denial of Palestinians' Freedom of Movement in the West Bank.* August 2007.
Israeli Information Center for Human Rights in the Occupied Territories—B'Tselem. *Human Rights in the Occupied Territories: 2008 Annual Report.* Jerusalem, 2008.
Issacharoff, Avi, and Amos Harel. "Israeli Security Officials Laud PA Crackdown on Hamas." *Ha'aretz*, September 7, 2008.

"'It Will Be a Hot Summer.' Interview with Fatah's Intelligence Coordinator." *Speigel Online,* June 18, 2007.

Jamal, Amaney A. *Barriers to Democracy: The Other Side of Social Capital in Palestine and the Arab World.* Princeton, NJ: Princeton University Press, 2007.

Jensen, Michael Irving. "Islamism and Civil Society in the Gaza Strip," in Ahmad S. Moussalli, ed., *Islamic Fundamentalism: Myths and Realities.* Ithaca, NY: Ithaca Press, 1998.

Jensen, Michael Irving. "'Re-Islamising' Palestinian Society 'From Below': Hamas and Higher Education in Gaza." *Holy Land Studies* 5, May 2006.

Jensen, Michael Irving. *The Political Ideology of Hamas: A Grassroots Perspective.* London: I. B. Tauris, 2009.

Jubran, Michael, and Laura Drake. "The Islamic Fundamentalist Movement in the West Bank and Gaza Strip." *Middle East Policy* 2, no. 2, 1993.

Juergensmeyer, Mark. *Terror in the Mind of God: The Global Rise of Religious Violence.* Berkeley: University of California Press, 2000.

Kanwisher, Nancy, Johannes Huashofer, and Anat Bilitzki. "Reigniting Violence: How Do Ceasefires End?" *The Huffington Post,* January 6, 2009.

Katzman, Kenneth and Clyde Mark. *Hamas and Palestinian Islamic Jihad: Recent Developments, Source of Support and Implications for U.S. Policy.* Washington, DC: Congressional Research Service, Library of Congress, 1994.

Keddie, Nikki R. *Sayyid Jamal ad-Din "al-Afghani": A Political Biography.* Berkeley: University of California Press, 1972.

Keddie, Nikki R., ed. *Scholars, Saints and Sufis: Muslim Religious Institutions in the Middle East since 1500.* Berkeley: University of California Press, 1972.

Keddie, Nikki R. *An Islamic Response to Imperialism: Political and Religious Writings of Sayyid Jamal ad-Din "al-Afghani."* Berkeley: University of California Press, 1983.

Kedourie, Elie. *Democracy and Arab Political Culture.* London: Frank Cass, 1994.

Kedourie, Elie. *Afghani and 'Abduh: An Essay on Religious Unbelief and Political Activism in Modern Islam.* New York: Routledge, 2008 (originally published in 1966).

Kepel, Gilles. *Jihad: The Trail of Political Islam.* Cambridge, MA: Harvard University Press, 2002.

Kerr, Malcolm H. *Islamic Reform: The Political and Legal Theories of Muhammad 'Abduh and Rashid Rida.* Berkeley: University of California Press, 1966.

Khan, Mushtaq, George Giacaman, and Inge Amundsen, eds. *State Formation in Palestine: Viability and Governance during a Social Transformation.* London: Routledge Curzon, 2004.

Klein, Menachem. "Competing Brothers: The Web of Hamas-PLO Relations." *Terrorism and Political Violence* 8, Summer 1996.

Klein, Menachem. "Hamas in Power." *Middle East Journal* 61, Summer 2007.

Kramer, Gudrun. "Islamist Notions of Democracy." *Middle East Report,* July–August 1993.

Kristianasen, Wendy. "Challenge and Counterchallenge: Hamas' Response to Oslo." *Journal of Palestine Studies* 28, Spring 1999.

Kubursi, Atif, and Fadle Naqib. "The Palestinian Economy under Occupation: The Economics of Subjugation and Dynamics of Dependency." Paper presented at a conference at the University of London, School of Oriental and African Studies, London, January 27–28, 2007.

Kydd, Andrew, and Barbara Walter. "Sabotaging the Peace: The Politics of Extremist Violence." *International Organization* 56, Spring 2002.

Lapidus, Ira M. "The Separation of State and Religion in the Development of Early Islamic Society." *International Journal of Middle East Studies* 6, October 1975.

Laub, Karin. "Disagreements in Hamas Camps Laid Bare." Associated Press, October 22, 2007.

Laub, Karin. "Abbas Shuts Hamas Charities in the West Bank." Associated Press, December 3, 2007.

Lawrence, Bruce. *Shattering the Myth: Islam beyond Violence*. Princeton, NJ: Princeton University Press, 1998.

Lawrence, Bruce, ed. *Messages to the World: The Statements of Osama Bin Laden*. London: Verso, 2005.

Le More, Anne. *International Assistance to the Palestinians after Oslo: Political Guilt, Wasted Money*. New York: Routledge, 2008.

Legrain, Jean-Francois. "The Islamic Movement and the *Intifada*," in Roger Heacock and Jamal R. Nassar, eds., *Intifada: Palestine at the Crossroads*. New York: Praeger, 1990.

Legrain, Jean-Francois. "A Defining Moment: Palestinian Islamic Fundamentalism," in James Piscatori, ed., *Islamic Fundamentalisms and the Gulf Crisis*. Chicago: American Academy of Arts and Sciences, 1991.

Legrain, Jean-Francois. "Vers une Palestine Islamique?" *L'Arabisant* 35, 2001.

Leibowitz, Elia. "Maginot Mentality in Israel." *Ha'aretz*, July 11, 2003.

Levinson, Charles. "Hamastan Day One." *Conflict Blotter*, June 15, 2007.

Levitt, Matthew. *Hamas: Politics, Charity, and Terrorism in the Service of Jihad*. New Haven, CT, and Washington, DC: Yale University Press in cooperation with the Washington Institute for Near East Policy, 2006.

Levitt, Matthew. "Financial Setbacks for Hamas," Policy Watch no. 1436. Washington, DC: The Washington Institute for Near East Policy, December 3, 2008.

Levy, Gideon. "The General of Onions and Garlic." *Ha'aretz*, July 13, 2008.

Levy, Gideon. "Yes, Hate." *Ha'aretz*, October 26, 2008.

Lewis, Bernard. *The Shaping of the Modern Middle East*. New York: Oxford University Press, 1994.

Li, Darryl. "From Prison to Zoo: Israel's "Humanitarian" Control of Gaza." *Adalah's Newsletter* 44, January 2008.

Lia, Brynjar. *The Society of Muslim Brothers in Egypt: The Rise of an Islamic Mass Movement, 1928–1942*. Reading, UK: Ithaca Press, 1998.

Litvak, Meir. *The Islamization of Palestinian Identity: The Case of Hamas*. Tel Aviv: Moshe Dayan Center for Middle Eastern and African Studies, Tel Aviv University, 1996.

Litvak, Meir. "Hamas's Victory in Municipal Elections." *Tel Aviv Notes*, no. 156, December 26, 2005.

Lundblad, L. G. "Islamic Welfare, Discourse and Practise: The Institutionalization of Zakat in Palestine," in Nefissa Naguib and Inger Marie Okkenhaug, eds., *Interpreting Welfare and Relief in the Middle East*. Leiden: E. J. Brill, 2008.

Lybarger, Loren. "Hamas May Become Victim of Own Success: Isolating Group Further Serves No One's Interest." *San Francisco Chronicle*, June 24, 2007.

Lybarger, Loren. *Identity and Religion in Palestine: The Struggle between Islamism and Secularism in the Occupied Territories*. Princeton, NJ: Princeton University Press, 2007.

Macintyre, Donald. "Living off Scraps: The West Bank's Bitter Harvest." *The Independent*, September 14, 2007.

Makdisi, Saree. "The Strangulation of Gaza." *The Nation*, February 3, 2008.

Makovsky, David. "Are All Politics Local? A Look at Palestinian Municipal Election Results." Peace Watch no. 487. Washington, DC: Washington Institute for Near East Policy, December 2004.

Malka, Haim. "Forcing Choices: Testing the Transformation of Hamas." *The Washington Quarterly*, Autumn 2005.

Malka, Haim. "Hamas: Resistance and Transformation of Palestinian Society," In Jon B. Alterman and Karin von Hippel, eds., *Understanding Islamic Charities*. Washington, DC: Center for Strategic and International Studies Press, 2007.

Malley, Robert, and Henry Siegman. "The Hamas Factor." *International Herald Tribune*, December 27, 2006.

Maoz, Zeev. *Defending the Holy Land: A Critical Analysis of Israel's Security and Foreign Policy*. Ann Arbor: University of Michigan Press, 2006.

McCarthy, Rory. "Closed Crossings Pushing Gaza into Disaster, Says UN." *The Guardian*, July 19, 2007.

"Meshal Signals Readiness to Accept 1967 Borders—Look at the Program on the Table." *The Daily Star*, April 4, 2008.

Miller, Judith. "The Challenge of Radical Islam." *Foreign Affairs* 72, 1993.

Milne, Seumas. "Too Late for Two States?" *The Guardian*, January 24, 2004.

Milton-Edwards, Beverly. *Islamic Politics in Palestine*. London: I. B. Tauris, 1996.

Milton-Edwards, Beverly. "Prepared for Power: Hamas, Governance, and Conflict." *Civil Wars* 7, 2005.

Milton-Edwards, Beverly. "The Ascendance of Political Islam: Hamas and Its Consolidation in the Gaza Strip." *Third World Quarterly* 29, 2008.

Milton-Edwards, Beverly, and Alastair Crooke. "Costly Choice: Hamas, Cease-fires and the Palestinian-Israeli Peace Process." *World Today* 59, November 2003.

Milton-Edwards, Beverly, and Alastair Crooke. "Elusive Ingredient: Hamas and the Peace Process." *Journal of Palestine Studies* 33, Summer 2004.

Milton-Edwards, Beverly, and Alastair Crooke. "Waving, Not Drowning: Strategic Dimensions of Ceasefires and Islamic Movements." *Security Dialogue* 35, September 2004.

Milton-Edwards, Beverly, and Stephen Farrell. *Hamas: The Islamic Resistance Movement*. Cambridge: Polity Press, 2010.

Mishal, Khalid. "We Will Not Sell Our People or Principles for Foreign Aid." *The Guardian*, January 31, 2006.

Mishal, Shaul. "The Pragmatic Dimension of the Palestinian Hamas: A Network Perspective." *Armed Forces & Society* 29, Summer 2003.

Mishal, Shaul, and Avraham Sela. *The Palestinian Hamas: Vision, Violence and Coexistence*. New York: Columbia University Press, 2000, 2006.

Mitchell, Richard P. *The Society of Muslim Brothers*. 2nd edition. New York: Oxford University Press, 1993.

Mithaq Harakat al-Muqawama al-Islamiyya (Hamas) [Charter of the Islamic Resistance Movement (Hamas)]. August 18, 1988.

Mneimneh, Hassan. "Convergence? The Homogenization of Islamist Doctrines in Gaza." *Current Trends in Islamist Ideology* 9, December 2009.

Moaddel, Mansoor, and Kamran Talattof, eds. *Contemporary Debates in Islam: An Anthology of Modernist and Fundamentalist Thought*. New York: St. Martin's Press, 2000.

Moussalli, Ahmad S. "Modern Islamic Fundamentalist Discourses on Civil Society, Pluralism and Democracy," in Augustus Richard Norton, ed., *Civil Society in the Middle East*, vol. 1. Leiden and New York: E. J. Brill, 1995.

Moussalli, Ahmad S., ed. *Islamic Fundamentalism: Myths and Realities*. Ithaca, NY: Ithaca Press, 1998.

Mughrabi, Nidal al-. "Gaza Businesses Risk Collapse Despite Calm." Reuters, July 12, 2007.

Muslih, Muhammad. "Palestinian Civil Society," in Augustus Richard Norton, ed., *Civil Society in the Middle East*, vol. 1. Leiden E. J. Brill, 1995.

Muslih, Muhammad. *The Foreign Policy of Hamas*. New York: Council on Foreign Relations, 1999.

Naguib, Nefissa, and Inger Marie Okkenhaug, eds. *Interpreting Welfare and Relief in the Middle East*. Leiden: E. J. Brill, 2008.

Nasaw, Daniel. "Leaders of Muslim Charity in U.S. Found Guilty of Providing Funds to Hamas." *The Guardian*. November 24, 2008.

Niblock, Tim. "Islamic Movements and Sudan's Political Coherence," in Herve Bleuchot, Christian Delmet, and Derek Hopwood, eds., *Sudan: History, Identity, Ideology*. Reading, PA: Ithaca Press, 1991.

Norton, Augustus Richard. "Introduction," in Augustus Richard Norton, ed., *Civil Society in the Middle East*, vol. 1. Leiden and New York: E. J. Brill, 1995.

Norton, Augustus Richard, ed. *Civil Society in the Middle East*, 2 vols. Leiden and New York: E .J. Brill, 1995, 1996.

Norton, Augustus Richard. "Thwarted Politics: The Case of Egypt's Hizb al-Wasat," in Robert W. Hefner, ed., *Remaking Muslim Politics: Pluralism, Contestation, Democratization*. Princeton, NJ: Princeton University Press, 2005.

Norton, Augustus Richard. *Hezbollah: A Short History*. Princeton, NJ: Princeton University Press, 2007.

Nusse, Andrea. *Muslim Palestine: The Ideology of Hamas*. Amsterdam: Harwood Academic Publishers, 1998.

Office of the Press Secretary, White House. "President Announces Progress on Financial Fight against Terror: Remarks by the President on Financial Fight Against Terror, the Rose Garden," December 4, 2001. www.whitehouse.gov/news/releases/2001/12/print/20011204-8.html.

Olsen, Norman H., and Matthew N. Olsen. "An Inside Story of How the US Magnified Palestinian Suffering." *Christian Science Monitor*, January 12, 2009.

Oxfam. "Poverty in Palestine: The Human Cost of the Financial Boycott." April 2007.
Oxfam International. "Forgotten Villages: Struggling to Survive under Closure in the West Bank." Oxfam Briefing Paper, September 2002.
"PA dismantles Hamas 'Charities.'" Arutz Sheva/IsraelNationalNews.com, October 19, 2007.
"PA Officials Have Fewer Powers Than a Swiss Local Council—UN Body." *The Daily Star*, September 9, 2008.
Palestine Center. "Gaza's Humanitarian Crisis—Edited Transcript of Remarks by Saahir Lone." *For the Record*, no. 281, Washington, DC, July 5, 2007.
Palestinian Centre for Human Rights. "'El-Ata Charitable Society' Burned in Beit Hanoun." Gaza, April 11, 2007.
Palestinian Centre for Human Rights. "PCHR Publishes 'Black Days in the Absence of Justice: Report on Bloody Fighting in the Gaza Strip from 7 to 14 June 2007.'" Gaza Strip, October 2007.
Palestinian Centre for Human Rights. "Explosive Device Detonated in Yabous Benevolent Society and Rafah Service Club in Southern Gaza." Gaza, July 13, 2008.
Palestinian Centre for Human Rights. "PCHR Condemns Attacks on Civil Society Organizations and the Continued Arrests against Hamas Members in the West Bank." Gaza, August 10, 2008.
Palestinian Media Watch. "Fatah Declared "Illegal Organization' by Hamas in Gaza." *Bulletin*, November 25, 2008, www.pmw.or.il.
Paz, Reuven. "Higher Education and the Development of Palestinian Islamic Groups." *Middle East Review of International Affairs* 4, June 2000.
Pelham, Nicolas. "Hamas Back Out of Its Box." *Middle East Report Online*, September 2, 2010, www.merip.org/mero/mero090210.html.
Perry, Mark. "Israeli Offensive Disrupts US-Hamas Contacts." *Palestine Report*, October 9, 2002.
Perry, Mark and Paul Woodward. "Document Details 'U.S.' Plan to Sink Hamas. *Asia Times*, May 16, 2007.
Physicians for Human Rights—Israel and Dan Magen. "'Ill Morals': Grave Violations of the Right to Health during the Israeli Assault on Gaza." Israel, March 2009.
Pipes, Daniel. *In the Path of God: Islam and Political Power*. New York: Basic Books, 1983.
Qutb, Sayyid. *Social Justice in Islam*. Translated from the Arabic by John B. Hardie. Washington, DC: American Council of Learned Societies, 1953.
Qutb, Sayyid. *Islam and Universal Peace*. Plainfield, IN: American Trust Publications, 1993.
Rabbani, Mouin. "A Hamas Perspective on the Movement's Evolving Role: An Interview with Khalid Mishal (Part II)." *Journal of Palestine Studies* 37, Summer 2008.
Rappaport, Meron. "On Israel's Separation Fence." *Yediot Ahronoth*, May 31, 2003.
Rashad, Ahmad. "Hamas: Palestinian Politics with an Islamic Hue." Occasional Paper no. 2. Springfield, VA: United Association for Studies and Research, December 1993.

Ravid, Barak. "In 2006 Letter to Bush, Haniyeh Offered Compromise with Israel." *Ha'aretz*, November 14, 2008.
Ravid, Barak. "Disinformation, Secrecy, and Lies: How the Gaza Offensive Came About." *Ha'aretz*, December 28, 2008.
Reuters. "World Bank: Gaza Strip May Face 'Irreversible' Economic Collapse." *Ha'aretz*, July 12, 2007.
Robinson, Glenn E. *Building a Palestinian State: The Incomplete Revolution*. Bloomington: Indiana University Press, 1997.
Robinson, Glenn E. "Can Islamists Be Democrats?" *Middle East Journal* 51, Summer 1997.
Robinson, Glenn E. "Hamas as Social Movement," in Quintan Wiktorowicz, ed., *Islamic Activism: A Social Movement Theory Approach*. Bloomington: Indiana University Press, 2004.
Rome, Barbara Opall. "Marines to Train at New Israeli Combat Center." *Marine Corps Times*, June 25, 2007.
Rose, David. "The Gaza Bombshell." *Vanity Fair*, April 2008.
Rosefsky Wickham, Carrie. *Mobilizing Islam: Religion, Activism, and Political Activism in Egypt*. New York: Columbia University Press, 2002.
Roussillon, Alain. "Entre al-Jihad et al-Rayyan," in *Modernisation et nouvelles formes de mobilization sociale*. Cairo, Egypt: Dossiers du Centre d'Etudes et de Documentation Economiques, 1991.
Roy, Olivier. *The Failure of Political Islam*. Cambridge, MA: Harvard University Press, 1994.
Roy, Sara. "Beyond Hamas: Islamic Activism in the Gaza Strip." *Harvard Middle Eastern and Islamic Review* 2, Fall 1995.
Roy, Sara. *The Gaza Strip: The Political Economy of De-development*. Washington, DC: Institute for Palestine Studies, 1995, 2001.
Roy, Sara. "Civil Society in the Gaza Strip: Obstacles to Social Reconstruction," in Augustus Richard Norton, ed., *Civil Society in the Middle East*, vol. 2. Leiden: E. J. Brill, 1996.
Roy, Sara. "Professionalization versus Politics: The Transformation of Islamic NGOs in Palestine." *Middle East Report* 214, Spring 2000.
Roy, Sara. "The Crisis Within: The Struggle for Palestinian Society." *Critique: Journal for Critical Studies of the Middle East*, no. 17, Fall 2000.
Roy, Sara. "Hamas and the Transformation(s) of Political Islam in Palestine." *Current History*, January 2003.
Roy, Sara. "The Palestinian-Israeli Conflict and Palestinian Socioeconomic Decline: A Place Denied." *International Journal of Politics, Culture and Society* 17, Spring 2004.
Roy, Sara. "Religious Nationalism and the Palestinian-Israeli Conflict: Examining Hamas and the Possibility of Reform." *Chicago Journal of International Law* 5, Summer 2004.
Roy, Sara. "A Dubai on the Mediterranean." *London Review of Books* 27, November 3, 2005.
Roy, Sara. *Failing Peace: Gaza and the Palestinian-Israeli Conflict*. London: Pluto Press, 2007.
Roy, Sara. "If Gaza Falls...." *London Review of Books*, January 1, 2009.

Rubin, Barry. *Islamic Fundamentalism in Egyptian Politics: Updated Edition.* New York: Palgrave Macmillan, 2002.

Rubinstein, Danny. "The New Message of Hamas." *Ha'aretz*, February 10, 1993. Translated by Israel Shahak in *From the Hebrew Press*, March 1993.

Rustow, Dankwart. "Transitions to Democracy." *Comparative Politics* 2, no. 3, 1970.

Said, Edward. *Orientalism.* New York: Vintage, 1978.

Said, Edward. "Palestinians under Siege." *London Review of Books*, December 14, 2000.

Salam, Nawaf. "The Emergence of Citizenship in Islamdom." *Arab Law Quarterly* 12, 1997.

Salam, Nawaf. *Civil Society in the Arab World: The Historical and Political Dimensions.* Occasional Publications 3, Islamic Legal Studies Program, Harvard Law School, Cambridge, MA, October 2002.

Salame, Ghassan, ed. *Democracy without Democrats: The Renewal of Politics in the Muslim World.* London: I. B. Tauris, 1994.

Salvatore, Armando, and Dale F. Eickelman, eds. *Public Islam and the Common Good.* Leiden: E. J. Brill, 2004.

Samhouri, Mohammed. "Looking beyond the Numbers: The Palestinian Socioeconomic Crisis of 2006." Middle East Brief 16. Crown Center for Middle East Studies, Brandeis University, February 2007.

Sarraj, Eyad al-. "Suicide Bombers: Dignity, Despair, and the Need for Hope—an Interview with Eyad El Sarraj." *Journal of Palestine Studies* 31, Summer 2002.

Sayigh, Yezid. "Hamas Rule in Gaza: Three Years On." Middle East Brief 41, Crown Center for Middle East Studies. Brandeis University, March 2010.

Sayyid, Mustapha K. al-. "A Civil Society in Egypt." *Middle East Journal* 47, Spring 1993.

Schaublin, Emmanuel. *The West Bank Zakat Committees (1977–2009) in the Local Context.* Geneva: Centre on Conflict, Development and Peacebuilding, The Graduate Institute, November 2009.

Seligman, Adam B. *The Idea of Civil Society.* New York: Free Press, 1992.

Shadid, Mohammed. "The Muslim Brotherhood Movement in the West Bank and Gaza." *Third World Quarterly* 10. April 1988.

Shafiq, Munir. "Secularism and the Arab-Muslim Condition," in John L. Esposito and Azzam Tamimi, eds., *Islam and Secularism in the Middle East.* New York: New York University Press, 2000.

Shepard, William E. *Sayyid Qutb and Islamic Activism: A Translation and Critical Analysis of Social Justice in Islam.* Leiden: E. J. Brill, 1996.

Shils, Edward. "The Virtue of Civil Society." *Government and Opposition* 26, Winter 1991.

Siegman, Henry. "US Hamas Policy Blocks Middle East Peace." *Noref Reports* 8. Oslo: Norwegian Peacebuilding Centre, September 2010.

Silk, Andrew, ed. *Research on Terrorism: Trends, Achievements and Failures.* London: Frank Cass, 2004.

Singer, Amy. *Charity in Islamic Societies.* Cambridge: Cambridge University Press, 2008.

Singerman, Diane. *Avenues of Participation: Family, Politics, and Networks in Urban Quarters of Cairo.* Princeton, NJ: Princeton University Press, 1995.

Sivan, Emmanuel. *Radical Islam: Medieval Theology and Modern Politics.* New Haven, CT: Yale University Press, 1990.

Sivan, Emmanuel. "Eavesdropping on Radical Islam." *Middle East Quarterly* 2, 1995.

Slater, Jerome. "A Perfect Moral Catastrophe: Just War Philosophy and the Israeli Attack on Gaza." *Tikkun,* March–April 2009.

Starrett, Gregory. *Putting Islam to Work: Education, Politics, and Religious Transformation in Egypt.* Berkeley: University of California Press, 1998.

State of Israel. *The Civilian Policy toward the Gaza Strip.* Tel Aviv: Coordinator of Government Activities in the Territories, Ministry of Defense, 2010.

Steele, Jonathan. "Hamas Acted on a Very Real Fear of a US-Sponsored Coup." *The Guardian,* June 22, 2007.

Strasler, Nehemia. "Talk to Hamas." *Ha'aretz,* March 4, 2008.

Swirski, Shlomo. *The Cost of Occupation: The Burden of the Israeli-Palestinian Conflict, 2008 Report.* Tel Aviv: Information of Equality and Social Justice in Israel, ADVA, June 2008.

Tamimi, Azzam. *Rachid Ghannouchi: A Democrat within Islamism.* Oxford: Oxford University Press, 2001.

Tamimi, Azzam. *La Vanguardia Dossier.* Special issue on the Palestinians, October/December 2003.

Tamimi, Azzam. *Civil Society in Islamic Political Thought.* Institute of Islamic Political Thought, January 21, 2005.

Tamimi, Azzam. "Appendix VI: Hamas Election Manifesto for the Legislative Elections Held on 25 January 2006," in Azzam Tamimi, *Hamas: Unwritten Chapters.* London: Hurst and Company, 2007.

Tamimi, Azzam. *Hamas: A History from Within.* Northampton, MA: Olive Branch Press, 2007.

Taraki, Lisa. "Enclave Micropolis: The Paradoxical Case of Ramallah/Al Bireh." *Journal of Palestine Studies* 37, Summer 2008.

Tibi, Bassam. *The Challenge of Fundamentalism: Political Islam in the New World Disorder.* Berkeley: University of California Press, 1998.

Tilley, Virginia. "A Beacon of Hope: Apartheid Israel." *Counterpunch,* December 5, 2006.

"Transcript: Interview With Khaled Meshal of Hamas." *New York Times,* May 5, 2009.

Turki, Fawaz. "Palestinian Self-Criticism and the Liberation of Palestinian Society." *Journal of Palestine Studies* 25, Winter, 1996.

United Nations Conference on Trade and Development. *The Palestinian War Torn Economy.* Geneva, April 2006.

United Nations Office for the Coordination of Humanitarian Affairs. *Gaza Humanitarian Situation Report—the Impact of the Blockade on the Gaza Strip: A Human Dignity Crisis.* Jerusalem: OCHA, December 15, 2008.

United Nations Special Coordinator's Office. *The Impact on the Palestinian Economy of Confrontation, Border Closures and Mobility Restrictions, 1 October 2000–30 September 2001.* Gaza, October 2001.

United States District Court for the Northern District of Texas, Dallas Division. *United States of America versus Holy Land Foundation, Et Al.,* Number 3:

04-240-G, July 25, 2007. Vol. 2, Transcript of Trial Before the Honorable A. Joe Fish.

"UNRWA Chief: Gaza on Brink of Humanitarian Catastrophe." *Ha'aretz*, November 21, 2008.

Usher, Graham. "What Kind of Nation? The Rise of Hamas in the Occupied Territories," in Graham Usher, ed., *Dispatches from Palestine: The Rise and Fall of the Oslo Peace Process*. Alberta: University of Alberta, 1998.

Usher, Graham. "The New Hamas: Between Resistance and Participation." *al-Ahram Weekly*, August 21, 2005.

Voice of America. "Palestinian Forces Shut Down Hamas-Linked Charities, Shops." August 9, 2008.

Voll, John O. "Fundamentalism in the Sunni Arab World: Egypt and Sudan," in R. Scott Appleby, ed., *Fundamentalisms Observed*. Chicago: University of Chicago Press, 1994.

Voll, John O. *Islam, Continuity and Change in the Modern World*. Syracuse, NY: Syracuse University Press, 1994.

Walzer, Michael. "On Proportionality." *The New Republic*, January 8, 2009.

Washington Institute for Near East Policy. *The Palestinian Legislative Council: A Handbook*. Washington, DC: WINEP, 2007.

Waterbury, John. "Democracy without Democrats?—The Potential for Political Liberalization in the Middle East," in Ghassan Salame, ed., *Democracy without Democrats—The Renewal of Politics in the Muslim World*. London: I. B. Tauris, 1994.

Weizman, Eyal. *Hollow Land: Israel's Architecture of Occupation*. London: Verso, 2007.

White, Jenny B. *Islamist Mobilization in Turkey: A Study in Vernacular Politics*. Seattle: University of Washington Press, 2002.

White, Jenny B. "The End of Islamism? Turkey's Muslimhood Model," in Robert W. Hefner, ed., *Remaking Muslim Politics: Pluralism, Contestation, Democratization*. Princeton, NJ: Princeton University Press, 2005.

Wiesman, Itzchak. "Sa'id Hawwa—the Making of a Radical Muslim Thinker in Modern Syria." *Middle Eastern Studies* 29, October 1993.

Wiesman, Itzchak. "Sa'id Hawwa and Islamic Revivalism in Bathist Syria." *Studia Islamica* 85, 1997.

Wiktorowicz, Quitan. *The Management of Islamic Activism: Salafis, the Muslim Brotherhood and State Power in Jordan*. Albany: State University of New York Press, 2001.

Wiktorowicz, Quintan, ed. *Islamic Activism: A Social Movement Theory Approach*. Bloomington: Indiana University Press, 2004.

Wiktorowicz, Quintan. "Islamic Activism and Social Movement Theory," in Quintan Wiktorowicz, ed., *Islamic Activism: A Social Movement Theory Approach*. Bloomington: Indiana University Press, 2004.

Wilson, Scott. "Hamas's New Order Exacts Toll on Gazans—Party Cements Grip with Harsh Tactics." *Washington Post*, September 17, 2007.

World Bank and Bisan Center for Research and Development. *The Role and Performance of Palestinian NGOs in Heath, Education and Agriculture*. Washington, DC, December 31, 2006.

Yousef, Ahmed. "Engage with Hamas." *Washington Post*, June 20, 2007.
Zakariyya, Fouad. *Myth and Reality in the Contemporary Islamist Movement*. London: Pluto Press, 2005.
Zaman, Muhammad Qasim. "The 'Ulama of Contemporary Islam and Their Conceptions of the Common Good," in Armando Salvatore and Dale F. Eickelman, eds., *Public Islam and the Common Good*. Leiden: Brill, 2004.
Zaman, Muhammad Qasim. *The Ulama in Contemporary Islam: Custodians of Change*. Princeton, NJ: Princeton University Press, 2007.
Ze'evi, Dror. "My Talks with Hamas: Israeli Leaders Should at Least Consider Hamas Proposals for Long-Term Ceasefire." *Israel Opinion*, January 23, 2008.
Zubaida, Sami. "Islamic Fundamentalism in Egypt and Iran," in Lionel Caplan, ed., *Studies in Religious Fundamentalism*. London: Macmillan, 1987.
Zubaida, Sami. "Islam, the State and Democracy: Contrasting Conceptions of Society in Egypt." *Middle East Report* 179, November–December 1992.
Zubaida, Sami. *Islam, the People and the State: Political Ideas and Movements in the Middle East*. London: I. B. Tauris, 1993

INDEX

Abbas, Mahmoud, 3, 209; antagonism toward Hamas, 43–47, 215–216; and attacks on Islamic social institutions, 85–86, 215–216, 235; electoral process and, 40, 46; peace process and, 43, 236; power-sharing with Hamas, 44, 196, 199, 210–211
Abduh, Muhammad, 53, 63
Abrams, Elliot, 43
Abu Asaker, Mohammad, 125
Abu Baker, Shukri, 98
Abu Hisham (head of QCS), 104–108, 118, 122, 134, 168, 169, 170
Abu Jihad (Khalil al-Wazir), 22
Abu Majid (director of Gaza *zakat*), 115–117
Abu Murzuq, Musa, 245n49
Abu Mussameh, Sayyid, 268n9
Abu Nasser Kujuk, Mr., 129, 262n54
Abu Rayya Rehabilitation Center, 152
Abu-Salam, Hamis, 197
Abu Shanab, Ismail, 64, 161; assassination of, 40, 197; on Islam and the social agenda, 74, 102, 136, 142–143, 162, 257n40; on organization and membership of Hamas, 25, 26, 182; on political objectives of Hamas, 208
accommodation, Hamas and, 7, 48–49; ideology and, 36–37, 60, 144, 163–165, 182; ISI and compliance with Law No. 1, 137–138; political, 198, 204; social agenda and, 85, 87–95, 163, 177, 188–189, 204
adoption services, 101, 128–130, 262n58
el-Affendi, Abdelwahab, 62–63, 68, 175
al-Afghani, Jamal al-Din, 63
agriculture, 231–232
al-Ahli Hospital, 169, 170, 176, 219
American Muslim Society, 99
American Near East Refugee Aid (ANERA), 130, 140
anti-Semitism, 10, 159–160
al-Anwar al-Ibrahimiyya Library for Children, 173–174

al-Aqsa Martyrs Brigade, 200, 272n8, 273n35
al-Aqsa Mosque massacre (1990), 31
Arafat, Yasir, 85, 137; antagonism toward Hamas, 35–39, 85, 277n83; death of, 199; Gulf War policies and, 30; and ISIs, 113, 137; and militarization of the second Intifada, 194; Oslo Accords and leadership of, 33–34, 277n83; and political legitimacy, 195–196, 199, 201–202; popular support for, 32–33, 195; and renunciation of terrorism, 27
arrests: of Hamas activists and leaders, 29, 36, 38, 39, 46, 84, 85, 196–197, 216, 219, 235; of legislators affiliated with Hamas, 41; of Muslim Brotherhood leaders, 24–25
assassination: of Abu Shanab, 40; of Ayyash, 38; of al-Aziz al-Rantisi, 40, 197; of Rabin, 37; of al-Shaqaqi, 38; of Yassin, 40
autonomy: of civil institutions, as principle, 54–55, 66–67; of ISIs, 127–128, 139–140, 159, 164, 168–169, 184; and lack of mobilizing vision, 185
awqaf (Islamic charitable trusts), 54, 57
al-'Awwa, Muhammad Salim, 52–53, 65–66, 175
Ayyash, Yahia, 38
al-Aziz al-Rantisi, Dr. Abd, 40, 197
al-Aziz Awda, Sheikh Abd, 24

Bahar, Ahmad, 74, 139, 172
banking, financial institutions, 232; Islamic banking network, 89–90
al-Banna, Hassan, 20, 63–66, 72, 162, 169
al-Bardawil, Salah, 205
Barel, Zvi, 229–230
Barghouti, Marwan, 198, 200
Beirut Declaration (March, 2002), 210
Bethlehem Charitable Society (BCS), 172, 179
Black Friday, 36
Boim, David, 99

boycott, international, 2, 16, 31, 41, 45, 211–213, 228–229, 231–234
Brown, Nathan, 208
Burke, Edmund, III, 161
Bush, George W. and U.S. policy, 1–2, 41–44, 196

Cairo Agreement, 35
Caliphate, 53
cease-fires, 28, 199–200, 205, 213–214, 228, 273n23, 274n40, 275n57; accommodation and proposed, 35–37, 40–41, 192; Israel's assassination campaign during, 197
centrism. *See* moderates
charitable institutions: *awqaf* (charitable trusts), 54, 57; coordination among, 168–169, 179; as fronts for terrorism, 3, 97–100, 178; Hamas and social agenda, 11, 92, 202, 206; Islamic charities blacklisted by U.S. government, 103; Law No. 1 and registration of, 137; PNA and closure of Hamas's, 38, 92, 213, 216, 235–236; U.S. actions to freeze assets of Islamic, 1–2, 97–99; *zakat* committees and, 113, 114, 117, 118, 179. *See also* Islamic social institutions (ISI)
Charter, Hamas (1988), 79–80
children: adoption services, 101, 128–130, 262n58; brain injuries and medical treatment of, 107, 154; illegitimate births, 128–130, 262n54; orphans, support for, 80–81, 82, 97, 101, 104–105, 111–114, 116–117, 119–123, 130; vocational training for, 107
civil society, Islamic, 52–56; institutional autonomy and, 51–57, 66–67; and Islamic state (political authority), 52; Islamic values and, 51, 67–68; legislative role or legal function of, 55–56; political theory and, 52–53; radical stance on legitimate civil institutions, 62–63; religion and, 51, 55–56, 57, 167–168; the state or political authority and, 52; *ulama* and, 55–58; *umma* and, 51, 53–54; *vs.* Western political concepts of, 52, 53
civism, 9, 12, 15; *umma* (Muslim social community), 20, 51, 53–55, 57, 161–162; violent resistance and, 249n6
clan or tribal disputes, 75, 194, 209, 214, 236, 271n5

clientelism, 186, 192
clients: as active participants *vs.* passive recipients, 102, 123, 171–172, 184–185; constituency contrasted with, 132; elder-care facilities, 151–152; inclusive service policies, 80–82, 108, 110, 125, 132–133, 172, 186, 187; indoctrination and recruitment among, 1–4; as local community, 170; number served, 101, 107, 114, 123, 125, 173–174; reasons for selecting ISIs as service providers, 175–176, 177
Clinton, Bill, 2
collaborators, 24, 32, 80–81, 131
colonialism, 9–10, 20, 57, 62, 66
community: communal development as priority for Hamas, 92–93, 185, 193; erosion of collective or communal identity in Gaza, 224–225; Islamic social services as communal development, 91; as Islamic value, 53, 67; and legitimacy, 64
Community Based Rehabilitation Team, 157
computer literacy, 74, 82, 101, 103, 108, 111, 123–124, 174
consensus *(ijma')*, 64, 65, 68, 171
conservative ideology: and imposition of cultural norms, 77, 134, 221–224; Muslim Brotherhood and, 25, 72; social agenda and, 72, 79, 83–84, 134, 187
constituencies *vs.* clientele, 132–133
Crooke, Alistair, 45
cultural Islam, 77, 86, 165–166; mobilization and, 184–185
curriculum in Islamic schools, 80, 81–82, 88–89, 112, 123–124, 168

Dahlan, Mohammed, 44–45, 272n9
da'wa (work toward Islamization of society), 70, 72, 99, 161–162, 185, 223
Dayton, Keith, 43
Decision no. 48/2010, 220
Declaration of Principles, 33
democracy, 66; intermediary model as precursor for, 57; Islamic society as context for, 60, 68; transition to, 58. *See also* elections
deportations, 29, 32, 113–114
de Soto, Alvaro, 42–43
diversity, 66–67
dual contract (social/divine), 65

INDEX 353

Dukkhan, Sheikh Abdel Fatteh, 160–162
Duweiq, Aziz, 134, 136, 169, 183–184

economic sector: agricultural production, 231–232; banking, 89–90, 232; black market and smuggling, 232–233; competition within, 149–150; destruction of Gaza's, 191, 231–232 (*see also* economic sector: international boycott and blockage of Gaza); employment, 42; financial institutions, 232; informalization of, 178, 232–233; international boycott and blockade of Gaza, 2, 16, 31, 41, 45, 211–213, 228–229, 231–234; "Islamic" economic entities (IEEs), 89–90, 144–155; Islamic social organizations and, 11–12; Israel as market, 144–145, 151; manufacturing, 145–150, 179, 231, 234; personal relationships and ties within, 150–151; trade restrictions, 147, 231, 233–234; unemployment rates, 41–42, 233, 271n7; U.S. aid policies as political instrument, 46–47; women and participation in, 147. *See also* socioeconomics
education: college and university establishment, 23; curriculum in Islamic schools, 80, 81–82, 88–89, 112, 123–124, 168; demographic diversity of constituency, 132–133; gender segregation and, 103, 112–113, 222; as indoctrination, 124; libraries and, 173–174; as mission, in Hamas Charter, 79–80, 81; for refugee camp residents, 81–82; travel restrictions and access to, 234; tutoring services, 82; as value, xvi; vocational training, 101, 107, 108–109, 212. *See also* schools and universities
Egypt, 21
Eickelman, Dale, 162
Eid Misk, Mohammed, 173
Elashi, Ghassan, 98
elections, 2–3, 14, 88; exclusion of Hamas from political process, 46, 48–49, 201; Hamas and participation in, 40; Hamas as democratically elected power, 2–3, 10, 41, 47–48, 189, 192; Hamas boycott of, 37; as instrument of U.S. policy, 210–211; of leaders/administrators of charities, 138; political legitimacy and, 199
employment, 42; in IEEs, 149–151; unemployment, 41–42, 233, 271n7;

vocational training, 83, 101, 107, 108–109, 212
empowerment: of disenfranchised or marginalized groups, 75; ISIs and, 187–188; militarism as, 209, 213; as objective of social development, 88, 102, 119, 171, 187–188, 192; of women, 101, 122–123, 134–135, 171–172
evidence-based policy, 49–50
exclusion: of Hamas from peace process, 193; from political participation, 69
Executive Order 12947 (US), 1
"extremism," 11–12

factionalism, 31–33, 44, 163, 195, 217, 221, 224–225, 236, 272n9; factional violence, 14, 31, 42, 192, 194–195, 210–213, 236, 246n79, 271n5; national strategy document and cooperation, 283n151; and "politicide," 196; power sharing agreements and, 200–201, 210–211, 274n40, 277n82
Fatah: Hamas as rival, 2–3, 14, 26–27, 31–33, 37, 42–44, 79, 92, 195; internal factionalism or power struggles, 271n8, 272n9; lack of public support and political legitimacy of, 41; militarization and, 191; origins of, 22; U.S. policy and, 41–44
Fayyad, Salam, 2–3, 45–46, 215–217
fedayeen movement, 23, 71
first Intifada (1987), 25, 26–33, 72; as context for emergence of Hamas, 78–79, 94; establishment of Hamas and, 19
freedom: of association, 66–67, 68; community and, 55; as Islamic value, 52–53, 59, 66–68; Muslim societies as context for, 68; radicalism and constructions of, 61; sharia and individual, 59, 252n67; social contract and protection of personal, 65; tolerance and pluralism, 254n97
fundamentalism: Hamas as moderate, 196–197; moderate fundamentalists, 69; radical fundamentalists, 60–61; Salafism and Islamization in Gaza, 221–224
funding, 113; audits of ISIs, 120; entrepreneurial actions of ISIs, 114; fees charged clients, 73, 81, 83, 100, 103–105, 110, 123, 124, 262n47; Gulf War as context for support of Hamas, 30–31; for Hamas, 138–139; interpersonal

354   INDEX

funding (cont'd)
  donor-recipient relationships, 120; Israeli financial assistance, 73; Law No. 1 and transparency regarding movement of funds, 138; for medical clinics, 125; redirection of funds through the PNA, 105; of social sector by Hamas, 139; state sources, 154–155; U.S. actions to freeze assets of Islamic charitable institutions, 1–2, 97–99; USAID and, 47, 90, 118, 125, 131, 141–142, 211, 212. *See also zakat*

Gaza Community Mental Health Program, 122–123
Gaza Strip, maps of, 96, 190; as research site, 4–5
gender segregation, 103, 112–113, 132, 147, 170–171, 222
Ghalyun, Burhan, 55
al-Ghannouchi, Rachid, 53, 57–58, 64–67, 68, 173, 175
al-Ghazali, Muhammad, Sheikh, 65–66
Ging, John, 222
Gulf War (1990), 30–31, 138
Gunning, Jeroen, 25, 65, 88, 135, 138, 142, 183, 206, 256n24, 271n5

Habib, Kamal, 58
al-Halabi, Abdel Raouf, 223
Halevy, Efraim, 209–210, 228
Hamas Charter, 10, 28, 79–80, 138, 244n41
Hamdan, Usama, 41
Hamzawy, Amr, 51–52, 63, 91, 163, 182
Haniyeh, Ismail, 44–45, 102
Harel, Dan, 235
Hass, Amira, 231
Hatina, Meir, 57, 59
Hawwa, Sa'id, 66–67
Hebron Women's Union (Hebron Young Women's Club), 134
Hefner, Robert, 165–166
Helfont, Samuel, 60
Hijazi, Ahmad, 108
el-Hindi, Mohammed, 144
Hizb al-Khalas Political Bureau, 168–169, 269n30
Hizballah, 14, 24, 249n6; Hamas and, 6, 32, 139, 199
Hoffman, Bruce, 98
Holy Land Foundation for Relief and Development (HLF), 1–2, 97–98, 140, 203

House of the Book and the Sunna (HBS), 103–104, 112, 136, 176
Hroub, Khaled, 11, 19–20, 22, 28, 78–79, 92, 244n41
al-Huda girls' school, 3
al-Huda Health Clinic, 126–128
human rights: education and, 135; Islamic society and protection of, 66–67; violation of, 48; women's rights in Islam, 134–135
Hume, John, 236

Ibrahimi Mosque massacre (1994), 35–36
identity, xv–xvii; civic work and, 5; collective Islamic, 11, 178, 181–183; nationalism and, 23; "oppositional Muslimness," 177–178, 182; Palestinian, 180–181, 182; self-definition of social organizations as "Islamic," 11, 135–137, 161–162, 171, 173, 176, 186, 188
ideology: accommodation and, 36–37, 60, 144, 163–165, 182; *vs.* affiliation as motive for mobilization, 142; cultural norms and conservative, 77, 134, 221–224; and education as mission of Hamas, 79–80; and emergence of Hamas, 19–20; evolution of Hamas's, 4, 33, 88, 92–95; Islamism and nationalism and rival ideologies, 70–71, 78, 84, 85; of Muslim Brotherhood, 19, 22–23, 25, 71–72; occupation and resistance as context for, 87, 164–165; political sector and Islamic social institutions, 13; social agenda and, 72, 79, 83–84, 134, 187; of violent resistance, 24, 251n46
al-Ihsan Association for Disabled Children, 108, 117, 171–172
al-Ihsan Charitable Society, 108, 117, 140
ijma' (consensus), 64, 65, 68, 136, 171
ijtihad (interpretation), 63–67, 162, 171, 187–188
al-Ikhwan al-Muslimun. *See* Muslim Brotherhood
illegitimate births, 128–130
'Imara, Muhammad, 65–66
inclusion: and education sector, 132–133; Hamas as inclusive organization, 12; and provision of social services to clients, 80–82, 108, 110, 125, 132–133, 172, 186, 187; staff hiring policies, 104, 126; tolerance of difference, 65; *umma* and Islamic vision of community, 54

indoctrination, 163, 186; social institutions as instruments for, 1–3, 91, 124, 186, 221–224
informalization of economic sector, 178–179, 232–234
institution building (social): context for period of, 23–24; Hamas and social institutions as priority, 25, 37; as instrumental, 87; Muslim Brotherhood and, 72–73
International Crisis Group (ICG), 101, 203, 214
interpretation: and diverse institutional philosophies of ISIs, 168–169; *ijtihad* (interpretation) and innovation, 63–67, 162, 171, 187–188; of Islamic law, 63–64
Intifada. *See* first Intifada (1987); second Intifada (2000 to present)
Islamic Association for Palestine-National, 99
Islamic Center (al-Mujamma al-Islami). *See* al-Mujamma al-Islami (Islamic Center)
Islamic Charitable Society (ICS), 3, 111–114, 173–174, 203, 219
Islamic economic entities (IEEs), 89–90, 144–155
Islamic Jihad, 8, 24, 36, 38, 76–77, 128, 200, 277n82; affiliates of, 108, 134, 144, 263n68
Islamic movement, 8–9; socioeconomics and, 11, 49–50, 188–189
Islamic social institutions (ISI): accommodation and coexistence with other institutions, 163; as apolitical, 90–91, 177; attacks on, 235; audits and PNA oversight of, 120; autonomy of, 74, 127–128, 139–140, 159, 164, 168–169, 170, 184; community development and, 170, 185–186, 187; cooperation or coordination among, 114, 118, 127–128, 133–134, 168–169; cooperation with government, 90; as cultural phenomenon, 186; decentralized approach, 127–128, 133, 168–169, 184; developmental/activist type, 102, 119–131; as fronts for political activities or terrorism, 137–139, 186–187, 235; funding sources for, 138–141; general organizational structure of, 132–137; Hamas and funding for, 139; Hamas's relationship with, 91, 139, 163–164; inclusion, 187; indoctrination and, 1–3, 91, 124, 186, 221–224; institutional philosophy of, 168–169; and Islam as *Minhaj al-hayat* (all-encompassing system), 161–162, 176–177; as "Islamic" organizations, 11, 135–137, 161–162, 171, 173, 176, 186, 188; Israeli government and closure of, 108, 113–114, 191–192; legal status of, 110, 137–138, 175; licensing, registration, or regulation of, 75, 108, 113, 123, 124, 137–138, 187, 220; local or community orientation of, 127–128, 133, 140, 143, 146–148, 165, 168–170, 180; marginalization of, 191–192; number of clients served by, 101, 107, 114, 123, 125, 173–174; occupation as context for, 184; pluralism and, 187; PNA and, 110, 113; political affiliation and, 141–144; professionalism, 90, 107–108, 141, 158–159, 168, 173–174, 187; quality of services, 173, 177; relationship with state, 52, 113, 154–155, 163, 177; social agenda as alternative to violent resistance, 164–165, 188; staffing policies, 90; as terrorist infrastructure, 97–100; traditional/nonactivist type, 102–118; typologies for, 100–103.
Islamic University in Gaza (IUG), 75–76, 77, 142, 151, 156, 163; violence and, 256n24
Israel: closure and confiscation orders against ICS, 3, 113; Dec. 2008 assault on Gaza, 14, 192, 220, 226–229, 231–232, 234–235; destruction of Palestinian civic institutions by, 191–192; "disengagement" in 2005 from Gaza, 16; June 2008 truce, 229–230; licensing and legal recognition of Mujamma institutions, 75; Likud Party and policies of, 24; as market for Palestinian products, 151; as overwhelming power, 72, 198; settlement expansion policy, 31; settlements, map showing locations of, 190. *See also* occupation
Izz ad-Din al Qassam, Sheikh, 20–21
Izz ad-Din al Qassam Brigades, 31

Jabalya refugee camp, 26
Jabari, Iffat, 134–135, 136, 263n71
Jad, Islah, 169
Jaljalat, 222
al-Jam'iyya al-Islamiyya, 74, 85, 124, 133, 139, 168, 172

Jam'iyyat al-Shabbat al-Muslimat (Young Women's Muslim Society), 74, 108
Jam'iyyat Tahfiz al-Qur'an (Association for the Memorization of the Quran), 75
Jensen, Michael, 175–176
jihad, 79–80
Jonas, Barry, 98
Jordan, 21
Jund Ansar Allah (JAA Soldiers of the Supporters of God), 222
justice: absence of due process under PNA administration, 194–195; mediation of disputes, 75, 83–84; sharia law, 56–57, 59, 61, 63, 72, 112, 134, 166, 222, 252n67

Kawtharani, Wajih, 55
Kimmerling, Baruch, 196
kindergartens, 88–89, 109, 124, 171–172
Kramer, Gudrun, 60
al-Kurd, Ahmad, 119–120, 123–124, 136

Labor Party (Israel), 38
Lapidus, Ira M., 167
law: civil, 75, 224; customary, 75; flexibility of Islamic law in moderate thought, 63–64; mediatory role in disputes, 75; social norms and immorality, 74
Law No. 1 on Charitable Societies and Civic Associations, 137–138
leadership: dual leadership and decentralized organizational structure, 29–30; generational and ideological tensions within, 77–78, 86; of Mujamma, 72–75; power struggles over control of social institutions, 74. *See also* organizational structure
Lebanon: deportation of activists to, 29, 32, 113–114; expulsion of PLO from, 24
legitimacy: accountability and, 64–65; Arafat and Palestinian, 199, 201–202; of civil institutions in radical thought, 62–63; of civil society, 55–56; elections and political (*see* elections); of Fatah, 41; of Hamas as political actor, 3–4, 6, 10, 14, 41, 45–46, 78, 199, 201; of Islam as cultural and religious authority, 86; Israeli attempts to delegitimize Palestinians as political actors, 198–199; popular opinion and, 84; and principles of *shura* (consultation) and *ijma'* (consensus), 65; resistance and, 199; social agenda and,
177–178; social service infrastructure and, 89–90
Leibowitz, Avital, 235
Levin, Amiran, 235
Levitt, Matthew, 2, 259n3, 260n15
Levy, Gideon, 197
libraries, 131, 173–174
licensing or registration of institutions, 75, 108, 113, 123, 124, 137–138, 179, 187, 220
Likud party, 24, 38
literacy, 74, 101, 108–109, 121, 135, 166, 172
al-Lu'-lu', Taher, 126–128
Lybarger, Loren, 18

Madrid peace conference, 31–32
Malka, Haim, 142
al-Malki, Riyad, 3
massacres, 31, 35–36, 197
Mecca Agreement, 43
Medhat, Dr. (Director of al-Wafa, WMRH), 150–152, 154, 156, 159–160, 169
mediation or intermediary role, 54–55, 57, 75, 83–84, 139
medical services, 73; accessibility of, 125; to brain-injured children, 107–108; clinics in refugee camps, 73, 107, 125; drugs and pharmaceutical services, 104, 125, 126, 128, 212, 217; free clinics, 82, 127; al-Huda Health Clinic, 126–128; nursing home facilities, 72, 151–152, 157; psychological care, 122–123, 153, 157; quality of services at Islamic facilities, 89, 125; rehabilitative care, 151–157; sexuality, rehabilitative care and, 175; *zakat* committees and financial assistance for, 115, 118. *See also* al-Ahli Hospital; al-Wafa Medical Rehabilitation Hospital
Merken, Mette, 158–159
Meshal, Khaled, 10, 40, 44, 210, 215, 272n9
methodology, 7–8, 17–18
el-Mezain, Mohammed, 98
militancy, 20–21; demilitarization and de-radicalization, 85, 91–93; during first Intifada, 32; funding of militants, 3; Hamas and, 3, 91–93, 196, 239n8; Hizballah and, 32; Islamic movement and, 192; of al-Majid, 24; militarization

of the second Intifada, 196; of al-Mujahideen, 24; Qutb and militant paradigm, 58; Salafism and, 221–224; in West Bank vs. Gaza, 21. *See also* violent resistance
Milton-Edwards, Beverly, 71, 72
Minhaj al-hayat (all-encompassing system), 161–162, 176–177
Ministry of Health (MOH), 121, 128, 154–155, 212, 217–218
Mishal, Shaul, 25, 28, 35, 79, 92
mobilization, 12; collective action and, 13, 93–95, 183, 185, 189; communal orientation of, 185; cultural Islam and, 184–185; decentralization and lack of mobilizing vision, 183–184; identity and, 181–183; ideology vs. affiliation as motive for, 142; informal networks and, 178–179; lack of organizational infrastructure for, 174–175, 183; lack of religious framework for, 167; of Muslim Brotherhood, 24–25; occupation as context for, 182–185, 189; political organizations and, 102, 162, 194; and self-interest as priority, 185; social strategy and, 4, 15, 87, 91, 93, 99–100, 167, 180, 184, 215
moderates, 59–67
modernity: colonialism and modernization, 57; democracy and, 58; Hamas and, 165, 186–187; Islam and, 51, 53–54, 58–60, 62–64, 136, 165–166, 171; moderate fundamentalism and, 60; reform tradition and, 53–54, 62–64, 171; values linked to, 51, 67, 171, 175
Mohmmadi, Majid, 68
morality: illegitimate births as social dilemma, 128–130; as pillar of Islam and, 67; Salafists and imposition of fundamentalist, 221–224; social Islam and, 177; *ulama's* role in defining public, 56
mosque building, period of, 23, 73
Moussalli, Ahmad, 53–54, 60, 69, 254n97
al-Mujamma al-Islami (Islamic Center), 23–24, 54, 72–73; closure of institutions operated by, 85–86; education and schools operated by, 89, 141, 168; establishment of Young Women's Muslim Society by, 74, 108; funding of, 115; Hamas and, 85–86, 102, 141, 168; IUG and education, 75–76; leadership in, 72; licensing and legitimacy of, 75; Muslim Brotherhood and, 74–77;

political activism, 76–77; as politicized and militant, 77–78
Musa, Yahya, 168–169, 184
Muslim Brotherhood, 19; al-Banna and ideological origins of, 19; *da'wa* as priority of, 72; Gaza vs. West Bank organizations, 23; Hamas and the, 25–27, 72, 77–78, 78–80; ideology and objectives of, 22–23, 25, 71–72; infrastructure created by, 77; membership and recruitment, 21–22; occupation as context for, 71; Palestinian orientation of, 19–20, 72; social agenda and, 77–80; violent resistance and, 71
Muslim Brotherhood International, 138
Muslim Women's Youth Center (MWYC), 119
Mustafa, Shukri, 253n71

An-Najah University, 235
Nassar, Gamal Abdel, 21, 22
nationalism, 33, 77; Arab, 22–23, 72; Hamas as nationalist movement, 25–26; Islamic vs. Arab, 22–23; Islamism as ideological rival to, 70–71, 78, 84, 85; Israeli policies and Islamic, 24
Natsheh, Abdel Kaleq, 111, 113–114
Netanyahu, Benjamin, 38, 236
non-governmental organizations (NGOs), 101; international (INGOs), 130, 220–221; Islamic (*see* Islamic social institutions (ISI)); secular, 101.
normalization, Hamas and pursuit of, 94–95
Norton, Augustus Richard, 17
nursery schools and day cares, 72–73, 81–82, 109, 118, 131
Nuseirat refugee camp, 81–83, 106, 257n36
Nuseirat Rehabilitation Center, Nuseirat refugee camp, 107

objectives for social agenda: fostering Islamic values and culture, 84–85
occupation: as context for Muslim Brotherhood in Gaza, 23–24; as context for research, 5; fragmentation and atomization of society during, 184; *jihad* as religious obligation in response to, 79–80; Muslim mobilization in context of, 182–183, 189; opposition Muslim identity formed in, 182–183; Oslo period and, 191; peace

occupation (cont'd)
  process and intensification of, 193–194; political assassinations and justification of, 198; terrorism and the, 111
Odeh, Abdulrahman, 98
Olmert, Ehud, 43, 46
"oppositional Muslimness," 177–178, 182
organizational structure, 183–184; coordination among ISIs, 114, 118, 127–128; coordination among *zakat* committees, 116; decentralized approach, 29–30, 127–128, 133–134, 135, 183–184; dual leadership and, 29–30; evolution of Hamas, 4, 6–7, 92–93; general structure of ISIs, 132–137; of Hamas, 79; horizontal connection between institutions, 133–134; informal networks of economic entities, 150–151; mobilization and organizational infrastructure, 174–175, 183; of Mujamma, 72–75; religion and, 167
orphans, support for, 80–81, 82, 97, 101, 104–105, 111–114, 116–117, 119–123, 130
Oslo peace accords/Oslo period, 33–39; Arafat and, 277n83; escalation of violence during, 193–194; evolution of Hamas and social institutions during, 70, 85–95; and fragmentation of Palestinian lands, 30, 193; Hamas and rejection of, 33–34; and institution building, 6–7, 15, 30; and the occupation, 193–194; as research context, 6–7; and social agenda of Hamas, 94, 188–189

Palestine Monetary Authority (PMA), 89
Palestine National Council (PNC), 27–28
Palestinian Liberation Organization (PLO), 6; funding sources for, 30–31; Hamas as political rival of, 19, 26–27, 30–34, 36–37, 79, 196, 199–200, 211; militarization of, 22; Muslim Brotherhood and, 71, 76, 77; nationalism and, 23; Oslo accords and, 33–34, 46; PNA and the, 33, 209; role in Oslo accords, 33. *See also* Fatah
Palestinian Ministry of Health (MOH), 121, 128, 154–155, 212, 217–218
Palestinian National Authority (PNA): establishment of, 7; as existential threat to Hamas, 92; Hamas and participation in administration of, 34–35; Hamas as rival to, 35–36; Hamas assets frozen by, 2; militarization of society by, 86–87; oversight of ISIs, 120; policy regarding Hamas and Jihad, 35–36; relationship with ISIs, 110; responsibilities assigned to, 194; and social deterioration during occupation, 194
participation: choice and engagement in social sector, 172; civil society and, 68; community engagement as Islamic value, 67; Hamas and power sharing, 200–201; Hamas excluded from political process, 46, 48–49, 200, 201; of Hamas in PNA administration, 34–35; of ISI clientele in community development, 102; Islamic society and political, 66–67; radicalism and exclusionary ideology, 61–62; shura (participation qua consultation) and, 61, 65–67
Paz, Reuven, 139
Peres, Shimon, 28, 38
Pharmacists Without Borders, 104, 128
Piscatori, James, 162
pluralism, 54, 60–62, 66, 91, 164, 166, 173, 187, 254n97
politics: autonomy of civil society, 54–55, 66–67; centrism, 59; Change and Reform Party, 40; civil society and the Islamic state, 52; cultural Islam and Palestinian, 116; erosion of political support for Hamas, 205–206; exclusion from political participation, 69; factional violence in Gaza, 192; Hamas and PLO as rival political factions, 19, 26–27, 30–34, 36–37, 79, 196, 199–200, 211; Hamas excluded from political process, 46, 48–49, 200, 201; legitimacy of Hamas as political actor, 3–4, 6, 10, 14, 35, 41, 45–46, 78–79, 199, 201; mobilization, political, 183–185; participation of citizens, 88; pluralism and multiparty system, 65–66; political alienation of populace, 86–87; "politicide" and factionalism, 196; power sharing, 44, 196, 199, 209–211, 274n40, 277n82; religiosity and, 72; social agenda as political instrument, 1–4, 88–90, 91, 124, 162, 186, 221–224; strategic participation in, 35, 36–37
Posner, Richard, 99
power sharing, 42, 44, 196, 199–201, 210–211, 274n40, 277n82

pragmatism, 26, 28, 48–49, 60, 165–166, 257n41
professionalism, 90, 107–108, 125, 141, 158–159, 168, 173–174, 187, 218
public opinion: cease-fire as response to, 275n57; political alienation and, 86; social services and, 4, 79; and support for Hamas, 10, 27, 28, 31–34, 40, 47–48, 86, 92, 191, 205–208, 244n38; toward violent resistance, 28, 86, 163, 275n57

al-Qaeda, 179, 199, 201, 221–222
al-Qaradawi, Sheikh Yusef, 58, 65–66, 251n47, 252n49
Qassam, Sheikh Naim, 139
Qassam Brigades, 20, 31, 35–36, 39, 45, 222, 236, 245n53, 277n83
Qatar Charitable Society (QCS), 104–108
Qur'anic Literacy Institute, 99
Quranic recitation, 81, 109–110, 124
Qutb, Sayyid, 58, 60–63, 66; Hamas's ideology and, 252n67; ideology of Muslim Brotherhood and influence of, 71–72; violent resistance and ideology of, 251n46

Rabbani, Mouin, 199
Rabin, Yitzhak, 34, 37
racism, 10, 28, 244n41
radicalism, 59–62
al-Rahma (Mercy for Children) Association, 119, 128–131, 141, 168–169, 175
recruitment, social services as instrument for, 3–4, 88–89, 91, 97–100, 162, 177
reform, Islamic, 13, 15, 20–21, 24–25, 29, 40, 58–59, 163; Change and Reform Party and, 40; community orientation of, 91; *ijtihad* (interpretation) and innovation, 63–67, 162, 169, 171, 187–188; and Islam as an all-encompassing system, 161–162; Mujamma and spread of, 72–73; Muslim Brotherhood and, 71–73, 77–78; and reinterpretation in modern contexts, 67–68, 87–88 (*see also* reform, Islamic: *ijtihad* (interpretation))
refugee camps: Askar refugee camp slayings, 197; children's services in, 73, 80–81, 82, 107, 110–111, 119; institutional and social infrastructure in, 72–73; map showing locations of, 190; medical clinics in, 73, 107, 125; and Muslim Brotherhood recruitment, 21, 25; organization of Islamic committees to provide service in, 73, 81; population in, 81; QCS and services in, 106–107; social programs provided in, 72–74, 80–81; women's programs in, 179
registration. *See* licensing or registration of institutions
resistance: social reform as, 24–25, 78–80, 85, 90–91, 164–165, 188. *See also* violent resistance
Rice, Condoleezza, 43, 210
Ricoeur, Paul, 18
Rida, Rashid, 63
Robinson, Glenn E., 25, 102
Rowan, Patrick, 98

al-Sadar, Faiz, 197
Salafism, 221–224
al-Salah Benevolent School, 123–124
al-Salah Islamic Association, 2–3, 82, 104, 107, 119–126, 133, 136, 137, 168–169, 203–204
Salam, Nawaf, 58
al-Sarraj, Eyad, 191
Sayigh, Yezid, 220
schools and universities: curriculum in Islamic, 80, 81–82, 88–89, 112, 123–124, 168; al-Huda girls' school, 3; Islamic University in Gaza (IUG), 75–76, 77, 142, 151, 156, 163; kindergartens, 88–89, 109, 124, 171–172; al-Mujamma al-Islami and operation of, 89, 141, 168; an-Najah University, 235; nursery schools and day cares, 72–73, 81–82, 109, 118, 131; al-Salah Benevolent School, 123–124
second Intifada (2000 to present), 39–49; militarization of, 191, 194–195; PNA's role during, 194–195
secularism, 207; clientelism and secular institutions, 186; Hamas's social agenda and, 188; Palestinian, 167; separation of religion and civic sphere, 167–168
secularization of religious discourse, 12, 91, 182
Sela, Avraham, 28, 79, 92
Sela, Zvi, 29
separation: of civil society and religion, 51, 55–56, 57, 167–168; of civil society and state, 93; of Gaza from the West Bank, 46–47, 157, 192, 193, 230, 234; Oslo and division into subdistricts, 30;

separation (cont'd)
  of religion and politics in Palestine, 167–168
Separation Wall, 14
sexuality, rehabilitative care and, 158–159, 175
Shafiq, Munir, 56–58, 64, 65
Shalit, Gilad, 41, 222
Shalom, Kerem, 233–234
al-Shaqaqi, Fathi, 24, 38
sharia, 56–57, 59, 61, 63, 72, 112, 134, 166, 222, 252n67
Sharon, Ariel, 23, 46, 197–199, 274n38
Shehada, Salah, 29–30, 40
shura (consultation), 61, 65–67, 171; democracy and, 66–67; shura council as legislative power, 254n79
Singerman, Diane, 173
Sirriyyah, Salih, 253n71
social institutions, Islamic. *See* Islamic social institutions (ISI)
social workers and social work, 16, 80, 87, 106, 121–122
Society of Muslim Brothers (al-Ikhwan al-Muslimun). *See* Muslim Brotherhood
socioeconomics: deteriorating situation in Gaza, 15, 86, 131, 188–189, 191–192; Hamas as socioeconomic actor, 5, 7, 10–11, 15, 183–185, 188–189, 207, 249n6; Islamic movement and, 11, 49–50, 188–189
Solana, Javier, 45
stability, social, 5, 9, 14–15, 53–54, 69, 94–95, 187, 192
staff: gender segregation and roles of, 132; inclusive hiring practices for, 104, 126; interpersonal relationships with clients, 82, 121, 122–123, 126–127; professionalism and quality of, 90, 107–108, 125–126, 173, 187; training and qualifications of, 123, 132, 133, 155–156, 157–159, 173–175
suicide bombings, 1–4, 35–36, 38–41, 99, 188, 196–198, 251n47, 272n19
Syria, 66

Taba Accord (Oslo agreement), 36
Taliban, 165, 199
taxation, 45, 57, 203, 221. *See also zakat* (as instituted in Islam)
terrorism, 70; American perceptions of Palestinians, xvi–xvii; Arafat and renunciation of, 27; charitable institutions targeted as "terrorist infrastructure," 85–86; designation of Hamas as terrorist organization, 1–2, 14, 212–213; Islamic charities as recruitment tool, 97–100; Islamic social sector as infrastructure for, 97–100; 9/11 as context for U.S. policy, 1; occupation as context for, 111; suicide bombings, 1–4, 35–36, 38–41, 99, 188, 196–198, 251n47, 272n19; U.S. actions to freeze assets of Islamic charitable institutions, 1–2, 97–99
tolerance, 65, 66–67
traditionalism, 60
travel restrictions, 157, 234
truces. *See* cease-fires
tunnels and tunnel economy, 232–233
al-Turabi, Hasan, 65–66, 254n97
two-state solution, 10, 27–28, 42–43, 210, 228, 230
tyranny, 59

ulama, 55–58, 165, 251n32
umma (Muslim social community), 20, 51, 53–55, 57, 161–162
Union of Good, 98–99, 138–139
United National Leadership of the Uprising (UNLU), 27–28
United Nations Relief and Works Agency (UNRWA), 82, 107, 110–111, 125, 133, 177, 203–204, 222, 245n52
United States: actions against Islamic charities, 1–2, 167–168; Bush administration policies, 1–2, 41–44, 196; designation of Hamas as terrorist organization by, 1–2, 14; diplomatic engagement of Hamas by, 196–197; elections as instrument of, 210–211; and exclusion of Hamas from peace process, 236; 9/11 as context for policy of, 1; support of Fatah over Hamas, 41–44
United States Agency for International Development (USAID), 47, 90, 118, 125, 131, 141–142, 211, 212

values, Islamic: charity, 119; community membership, 53, 171; creativity or innovation, 65, 66, 162, 187–188; *ijma'* (consensus), 64, 65, 68, 136, 171; Islam as all-encompassing system, 161–162, 176–177; mobilization and, 167;

modernity and, 51, 67, 171, 175; occupation as assault on, 163–164; respect for human worth, 175; *shura* (consultation), 61, 65–67, 136, 171; social agenda and fostering, 84–85

violence: assassinations, 37, 38, 40, 197; clan or tribal disputes, 75, 194, 209, 214, 236, 271n5; Israel's Dec. 2008 assault on Gaza, 14, 192, 220, 226–229, 231–232, 234–235; social norms enforced through, 74; 1967 War, 22. *See also* militancy; violent resistance

violent resistance, 85; civism and, 249n6; demilitarization of Hamas, 91–93; Hamas and strategy of, 29, 35, 78–79; ideology of, 24, 251n46; *jihad* as religious obligation, 79–80; moderates and rejection of, 66; Muslim Brotherhood and, 24–25, 71; Nasserism as context for, 251n46; paramilitary organizations, 24; popular opinion and engagement in, 28, 86, 163, 275n57; rejection of, 188; social agenda as alternative to, 24–25, 164–165, 188; suicide bombings, 1–4, 35–36, 38–41, 99, 188, 196–198, 251n47, 272n19

vocational training, 83, 101, 107, 108–109, 212

Voll, John, 53

al-Wafa Medical Rehabilitation Hospital, 90, 119, 131, 141, 151–160, 169, 175, 267n158, 267n159; autonomy of, 159; designation as "Hamas" institution, 159; January 15 assault on, 235

1967 War, 22

"war of the knives," 31

welfare system, 2–3, 31, 77; distribution of relief, 245n52; food aid distribution, 123; food aid provided by *zakat* committee, 115; Mujamma and, 72–73, 75

West Bank: Islamic social institutions in, 85–86, 101, 111–115, 132, 137, 192–193; militancy in, 12, 38–39; Muslim Brotherhood in, 21, 23, 25, 71, 75–77; Oslo period and impacts on, 30, 33, 35–36, 193; political control and administration in, 3, 21–22, 45, 192–193, 206–207, 209–210; as research site, 5, 7–8, 12, 17; separation from Gaza, 27–28, 46–47, 157, 192, 193, 230, 234; Wye River Accord and Israeli occupation of, 39–40

women: coercion and compliance with social norms, 84; dress, norms for, 117, 167, 170–171, 223–224; education of, 108, 135; emotional and psychological health of, 122–123; employment of, 147; empowerment and programs for, 82–83, 123, 134–135, 171–172; political participation of, 135; roles and interpretation of Islamic law, 169; traditional norms and, 134–135; vocational training for, 83, 108–109

Women's Islamic Association, 83

Worm, Klaus, 245n52

Wurmser, David, 43

Wye River Accord, 39

Yassin, Sheikh Ahmad, 23–27, 29, 32, 37, 39, 83–84, 183–184; assassination of, 40, 197, 198, 200; al-Mujamma al-Islami and, 23–24, 72–75

Yavuz, Hakan, 174, 177, 182

Yemen, 185

Young Women's Muslim Society (YWMS), 74, 108–111

al-Zahar, Ahmad, 128–131, 143–144, 262n54

al-Zahar, Mahmoud, 28, 29, 72

zakat (as instituted in Islam), 105, 114–115, 202; U.S. judicial actions to limit, 2

zakat committees: Hamas and, 30–31, 139, 219; Muslim Brotherhood and, 73–74; as organized institutions, 113–118, 134, 168, 170, 179, 203–204, 263n75; QCS and, 104

Ziyada, Khalid, 55, 57

GPSR Authorized Representative: Easy Access System Europe - Mustamäe tee
50, 10621 Tallinn, Estonia, gpsr.requests@easproject.com

www.ingramcontent.com/pod-product-compliance
Lightning Source LLC
Chambersburg PA
CBHW021149230426
43667CB00006B/307